T
Aah!
A BEER SURE TASTES GOOD AFTER BOXING!
*DON'T DRINK UNTIL YOU'RE OF AGE!
BEER
So much for my diet...

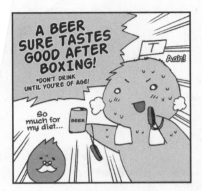

This is Taishi Tsutsui, and for some reason, I'm the chairman of the boxing club at my office.

Recently, I started playing a boxing game on my Nintendo Switch in order to get in shape. I roped in some colleagues, and we started playing every day after work. We get all sweaty and have fun and it seems to be going well!

I invite you all to give the boxing life a try!

Whether you're sad because you got a bit carried away shadowboxing and punched a pillar and it slightly impaired your ability to draw, or you're relieved because it wasn't your dominant hand, why not give this rom-com manga a try next time you need a warm-up before boxing?

• Taishi Tsutsui •

We Never Learn

We Never Learn

Volume 12 • SHONEN JUMP Manga Edition

STORY AND ART **Taishi Tsutsui**

TRANSLATION Camellia Nieh
SHONEN JUMP SERIES LETTERING Snir Aharon
GRAPHIC NOVEL TOUCH-UP ART & LETTERING Erika Terriquez
DESIGN Shawn Carrico
EDITOR John Bae

BOKUTACHI WA BENKYOU GA DEKINAI © 2017 by Taishi Tsutsui
All rights reserved.
First published in Japan in 2017 by SHUEISHA Inc., Tokyo.
English translation rights arranged by SHUEISHA Inc.

The stories, characters and incidents mentioned in this publication are entirely fictional.

Printed in Canada

Published by VIZ Media, LLC
P.O. Box 77010
San Francisco, CA 94107

10 9 8 7 6 5 4 3 2 1
First printing, October 2020

shonenjump.com

viz.com

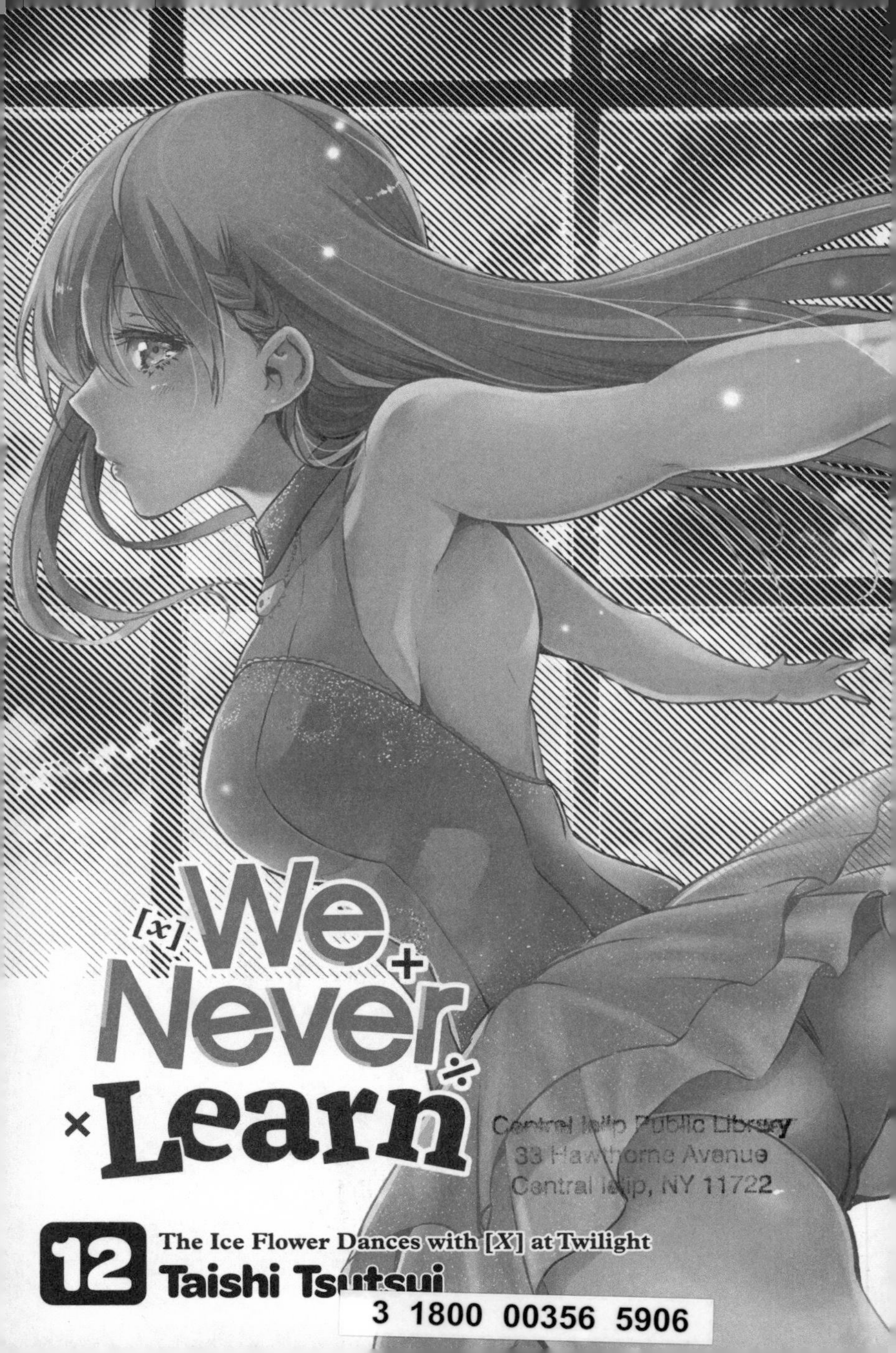
We Never Learn
12
The Ice Flower Dances with [X] at Twilight
Taishi Tsutsui

We Never Learn

Characters & Story

Nariyuki Yuiga and his family have led a humble life since his father passed away, with Yuiga doing everything he can to support his siblings. So when the principal of his school agrees to grant Nariyuki the school's special VIP recommendation for a full scholarship to college, he leaps at the opportunity. However, the principal's offer comes with one condition: Yuiga must serve as the tutor of Rizu Ogata, Fumino Furuhashi and Uruka Takemoto, the three girl geniuses who are the pride of Ichinose Academy! Unfortunately, the girls, while extremely talented in certain ways, all have subjects where their grades are absolutely rock-bottom. How will these three struggling students ever manage to pass their college entrance exams?!

Fumino stands up to her father with Nariyuki's support and finally persuades him to accept her chosen path. Meanwhile, Uruka tells Nariyuki of her plans to study abroad. Nariyuki is struggling as he compares himself to his friends, so he turns to Rizu for help. Will he give up the VIP recommendation in order to pursue his dreams?!

NARIYUKI YUIGA

CLASS:3-B

☺ Liberal Arts
☺ STEM
☹ Athletics

A bright student from an ordinary family. Nariyuki lacks genius in any one subject but manages to maintain stellar grades through hard work. Agrees to take on the role of tutor in return for the school's special VIP recommendation.

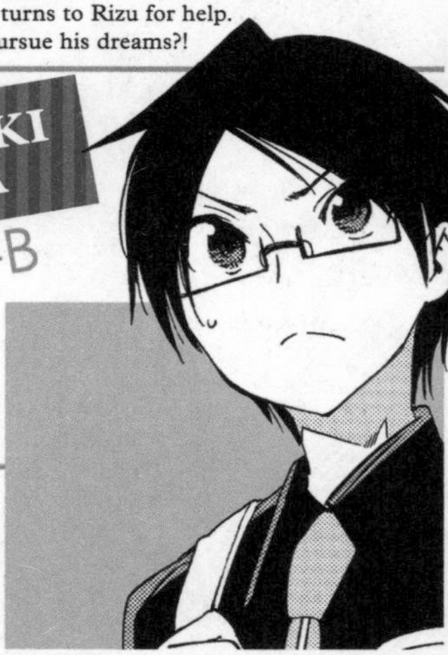

The Yuiga Family

A family of five consisting of Nariyuki, his mother and his siblings, Mizuki, Hazuki and Kazuki.

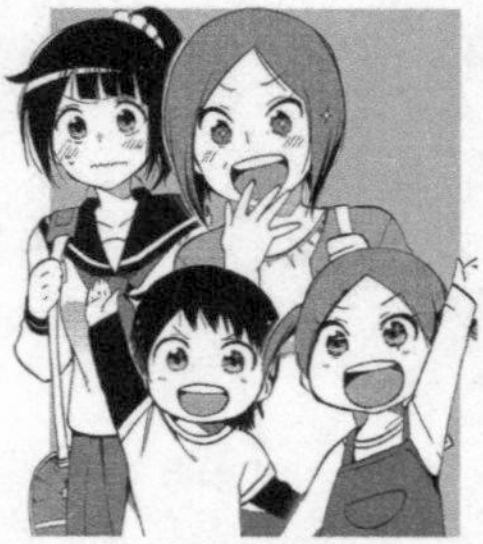

Kobayashi and Omori

Nariyuki's friends.

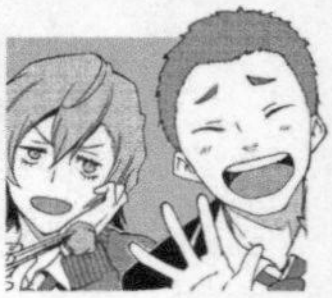

Miharu Kirisu

Kirisu Sensei's younger sister. Believes Nariyuki and her sister to be secret lovers.

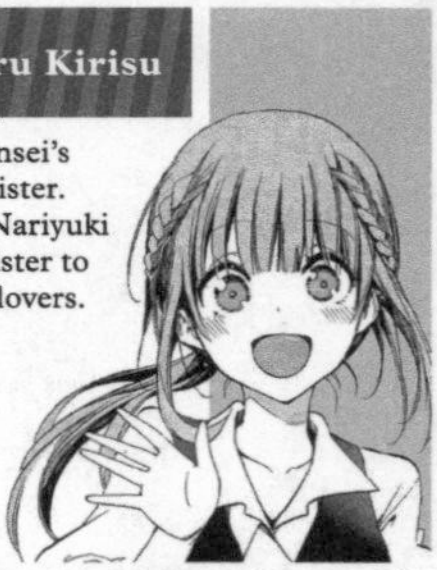

Kawase and Umihara

Uruka's friends.

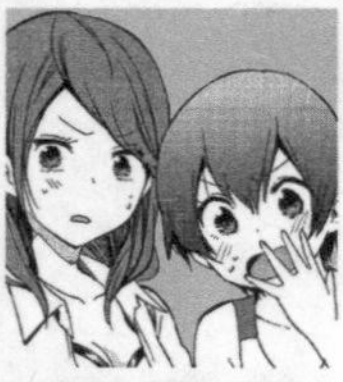

Sawako Sekijo

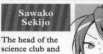

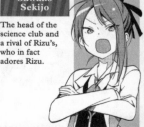

The head of the science club and a rival of Rizu's, who in fact adores Rizu.

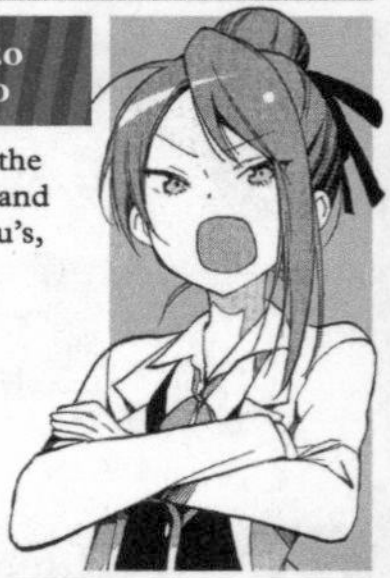

RIZU OGATA

CLASS:3-F

- 🙁 Liberal Arts
- 😊 STEM
- 🙁 Athletics

Known as the Thumbelina Supercomputer, Rizu is a math and science genius, but she's a dunce at literature, especially when human emotions come into play. She chooses a literary path to learn about human psychology—partially because she wants to become better at board games.

FUMINO FURUHASHI

CLASS:3-A

- 😊 Liberal Arts
- 🙁 STEM
- 😊 Athletics

Known as the Sleeping Beauty of the Literary Forest, Fumino is a literary wiz whose mind goes completely blank when she sees numbers. She chooses a STEM path because she wants to study the stars.

URUKA TAKEMOTO

CLASS:3-D

- 🙁 Liberal Arts
- 🙁 STEM
- 😊 Athletics

Known as the Shimmering Ebony Mermaid Princess, Uruka is a swimming prodigy but is terrible at academics. In order to get an athletic scholarship, she needs to meet certain academic standards. She's had a crush on Nariyuki since junior high.

MAFUYU KIRISU

TEACHER

- 😊 Pedagogy
- 🙁 Home Economics

A teacher at Ichinose Academy, and Rizu and Fumino's previous tutor. She believes people should choose their path according to their talents.

ASUMI KOMINAMI

OG

- 🙁 Science
- 😊 Service

A graduate of Ichinose Academy. Works at a maid cafe and attends cram school in order to get into medical school and take over her father's clinic one day.

TITLE

We Never Learn

CONTENTS

VOLUME **12** The Ice Flower Dances with [X] at Twilight

NAME **Taishi Tsutsui**

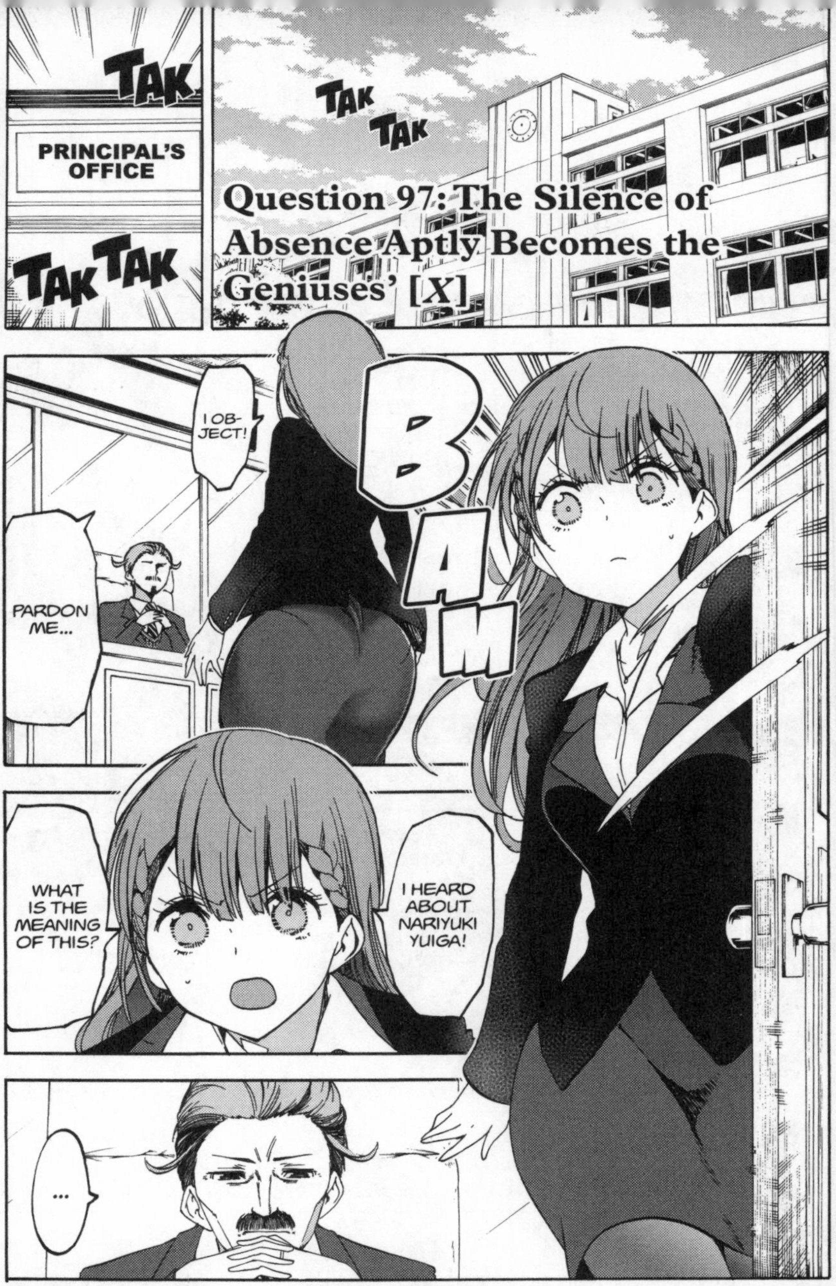
TAK
TAK
Question 97: The Silence of Absence Aptly Becomes the Geniuses' [X]
TAK
PRINCIPAL'S OFFICE
TAK TAK
BAM
I HEARD ABOUT NARIYUKI YUIGA!
I OB-JECT!
PARDON ME...
WHAT IS THE MEANING OF THIS?
...

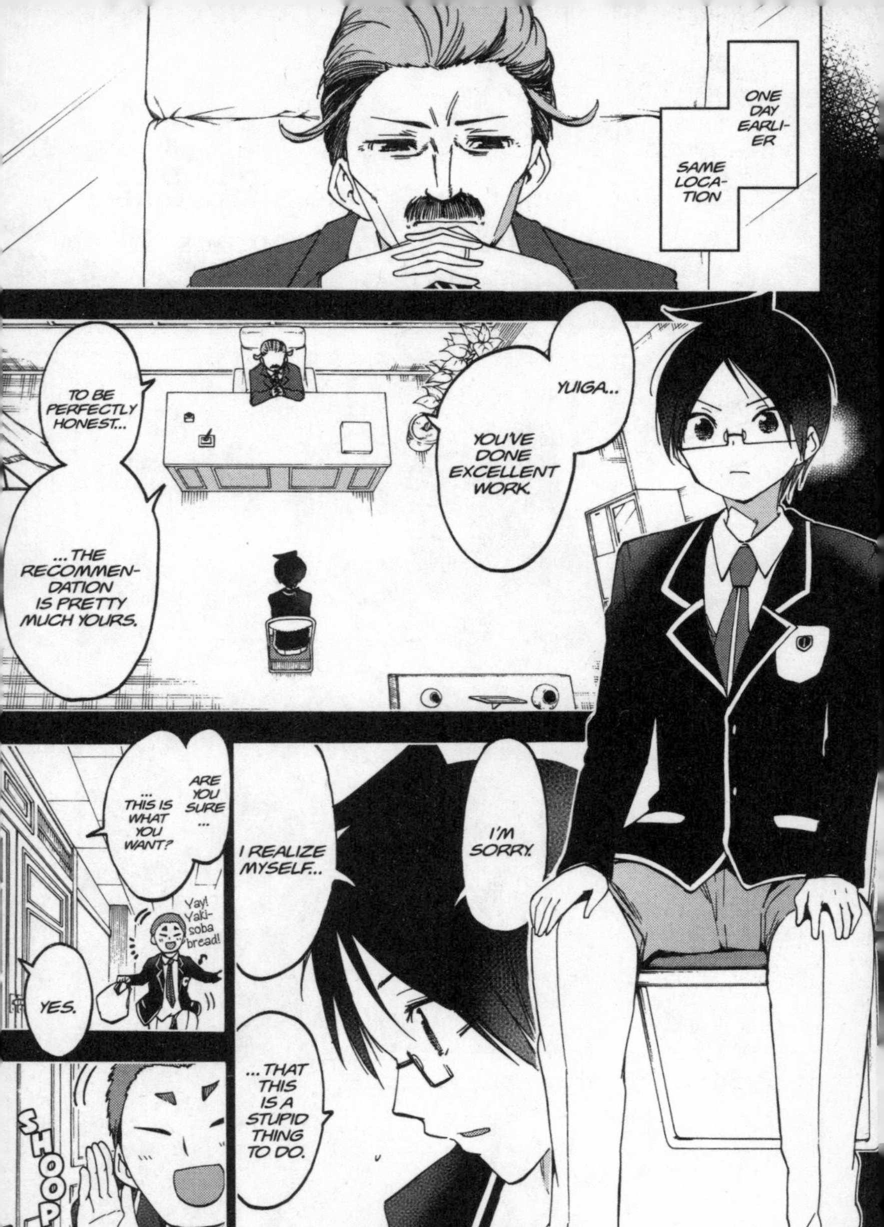
ONE DAY EARLIER
SAME LOCATION
YUIGA...
YOU'VE DONE EXCELLENT WORK.
TO BE PERFECTLY HONEST...
...THE RECOMMENDATION IS PRETTY MUCH YOURS.
I'M SORRY.
I REALIZE MYSELF...
...THAT THIS IS A STUPID THING TO DO.
ARE YOU SURE...
...THIS IS WHAT YOU WANT?
YES.
Yay! Yaki-soba bread!
SHOOP

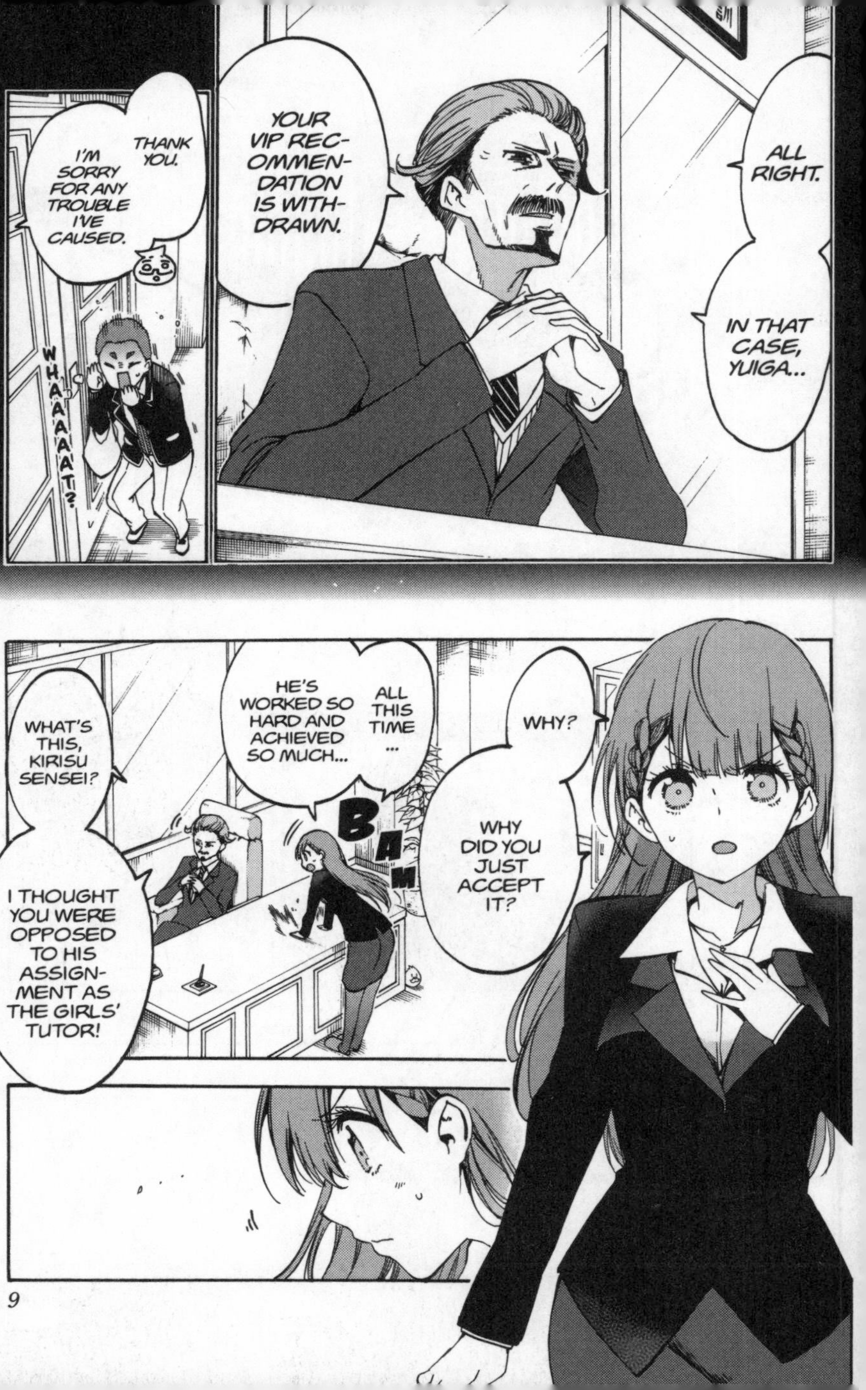
ALL RIGHT.
IN THAT CASE, YUIGA...
YOUR VIP RECOMMENDATION IS WITHDRAWN.
THANK YOU.
I'M SORRY FOR ANY TROUBLE I'VE CAUSED.
WHAAAAAAT?
WHY?
WHY DID YOU JUST ACCEPT IT?
ALL THIS TIME...
HE'S WORKED SO HARD AND ACHIEVED SO MUCH...
BAM
WHAT'S THIS, KIRISU SENSEI?
I THOUGHT YOU WERE OPPOSED TO HIS ASSIGNMENT AS THE GIRLS' TUTOR!

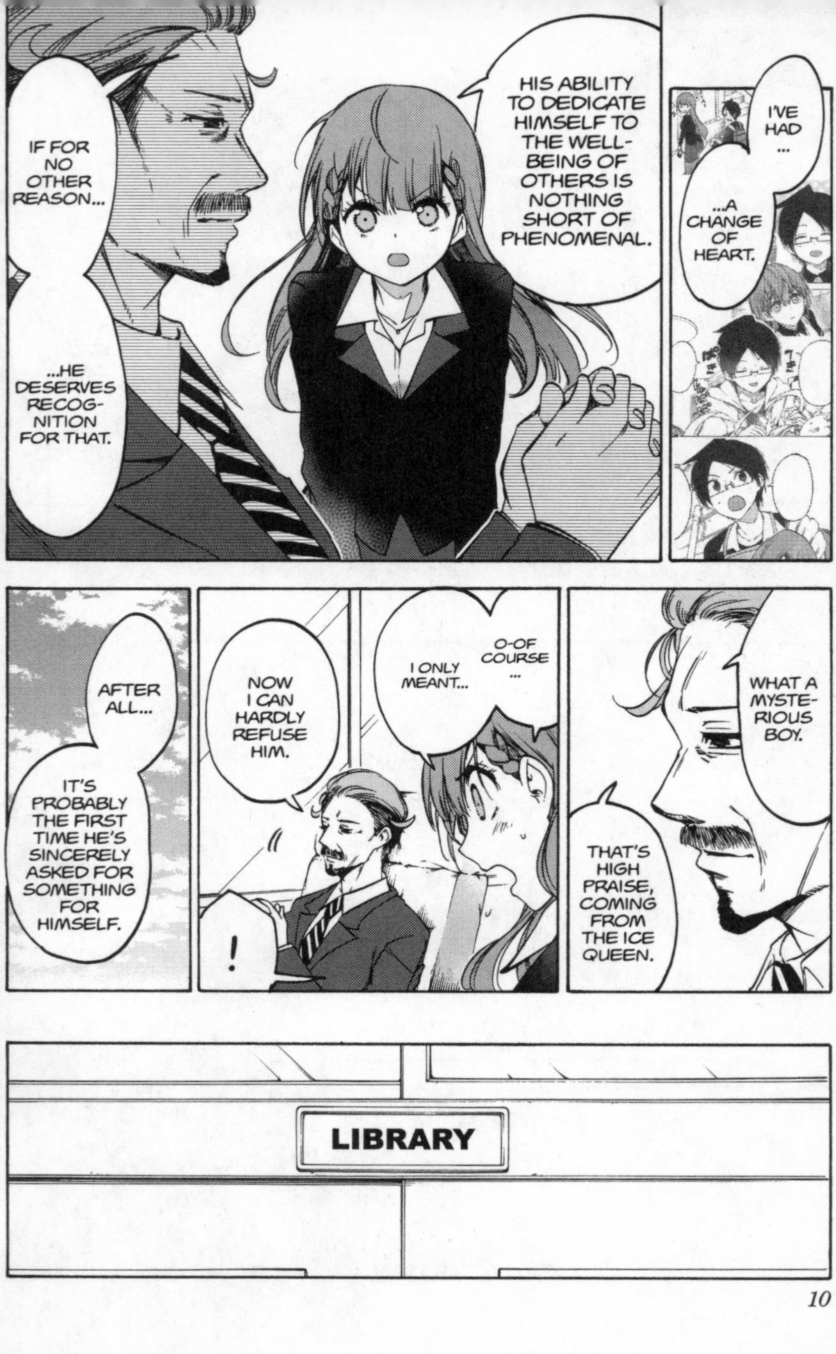
I'VE HAD ...
...A CHANGE OF HEART.
HIS ABILITY TO DEDICATE HIMSELF TO THE WELL-BEING OF OTHERS IS NOTHING SHORT OF PHENOMENAL.
IF FOR NO OTHER REASON...
...HE DESERVES RECOG-NITION FOR THAT.
WHAT A MYSTE-RIOUS BOY.
THAT'S HIGH PRAISE, COMING FROM THE ICE QUEEN.
O-OF COURSE ...
I ONLY MEANT...
NOW I CAN HARDLY REFUSE HIM.
!
AFTER ALL...
IT'S PROBABLY THE FIRST TIME HE'S SINCERELY ASKED FOR SOMETHING FOR HIMSELF.
LIBRARY

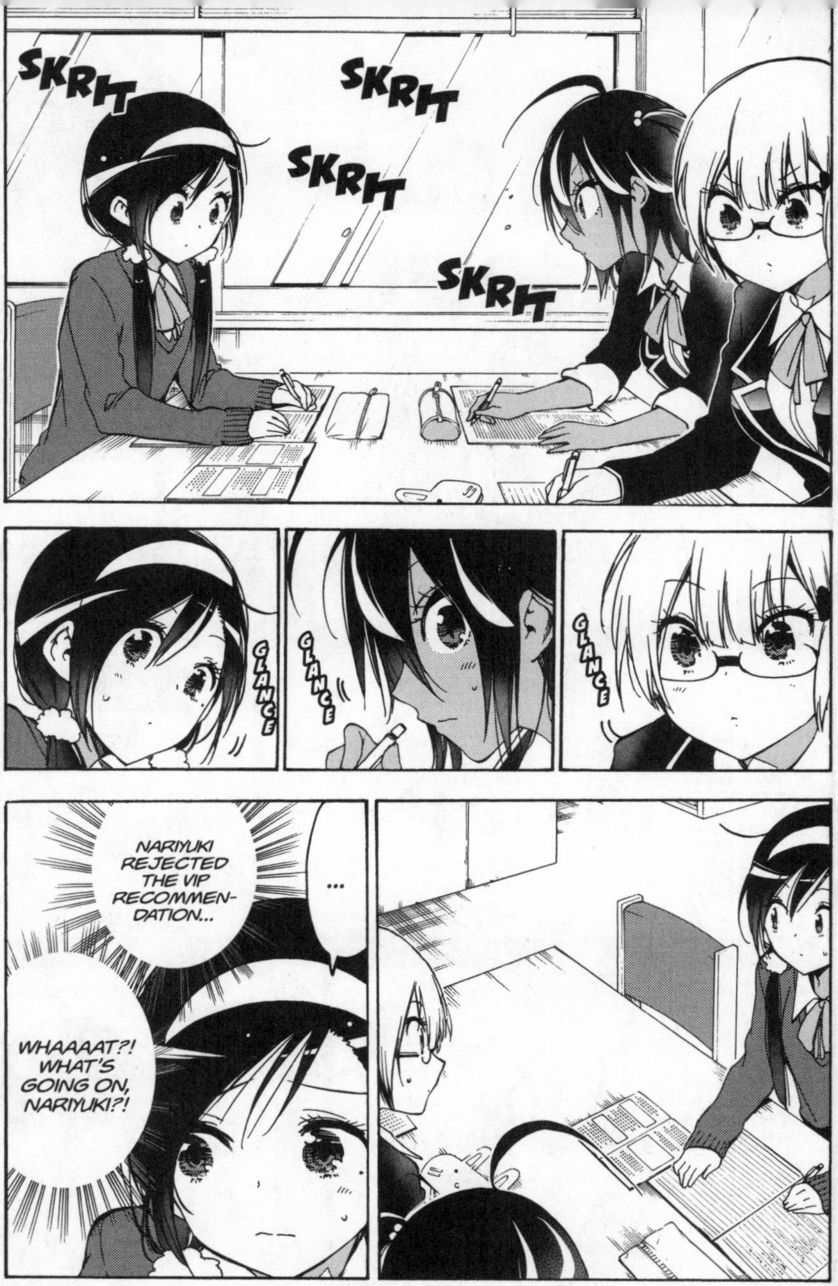
SKRITT
SKRITT
SKRITT
SKRITT
GLANCE
GLANCE
GLANCE
...
NARIYUKI REJECTED THE VIP RECOMMEN-DATION...
WHAAAAT?! WHAT'S GOING ON, NARIYUKI?!

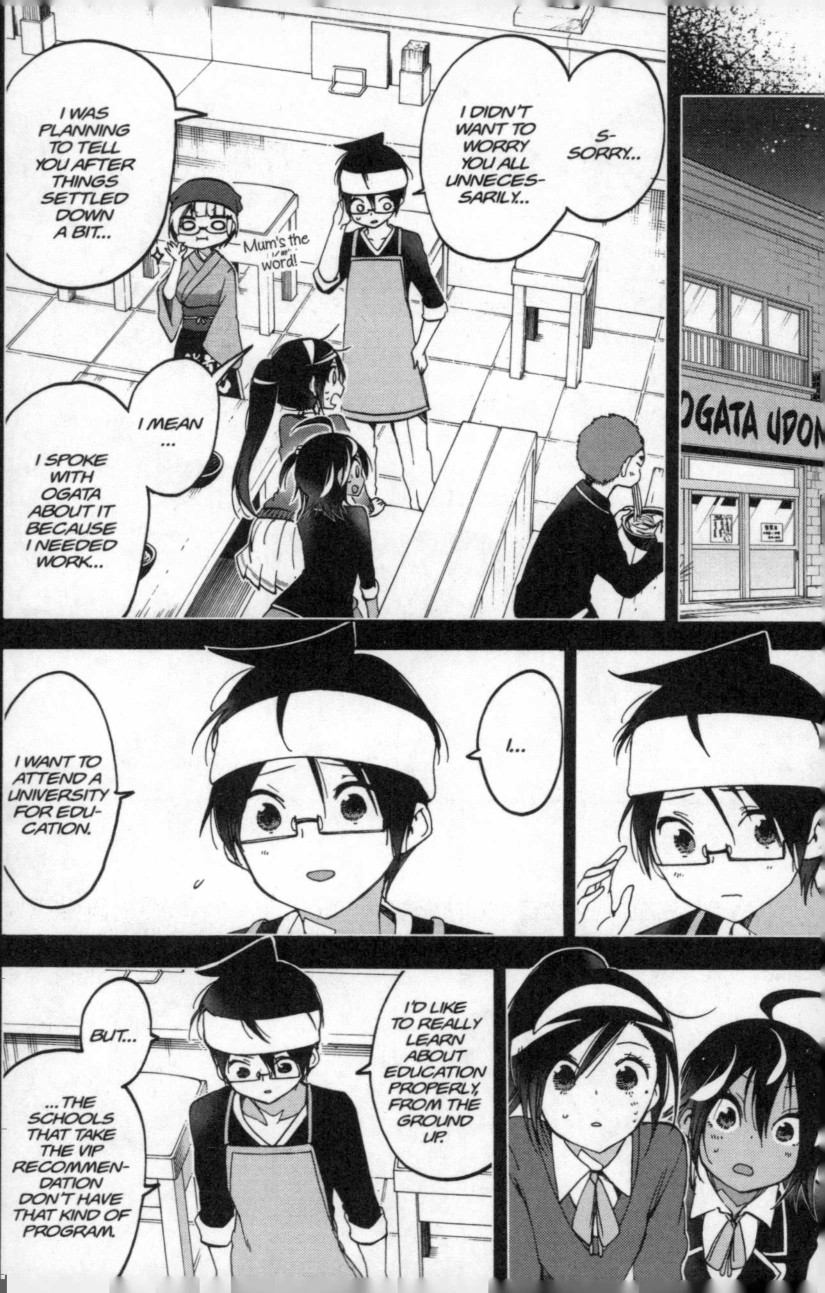
OGATA UDON
S-SORRY...
I DIDN'T WANT TO WORRY YOU ALL UNNECESSARILY...
I WAS PLANNING TO TELL YOU AFTER THINGS SETTLED DOWN A BIT...
Mum's the word!
I MEAN...
I SPOKE WITH OGATA ABOUT IT BECAUSE I NEEDED WORK...
I...
I WANT TO ATTEND A UNIVERSITY FOR EDUCATION.
I'D LIKE TO REALLY LEARN ABOUT EDUCATION PROPERLY, FROM THE GROUND UP.
BUT...
...THE SCHOOLS THAT TAKE THE VIP RECOMMENDATION DON'T HAVE THAT KIND OF PROGRAM.

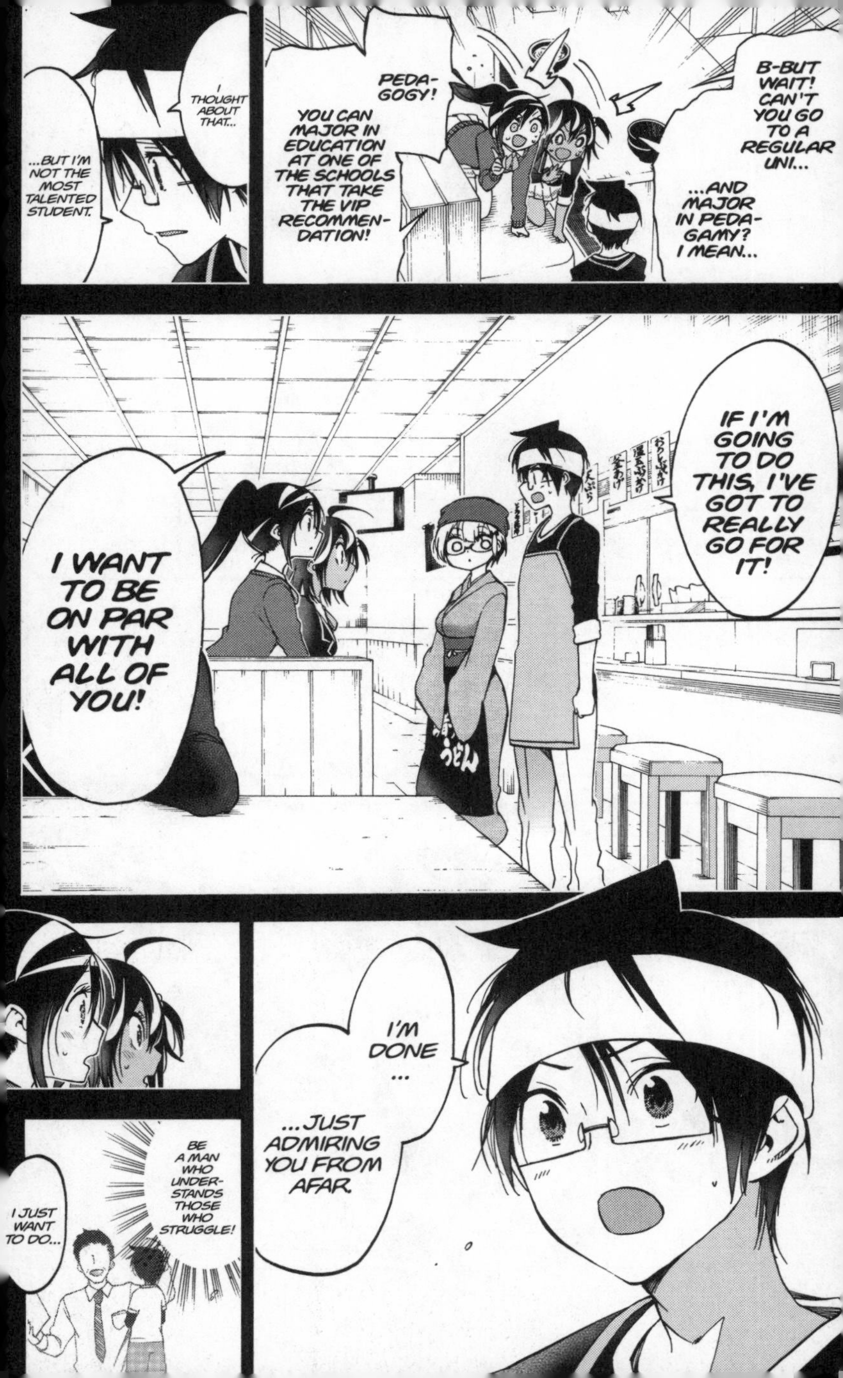
B-BUT WAIT! CAN'T YOU GO TO A REGULAR UNI...
...AND MAJOR IN PEDAGAMY? I MEAN...
PEDA-GOGY!
YOU CAN MAJOR IN EDUCATION AT ONE OF THE SCHOOLS THAT TAKE THE VIP RECOMMEN-DATION!
I THOUGHT ABOUT THAT...
...BUT I'M NOT THE MOST TALENTED STUDENT.
IF I'M GOING TO DO THIS, I'VE GOT TO REALLY GO FOR IT!
I WANT TO BE ON PAR WITH ALL OF YOU!
I'M DONE...
...JUST ADMIRING YOU FROM AFAR.
BE A MAN WHO UNDER-STANDS THOSE WHO STRUGGLE!
I JUST WANT TO DO...

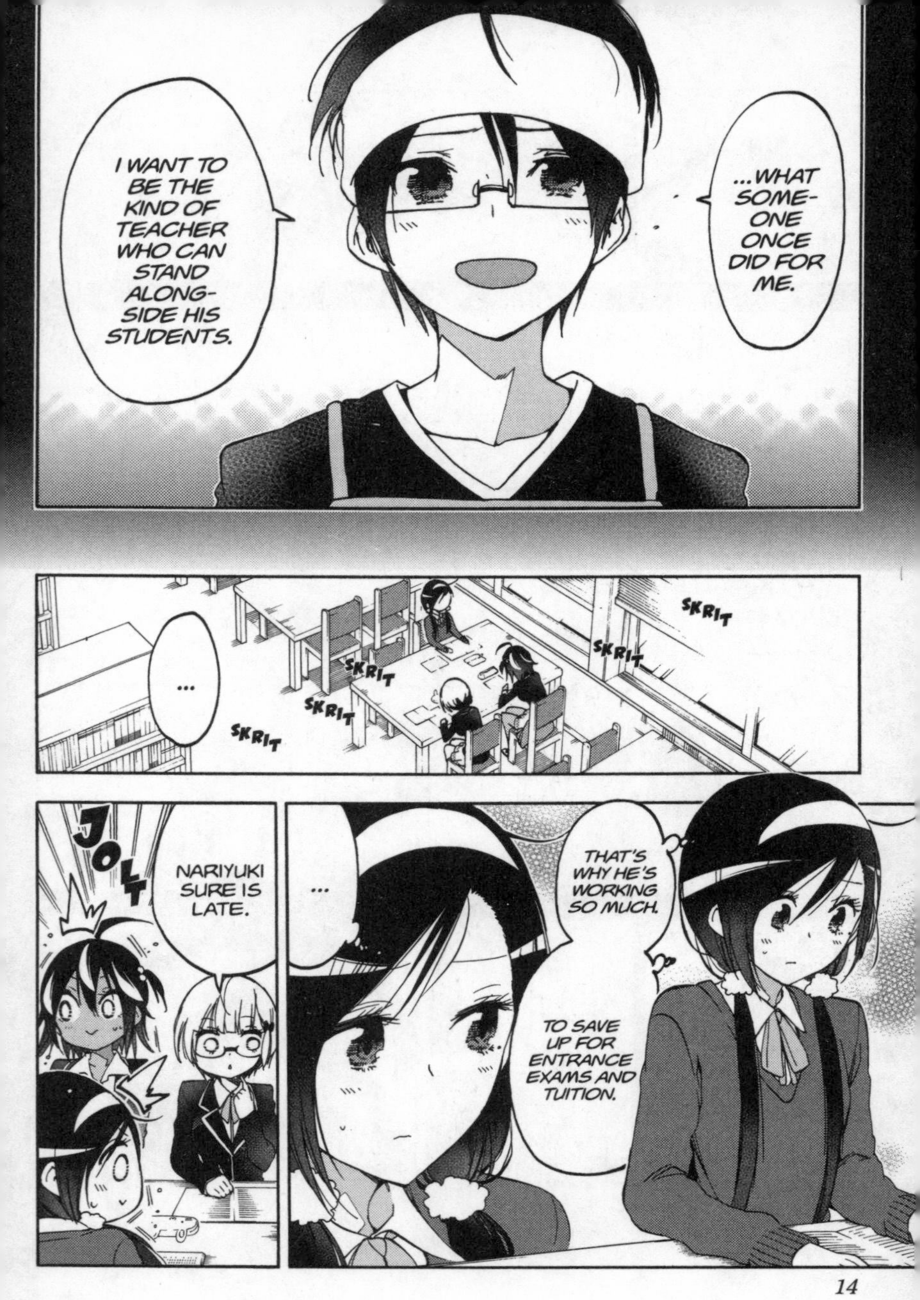
I WANT TO BE THE KIND OF TEACHER WHO CAN STAND ALONGSIDE HIS STUDENTS.
...WHAT SOMEONE ONCE DID FOR ME.
SKRIT
SKRIT
SKRIT
SKRIT
SKRIT
...
THAT'S WHY HE'S WORKING SO MUCH.
TO SAVE UP FOR ENTRANCE EXAMS AND TUITION.
...
NARIYUKI SURE IS LATE.
JOLT

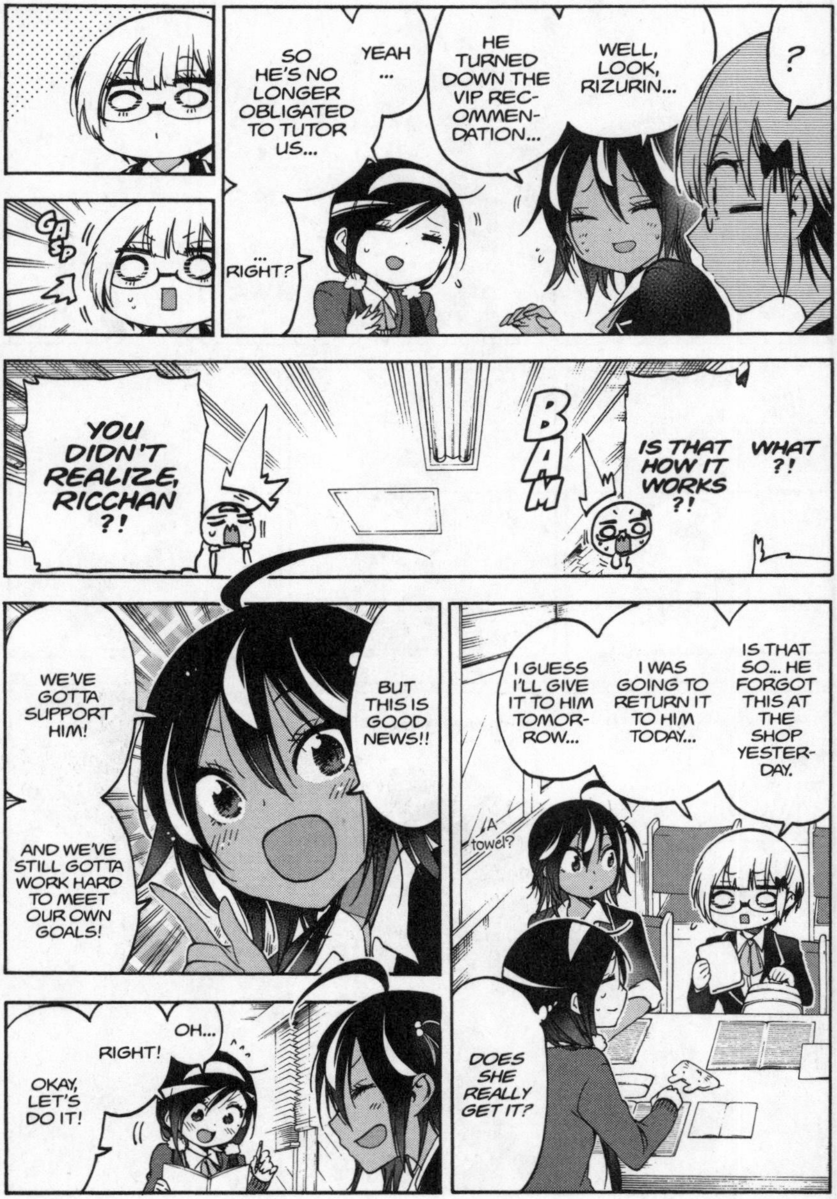
?
WELL, LOOK, RIZURIN...
HE TURNED DOWN THE VIP RECOMMENDATION...
YEAH ...
SO HE'S NO LONGER OBLIGATED TO TUTOR US...
... RIGHT?
GASP
WHAT ?!
IS THAT HOW IT WORKS ?!
BAM
YOU DIDN'T REALIZE, RICCHAN ?!
IS THAT SO... HE FORGOT THIS AT THE SHOP YESTERDAY.
I WAS GOING TO RETURN IT TO HIM TODAY...
I GUESS I'LL GIVE IT TO HIM TOMORROW...
A towel?
DOES SHE REALLY GET IT?
BUT THIS IS GOOD NEWS!!
WE'VE GOTTA SUPPORT HIM!
AND WE'VE STILL GOTTA WORK HARD TO MEET OUR OWN GOALS!
OH...
RIGHT!
OKAY, LET'S DO IT!

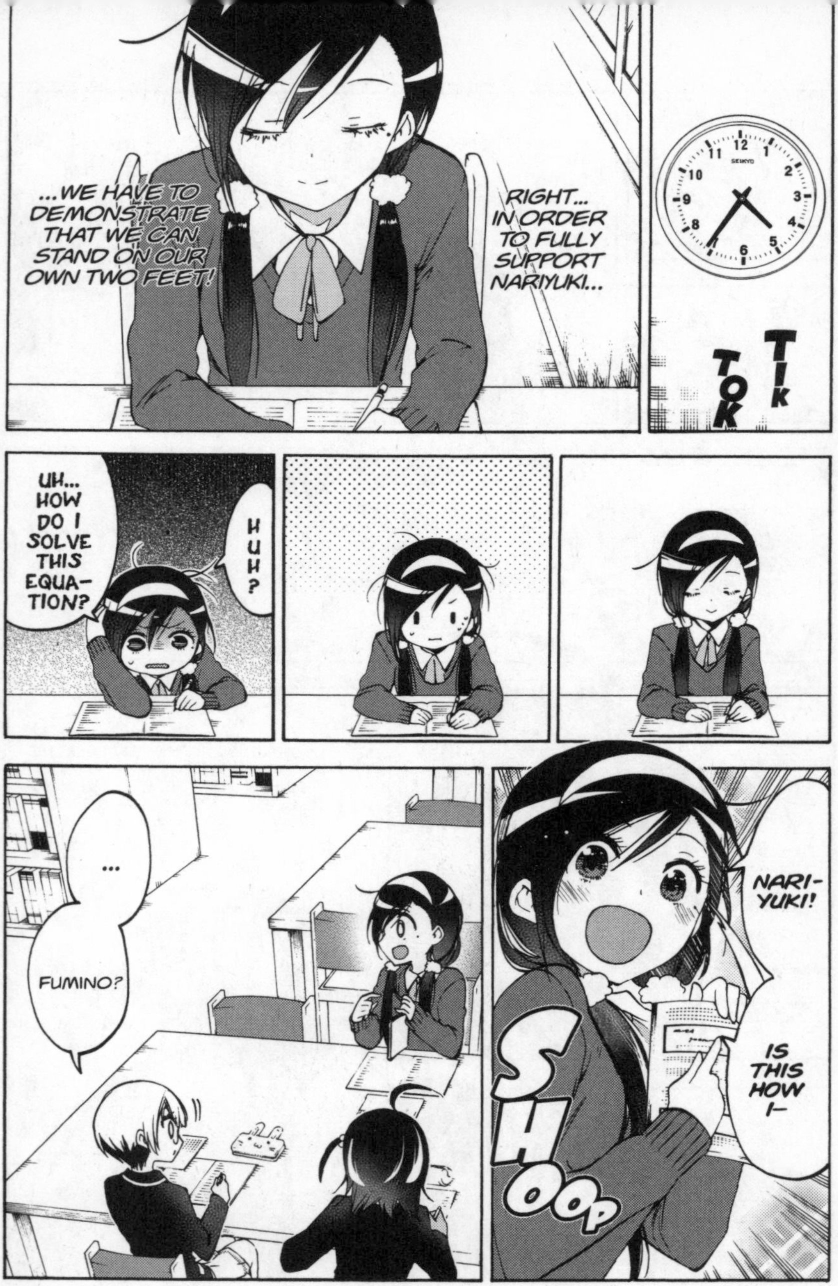
TIK
TOK
RIGHT... IN ORDER TO FULLY SUPPORT NARIYUKI...
...WE HAVE TO DEMONSTRATE THAT WE CAN STAND ON OUR OWN TWO FEET!
HUH?
UH... HOW DO I SOLVE THIS EQUA-TION?
NARI-YUKI!
SHOOP
IS THIS HOW I—
...
FUMINO?

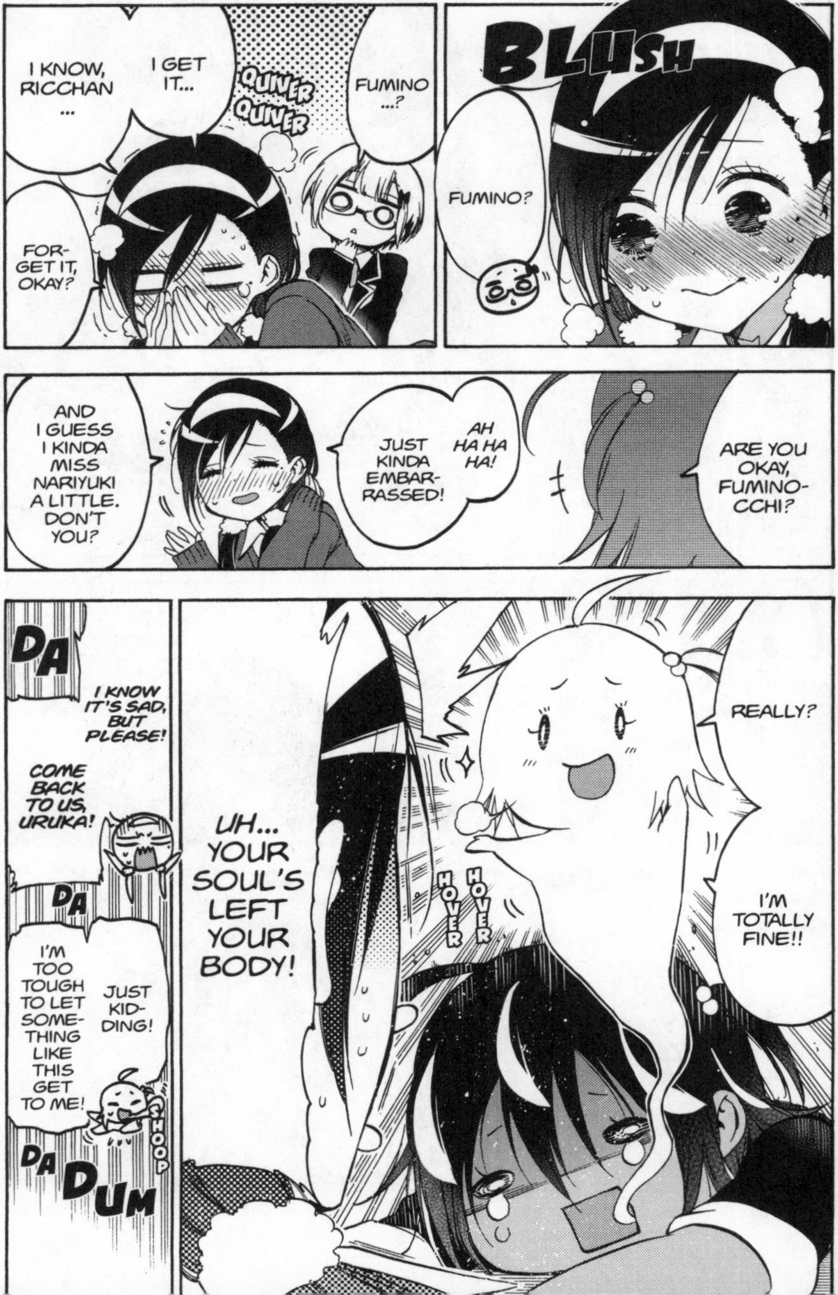
BLUSH
FUMINO?
FUMINO ...?
QUIVER QUIVER
I GET IT...
I KNOW, RICCHAN ...
FOR-GET IT, OKAY?
ARE YOU OKAY, FUMINO-CCHI?
AH HA HA HA!
JUST KINDA EMBAR-RASSED!
AND I GUESS I KINDA MISS NARIYUKI A LITTLE. DON'T YOU?
REALLY?
I'M TOTALLY FINE!!
HOVER HOVER
UH... YOUR SOUL'S LEFT YOUR BODY!
DA
I KNOW IT'S SAD, BUT PLEASE!
COME BACK TO US, URUKA!
DA
I'M TOO TOUGH TO LET SOME-THING LIKE THIS GET TO ME!
JUST KID-DING!
SHOOP
DA DUM

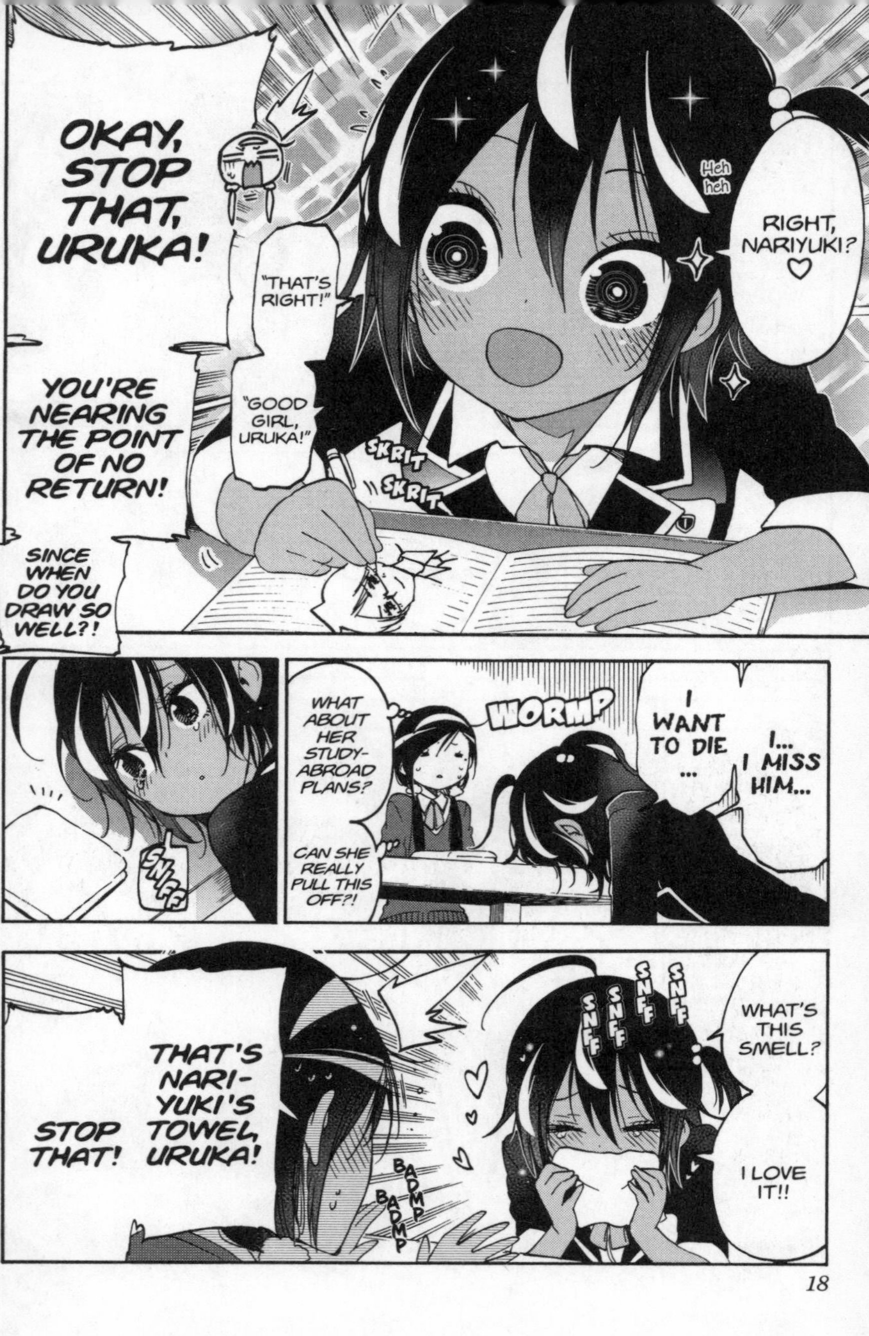
Heh heh
RIGHT, NARIYUKI? ♡
"THAT'S RIGHT!"
"GOOD GIRL, URUKA!"
SKRIT SKRIT
OKAY, STOP THAT, URUKA!
YOU'RE NEARING THE POINT OF NO RETURN!
SINCE WHEN DO YOU DRAW SO WELL?!
I... I MISS HIM...
I WANT TO DIE ...
WORMP
WHAT ABOUT HER STUDY-ABROAD PLANS?
CAN SHE REALLY PULL THIS OFF?!
SNIFF
WHAT'S THIS SMELL?
SNFF SNFF SNFF SNFF
I LOVE IT!!
BADMP BADMP
THAT'S NARI-YUKI'S TOWEL, URUKA!
STOP THAT!

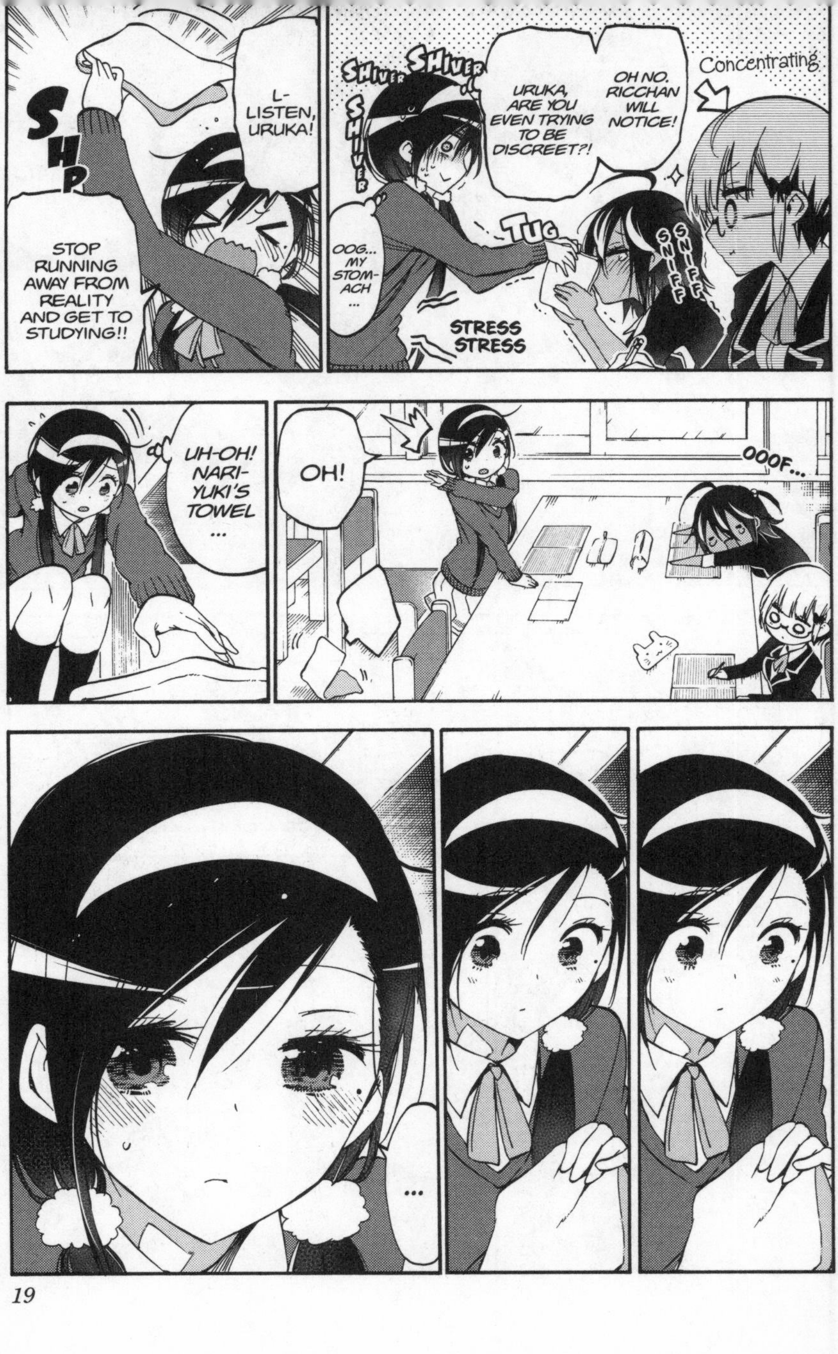
Concentrating
OH NO. RICCHAN WILL NOTICE!
URUKA, ARE YOU EVEN TRYING TO BE DISCREET?!
SHIVER SHIVER
SHIVER
SNIFF SNIFF
TUG
OOG... MY STOM-ACH ...
STRESS STRESS
L- LISTEN, URUKA!
SHP
STOP RUNNING AWAY FROM REALITY AND GET TO STUDYING!!
OOOF...
OH!
UH-OH! NARI-YUKI'S TOWEL ...
...

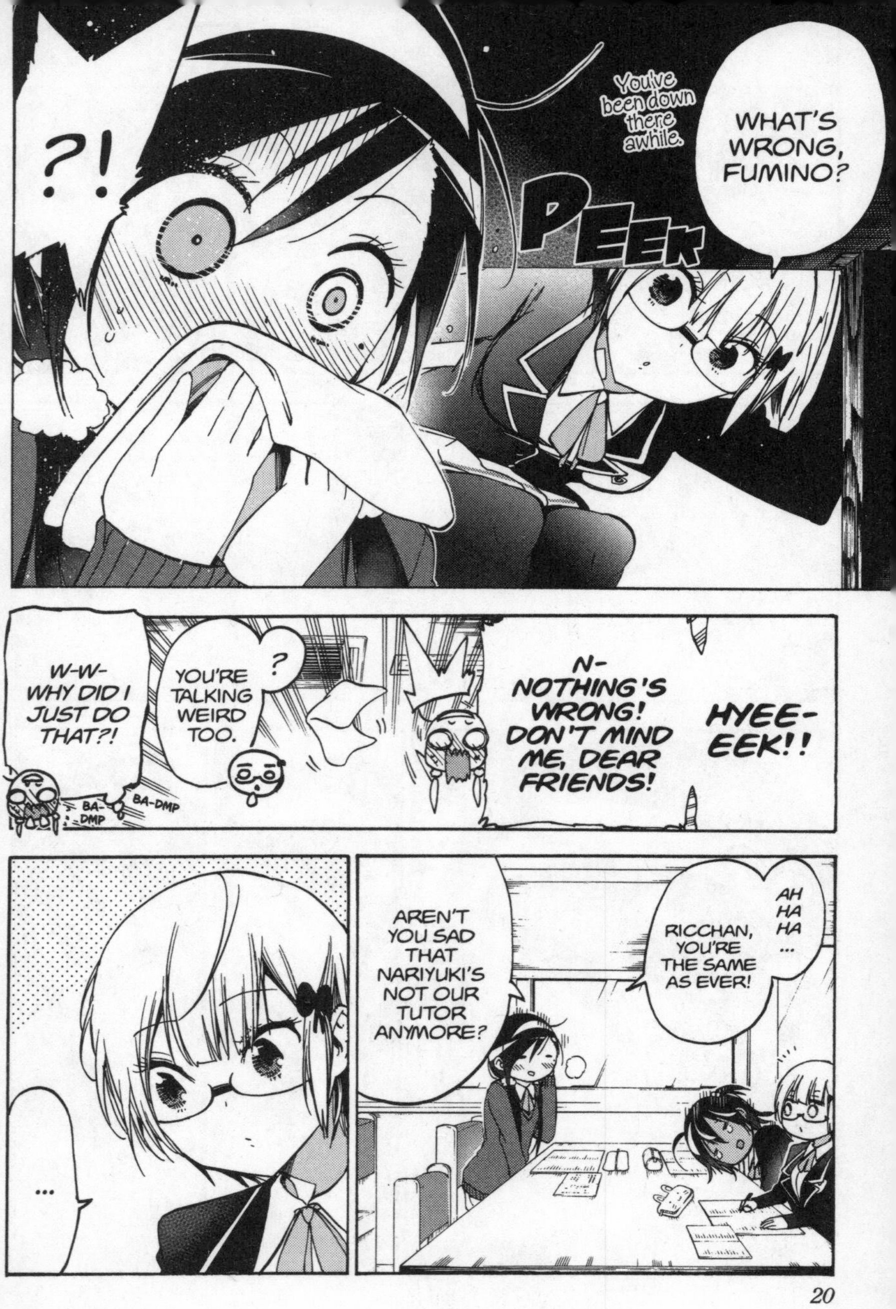
WHAT'S WRONG, FUMINO?
You've been down there awhile.
PEEK
?!
HYEEE-EEK!!
N-NOTHING'S WRONG! DON'T MIND ME, DEAR FRIENDS!
?
YOU'RE TALKING WEIRD TOO.
W-W-WHY DID I JUST DO THAT?!
BA-DMP
BA-DMP
RICCHAN, YOU'RE THE SAME AS EVER!
AH HA HA ...
AREN'T YOU SAD THAT NARIYUKI'S NOT OUR TUTOR ANYMORE?
...

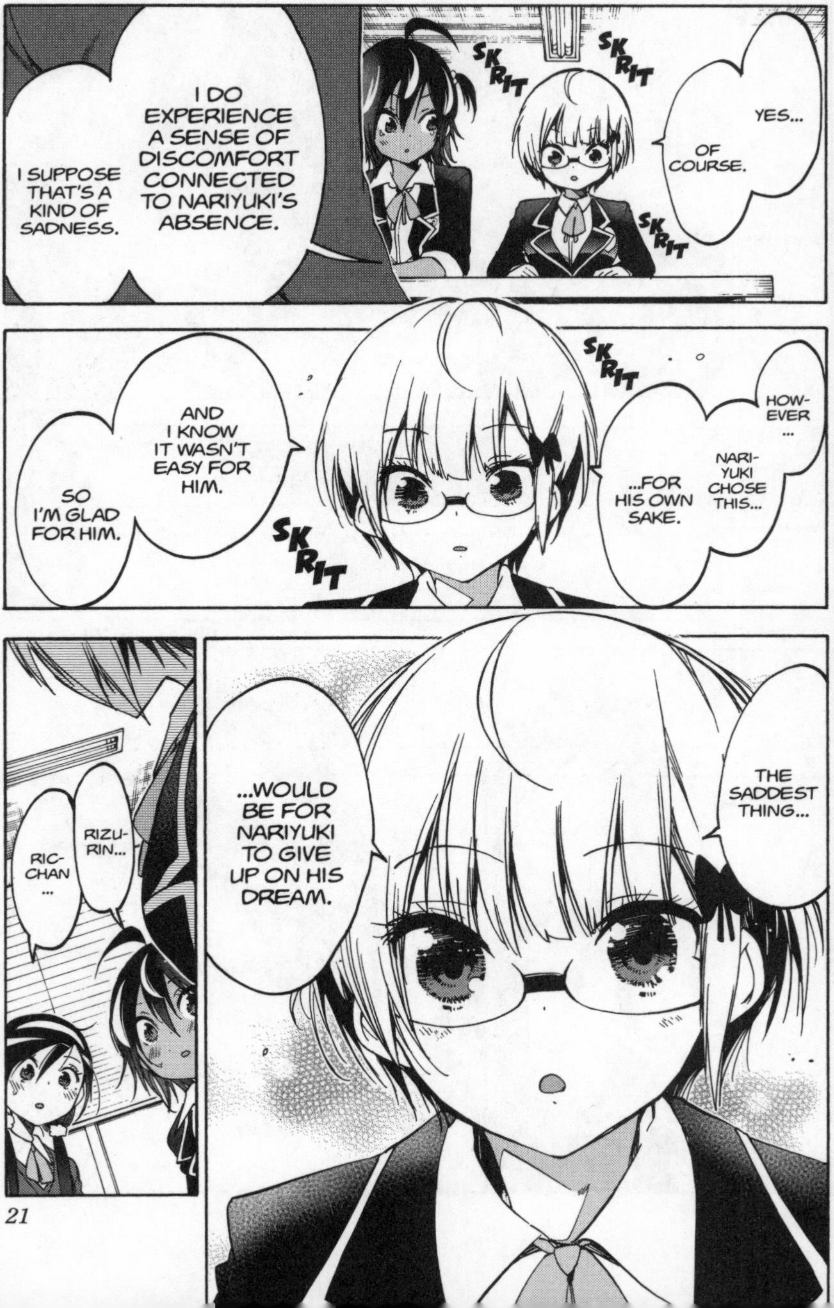
SKRIT
SKRIT
YES... OF COURSE.
SKRIT
I DO EXPERIENCE A SENSE OF DISCOMFORT CONNECTED TO NARIYUKI'S ABSENCE.
I SUPPOSE THAT'S A KIND OF SADNESS.
SKRIT
HOW-EVER... NARI-YUKI CHOSE THIS...
...FOR HIS OWN SAKE.
AND I KNOW IT WASN'T EASY FOR HIM.
SO I'M GLAD FOR HIM.
SKRIT
THE SADDEST THING...
...WOULD BE FOR NARIYUKI TO GIVE UP ON HIS DREAM.
RIZU-RIN...
RIC-CHAN...

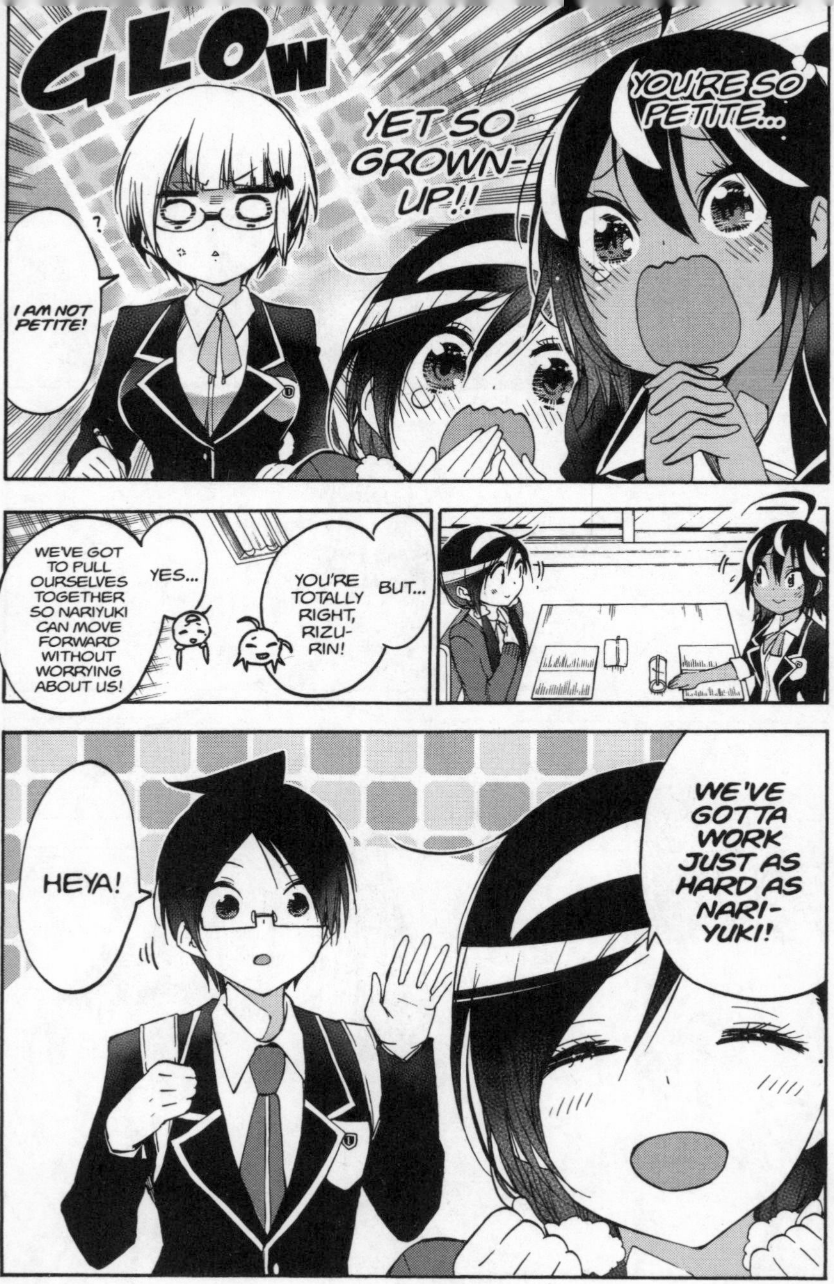
YOU'RE SO PETITE...
YET SO GROWN-UP!!
GLOW
?
I AM NOT PETITE!
YOU'RE TOTALLY RIGHT, RIZU-RIN!
BUT...
YES...
WE'VE GOT TO PULL OURSELVES TOGETHER SO NARIYUKI CAN MOVE FORWARD WITHOUT WORRYING ABOUT US!
WE'VE GOTTA WORK JUST AS HARD AS NARI-YUKI!
HEYA!

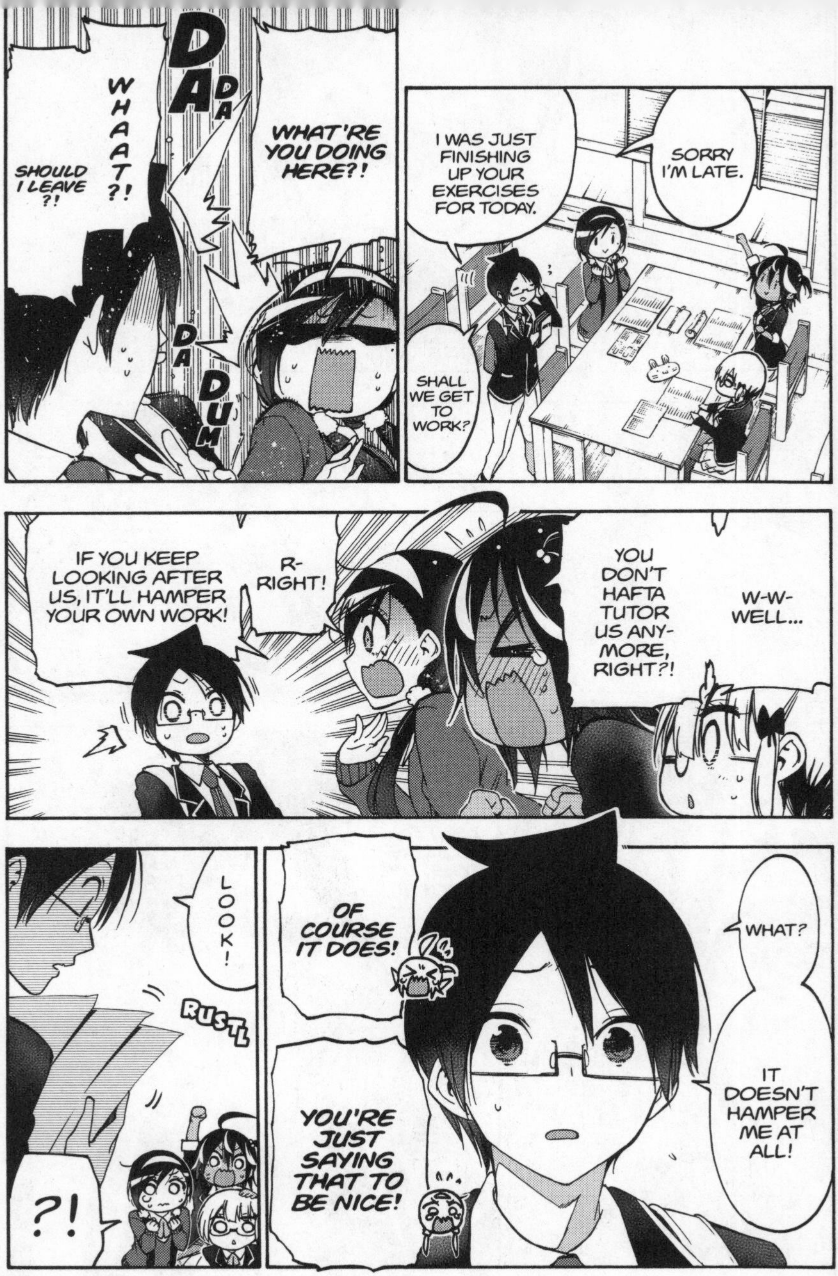
SORRY I'M LATE.
I WAS JUST FINISHING UP YOUR EXERCISES FOR TODAY.
SHALL WE GET TO WORK?
WHAT'RE YOU DOING HERE?!
DA DA
WHAAAT?!
SHOULD I LEAVE?!
DA DUM
W-W-WELL...
YOU DON'T HAFTA TUTOR US ANYMORE, RIGHT?!
R-RIGHT!
IF YOU KEEP LOOKING AFTER US, IT'LL HAMPER YOUR OWN WORK!
WHAT?
IT DOESN'T HAMPER ME AT ALL!
OF COURSE IT DOES!
YOU'RE JUST SAYING THAT TO BE NICE!
LOOK!
RUSTL
?!

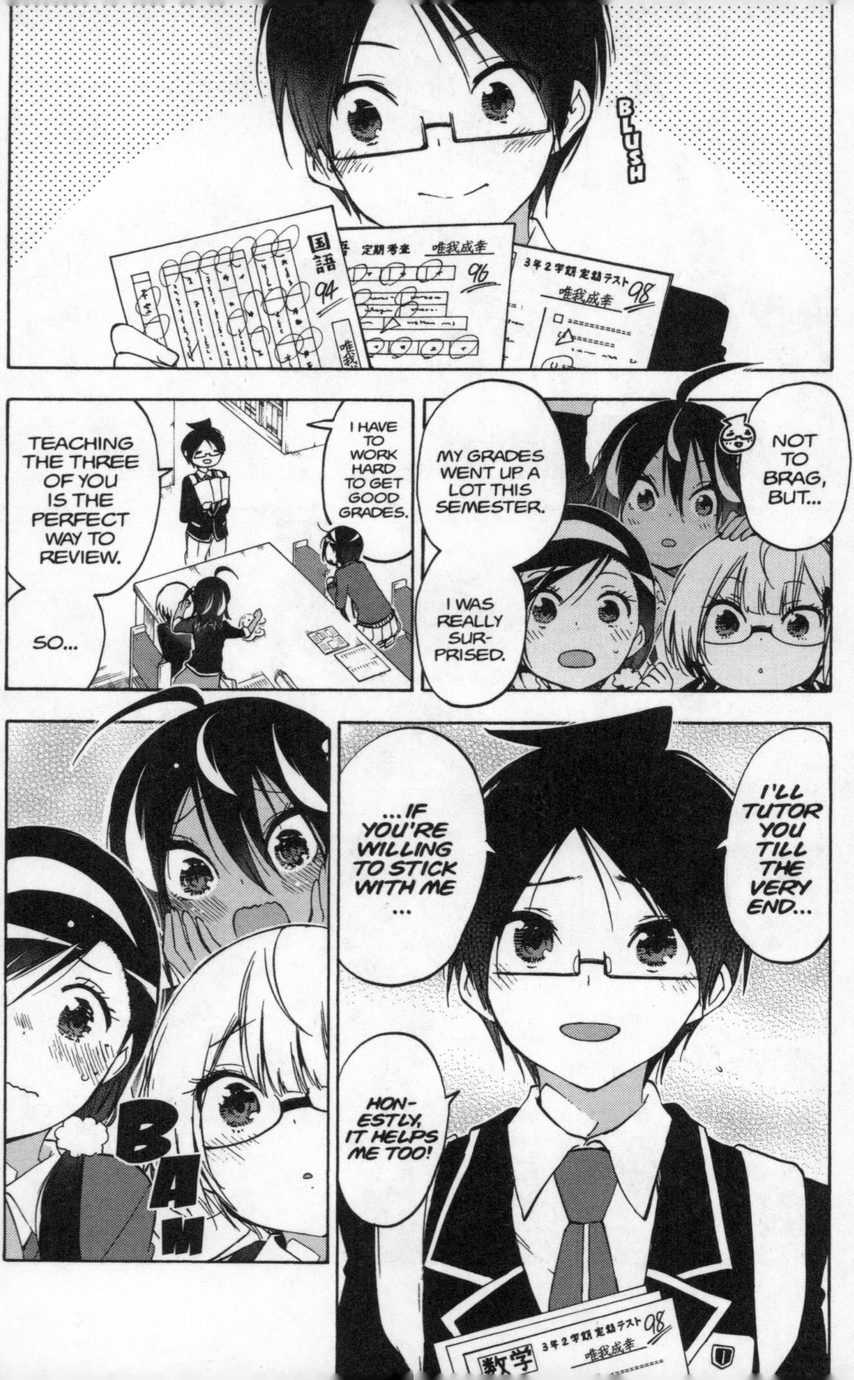
BLUSH
国語 94
定期考査 唯我成幸 96
3年2学期定期テスト 唯我成幸 98
NOT TO BRAG, BUT...
MY GRADES WENT UP A LOT THIS SEMESTER.
I WAS REALLY SURPRISED.
I HAVE TO WORK HARD TO GET GOOD GRADES.
TEACHING THE THREE OF YOU IS THE PERFECT WAY TO REVIEW.
SO...
I'LL TUTOR YOU TILL THE VERY END...
...IF YOU'RE WILLING TO STICK WITH ME ...
HON-ESTLY, IT HELPS ME TOO!
数学 3年2学期定期テスト 98 唯我成幸
BAM

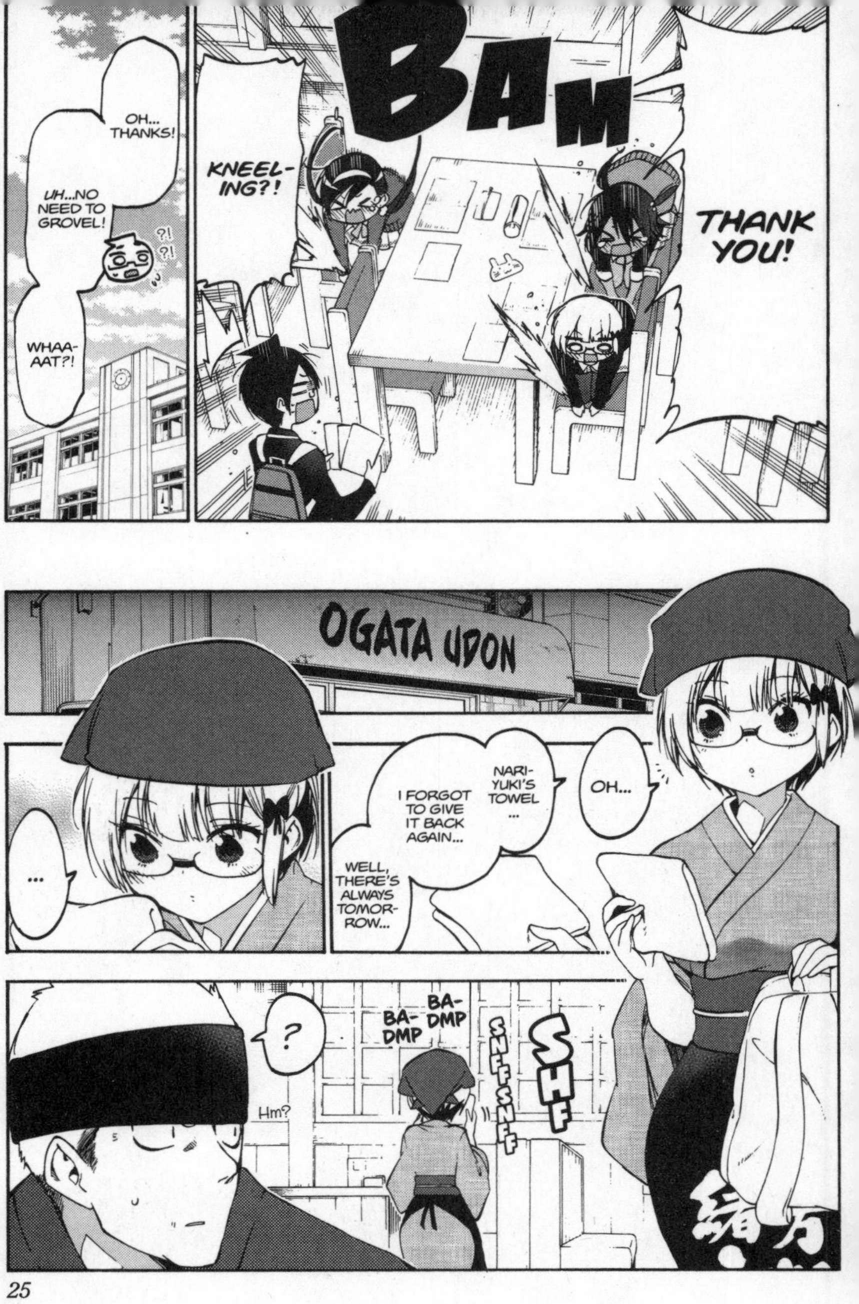
BAM
THANK YOU!
KNEEL-ING?!
OH... THANKS!
UH...NO NEED TO GROVEL!
?! ?!
WHAA-AAT?!
OGATA UDON
OH...
NARI-YUKI'S TOWEL ...
I FORGOT TO GIVE IT BACK AGAIN...
WELL, THERE'S ALWAYS TOMOR-ROW...
...
SHF
SNFFSNFF
BA-DMP
BA-DMP
?
Hm?
緒方

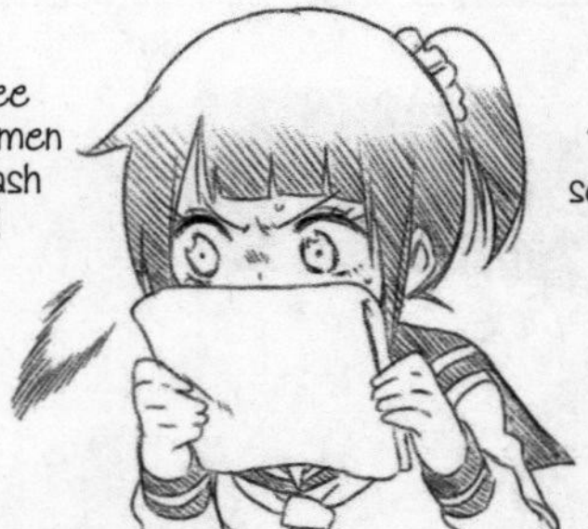
This scent...
...of three other women won't wash out?!

Question 98: Sometimes a Tome Lures Them to the [X] of Seduction

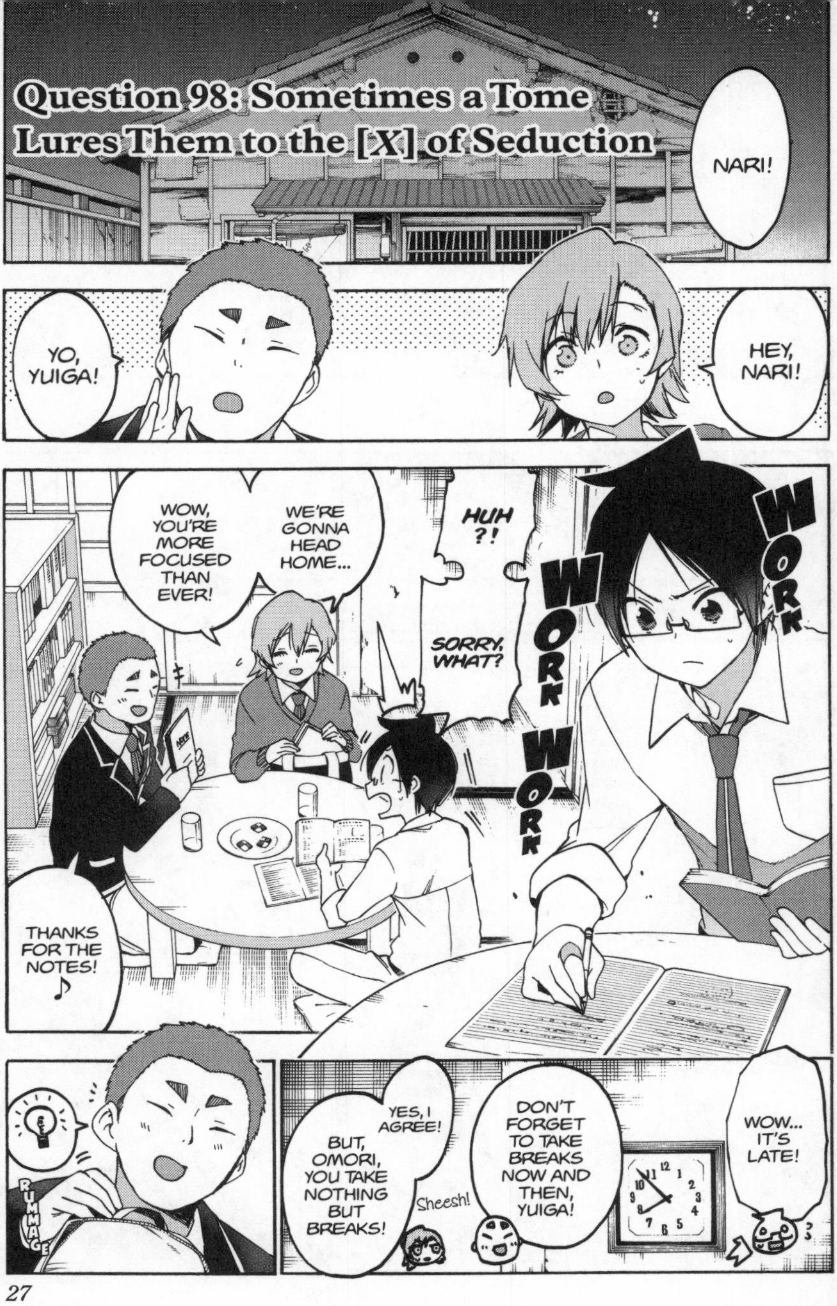

NARI!
HEY, NARI!
YO, YUIGA!
WORK WORK WORK WORK WORK
WE'RE GONNA HEAD HOME...
WOW, YOU'RE MORE FOCUSED THAN EVER!
HUH?!
SORRY, WHAT?
THANKS FOR THE NOTES! ♪
WOW... IT'S LATE!
DON'T FORGET TO TAKE BREAKS NOW AND THEN, YUIGA!
YES, I AGREE! BUT, OMORI, YOU TAKE NOTHING BUT BREAKS!
Sheesh!
RUMMAGE

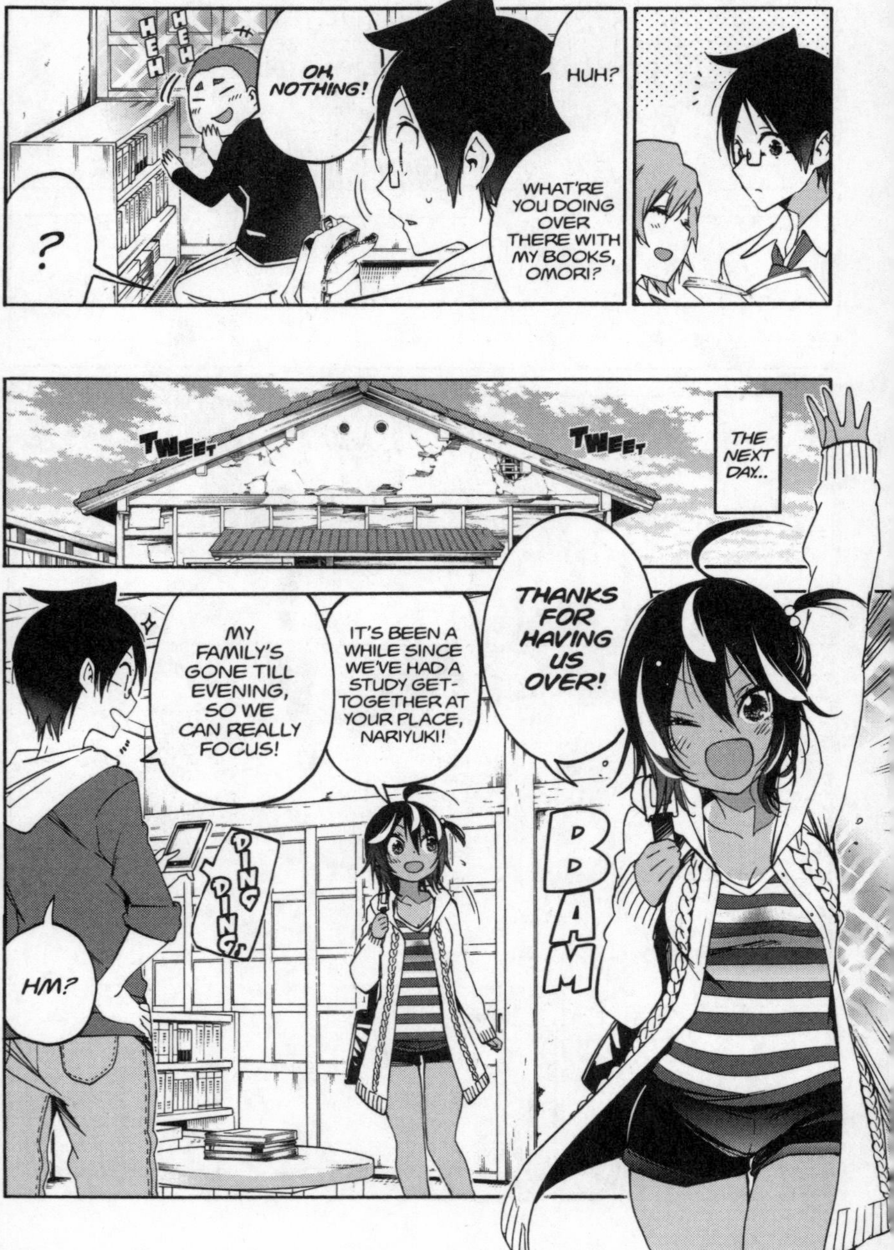
HUH?
WHAT'RE YOU DOING OVER THERE WITH MY BOOKS, OMORI?
OH, NOTHING!
HEH HEH
?
THE NEXT DAY...
TWEET
TWEET
THANKS FOR HAVING US OVER!
BAM
IT'S BEEN A WHILE SINCE WE'VE HAD A STUDY GET-TOGETHER AT YOUR PLACE, NARIYUKI!
MY FAMILY'S GONE TILL EVENING, SO WE CAN REALLY FOCUS!
DING DING
HM?

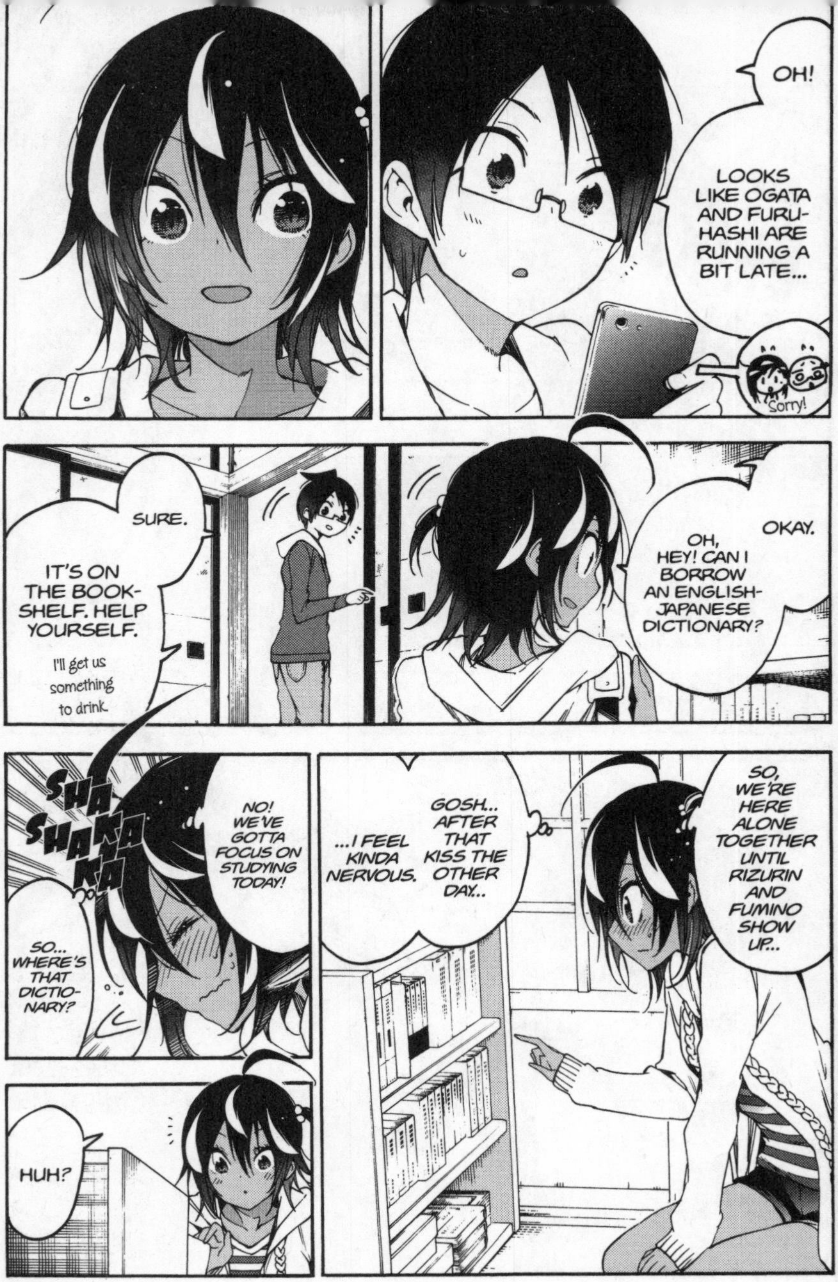
OH!
LOOKS LIKE OGATA AND FURU-HASHI ARE RUNNING A BIT LATE...
Sorry!
OKAY.
OH, HEY! CAN I BORROW AN ENGLISH-JAPANESE DICTIONARY?
SURE.
IT'S ON THE BOOK-SHELF. HELP YOURSELF.
I'll get us something to drink.
SO, WE'RE HERE ALONE TOGETHER UNTIL RIZURIN AND FUMINO SHOW UP...
GOSH... AFTER THAT KISS THE OTHER DAY...
...I FEEL KINDA NERVOUS.
NO! WE'VE GOTTA FOCUS ON STUDYING TODAY!
SHAKA SHAKA
SO... WHERE'S THAT DICTIONARY?
HUH?

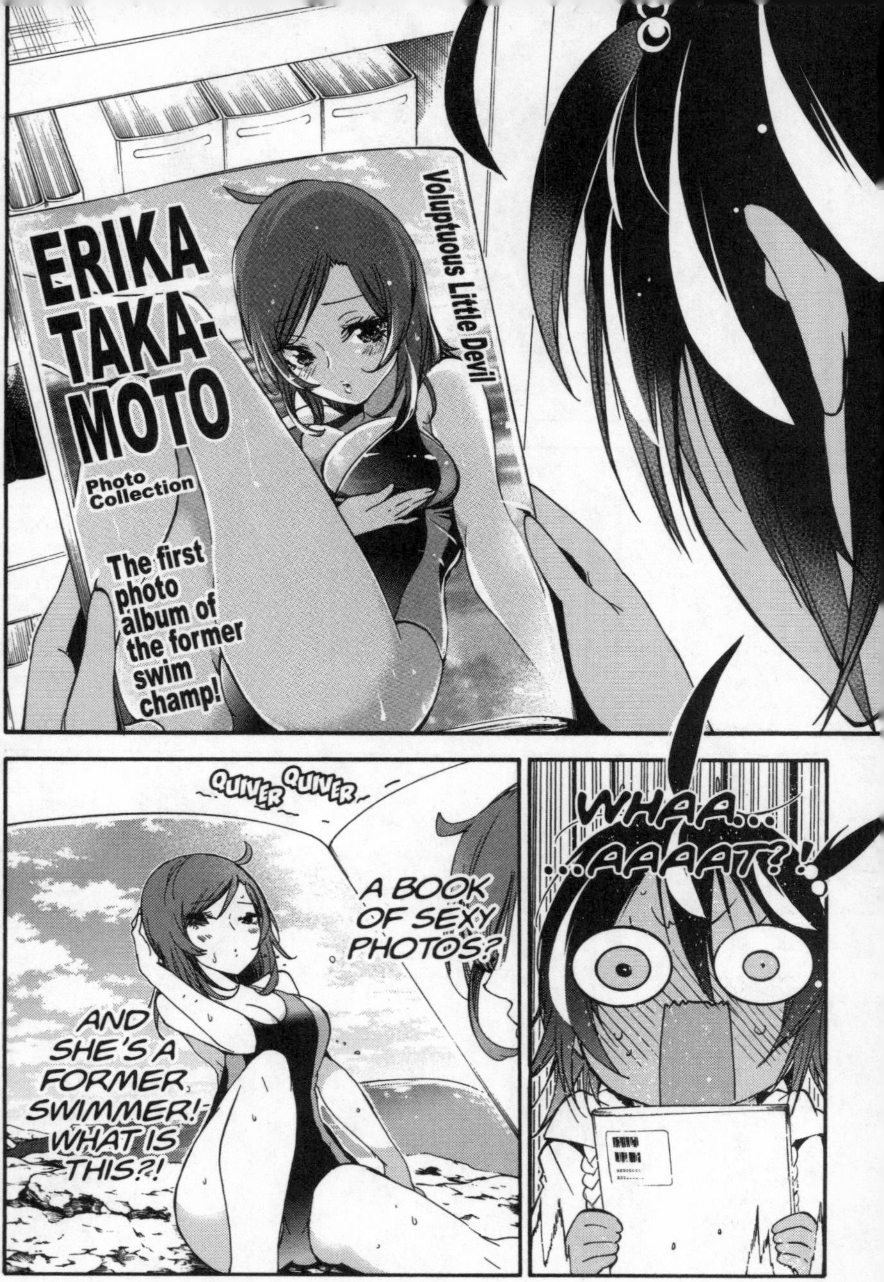
Voluptuous Little Devil
ERIKA TAKA-MOTO
Photo Collection
The first photo album of the former swim champ!
WHAA...
...AAAAT?!
QUIVER QUIVER
A BOOK OF SEXY PHOTOS?
AND SHE'S A FORMER SWIMMER! WHAT IS THIS?!

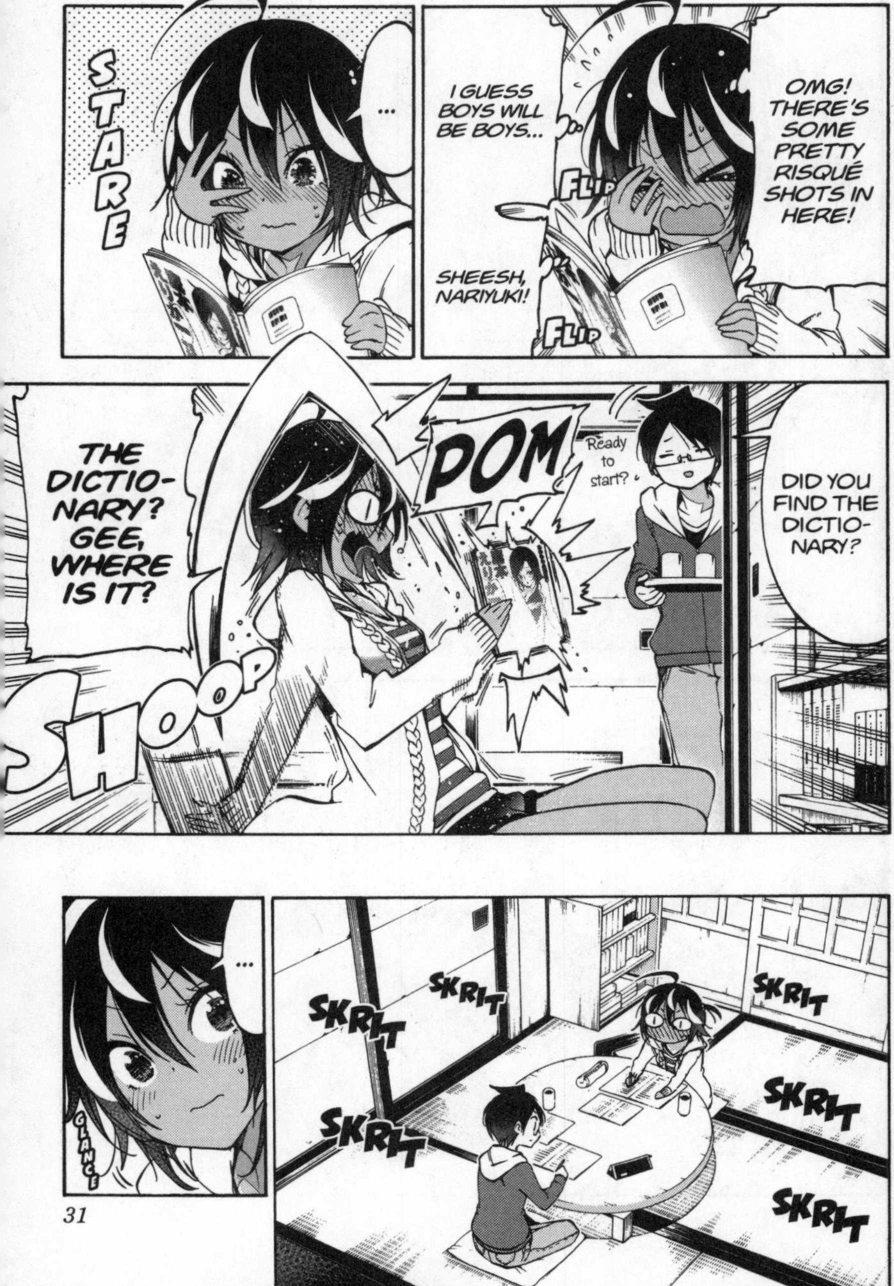
OMG! THERE'S SOME PRETTY RISQUÉ SHOTS IN HERE!
I GUESS BOYS WILL BE BOYS...
FLIP
SHEESH, NARIYUKI!
FLIP
...
STARE
DID YOU FIND THE DICTIONARY?
Ready to start?
POM
THE DICTIONARY? GEE, WHERE IS IT?
SHOOP
SKRIT
SKRIT
SKRIT
SKRIT
SKRIT
SKRIT
...
GLANCE

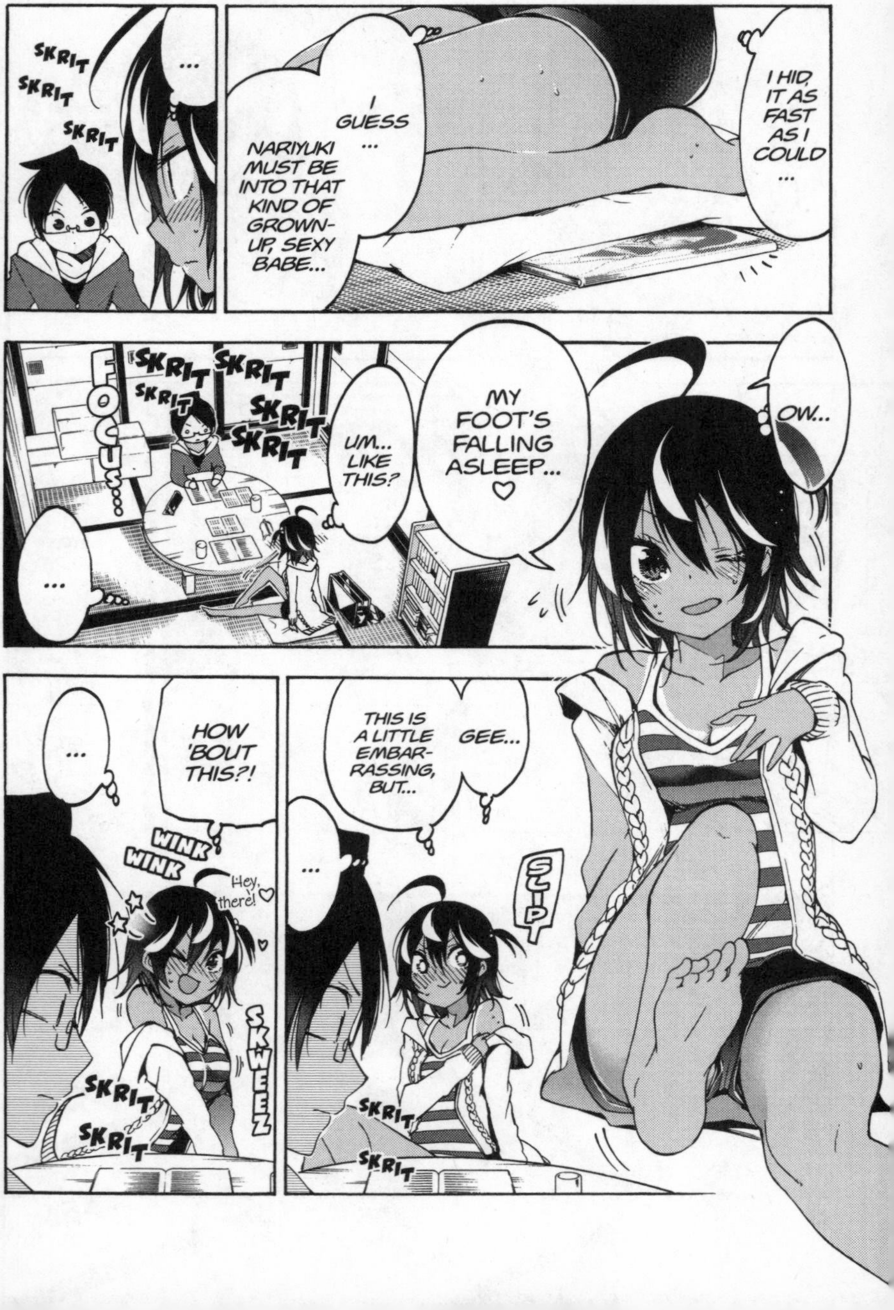
I HID IT AS FAST AS I COULD...
I GUESS... NARIYUKI MUST BE INTO THAT KIND OF GROWN-UP, SEXY BABE...
...
SKRIT
SKRIT
SKRIT
OW...
SLIP
MY FOOT'S FALLING ASLEEP... ♡
UM... LIKE THIS?
SKRIT SKRIT
SKRIT
SKRIT
SKRIT
FOCUS...
...
GEE...
THIS IS A LITTLE EMBARRASSING, BUT...
...
SKRIT
SKRIT
...
HOW 'BOUT THIS?!
WINK WINK
Hey, there! ♡
SKWEEZ
SKRIT
SKRIT

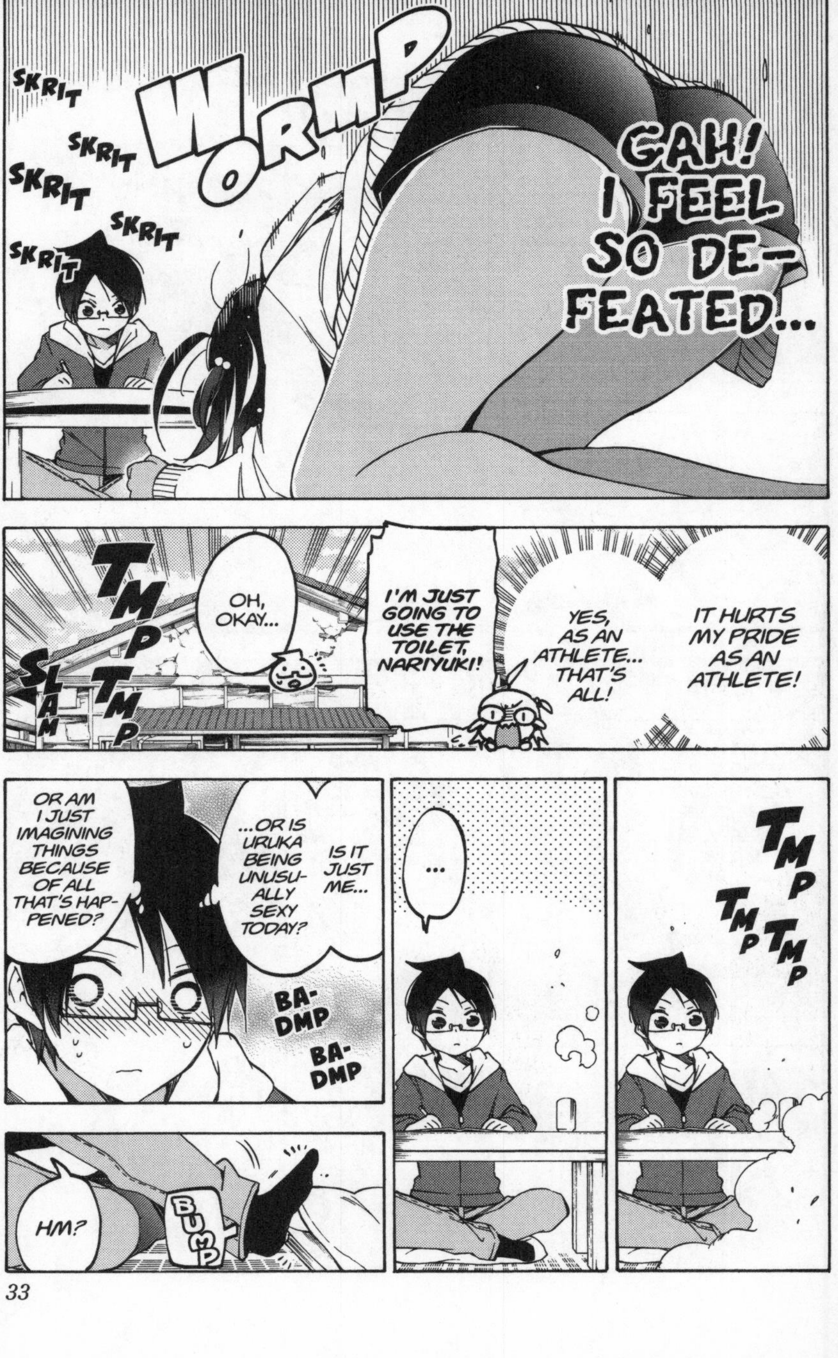
WORMP
GAH! I FEEL SO DE-FEATED...
SKRIT SKRIT SKRIT SKRIT SKRIT
IT HURTS MY PRIDE AS AN ATHLETE!
YES, AS AN ATHLETE... THAT'S ALL!
I'M JUST GOING TO USE THE TOILET, NARIYUKI!
OH, OKAY...
TMP TMP TMP
SLAM
TMP TMP TMP TMP
...
IS IT JUST ME...
...OR IS URUKA BEING UNUSU-ALLY SEXY TODAY?
OR AM I JUST IMAGINING THINGS BECAUSE OF ALL THAT'S HAP-PENED?
BA-DMP BA-DMP
BUMP
HM?

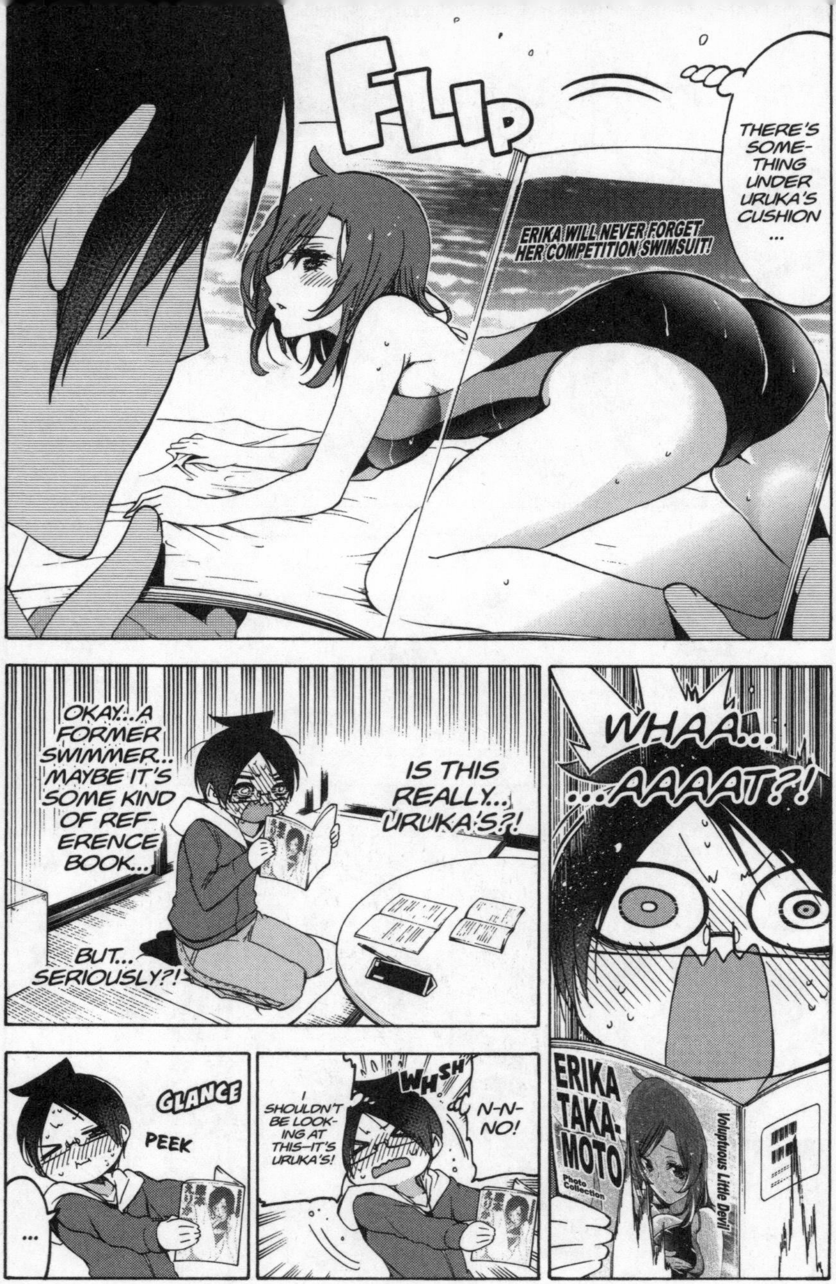
FLIP
THERE'S SOMETHING UNDER URUKA'S CUSHION ...
ERIKA WILL NEVER FORGET HER COMPETITION SWIMSUIT!
WHAA... ...AAAAT?!
ERIKA TAKA-MOTO
Photo Collection
Voluptuous Little Devil
IS THIS REALLY... URUKA'S?!
OKAY...A FORMER SWIMMER... MAYBE IT'S SOME KIND OF REFERENCE BOOK...
BUT... SERIOUSLY?!
WHSH
N-N-NO!
I SHOULDN'T BE LOOKING AT THIS—IT'S URUKA'S!
GLANCE
PEEK
...

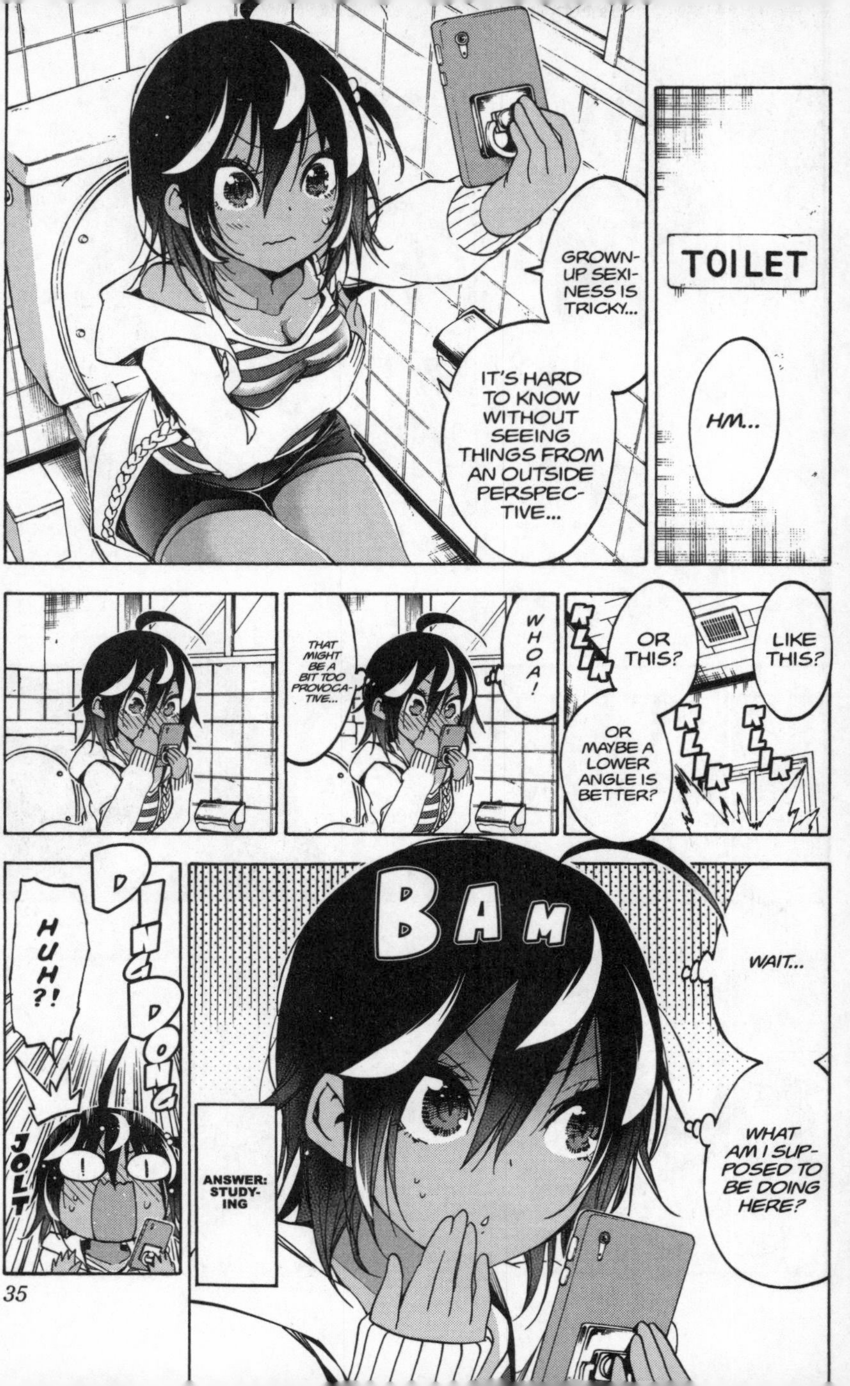
TOILET
HM...
GROWN-UP SEXINESS IS TRICKY...
IT'S HARD TO KNOW WITHOUT SEEING THINGS FROM AN OUTSIDE PERSPECTIVE...
LIKE THIS?
KLIK
KLIK
OR THIS?
KLIK
OR MAYBE A LOWER ANGLE IS BETTER?
WHOA!
THAT MIGHT BE A BIT TOO PROVOCATIVE...
BAM
WAIT...
WHAT AM I SUPPOSED TO BE DOING HERE?
ANSWER: STUDYING
DING DONG
HUH?!
JOLT

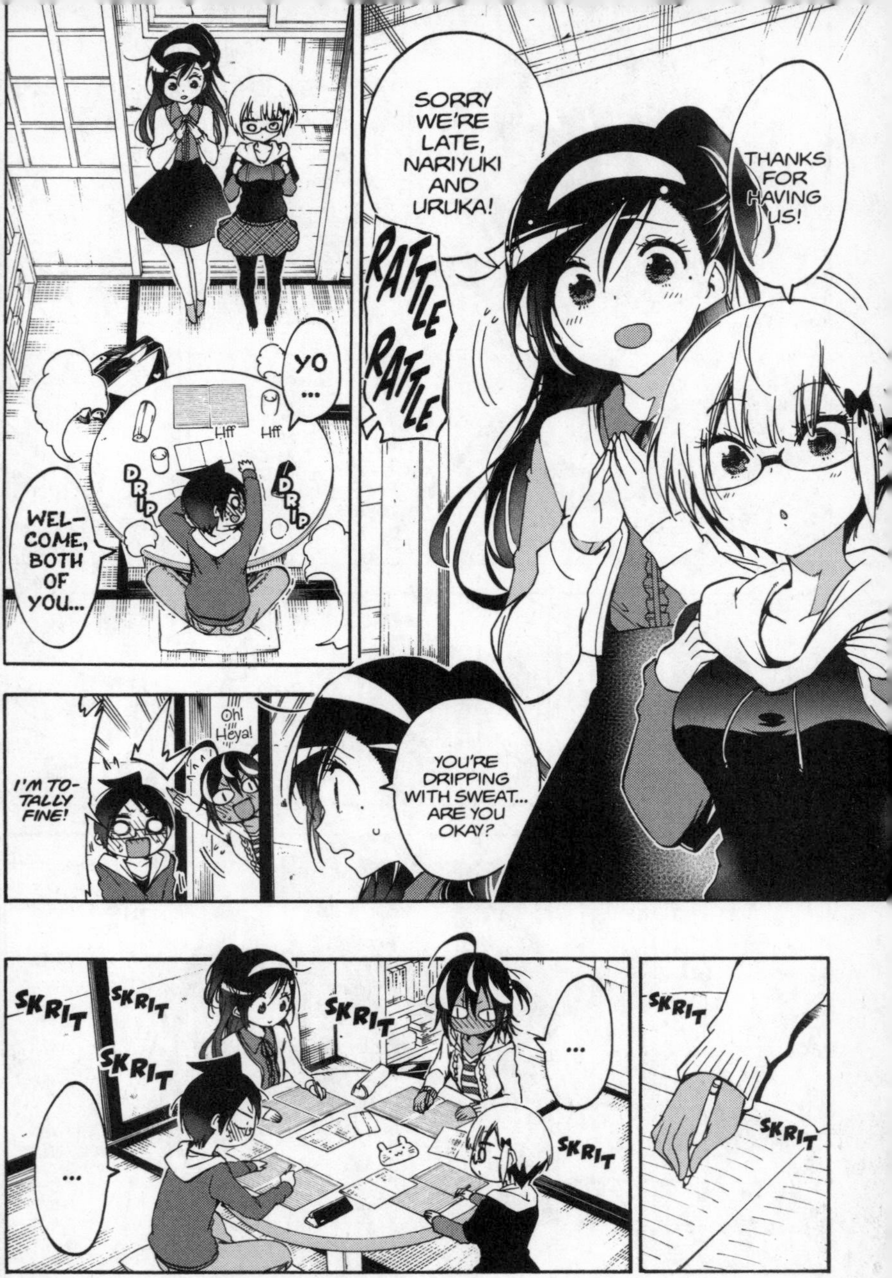
SORRY WE'RE LATE, NARIYUKI AND URUKA!
THANKS FOR HAVING US!
RATTLE RATTLE
YO ...
Hff Hff
DRIP DRIP
WEL-COME, BOTH OF YOU...
YOU'RE DRIPPING WITH SWEAT... ARE YOU OKAY?
Oh! Heya!
I'M TO-TALLY FINE!
SKRIT
SKRIT
...
SKRIT
SKRIT
SKRIT
SKRIT
SKRIT
...

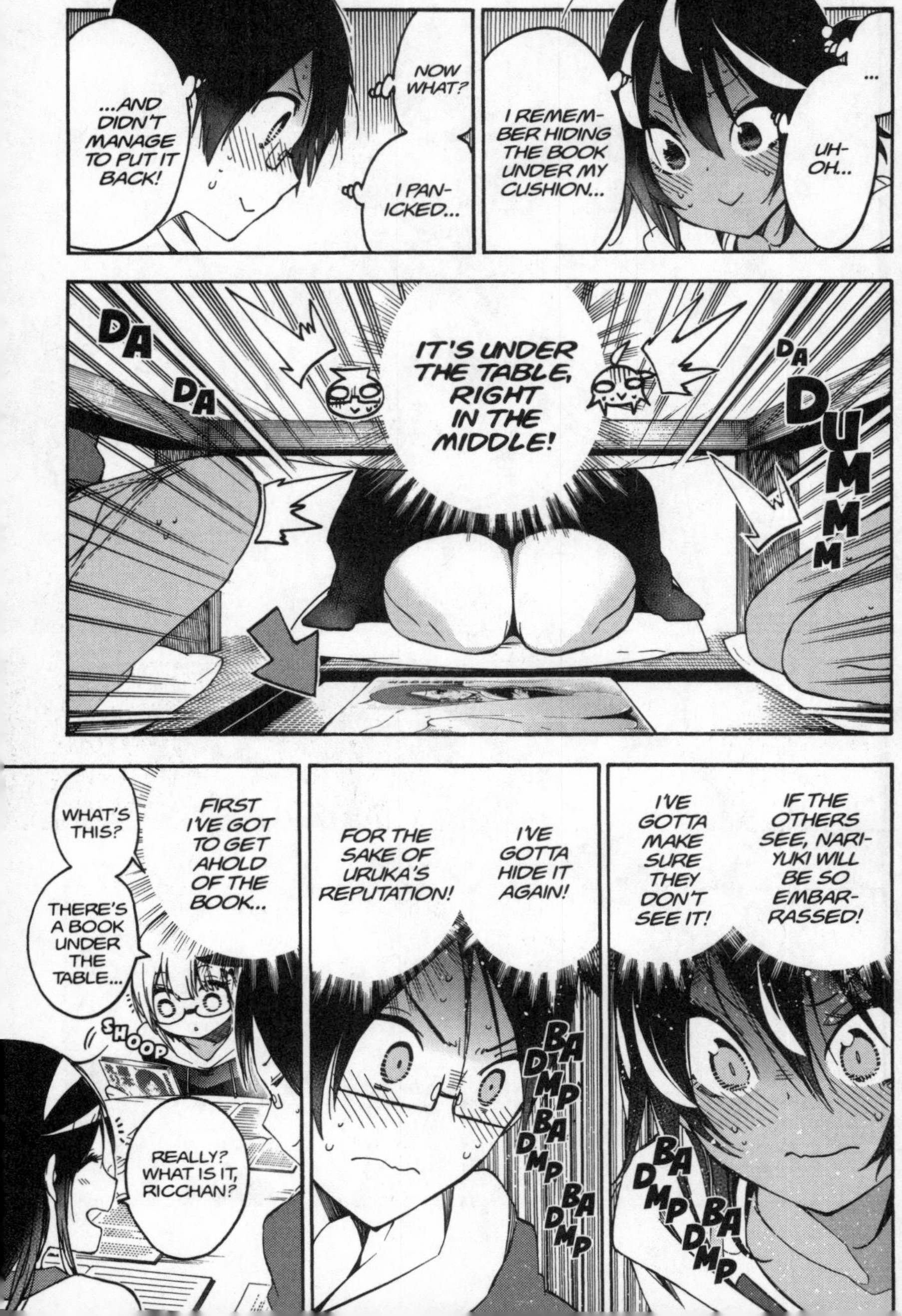
...
UH-OH...
I REMEMBER HIDING THE BOOK UNDER MY CUSHION...
NOW WHAT?
I PANICKED...
...AND DIDN'T MANAGE TO PUT IT BACK!
DA DUMMM
IT'S UNDER THE TABLE, RIGHT IN THE MIDDLE!
DA DA
IF THE OTHERS SEE, NARIYUKI WILL BE SO EMBARRASSED!
I'VE GOTTA MAKE SURE THEY DON'T SEE IT!
BA DMP BA DMP
I'VE GOTTA HIDE IT AGAIN!
FOR THE SAKE OF URUKA'S REPUTATION!
BA DMP BA DMP BA DMP
FIRST I'VE GOT TO GET AHOLD OF THE BOOK...
WHAT'S THIS?
THERE'S A BOOK UNDER THE TABLE...
SHOOP
REALLY? WHAT IS IT, RICCHAN?

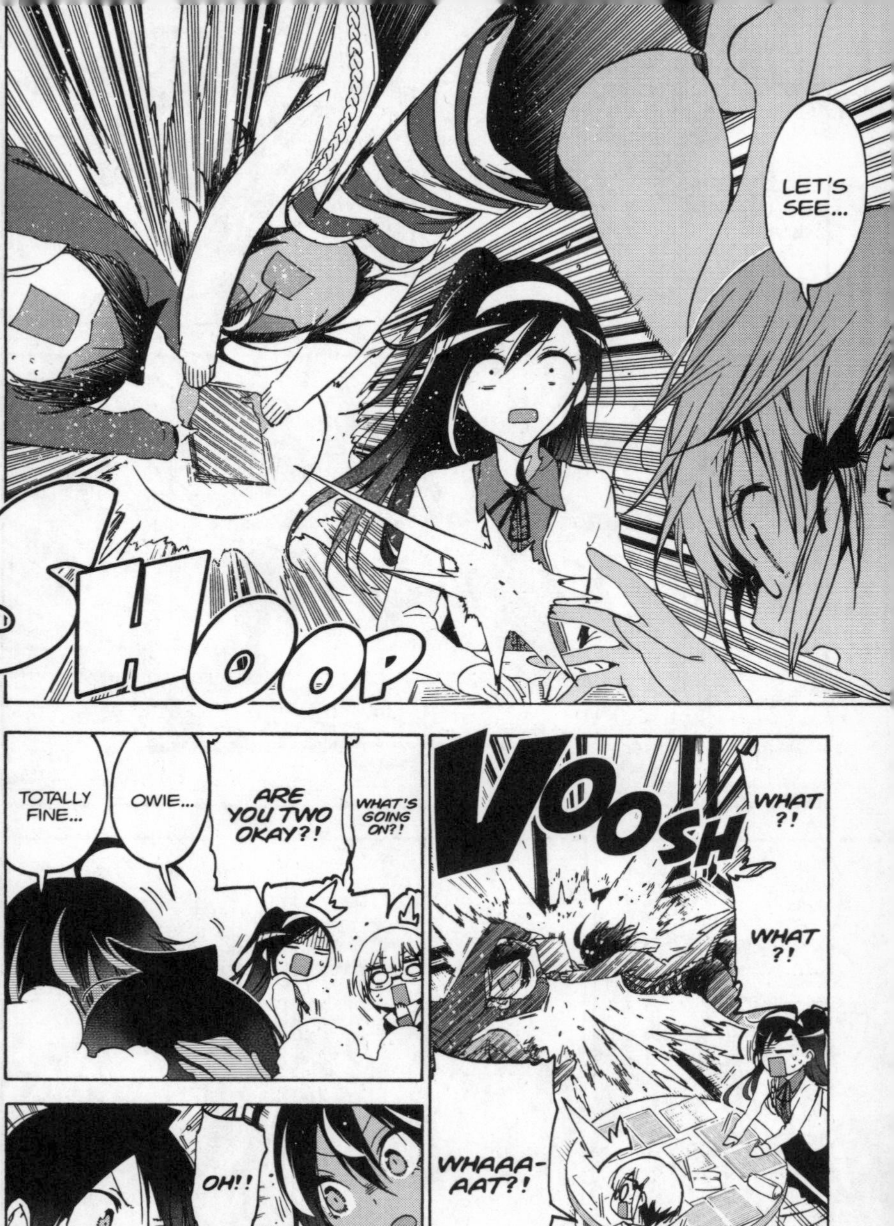
LET'S SEE...
WHOOP
VOOSH
WHAT?!
WHAT?!
WHAAA-AAT?!
WHAT'S GOING ON?!
ARE YOU TWO OKAY?!
OWIE...
TOTALLY FINE...
OH!!

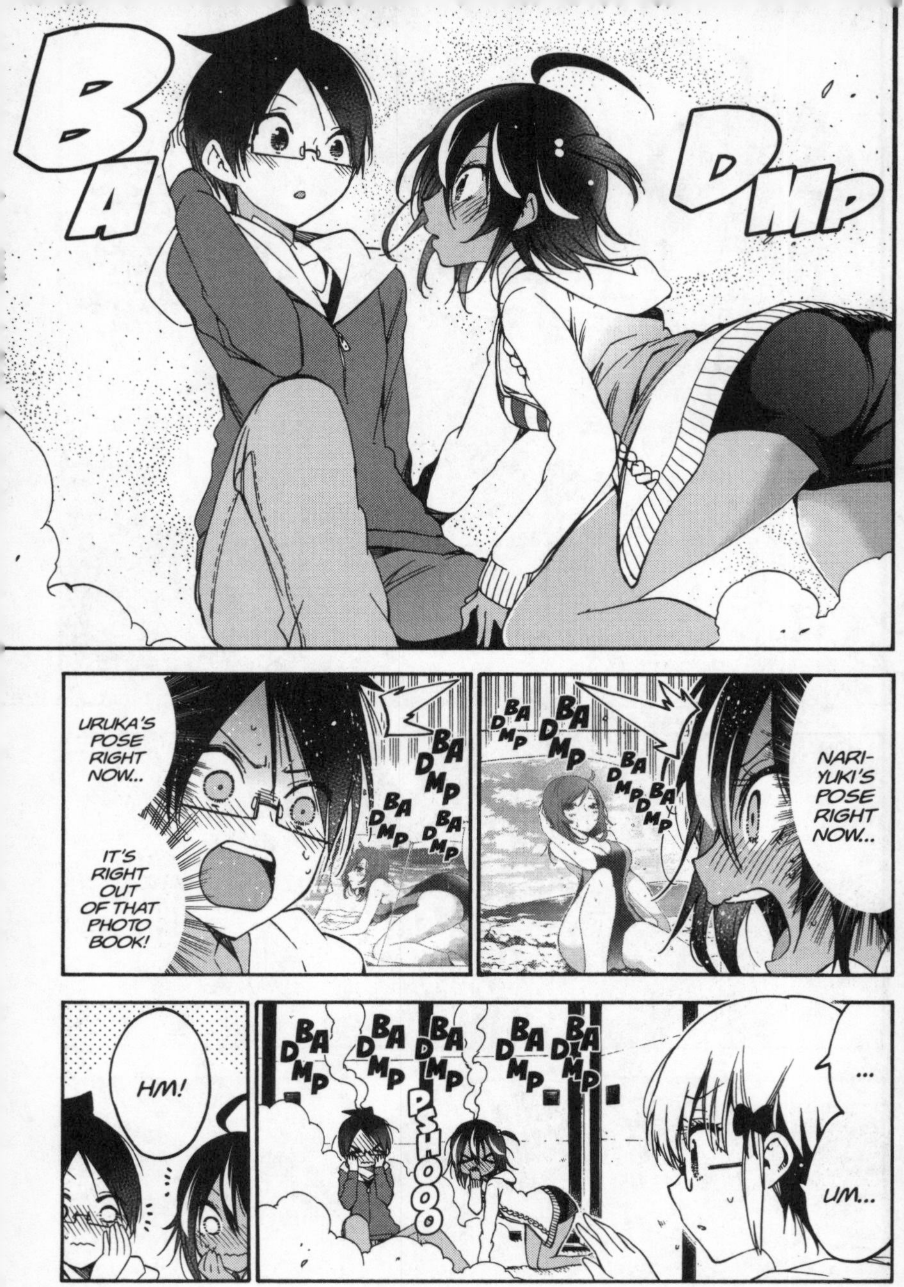
BA DMP
NARI-YUKI'S POSE RIGHT NOW...
BA DMP BA DMP BA DMP BA DMP
URUKA'S POSE RIGHT NOW...
IT'S RIGHT OUT OF THAT PHOTO BOOK!
BA DMP BA DMP BA DMP
...
UM...
BA DMP BA DMP BA DMP BA DMP BA DMP
PSHOOO
HM!

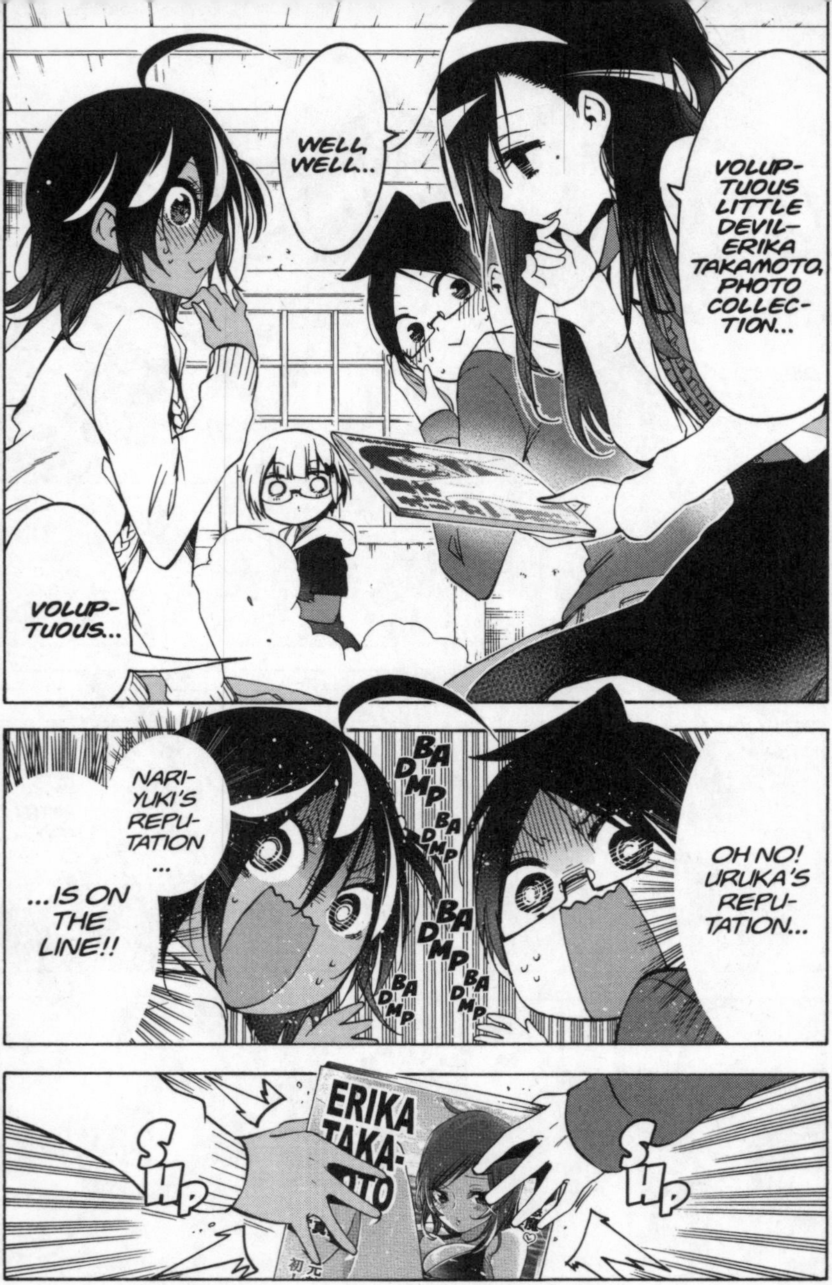
VOLUP-TUOUS LITTLE DEVIL-ERIKA TAKAMOTO, PHOTO COLLEC-TION...
WELL, WELL...
VOLUP-TUOUS...
OH NO! URUKA'S REPU-TATION...
BA DMP BA DMP
BA DMP BA DMP BA DMP
NARI-YUKI'S REPU-TATION ...
...IS ON THE LINE!!
SHP
ERIKA TAKA-
SHP

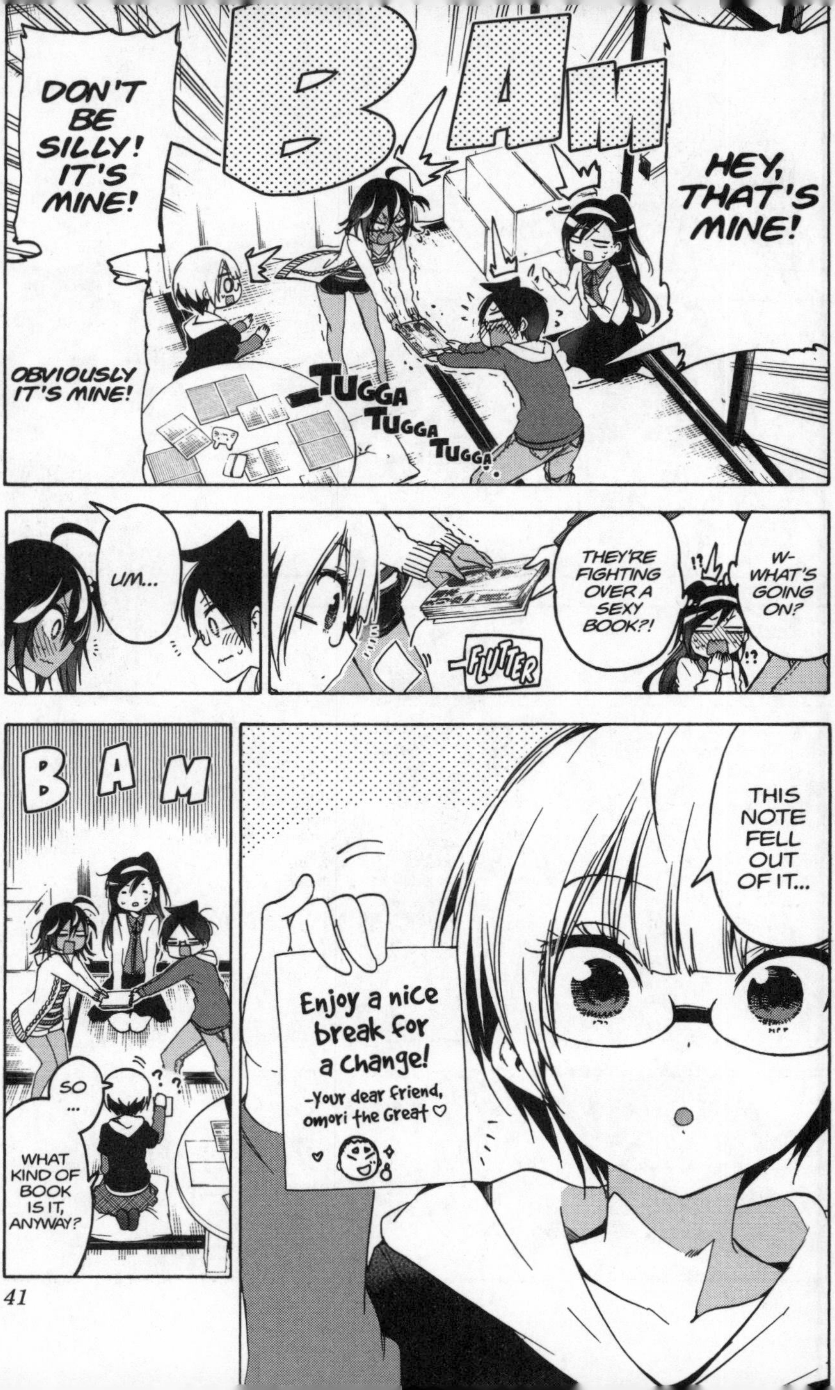
HEY, THAT'S MINE!
BAM
DON'T BE SILLY! IT'S MINE!
OBVIOUSLY IT'S MINE!
TUGGA TUGGA TUGGA
W- WHAT'S GOING ON?
THEY'RE FIGHTING OVER A SEXY BOOK?!
FLUTTER
UM...
THIS NOTE FELL OUT OF IT...
Enjoy a nice break for a change!
-Your dear friend, omori the Great
BAM
SO ...
WHAT KIND OF BOOK IS IT, ANYWAY?

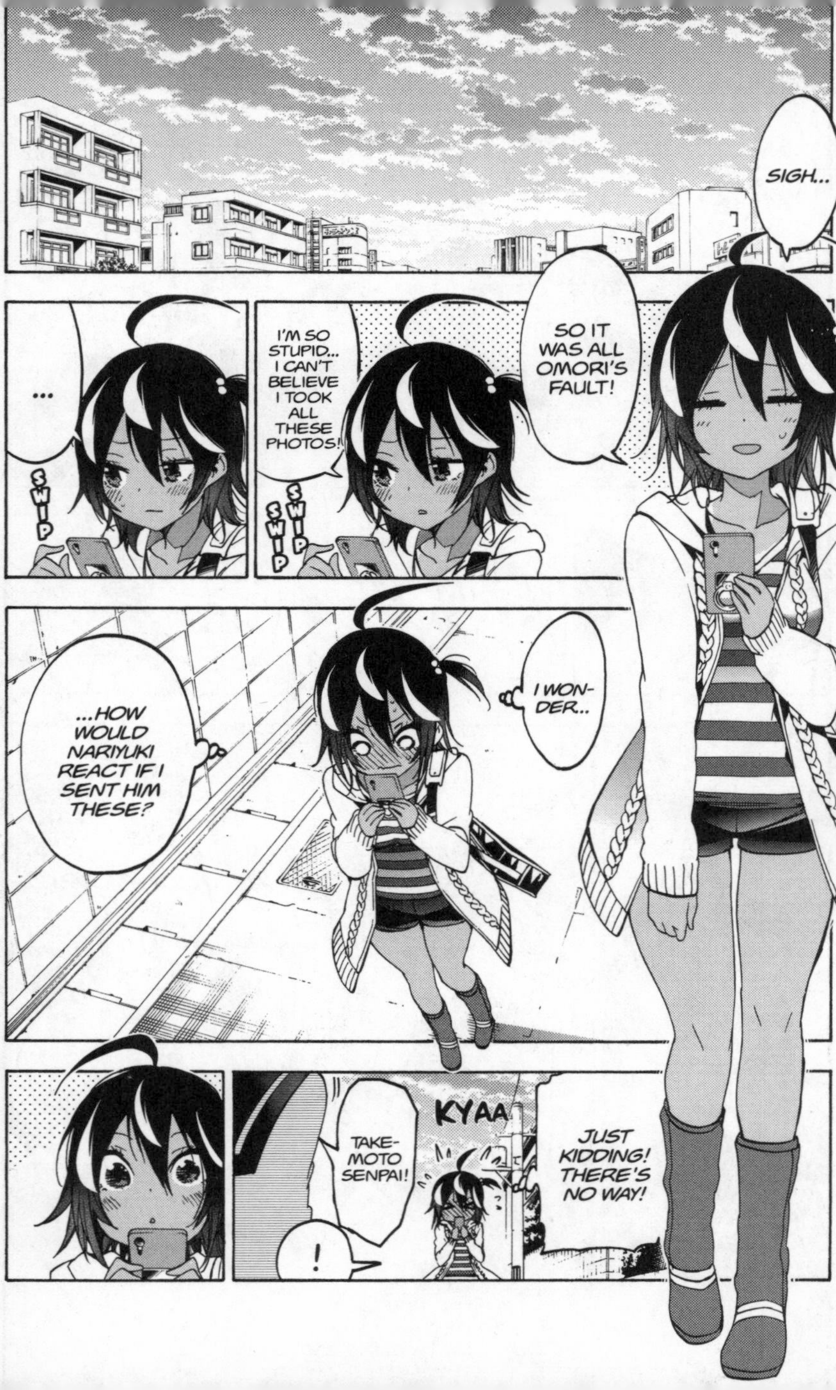

SIGH...
SO IT WAS ALL OMORI'S FAULT!
I'M SO STUPID... I CAN'T BELIEVE I TOOK ALL THESE PHOTOS!
SWIP SWIP
...
SWIP
I WON-DER...
...HOW WOULD NARIYUKI REACT IF I SENT HIM THESE?
JUST KIDDING! THERE'S NO WAY!
KYAA
TAKE-MOTO SENPAI!
!

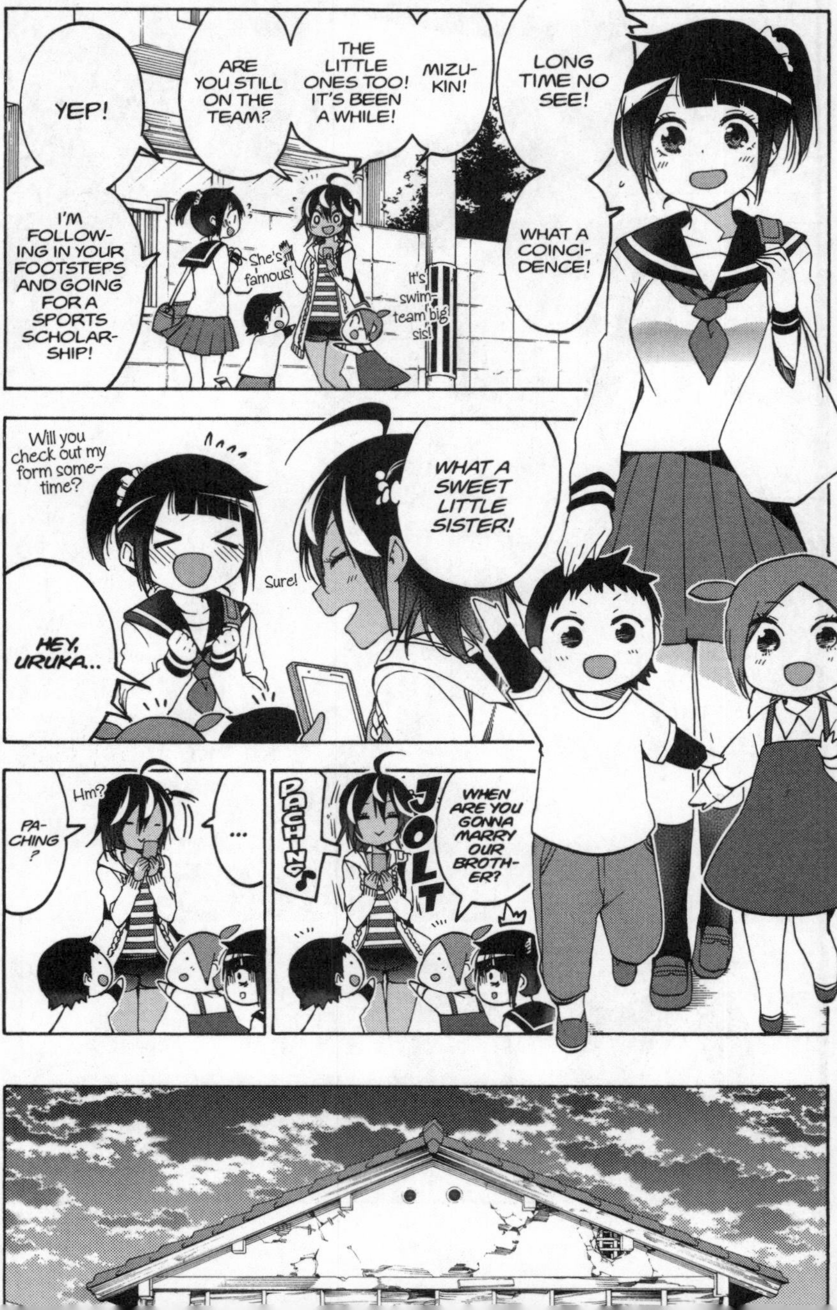
LONG TIME NO SEE!
WHAT A COINCIDENCE!
MIZU-KIN!
THE LITTLE ONES TOO! IT'S BEEN A WHILE!
ARE YOU STILL ON THE TEAM?
It's swim-team big sis!
She's famous!
YEP!
I'M FOLLOWING IN YOUR FOOTSTEPS AND GOING FOR A SPORTS SCHOLARSHIP!
WHAT A SWEET LITTLE SISTER!
Sure!
Will you check out my form sometime?
HEY, URUKA...
WHEN ARE YOU GONNA MARRY OUR BROTHER?
JOLT
PACHING
...
Hm?
PA-CHING?

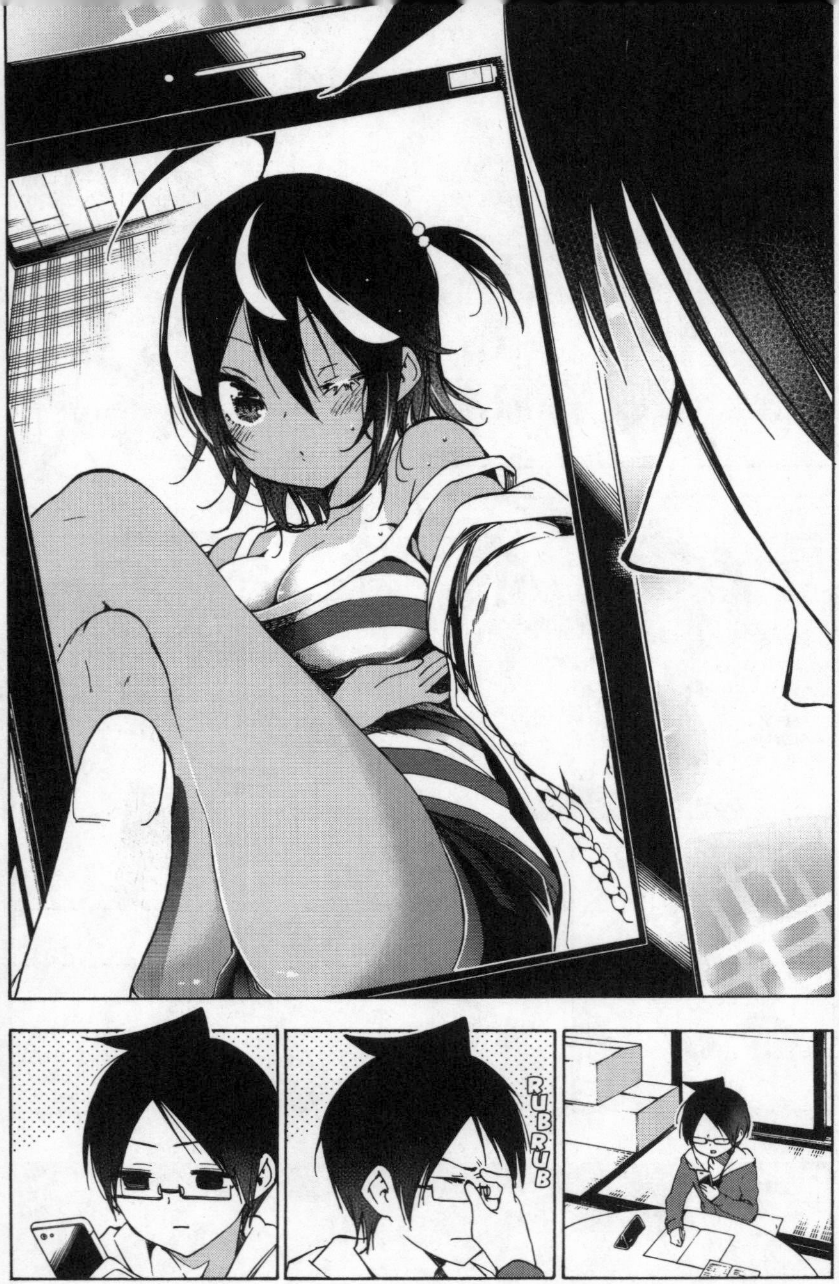
RUB RUB

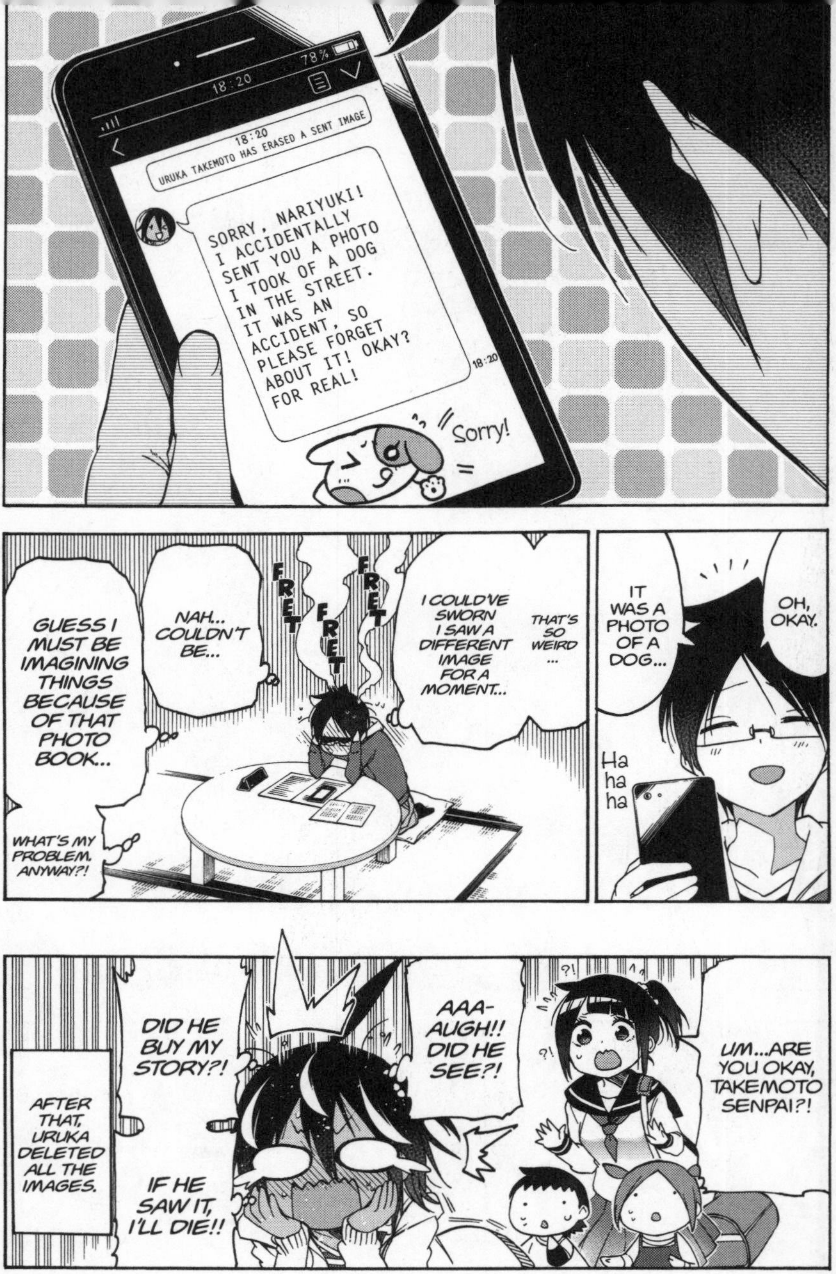
78%
18:20
18:20
URUKA TAKEMOTO HAS ERASED A SENT IMAGE
SORRY, NARIYUKI! I ACCIDENTALLY SENT YOU A PHOTO I TOOK OF A DOG IN THE STREET. IT WAS AN ACCIDENT, SO PLEASE FORGET ABOUT IT! OKAY? FOR REAL!
18:20
Sorry!
OH, OKAY.
IT WAS A PHOTO OF A DOG...
Ha ha ha
THAT'S SO WEIRD...
I COULD'VE SWORN I SAW A DIFFERENT IMAGE FOR A MOMENT...
FRET
FRET
FRET
NAH... COULDN'T BE...
GUESS I MUST BE IMAGINING THINGS BECAUSE OF THAT PHOTO BOOK...
WHAT'S MY PROBLEM, ANYWAY?!
UM...ARE YOU OKAY, TAKEMOTO SENPAI?!
?!
?!
AAA-AUGH!! DID HE SEE?!
DID HE BUY MY STORY?!
IF HE SAW IT, I'LL DIE!!
AFTER THAT, URUKA DELETED ALL THE IMAGES.

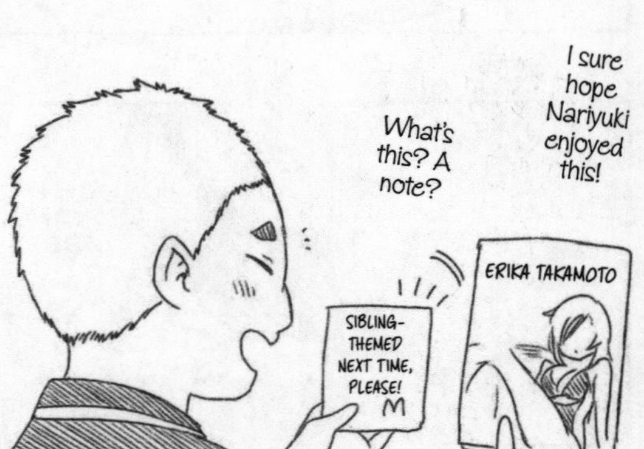
I sure hope Nariyuki enjoyed this!
What's this? A note?
ERIKA TAKAMOTO
SIBLING-THEMED NEXT TIME, PLEASE!
M

Question 99: Nonetheless, a Predecessor Imitates [X]'s Appearance Anticipating Tomorrow

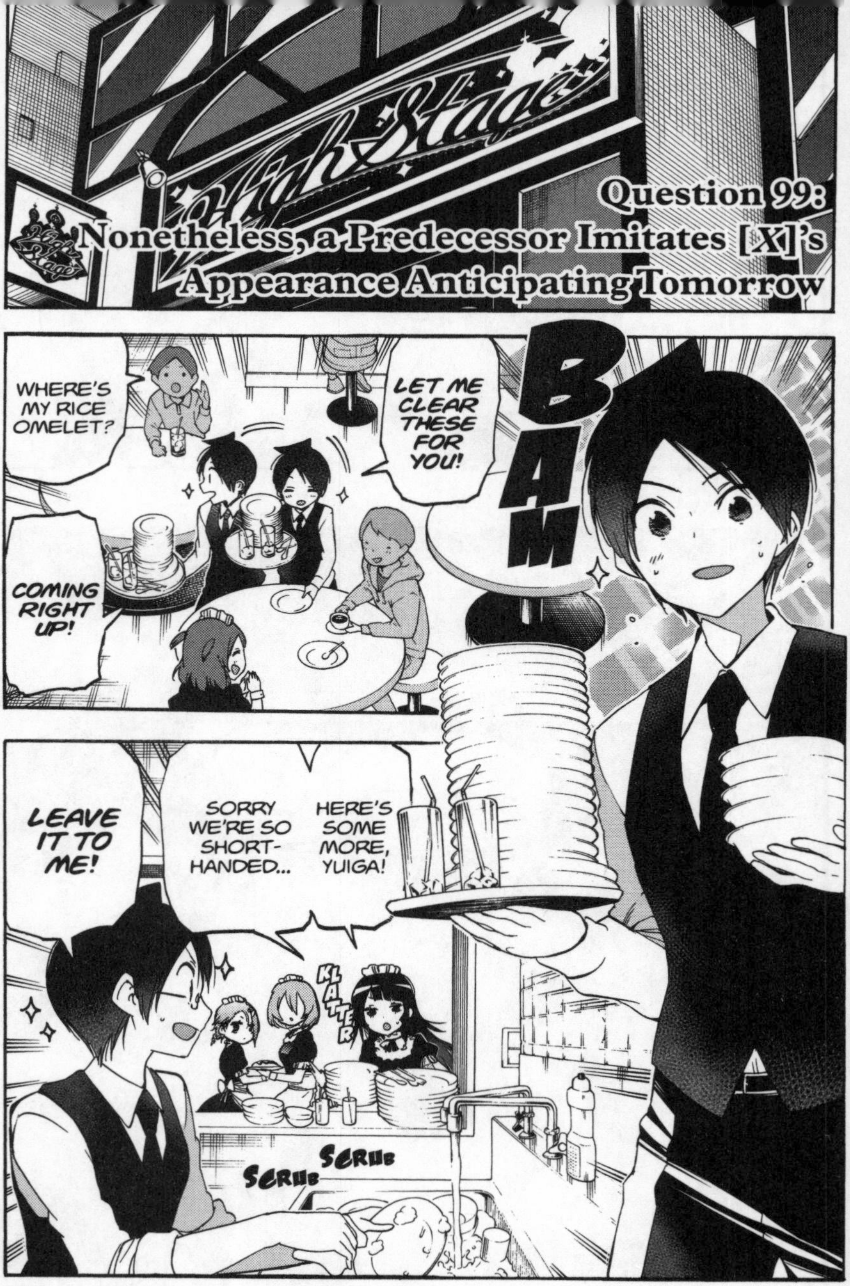

High Stage
BAM
LET ME CLEAR THESE FOR YOU!
WHERE'S MY RICE OMELET?
COMING RIGHT UP!
HERE'S SOME MORE, YUIGA!
SORRY WE'RE SO SHORT-HANDED...
LEAVE IT TO ME!
KLATTER
SCRUB
SCRUB

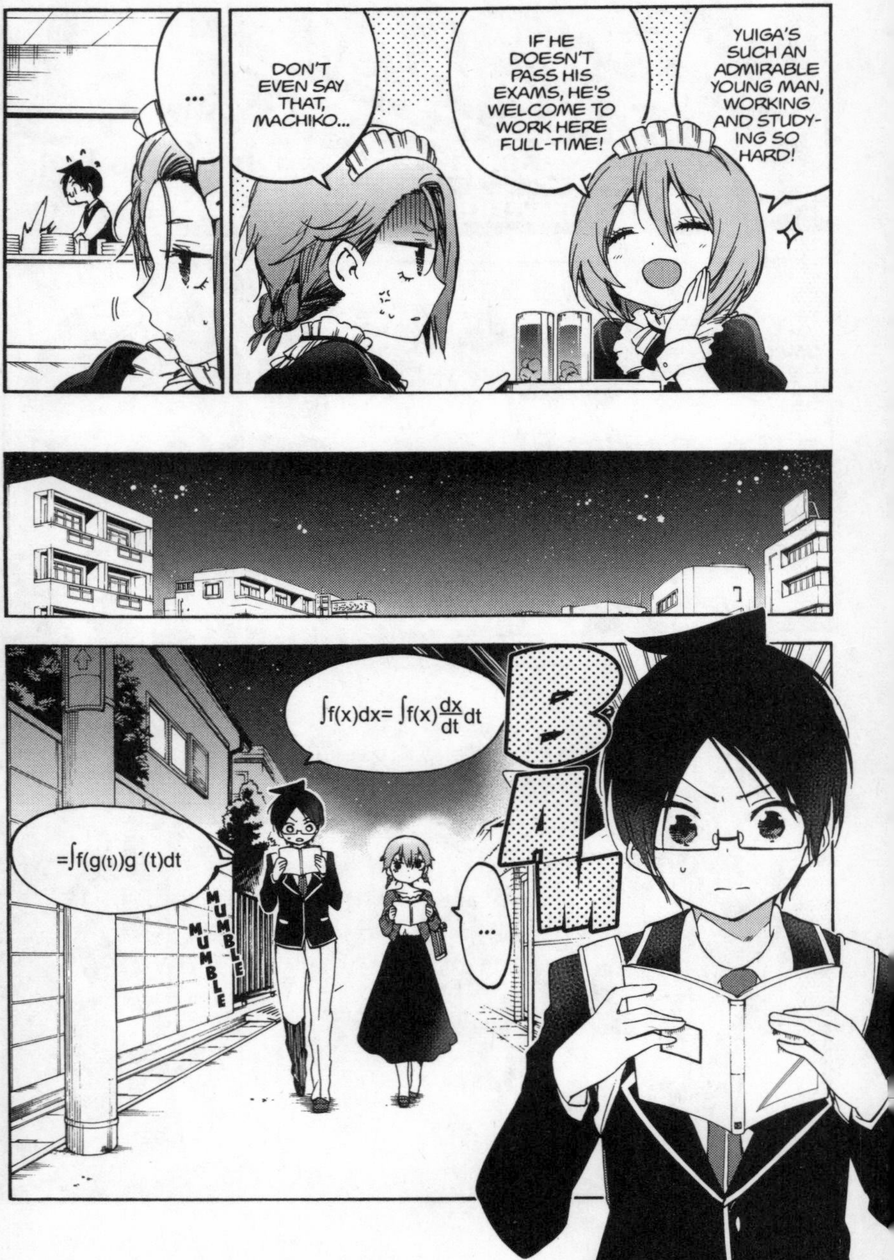
YUIGA'S SUCH AN ADMIRABLE YOUNG MAN, WORKING AND STUDYING SO HARD!
IF HE DOESN'T PASS HIS EXAMS, HE'S WELCOME TO WORK HERE FULL-TIME!
DON'T EVEN SAY THAT, MACHIKO...
...
BAM
$\int f(x)dx = \int f(x)\frac{dx}{dt}dt$
...
$= \int f(g(t))g'(t)dt$
MUMBLE MUMBLE

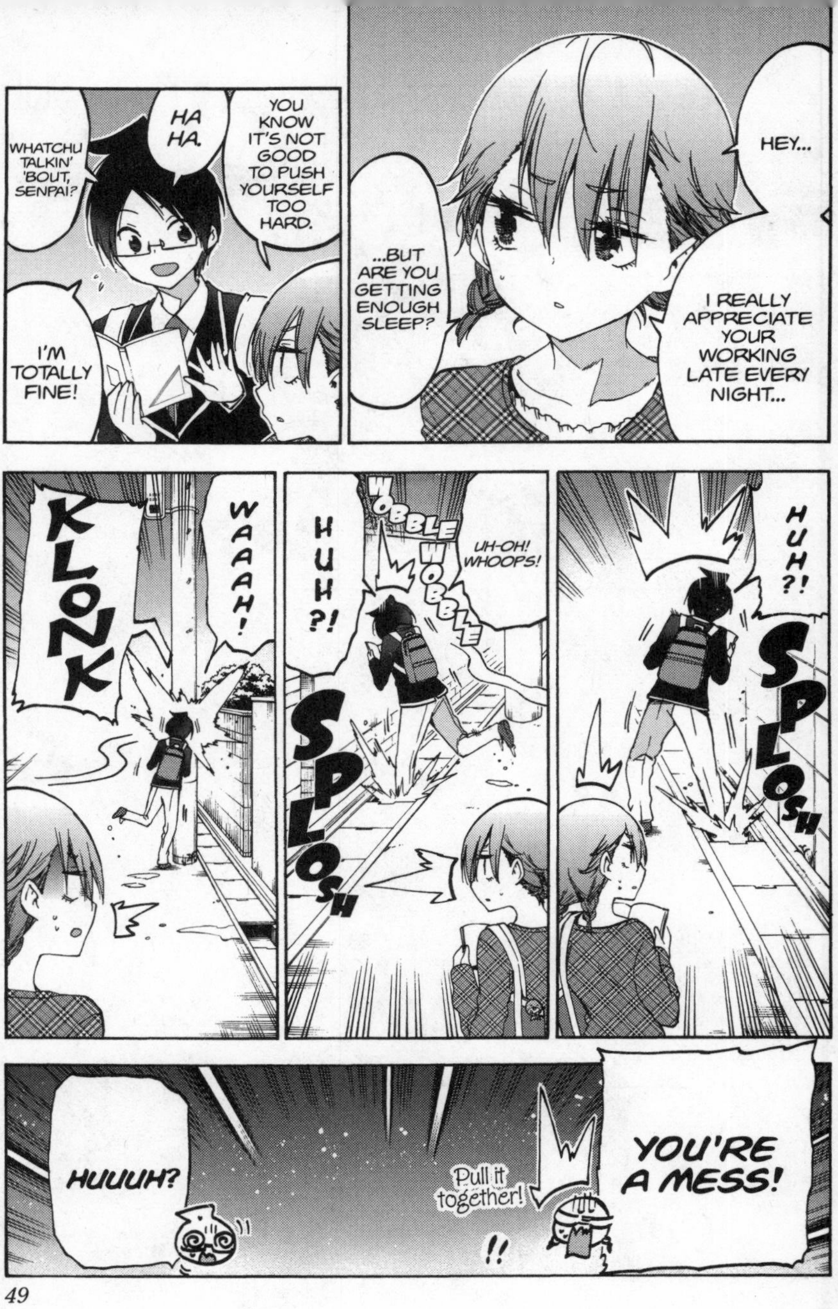
HEY...
I REALLY APPRECIATE YOUR WORKING LATE EVERY NIGHT...
...BUT ARE YOU GETTING ENOUGH SLEEP?
YOU KNOW IT'S NOT GOOD TO PUSH YOURSELF TOO HARD.
HA HA.
WHATCHU TALKIN' 'BOUT, SENPAI?
I'M TOTALLY FINE!
HUH?!
SPLOSH
WOBBLE WOBBLE
UH-OH! WHOOPS!
HUH?!
SPLOSH
WAAAAH!
KLONK
YOU'RE A MESS!
Pull it together!
!!
HUUUH?

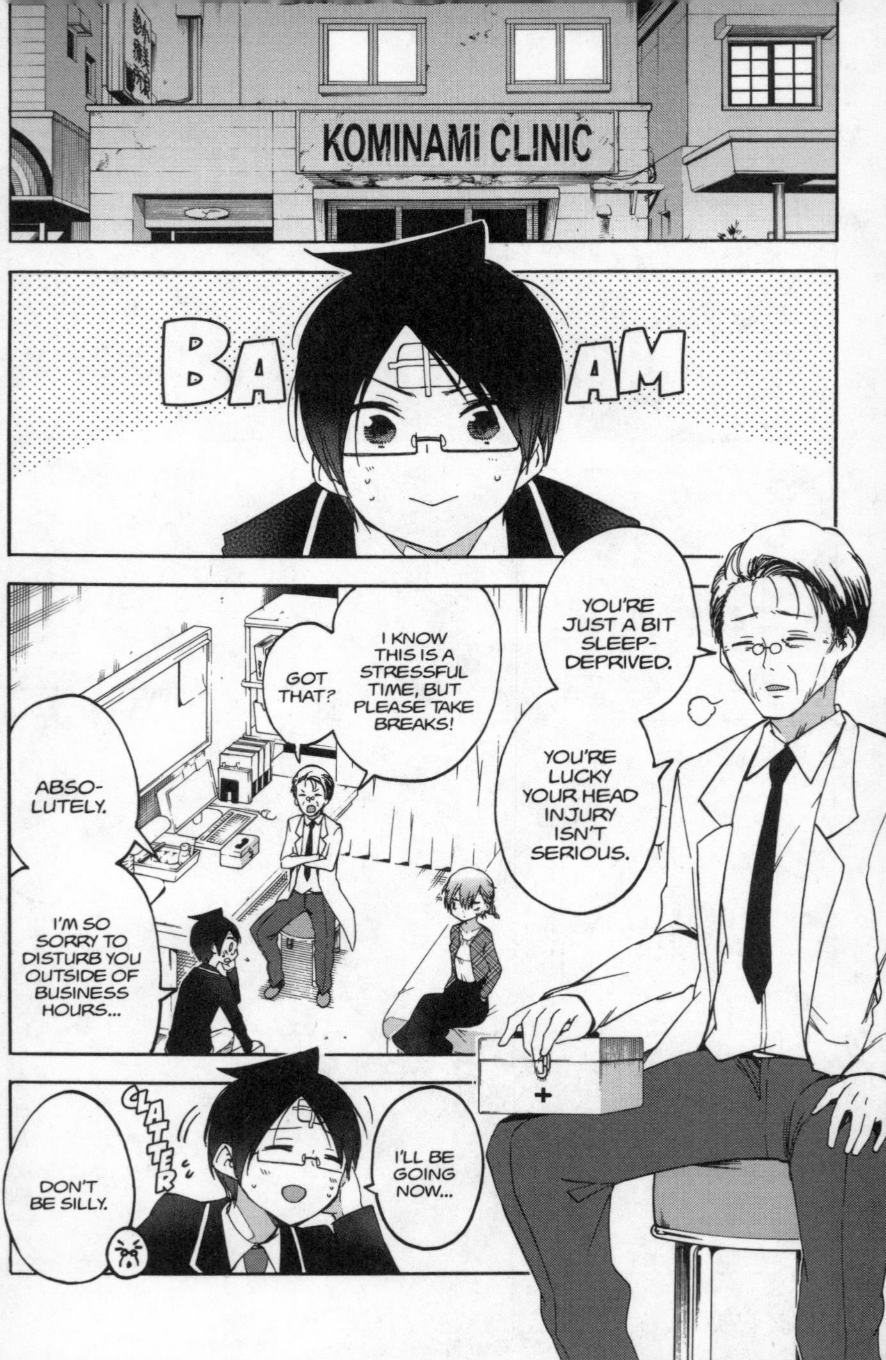
KOMINAMI CLINIC
BA AM
YOU'RE JUST A BIT SLEEP-DEPRIVED.
YOU'RE LUCKY YOUR HEAD INJURY ISN'T SERIOUS.
I KNOW THIS IS A STRESSFUL TIME, BUT PLEASE TAKE BREAKS!
GOT THAT?
ABSO-LUTELY.
I'M SO SORRY TO DISTURB YOU OUTSIDE OF BUSINESS HOURS...
I'LL BE GOING NOW...
CLATTER
DON'T BE SILLY.

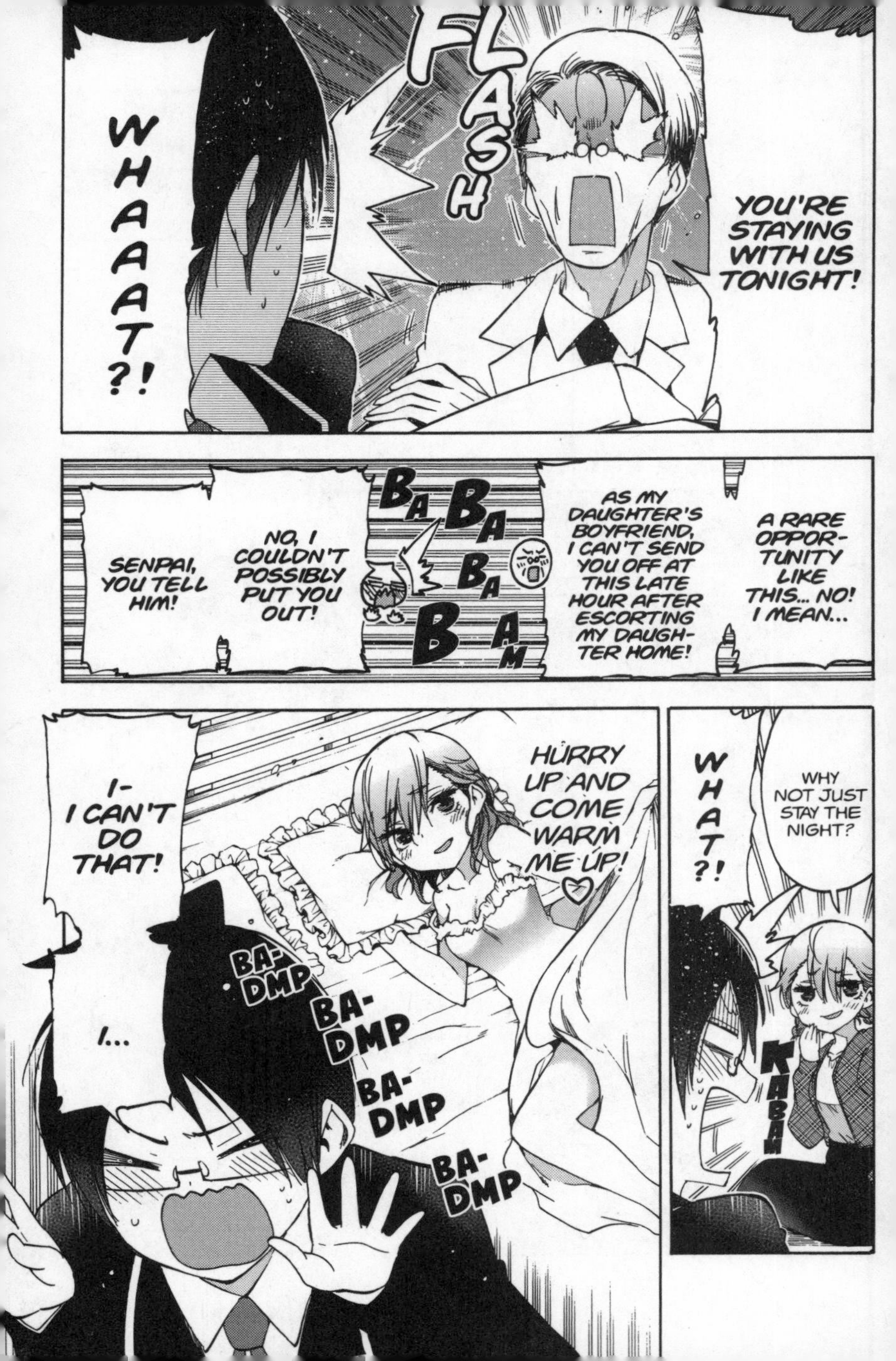

YOU'RE STAYING WITH US TONIGHT!
FLASH
WHAAAAT?!
A RARE OPPORTUNITY LIKE THIS... NO! I MEAN...
AS MY DAUGHTER'S BOYFRIEND, I CAN'T SEND YOU OFF AT THIS LATE HOUR AFTER ESCORTING MY DAUGHTER HOME!
BA BA BA BAM
NO, I COULDN'T POSSIBLY PUT YOU OUT!
SENPAI, YOU TELL HIM!
WHY NOT JUST STAY THE NIGHT?
WHAT?!
KABAM
HURRY UP AND COME WARM ME UP! ♥
I- I CAN'T DO THAT!
I...
BA-DMP
BA-DMP
BA-DMP
BA-DMP

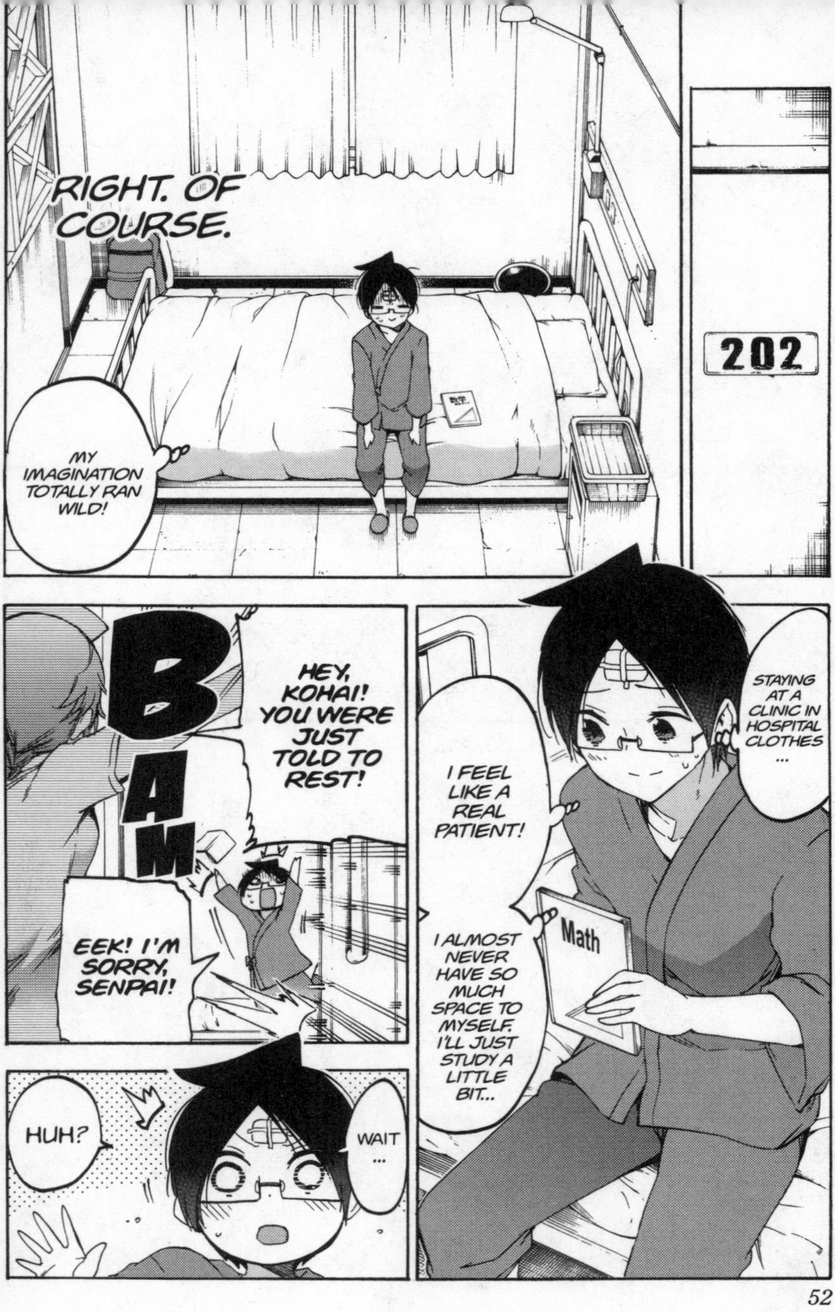
RIGHT. OF COURSE.
202
MY IMAGINATION TOTALLY RAN WILD!
STAYING AT A CLINIC IN HOSPITAL CLOTHES ...
I FEEL LIKE A REAL PATIENT!
I ALMOST NEVER HAVE SO MUCH SPACE TO MYSELF. I'LL JUST STUDY A LITTLE BIT...
Math
HEY, KOHAI! YOU WERE JUST TOLD TO REST!
BAM
EEK! I'M SORRY, SENPAI!
WAIT ...
HUH?

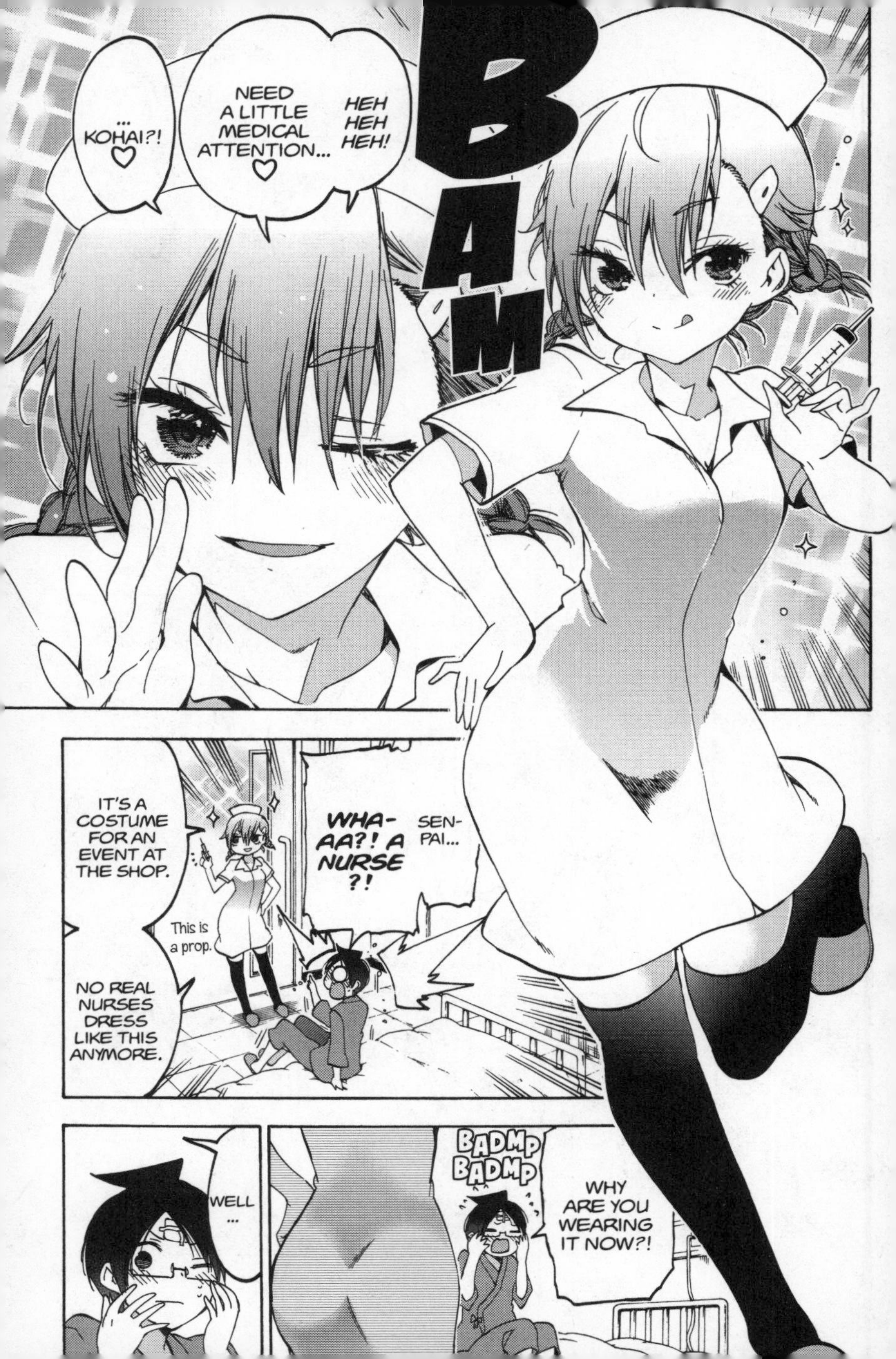
BAM
HEH HEH HEH!
NEED A LITTLE MEDICAL ATTENTION... ♡
... KOHAI?! ♡
SEN-PAI...
WHA-AA?! A NURSE?!
IT'S A COSTUME FOR AN EVENT AT THE SHOP.
This is a prop.
NO REAL NURSES DRESS LIKE THIS ANYMORE.
BADMP BADMP
WHY ARE YOU WEARING IT NOW?!
WELL ...

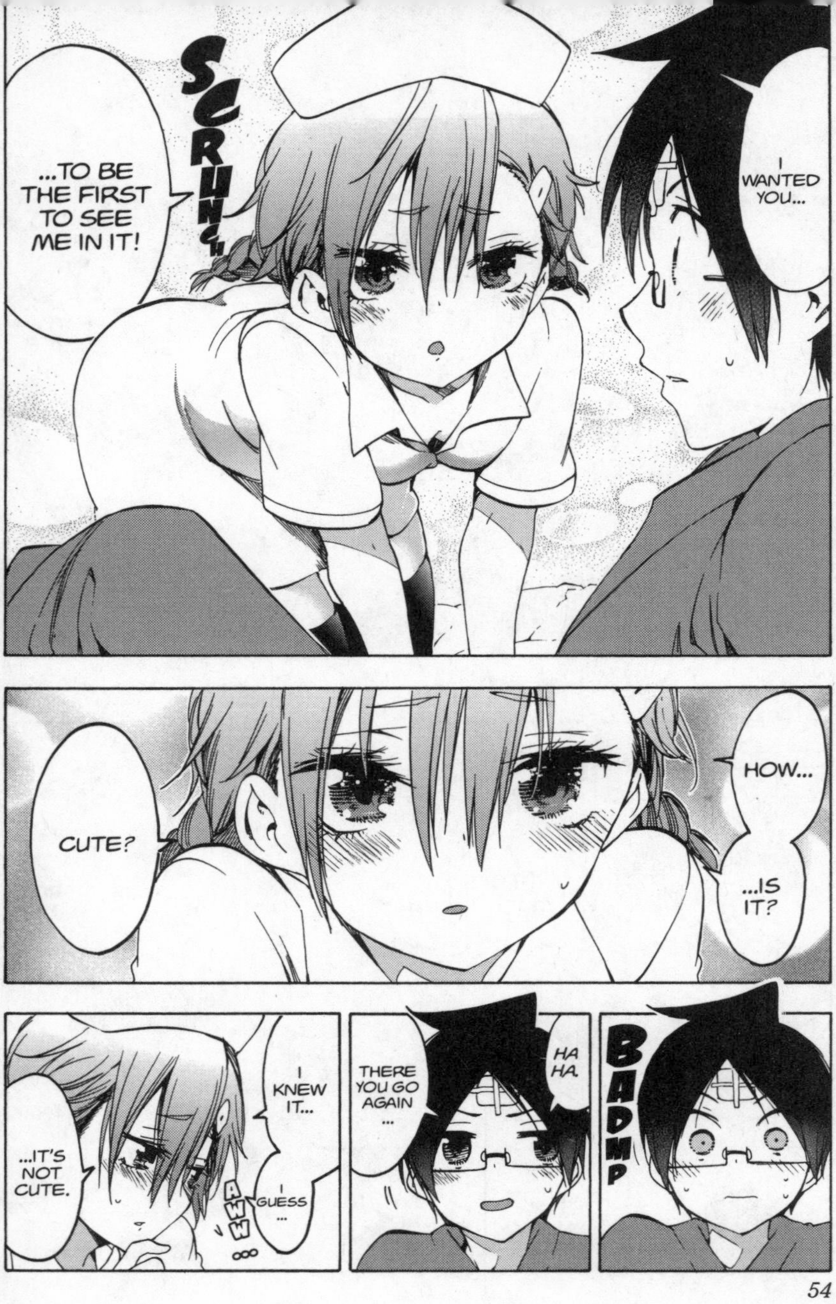
I WANTED YOU...
SCRUNCH
...TO BE THE FIRST TO SEE ME IN IT!
HOW...
...IS IT?
CUTE?
BADMP
HA HA.
THERE YOU GO AGAIN ...
I KNEW IT...
I GUESS ...
AWW...
...IT'S NOT CUTE.

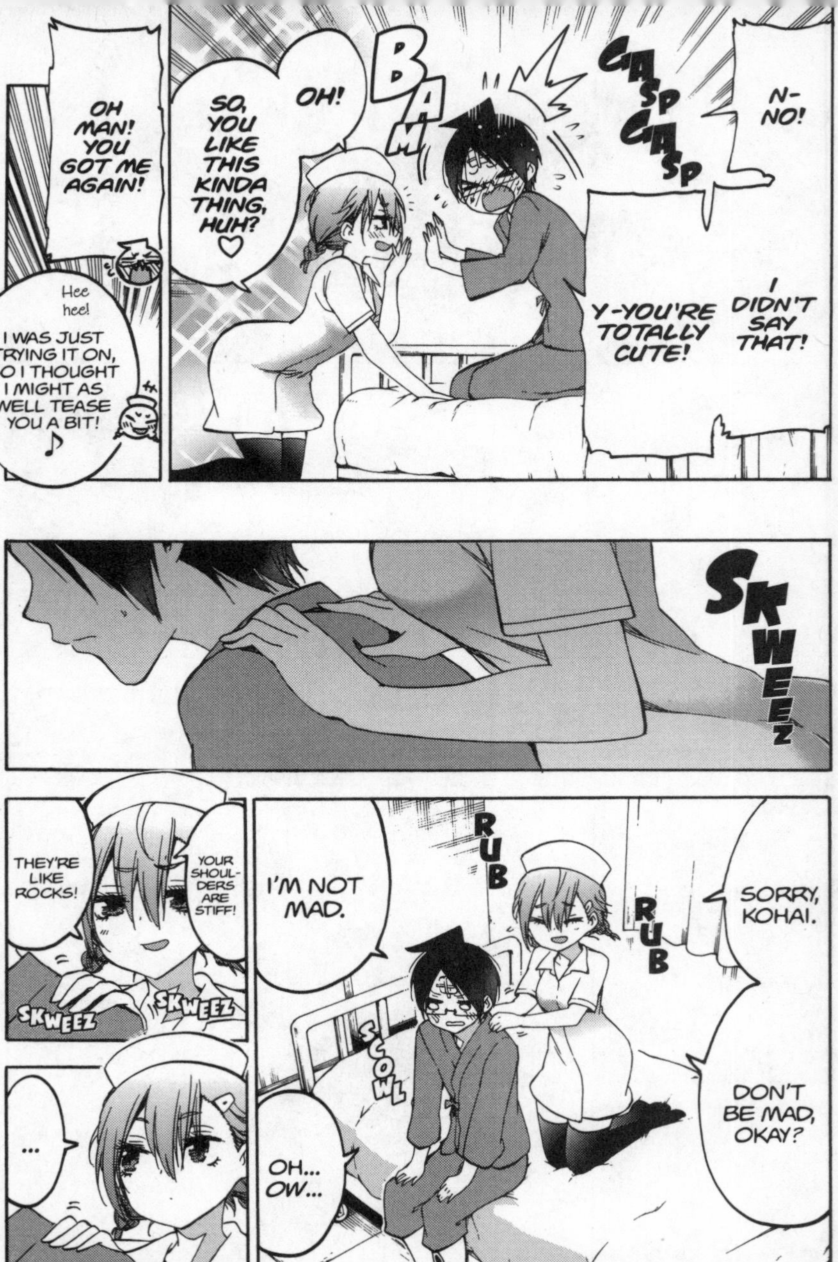
N- NO!
GASP GASP GASP
I DIDN'T SAY THAT!
Y-YOU'RE TOTALLY CUTE!
BAM
OH!
SO, YOU LIKE THIS KINDA THING, HUH? ♡
OH MAN! YOU GOT ME AGAIN!
Hee hee!
I WAS JUST TRYING IT ON, SO I THOUGHT I MIGHT AS WELL TEASE YOU A BIT! ♪
SKWEEZ
SORRY, KOHAI.
DON'T BE MAD, OKAY?
RUB
RUB
I'M NOT MAD.
SCOWL
OH... OW...
YOUR SHOUL-DERS ARE STIFF!
THEY'RE LIKE ROCKS!
SKWEEZ
SKWEEZ
...

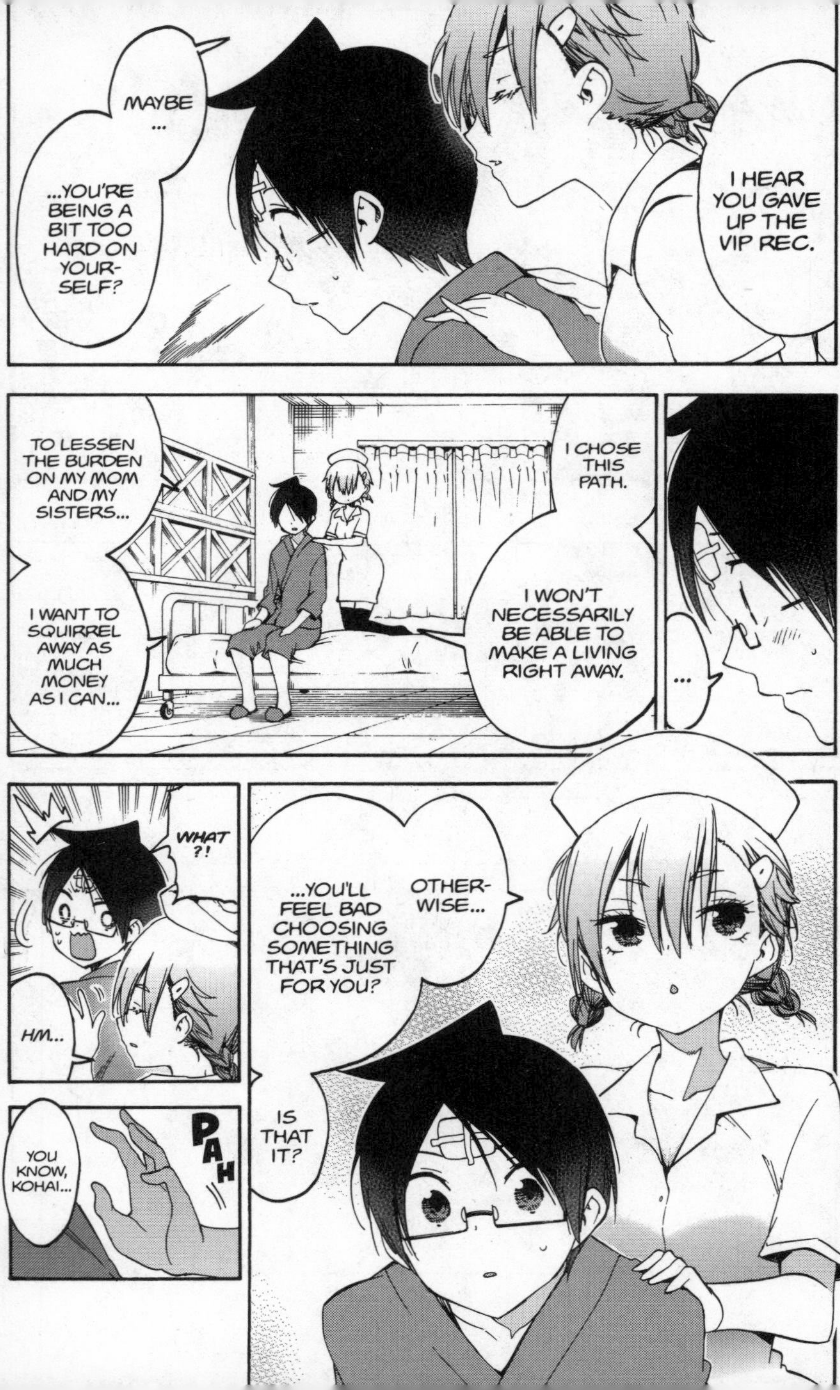
I HEAR YOU GAVE UP THE VIP REC.
MAYBE ...
...YOU'RE BEING A BIT TOO HARD ON YOURSELF?
...
I CHOSE THIS PATH.
I WON'T NECESSARILY BE ABLE TO MAKE A LIVING RIGHT AWAY.
TO LESSEN THE BURDEN ON MY MOM AND MY SISTERS...
I WANT TO SQUIRREL AWAY AS MUCH MONEY AS I CAN...
OTHERWISE...
...YOU'LL FEEL BAD CHOOSING SOMETHING THAT'S JUST FOR YOU?
IS THAT IT?
WHAT?!
HM...
PAH
YOU KNOW, KOHAI...

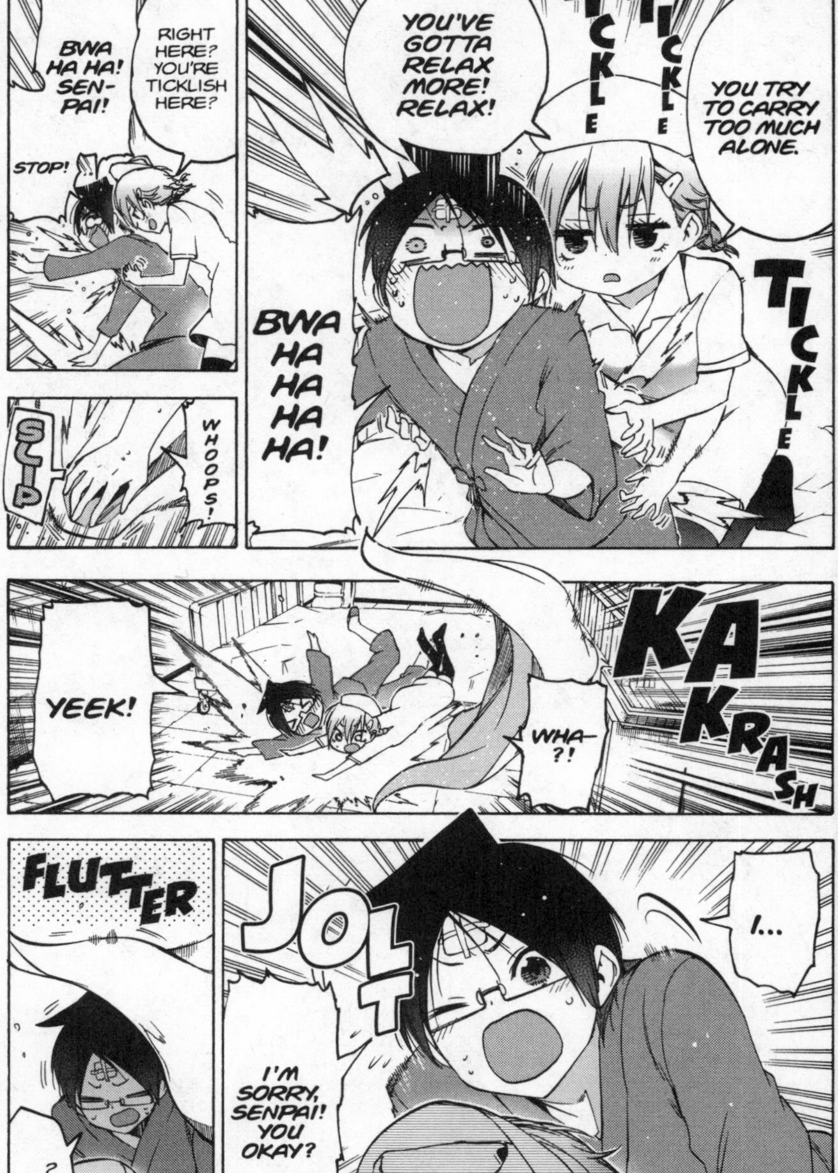
TICKLE
TICKLE
YOU TRY TO CARRY TOO MUCH ALONE.
YOU'VE GOTTA RELAX MORE! RELAX!
TICKLE
BWA HA HA HA HA HA!
RIGHT HERE? YOU'RE TICKLISH HERE?
BWA HA HA! SEN-PAI!
STOP!
WHOOPS!
SLIP
KA KRASH
WHA?!
YEEK!
I...
JOLT
I'M SORRY, SENPAI! YOU OKAY?
FLUTTER
...?

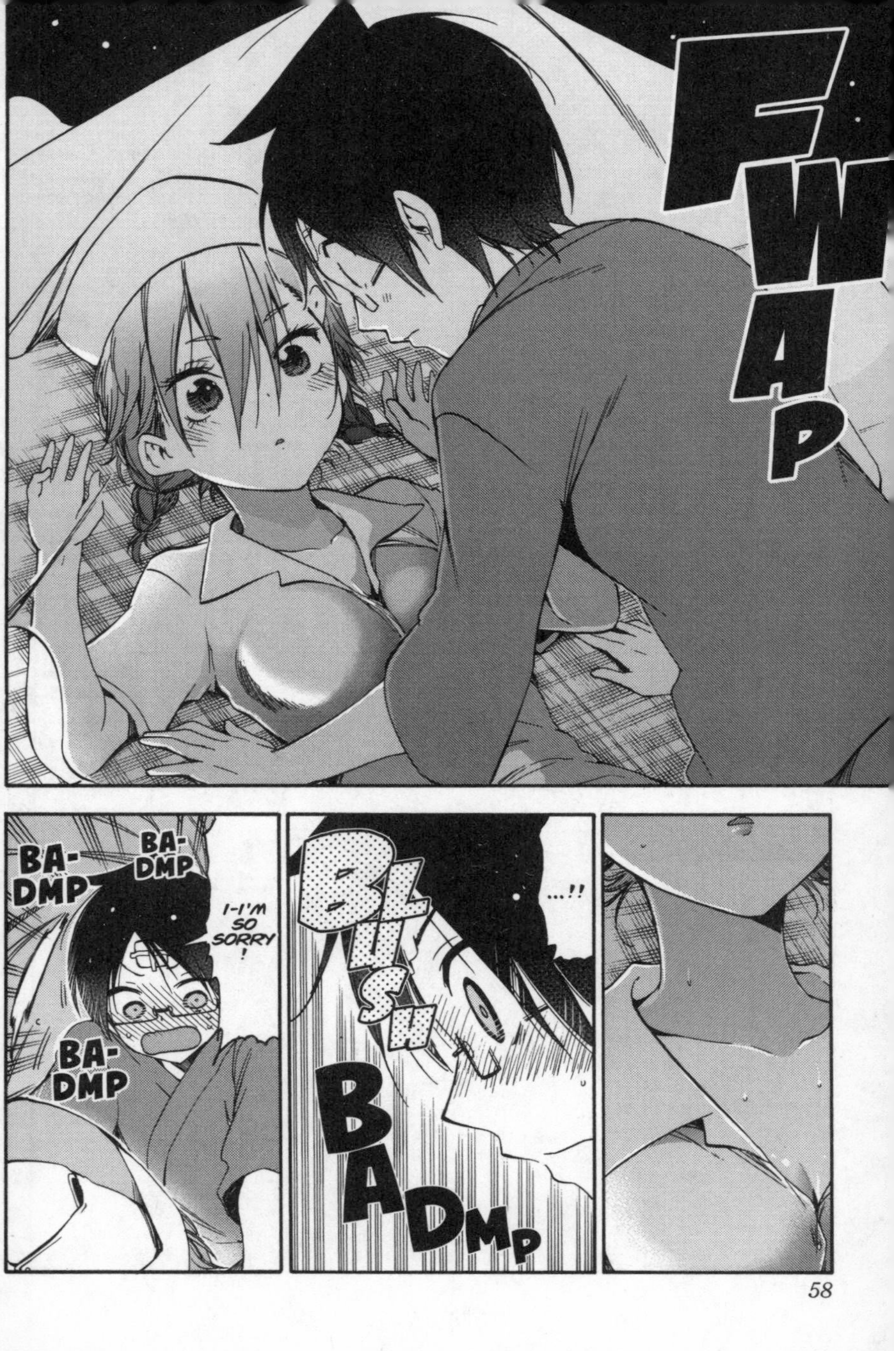
FWAP
...!!
BLUSH
BADMP
BA-DMP
BA-DMP
I-I'M SO SORRY!
BA-DMP

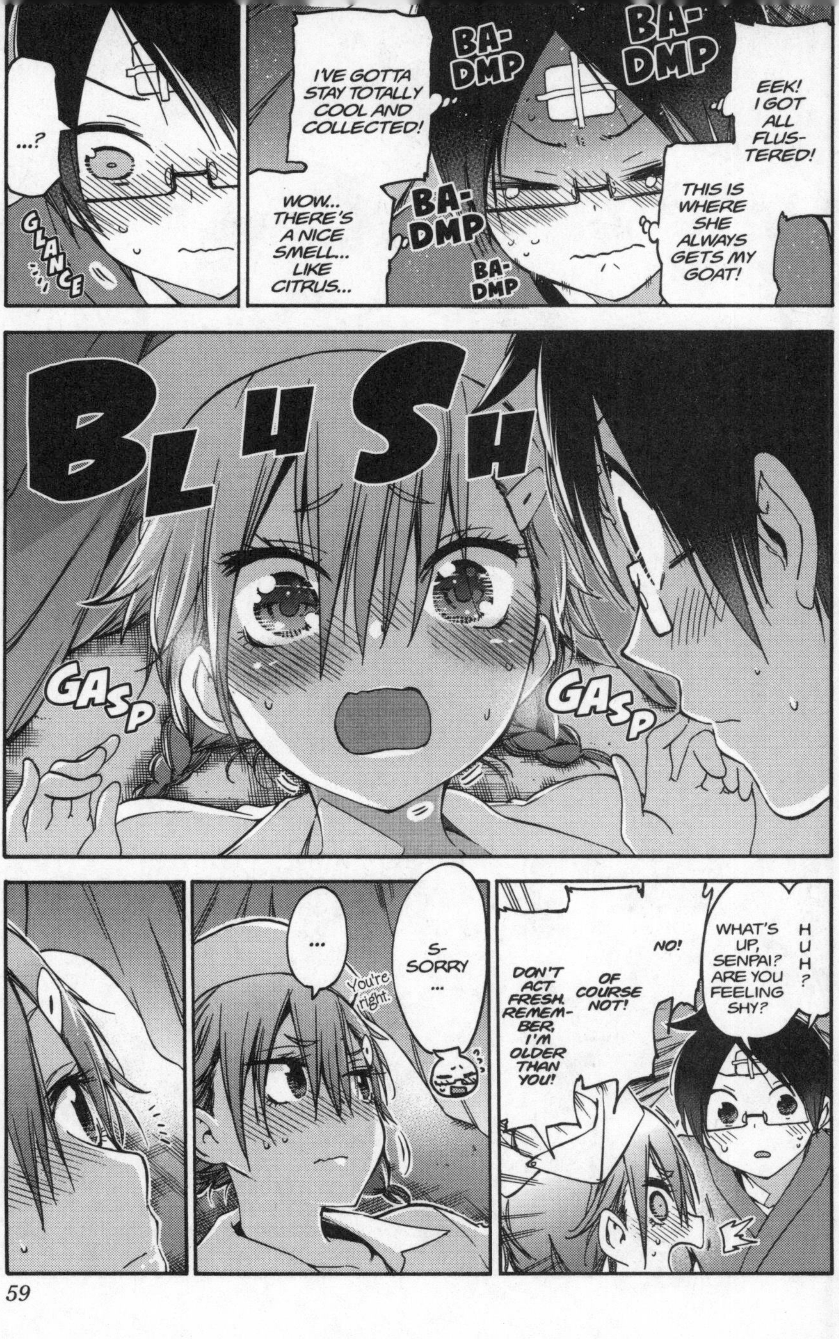
BA-DMP
EEK! I GOT ALL FLUS-TERED!
THIS IS WHERE SHE ALWAYS GETS MY GOAT!
BA-DMP
I'VE GOTTA STAY TOTALLY COOL AND COLLECTED!
BA-DMP
WOW... THERE'S A NICE SMELL... LIKE CITRUS...
BA-DMP
...?
GLANCE
BLUSH
GASP
GASP
HUH?
WHAT'S UP, SENPAI? ARE YOU FEELING SHY?
NO!
OF COURSE NOT!
DON'T ACT FRESH. REMEMBER, I'M OLDER THAN YOU!
S-SORRY ...
...
You're right.

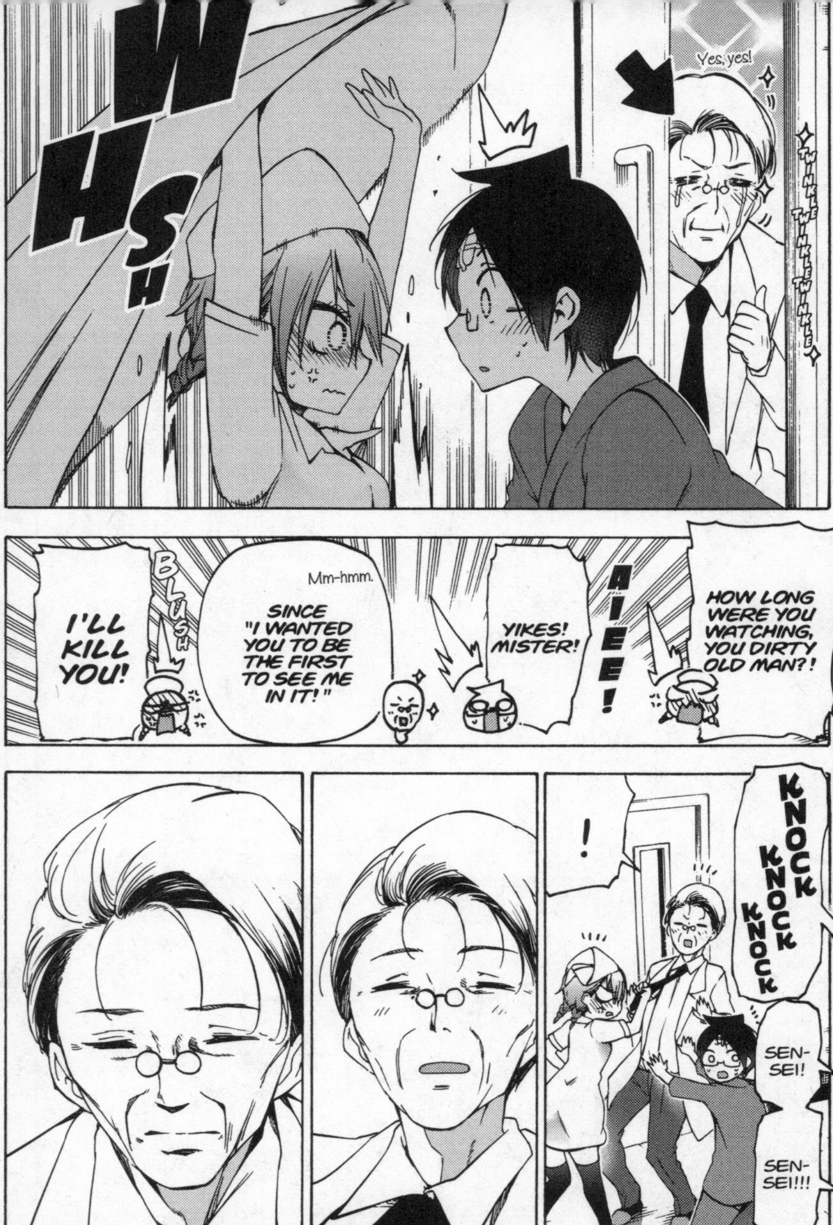
WHSH
Yes, yes!
TWINKLE TWINKLE TWINKLE
HOW LONG WERE YOU WATCHING, YOU DIRTY OLD MAN?!
AIEE!
YIKES! MISTER!
Mm-hmm.
SINCE "I WANTED YOU TO BE THE FIRST TO SEE ME IN IT!"
BLUSH
I'LL KILL YOU!
KNOCK KNOCK KNOCK
!
SEN-SEI!
SEN-SEI!!!

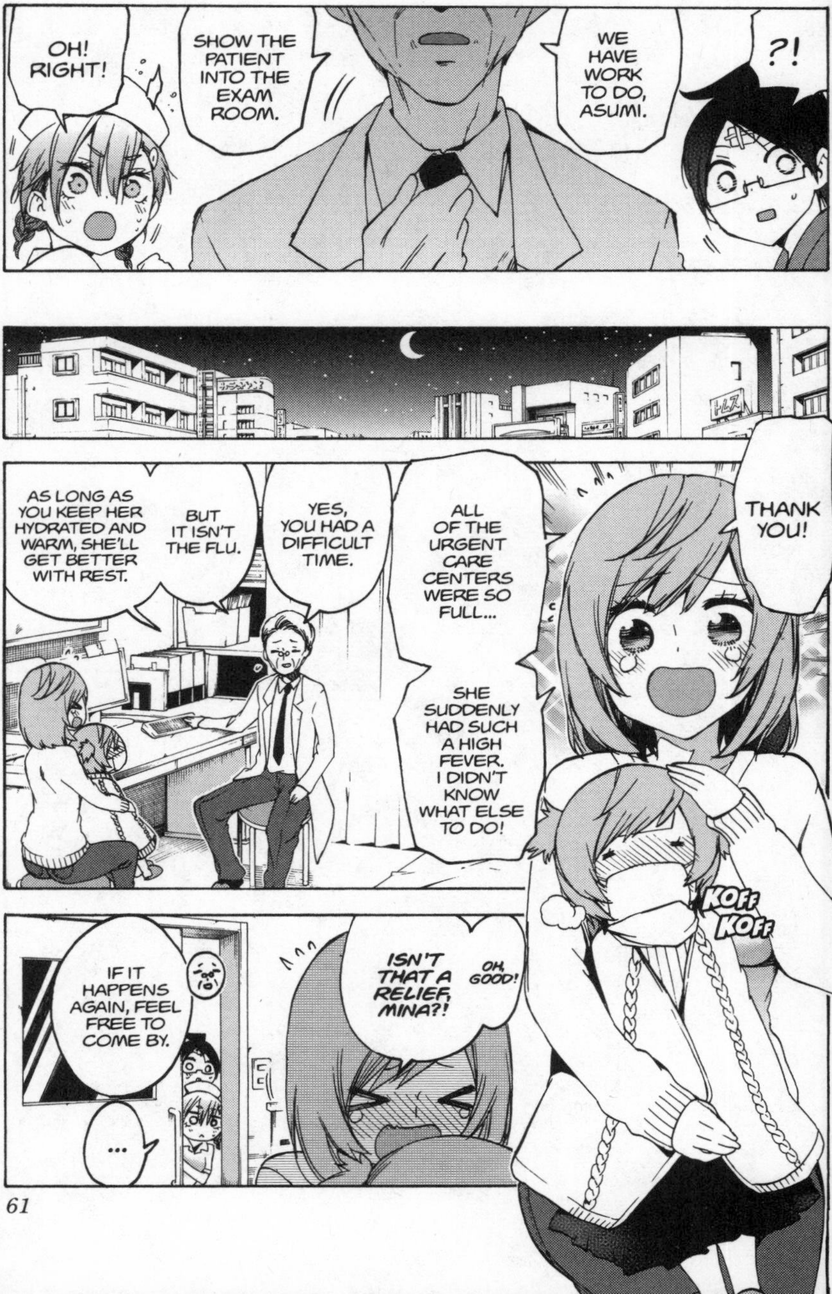
?!
WE HAVE WORK TO DO, ASUMI.
SHOW THE PATIENT INTO THE EXAM ROOM.
OH! RIGHT!
THANK YOU!
ALL OF THE URGENT CARE CENTERS WERE SO FULL...
SHE SUDDENLY HAD SUCH A HIGH FEVER. I DIDN'T KNOW WHAT ELSE TO DO!
YES, YOU HAD A DIFFICULT TIME.
BUT IT ISN'T THE FLU.
AS LONG AS YOU KEEP HER HYDRATED AND WARM, SHE'LL GET BETTER WITH REST.
KOFF KOFF
ISN'T THAT A RELIEF, MINA?!
OH, GOOD!
IF IT HAPPENS AGAIN, FEEL FREE TO COME BY.
...

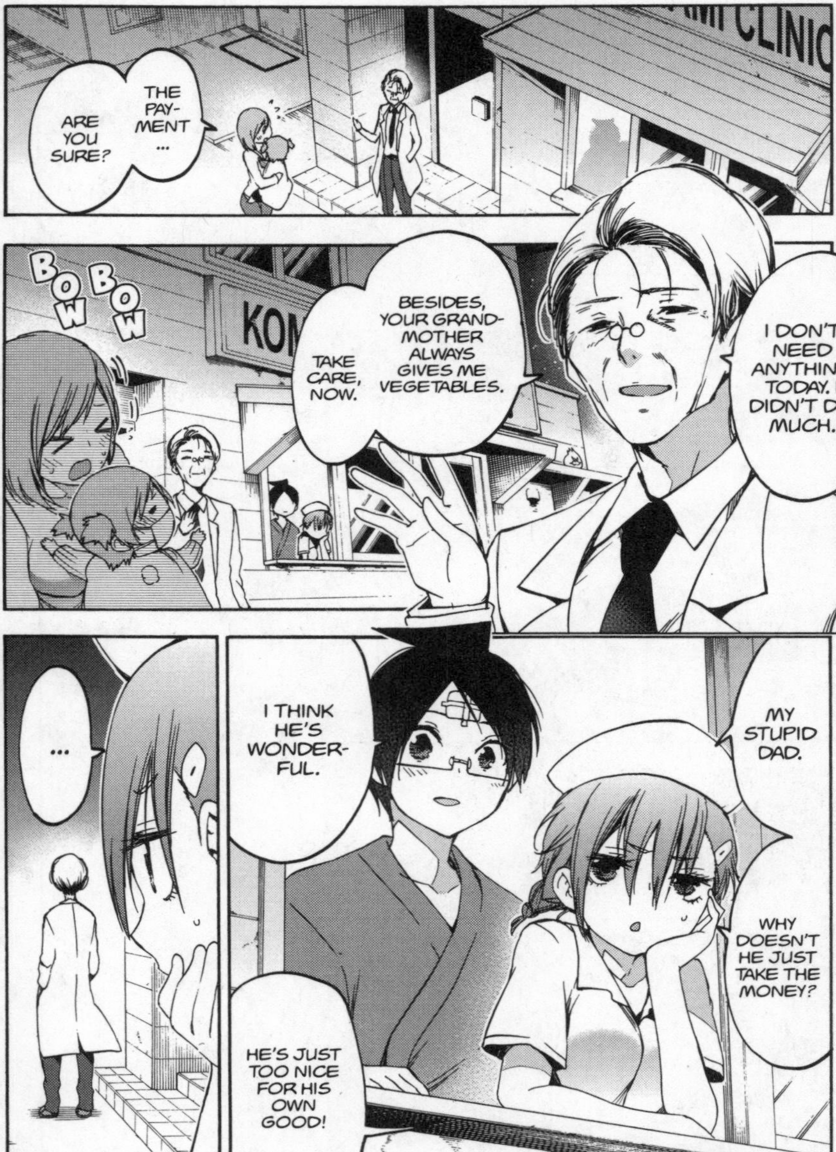
THE PAYMENT ...
ARE YOU SURE?
I DON'T NEED ANYTHING TODAY. I DIDN'T DO MUCH.
BESIDES, YOUR GRANDMOTHER ALWAYS GIVES ME VEGETABLES.
TAKE CARE, NOW.
BOW BOW
MY STUPID DAD.
I THINK HE'S WONDERFUL.
WHY DOESN'T HE JUST TAKE THE MONEY?
HE'S JUST TOO NICE FOR HIS OWN GOOD!
...

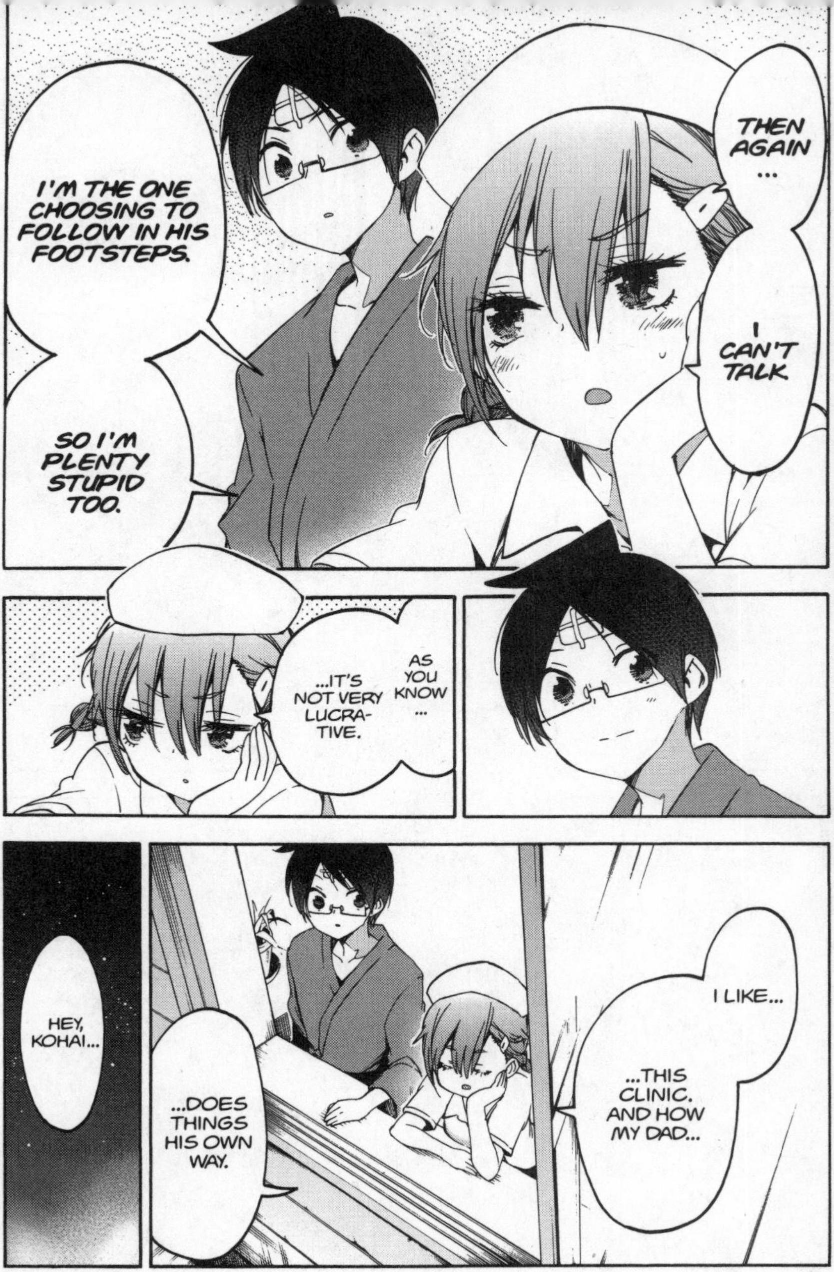
THEN AGAIN...
I CAN'T TALK
I'M THE ONE CHOOSING TO FOLLOW IN HIS FOOTSTEPS.
SO I'M PLENTY STUPID TOO.
AS YOU KNOW...
...IT'S NOT VERY LUCRA-TIVE.
I LIKE...
...THIS CLINIC. AND HOW MY DAD...
...DOES THINGS HIS OWN WAY.
HEY, KOHAI...

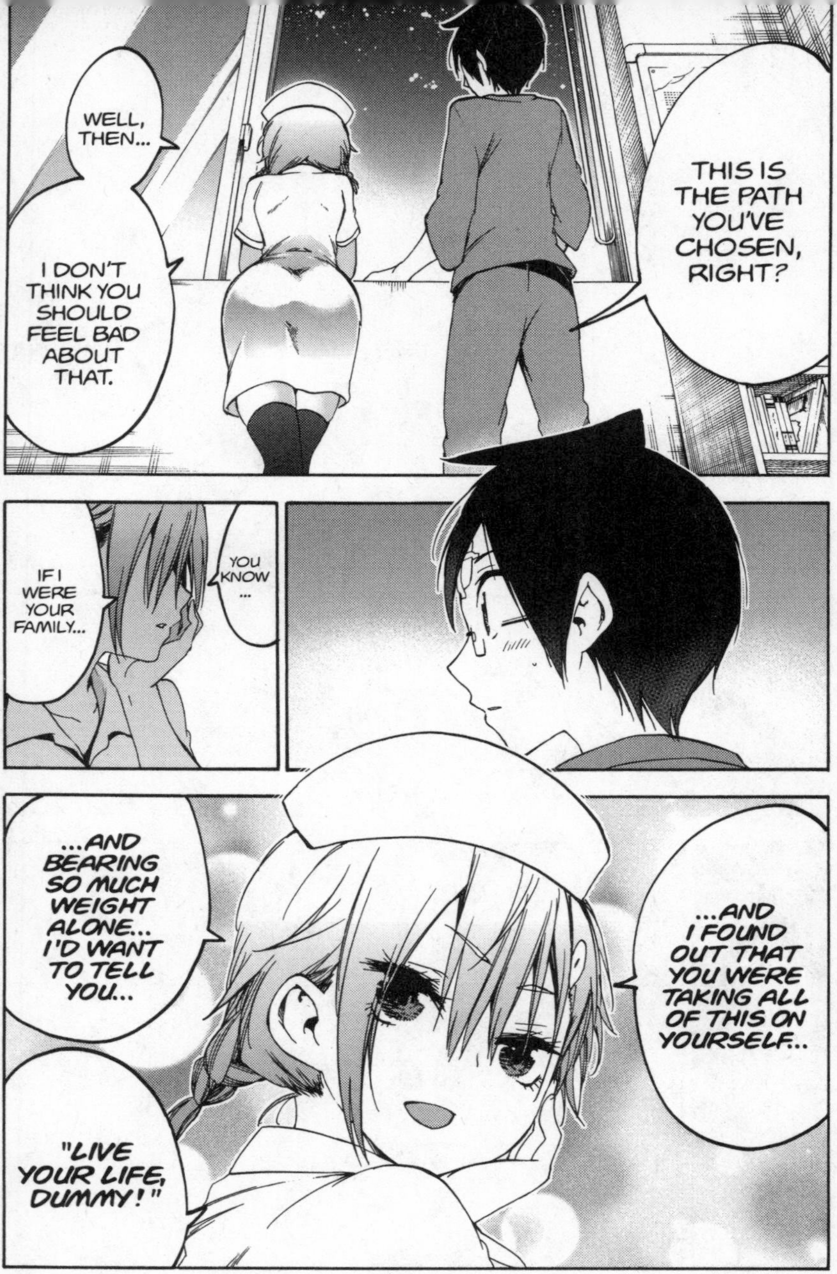
THIS IS THE PATH YOU'VE CHOSEN, RIGHT?
WELL, THEN...
I DON'T THINK YOU SHOULD FEEL BAD ABOUT THAT.
YOU KNOW ...
IF I WERE YOUR FAMILY...
...AND I FOUND OUT THAT YOU WERE TAKING ALL OF THIS ON YOURSELF...
...AND BEARING SO MUCH WEIGHT ALONE... I'D WANT TO TELL YOU...
"LIVE YOUR LIFE, DUMMY!"

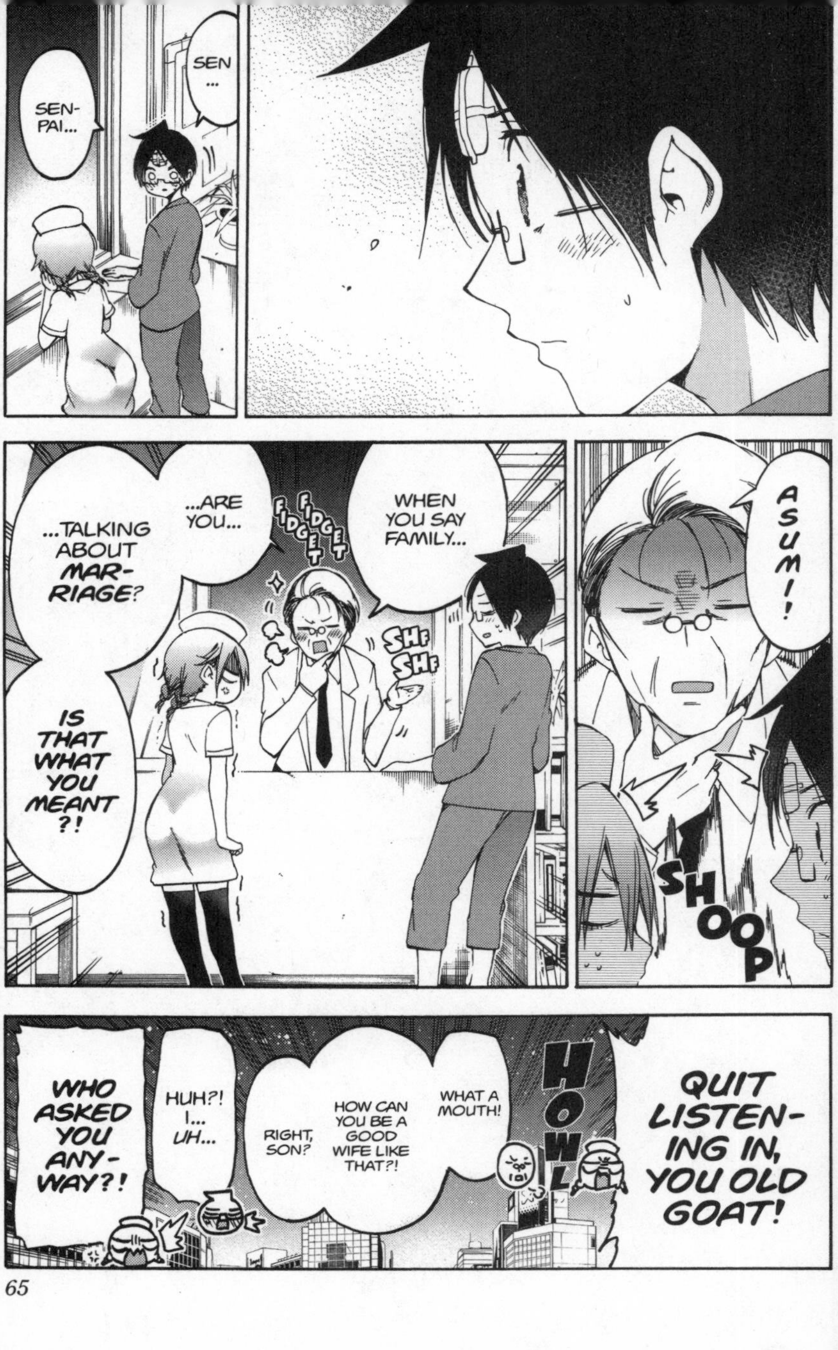
SEN ...
SEN-PAI...
ASUMI!
SHOOP
WHEN YOU SAY FAMILY...
FIDGET FIDGET
SHF SHF
...ARE YOU...
...TALKING ABOUT MARRIAGE?
IS THAT WHAT YOU MEANT?!
QUIT LISTENING IN, YOU OLD GOAT!
HOWL
WHAT A MOUTH!
HOW CAN YOU BE A GOOD WIFE LIKE THAT?!
RIGHT, SON?
HUH?! I... UH...
WHO ASKED YOU ANYWAY?!

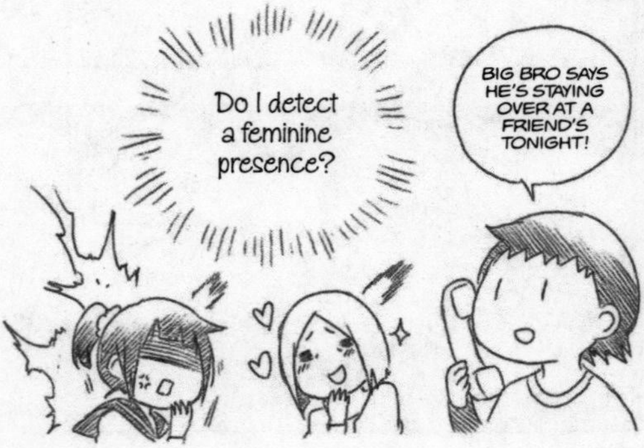
BIG BRO SAYS HE'S STAYING OVER AT A FRIEND'S TONIGHT!
Do I detect a feminine presence?

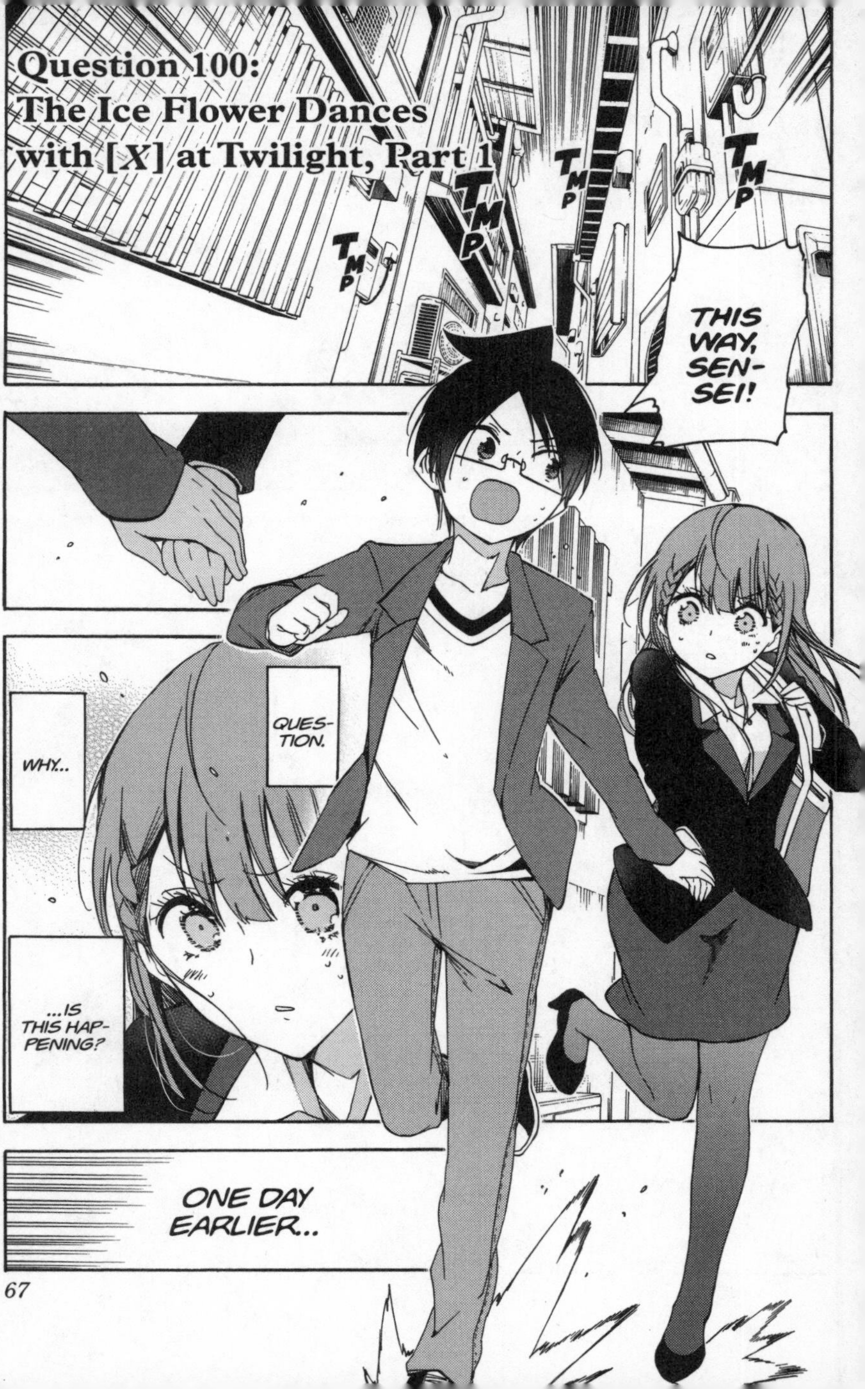
Question 100: The Ice Flower Dances with [X] at Twilight, Part 1
TMP
TMP
TMP
TMP
TMP
THIS WAY, SEN-SEI!
QUES-TION.
WHY...
...IS THIS HAP-PENING?
ONE DAY EARLIER...

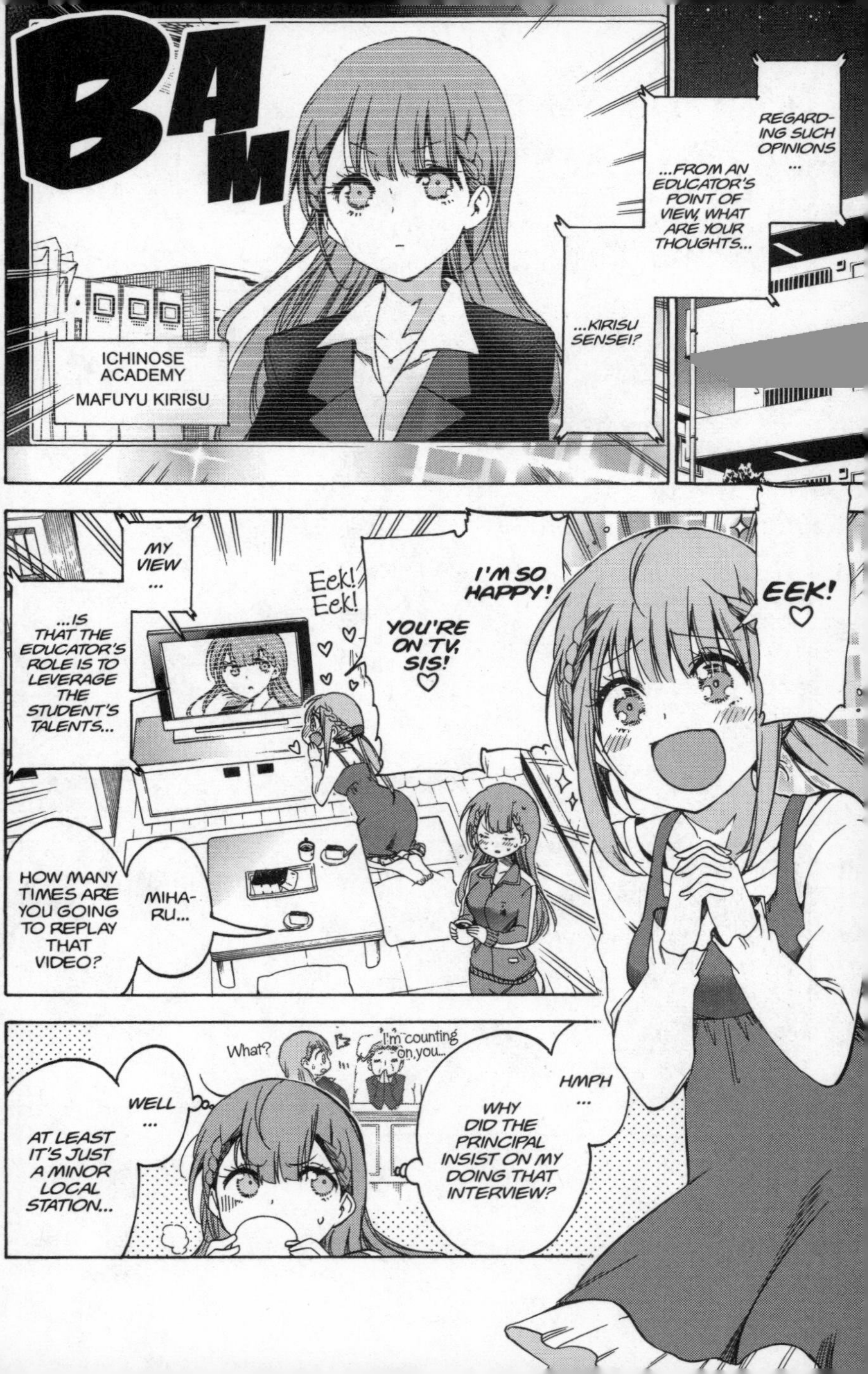
REGARDING SUCH OPINIONS...
...FROM AN EDUCATOR'S POINT OF VIEW, WHAT ARE YOUR THOUGHTS...
...KIRISU SENSEI?
BAM
ICHINOSE ACADEMY
MAFUYU KIRISU
EEK! ♡
I'M SO HAPPY!
YOU'RE ON TV, SIS! ♡
Eek! Eek!
MY VIEW...
...IS THAT THE EDUCATOR'S ROLE IS TO LEVERAGE THE STUDENT'S TALENTS...
MIHA-RU...
HOW MANY TIMES ARE YOU GOING TO REPLAY THAT VIDEO?
HMPH...
WHY DID THE PRINCIPAL INSIST ON MY DOING THAT INTERVIEW?
I'm counting on you...
What?
WELL...
AT LEAST IT'S JUST A MINOR LOCAL STATION...

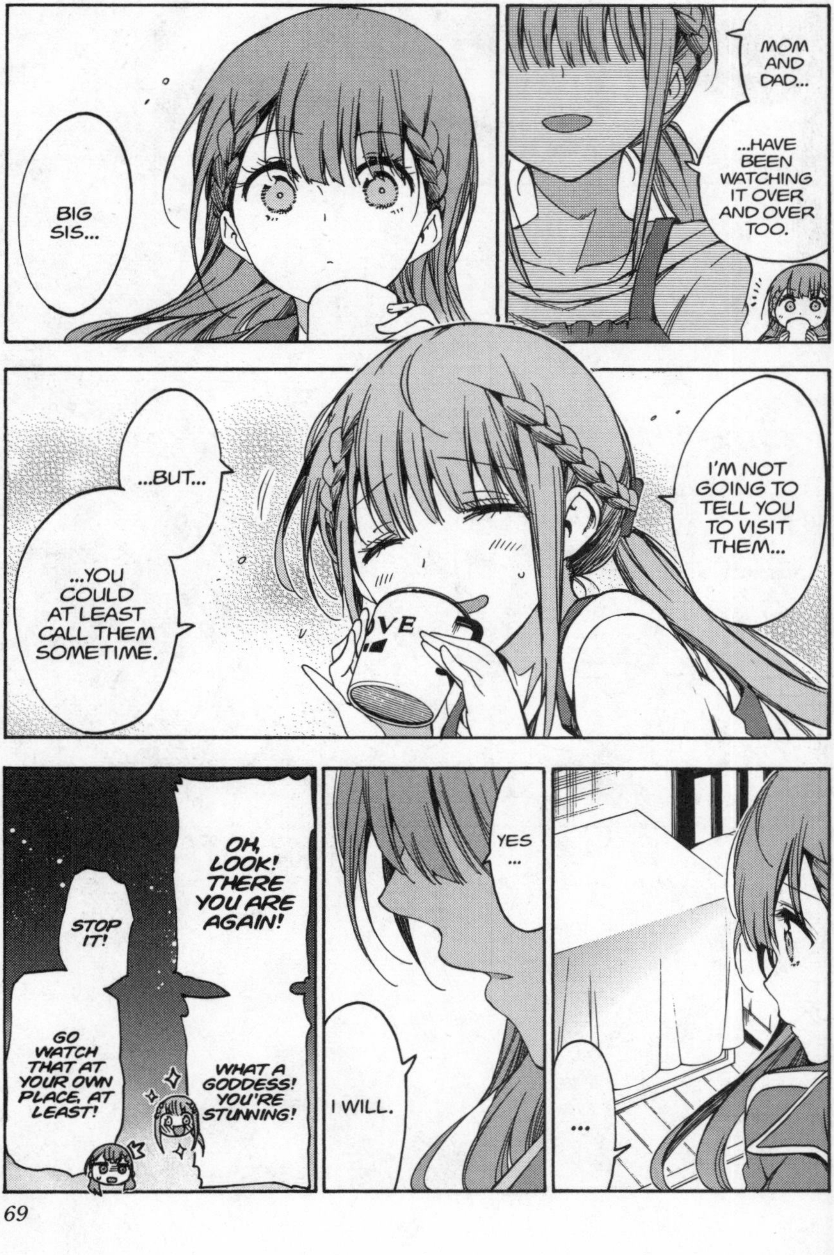
MOM AND DAD...
...HAVE BEEN WATCHING IT OVER AND OVER TOO.
BIG SIS...
I'M NOT GOING TO TELL YOU TO VISIT THEM...
...BUT...
...YOU COULD AT LEAST CALL THEM SOMETIME.
...
YES ...
I WILL.
OH, LOOK! THERE YOU ARE AGAIN!
WHAT A GODDESS! YOU'RE STUNNING!
STOP IT!
GO WATCH THAT AT YOUR OWN PLACE, AT LEAST!

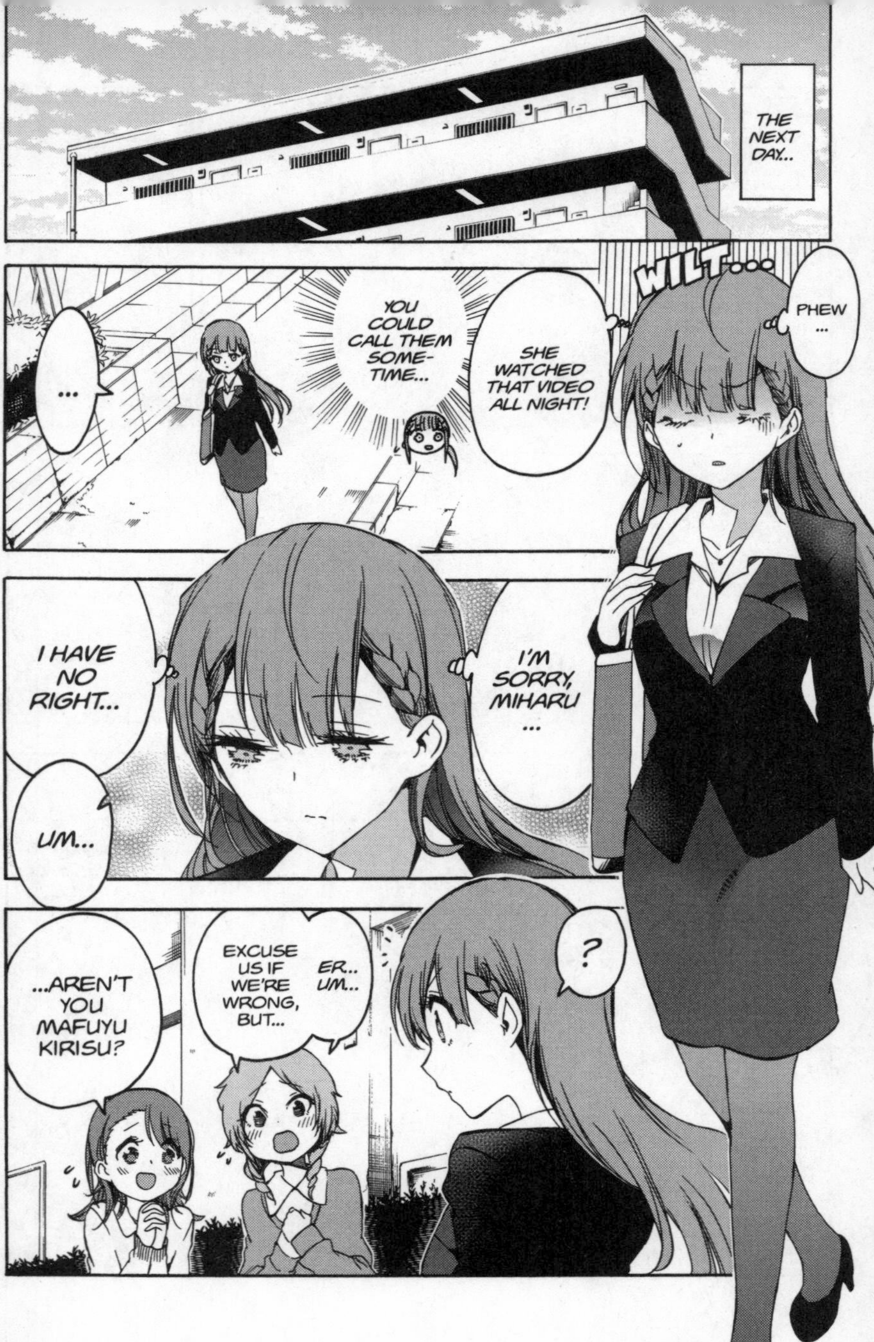
THE NEXT DAY...
WILT...
PHEW...
SHE WATCHED THAT VIDEO ALL NIGHT!
YOU COULD CALL THEM SOMETIME...
...
I'M SORRY, MIHARU...
I HAVE NO RIGHT...
UM...
?
ER... UM...
EXCUSE US IF WE'RE WRONG, BUT...
...AREN'T YOU MAFUYU KIRISU?

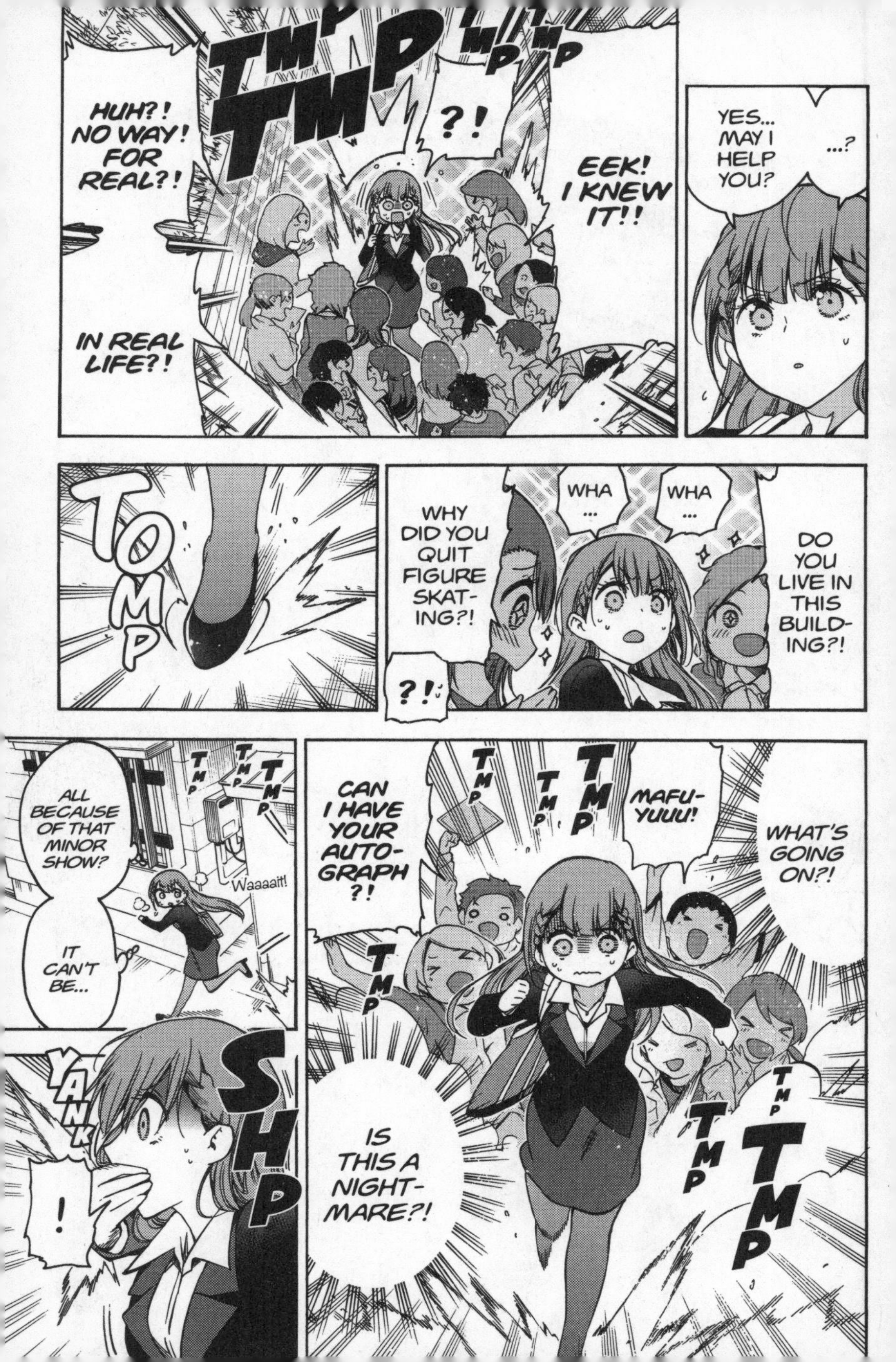
YES... MAY I HELP YOU?
...?
TMP TMP TMP TMP TMP
?!
EEK! I KNEW IT!!
HUH?! NO WAY! FOR REAL?!
IN REAL LIFE?!
DO YOU LIVE IN THIS BUILD-ING?!
WHA...
WHA...
WHY DID YOU QUIT FIGURE SKAT-ING?!
?!
TOMP
WHAT'S GOING ON?!
MAFU-YUUU!
TMP TMP TMP TMP
CAN I HAVE YOUR AUTO-GRAPH?!
TMP
IS THIS A NIGHT-MARE?!
TMP TMP TMP
TMP TMP TMP
ALL BECAUSE OF THAT MINOR SHOW?
Waaaait!
IT CAN'T BE...
SHP
YANK
!

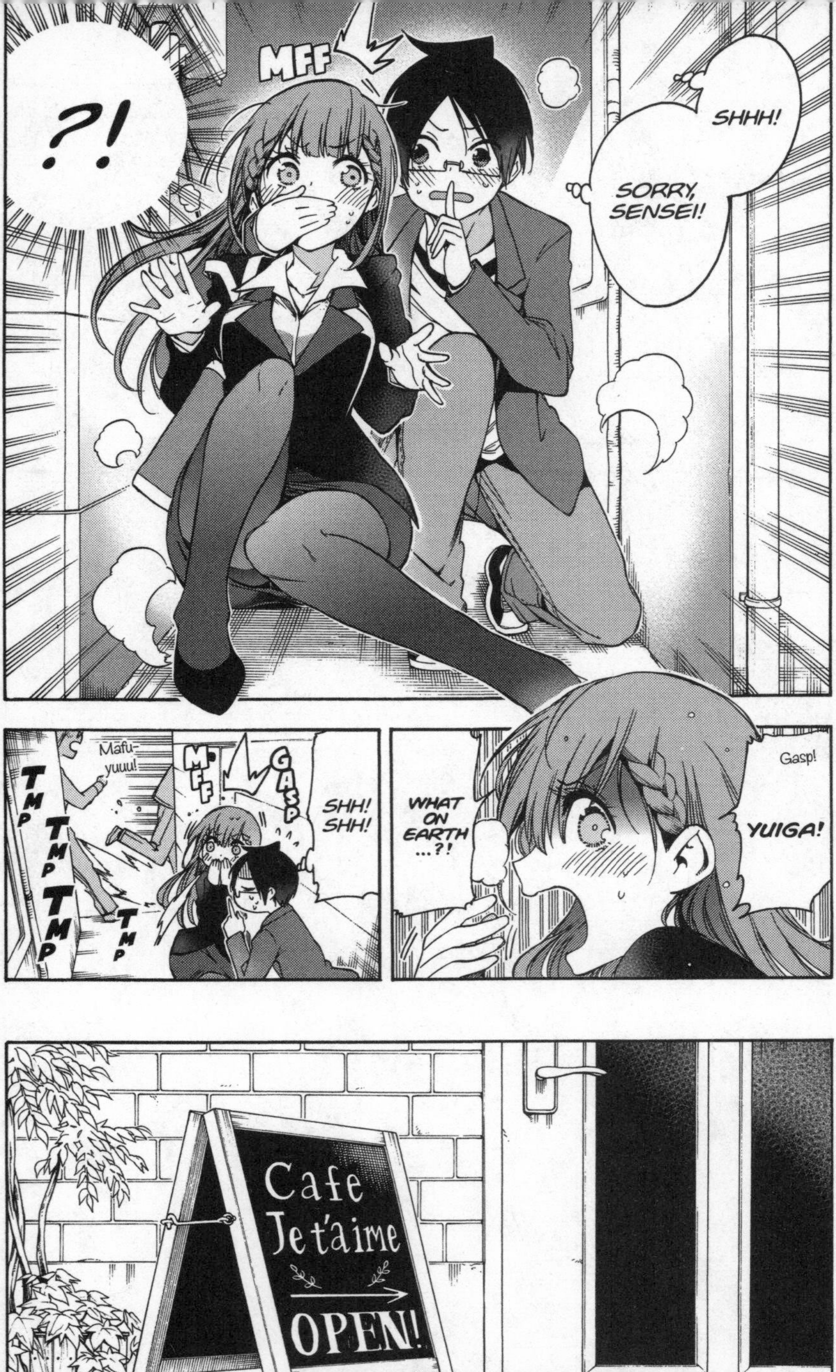
SHHH!
SORRY, SENSEI!
MFF
?!
Gasp!
YUIGA!
WHAT ON EARTH ...?!
SHH! SHH!
GASP
MFF
Mafu-yuuu!
TMP TMP TMP TMP TMP
Cafe
Je t'aime
OPEN!

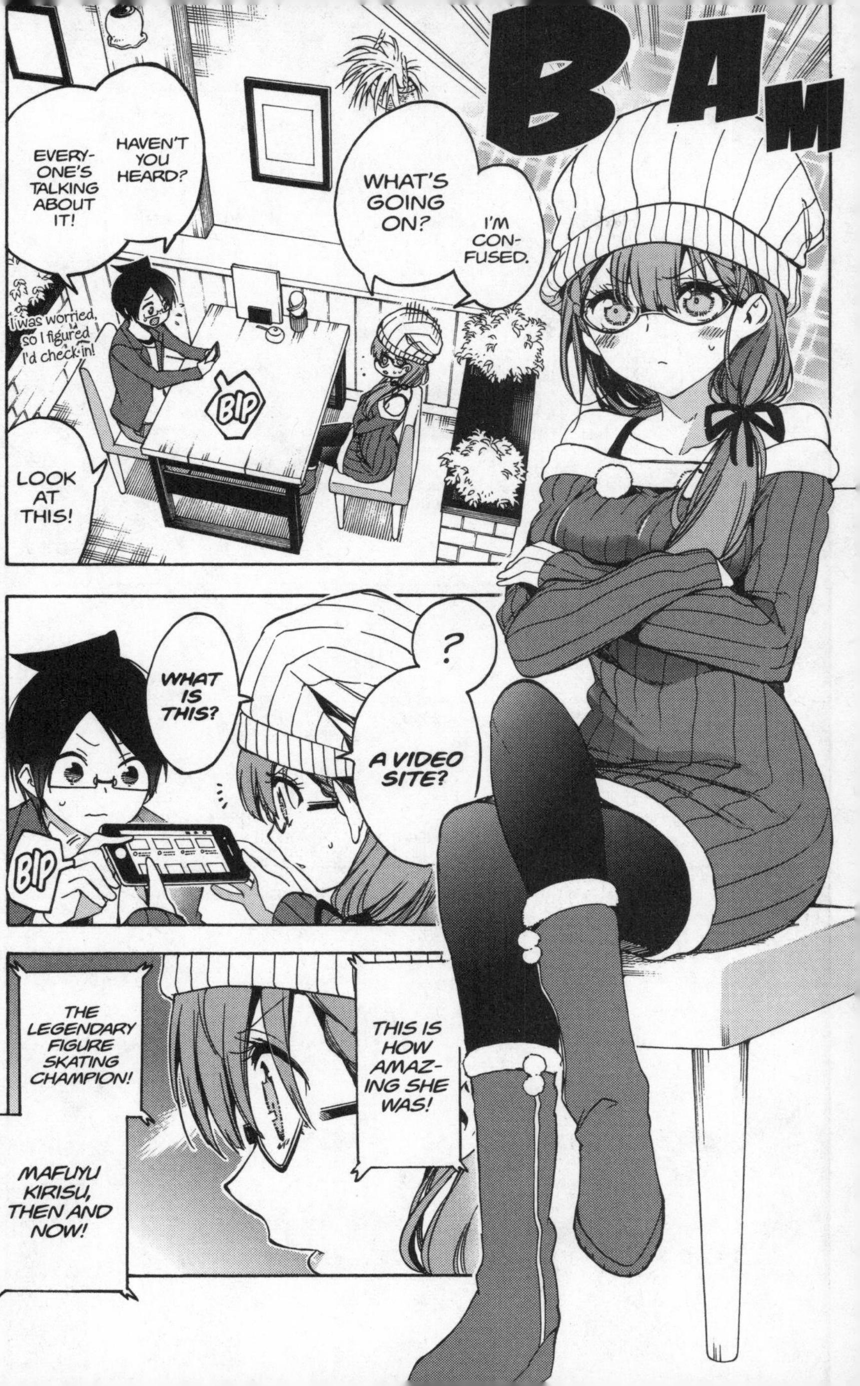
BAM
WHAT'S GOING ON?
I'M CON-FUSED.
HAVEN'T YOU HEARD?
EVERY-ONE'S TALKING ABOUT IT!
I was worried, so I figured I'd check in!
BIP
LOOK AT THIS!
?
A VIDEO SITE?
WHAT IS THIS?
BIP
THIS IS HOW AMAZ-ING SHE WAS!
THE LEGENDARY FIGURE SKATING CHAMPION!
MAFUYU KIRISU, THEN AND NOW!

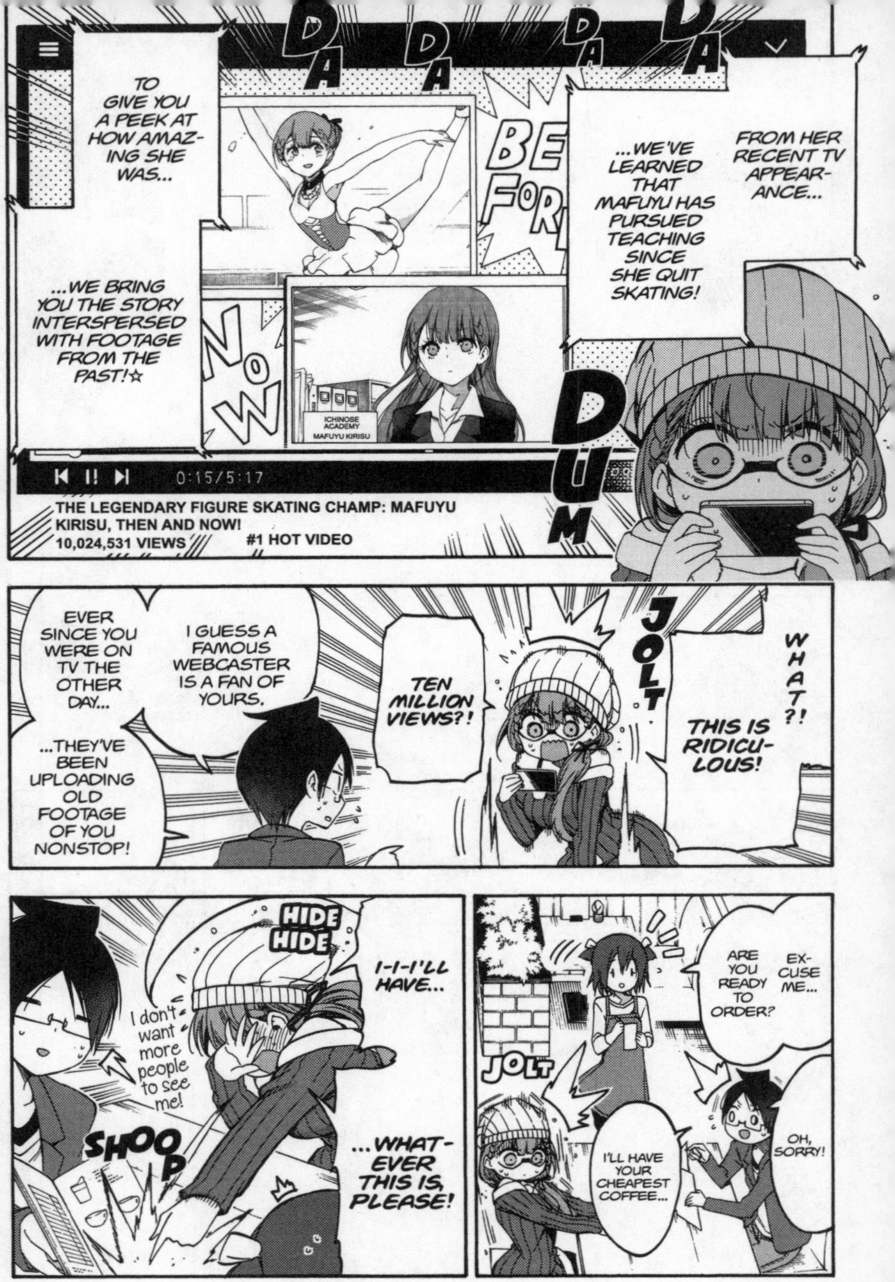
DA DA DA DA
FROM HER RECENT TV APPEARANCE...
...WE'VE LEARNED THAT MAFUYU HAS PURSUED TEACHING SINCE SHE QUIT SKATING!
BEFORE
NOW
TO GIVE YOU A PEEK AT HOW AMAZING SHE WAS...
...WE BRING YOU THE STORY INTERSPERSED WITH FOOTAGE FROM THE PAST!☆
ICHINOSE ACADEMY
MAFUYU KIRISU
0:15/5:17
THE LEGENDARY FIGURE SKATING CHAMP: MAFUYU KIRISU, THEN AND NOW!
10,024,531 VIEWS
#1 HOT VIDEO
DUM
WHAT?!
THIS IS RIDICULOUS!
JOLT
TEN MILLION VIEWS?!
I GUESS A FAMOUS WEBCASTER IS A FAN OF YOURS.
EVER SINCE YOU WERE ON TV THE OTHER DAY...
...THEY'VE BEEN UPLOADING OLD FOOTAGE OF YOU NONSTOP!
EXCUSE ME...
ARE YOU READY TO ORDER?
JOLT
OH, SORRY!
I'LL HAVE YOUR CHEAPEST COFFEE...
HIDE HIDE
I-I-I'LL HAVE...
...WHATEVER THIS IS, PLEASE!
I don't want more people to see me!
SHOOP

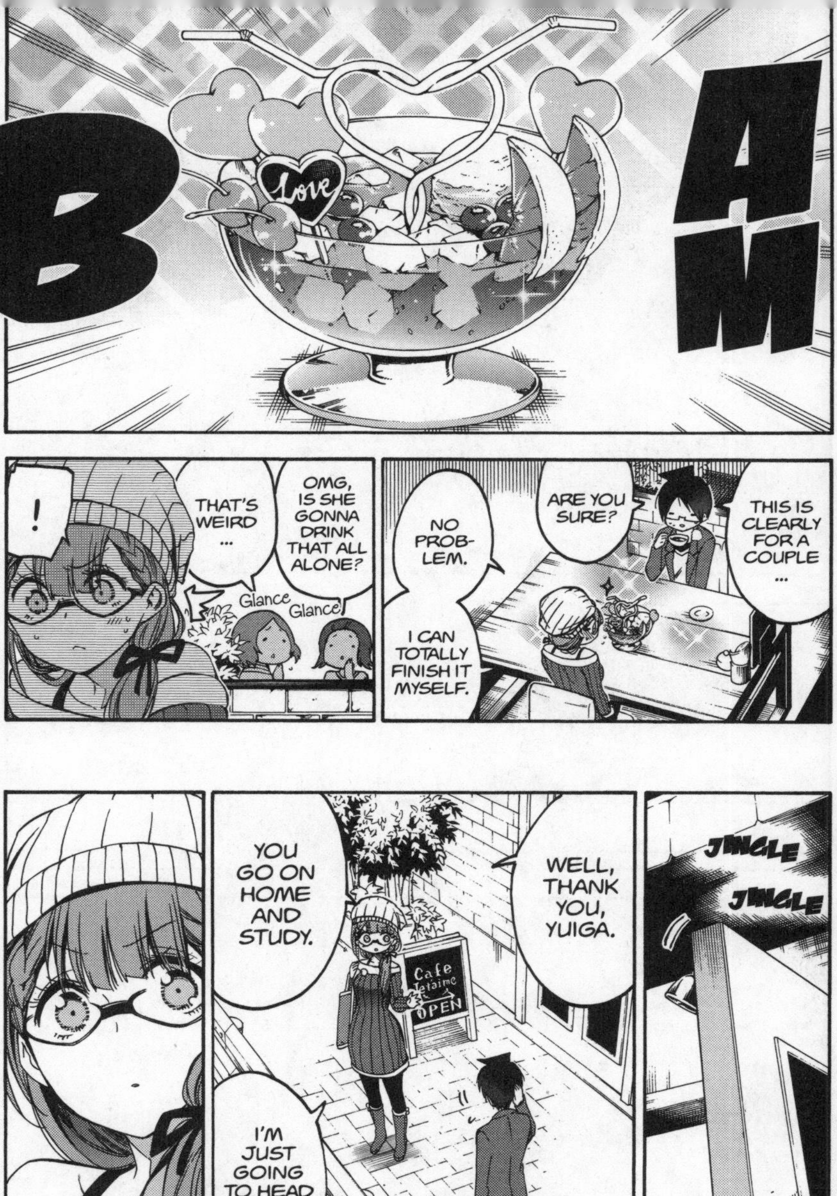
BAM
Love
THIS IS CLEARLY FOR A COUPLE ...
ARE YOU SURE?
NO PROBLEM.
I CAN TOTALLY FINISH IT MYSELF.
!
OMG, IS SHE GONNA DRINK THAT ALL ALONE?
THAT'S WEIRD ...
Glance Glance
JINGLE
JINGLE
WELL, THANK YOU, YUIGA.
YOU GO ON HOME AND STUDY.
Cafe Jetaime
OPEN
I'M JUST GOING TO HEAD HOME TOO.

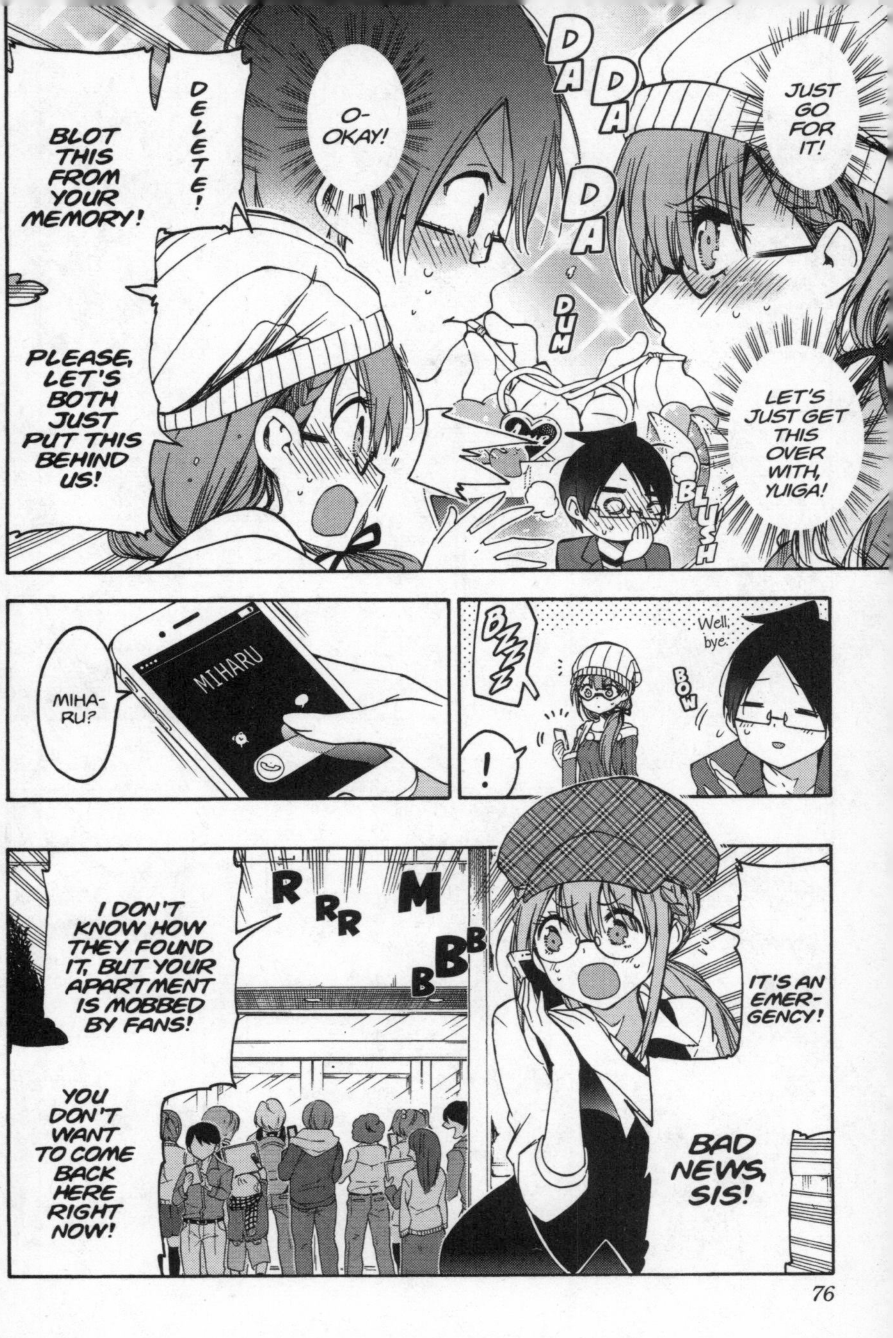
JUST GO FOR IT!
DA DA DA DA DA
O-OKAY!
DELETE!
BLOT THIS FROM YOUR MEMORY!
LET'S JUST GET THIS OVER WITH, YUIGA!
DUM
BLUSH
PLEASE, LET'S BOTH JUST PUT THIS BEHIND US!
Well, bye.
BOW
BZZZ
!
MIHARU
MIHA-RU?
IT'S AN EMERGENCY!
BAD NEWS, SIS!
RRR MBBB
I DON'T KNOW HOW THEY FOUND IT, BUT YOUR APARTMENT IS MOBBED BY FANS!
YOU DON'T WANT TO COME BACK HERE RIGHT NOW!

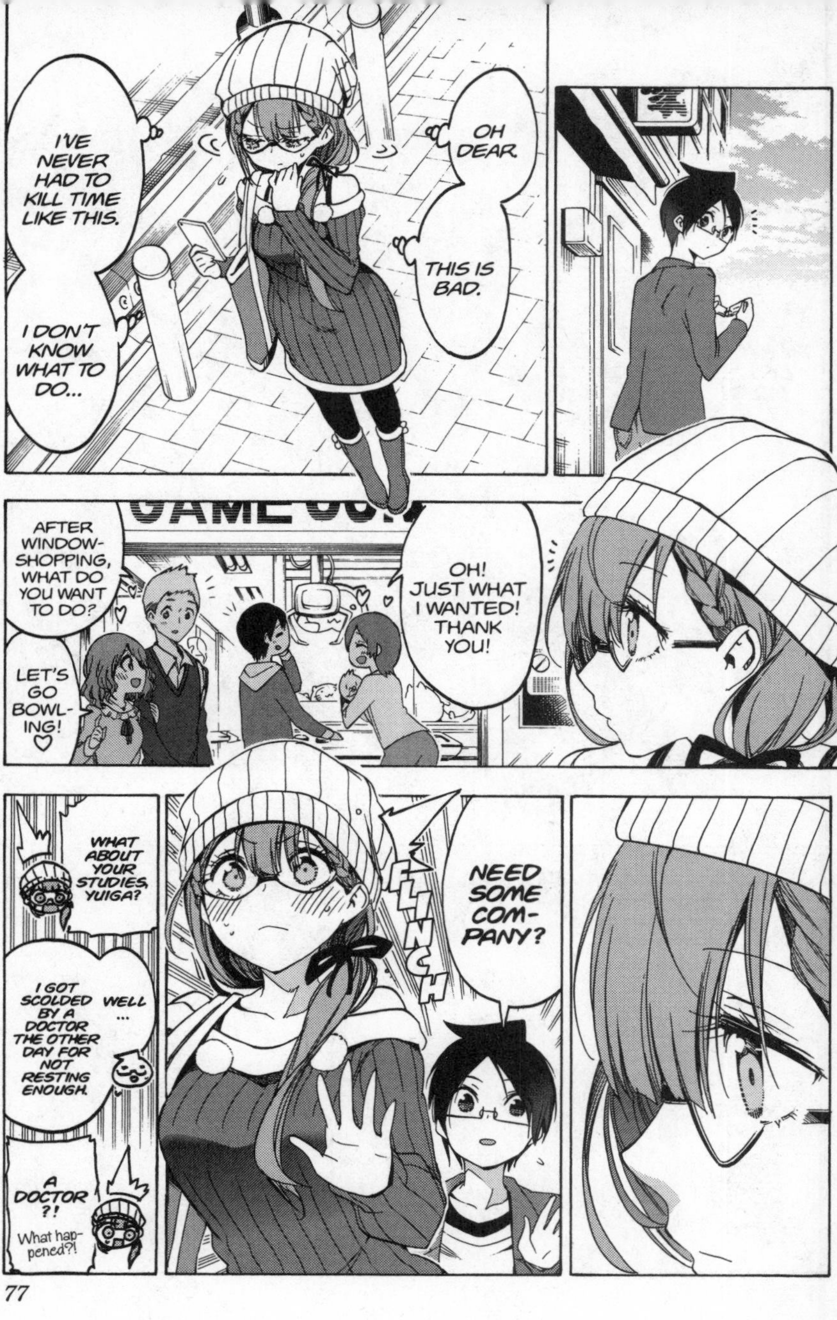
OH DEAR.
THIS IS BAD.
I'VE NEVER HAD TO KILL TIME LIKE THIS.
I DON'T KNOW WHAT TO DO...
OH! JUST WHAT I WANTED! THANK YOU!
AFTER WINDOW-SHOPPING, WHAT DO YOU WANT TO DO?
LET'S GO BOWL-ING! ♡
NEED SOME COM-PANY?
FLINCH
WHAT ABOUT YOUR STUDIES, YUIGA?
WELL...
I GOT SCOLDED BY A DOCTOR THE OTHER DAY FOR NOT RESTING ENOUGH.
A DOCTOR?!
What hap-pened?!

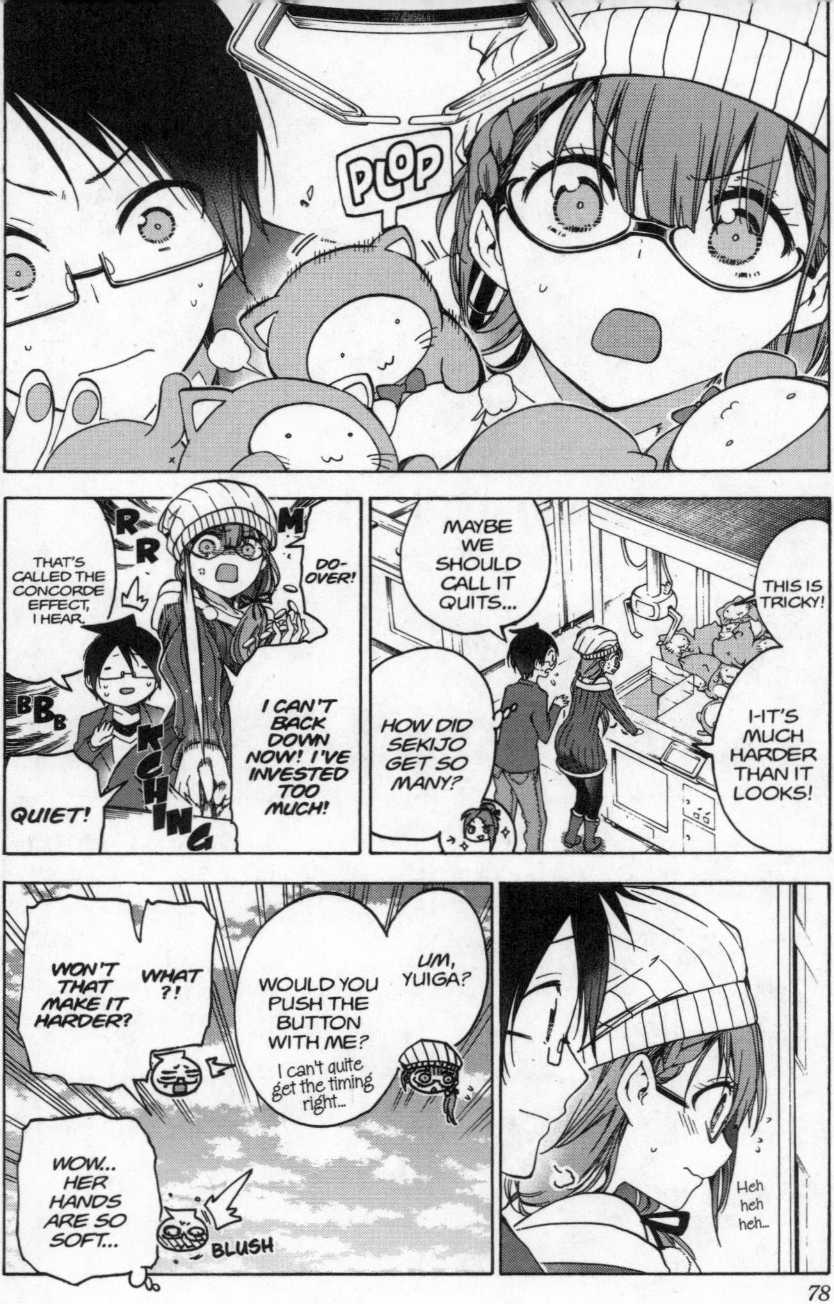
PLOP
THIS IS TRICKY!
MAYBE WE SHOULD CALL IT QUITS...
I-IT'S MUCH HARDER THAN IT LOOKS!
HOW DID SEKIJO GET SO MANY?
M
DO-OVER!
RRR
THAT'S CALLED THE CONCORDE EFFECT, I HEAR.
I CAN'T BACK DOWN NOW! I'VE INVESTED TOO MUCH!
KCHING
BBB
QUIET!
Heh heh heh...
UM, YUIGA?
WOULD YOU PUSH THE BUTTON WITH ME?
I can't quite get the timing right...
WHAT?!
WON'T THAT MAKE IT HARDER?
WOW... HER HANDS ARE SO SOFT...
BLUSH

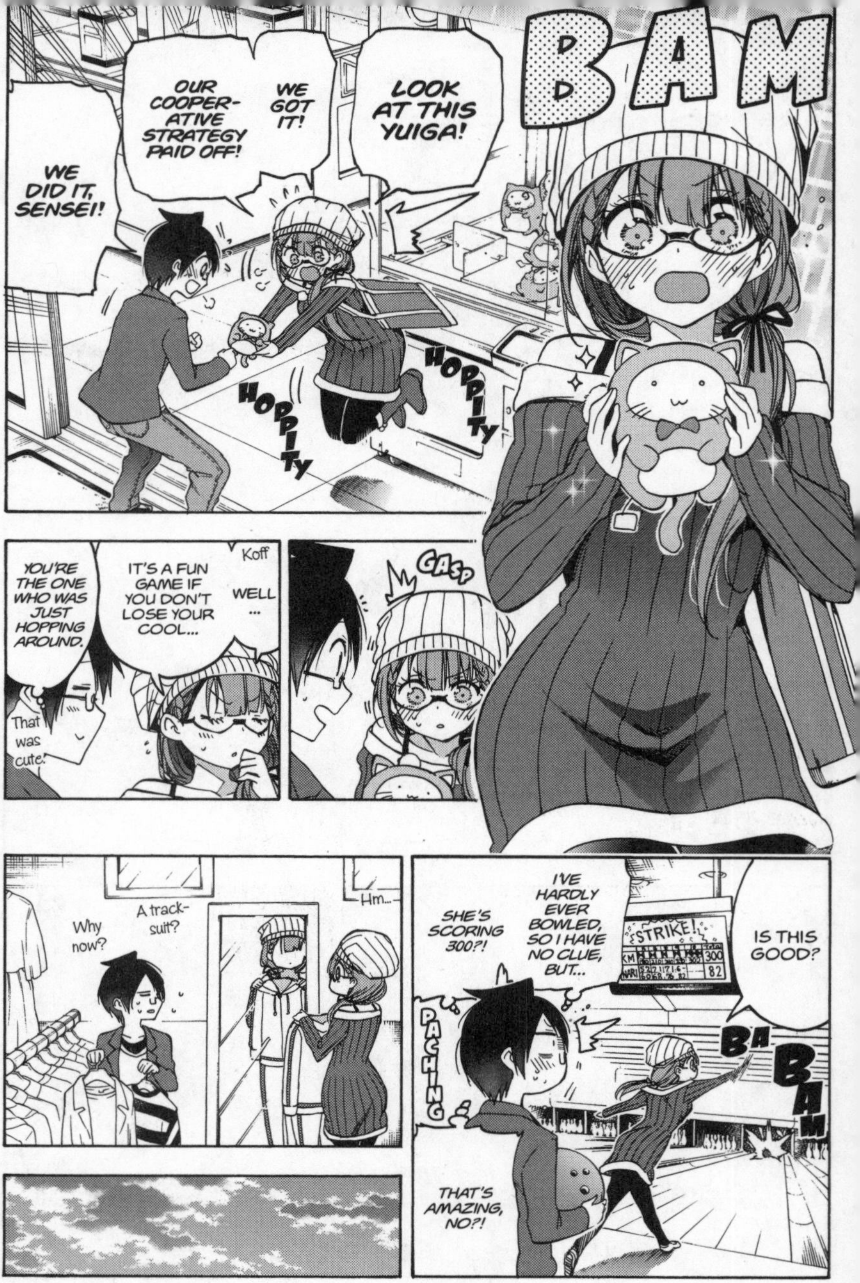
BAM
LOOK AT THIS YUIGA!
WE GOT IT!
OUR COOPERATIVE STRATEGY PAID OFF!
WE DID IT, SENSEI!
HOPPITY
HOPPITY
GASP
WELL ...
Koff
IT'S A FUN GAME IF YOU DON'T LOSE YOUR COOL...
YOU'RE THE ONE WHO WAS JUST HOPPING AROUND.
That was cute!
IS THIS GOOD?
STRIKE!
BA BAM
I'VE HARDLY EVER BOWLED, SO I HAVE NO CLUE, BUT...
SHE'S SCORING 300?!
PACHING
THAT'S AMAZING, NO?!
Hm...
A track-suit?
Why now?

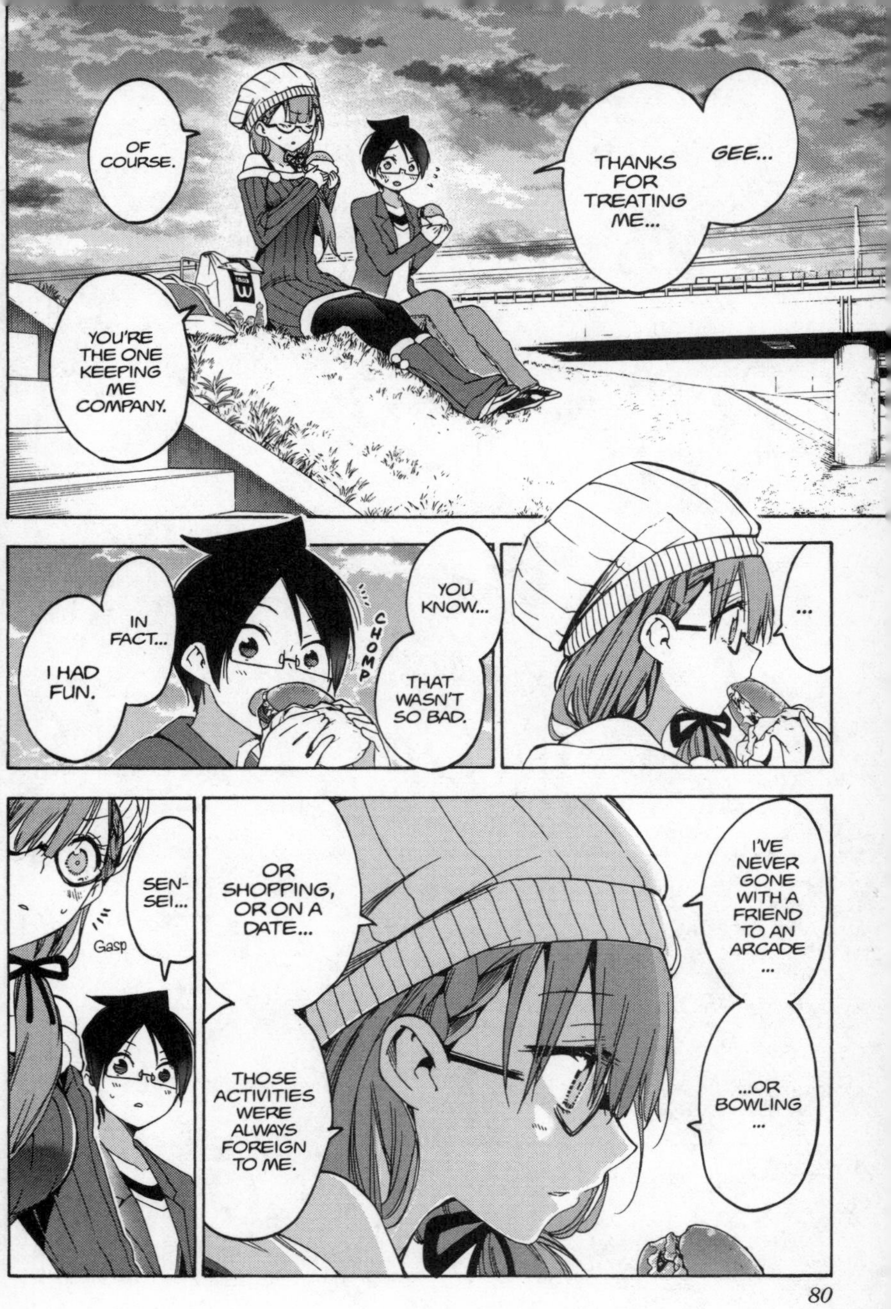
GEE...
THANKS FOR TREATING ME...
OF COURSE.
YOU'RE THE ONE KEEPING ME COMPANY.
...
YOU KNOW...
THAT WASN'T SO BAD.
CHOMP
IN FACT...
I HAD FUN.
I'VE NEVER GONE WITH A FRIEND TO AN ARCADE ...
...OR BOWLING ...
OR SHOPPING, OR ON A DATE...
THOSE ACTIVITIES WERE ALWAYS FOREIGN TO ME.
SEN-SEI...
Gasp

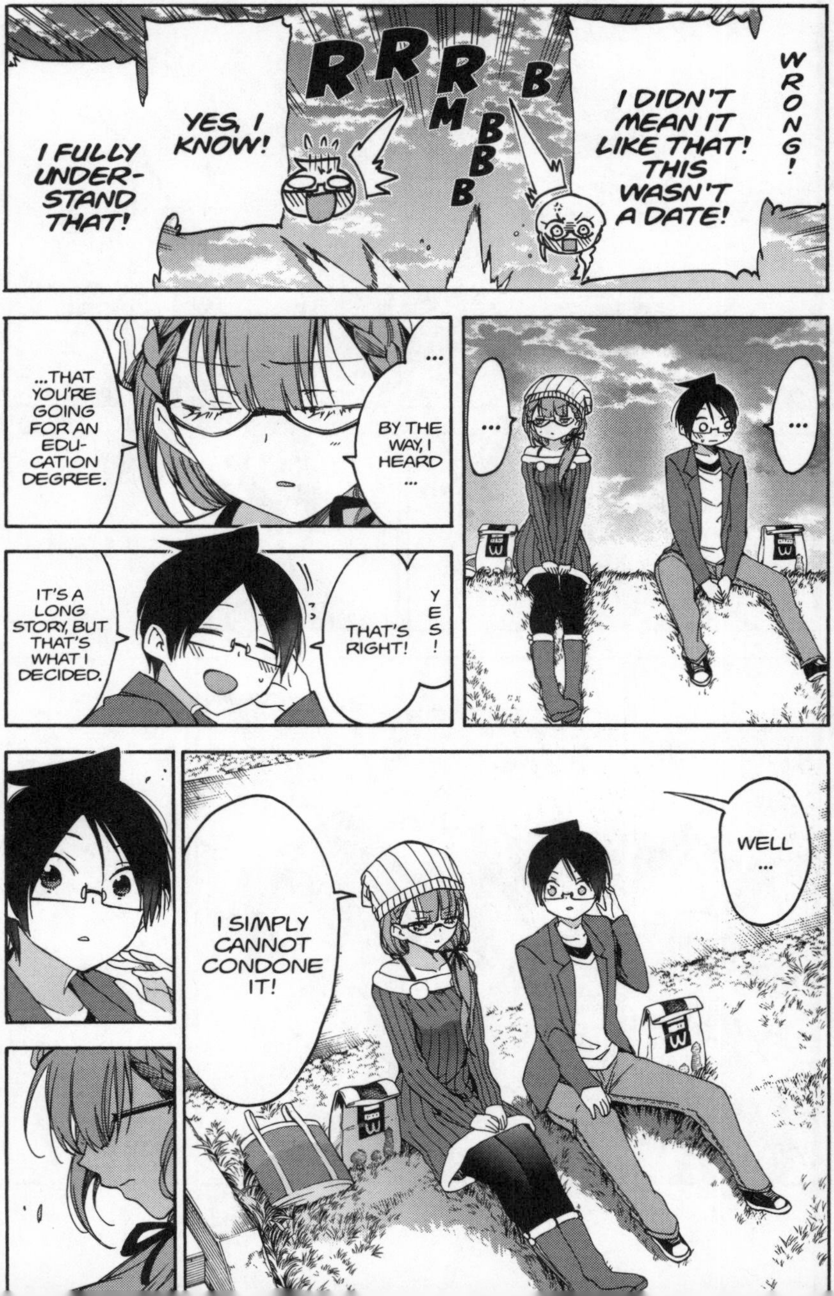
WRONG!
I DIDN'T MEAN IT LIKE THAT! THIS WASN'T A DATE!
RRRMBBBB
YES, I KNOW!
I FULLY UNDER-STAND THAT!
...
...
...
BY THE WAY, I HEARD ...
...THAT YOU'RE GOING FOR AN EDU-CATION DEGREE.
YES!
THAT'S RIGHT!
IT'S A LONG STORY, BUT THAT'S WHAT I DECIDED.
WELL ...
I SIMPLY CANNOT CONDONE IT!

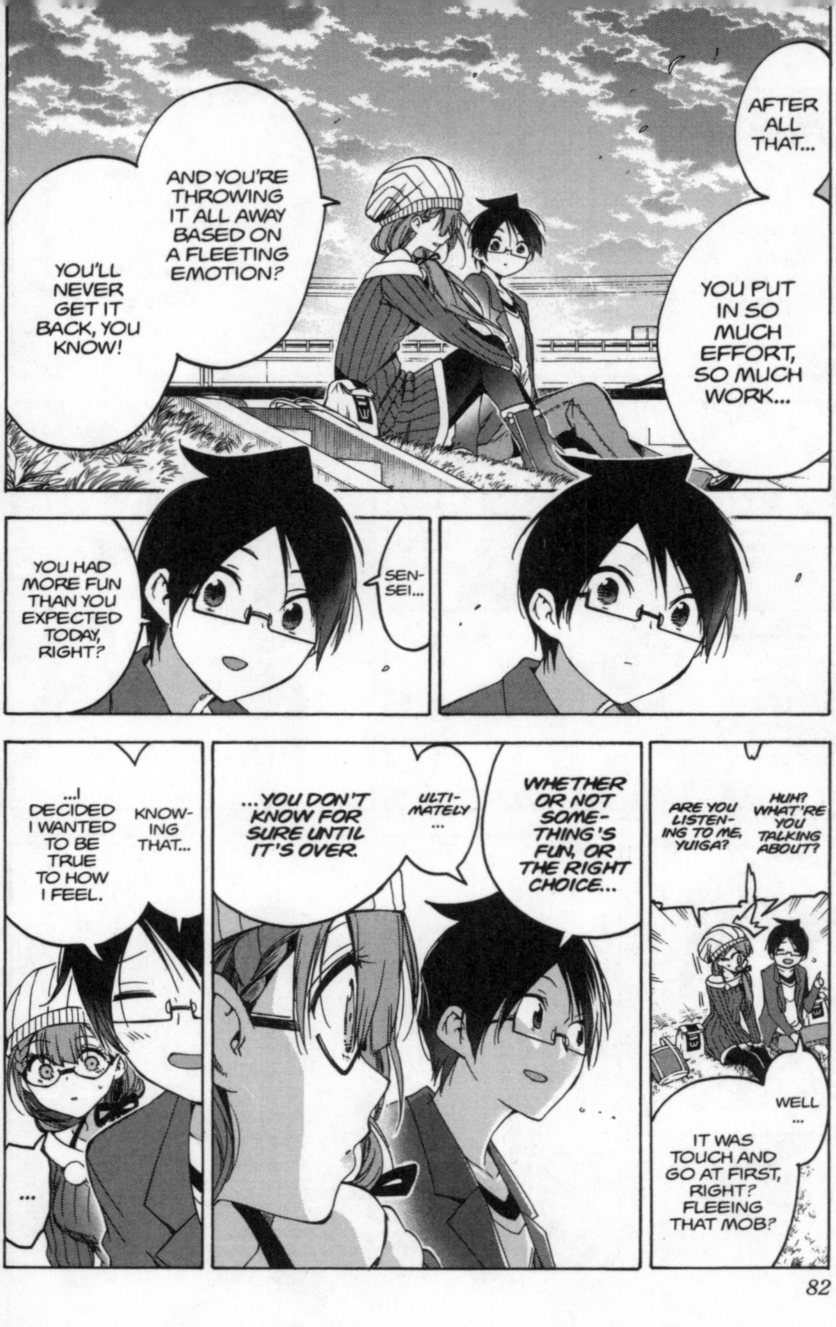
AFTER ALL THAT...
YOU PUT IN SO MUCH EFFORT, SO MUCH WORK...
AND YOU'RE THROWING IT ALL AWAY BASED ON A FLEETING EMOTION?
YOU'LL NEVER GET IT BACK, YOU KNOW!
SEN-SEI...
YOU HAD MORE FUN THAN YOU EXPECTED TODAY, RIGHT?
HUH? WHAT'RE YOU TALKING ABOUT?
ARE YOU LISTENING TO ME, YUIGA?
WELL...
IT WAS TOUCH AND GO AT FIRST, RIGHT? FLEEING THAT MOB?
WHETHER OR NOT SOMETHING'S FUN, OR THE RIGHT CHOICE...
ULTIMATELY...
...YOU DON'T KNOW FOR SURE UNTIL IT'S OVER.
KNOWING THAT...
...I DECIDED I WANTED TO BE TRUE TO HOW I FEEL.
...

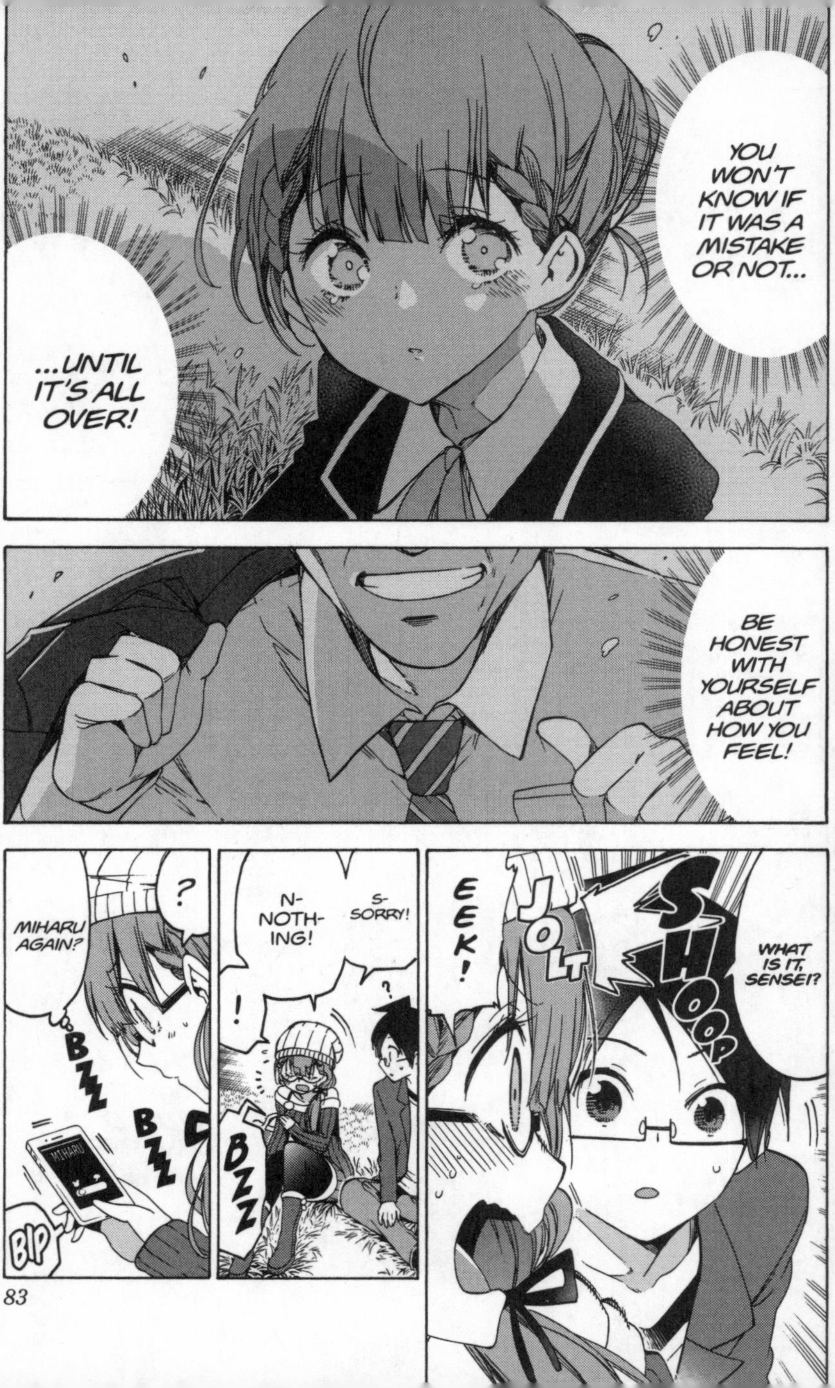
YOU WON'T KNOW IF IT WAS A MISTAKE OR NOT...
...UNTIL IT'S ALL OVER!
BE HONEST WITH YOURSELF ABOUT HOW YOU FEEL!
SHOOOP
WHAT IS IT, SENSEI?
JOLT
EEK!
S-SORRY!
N-NOTHING!
?
!
BZZ
?
MIHARU AGAIN?
BZZ
BZZ
MIHARU
BIP

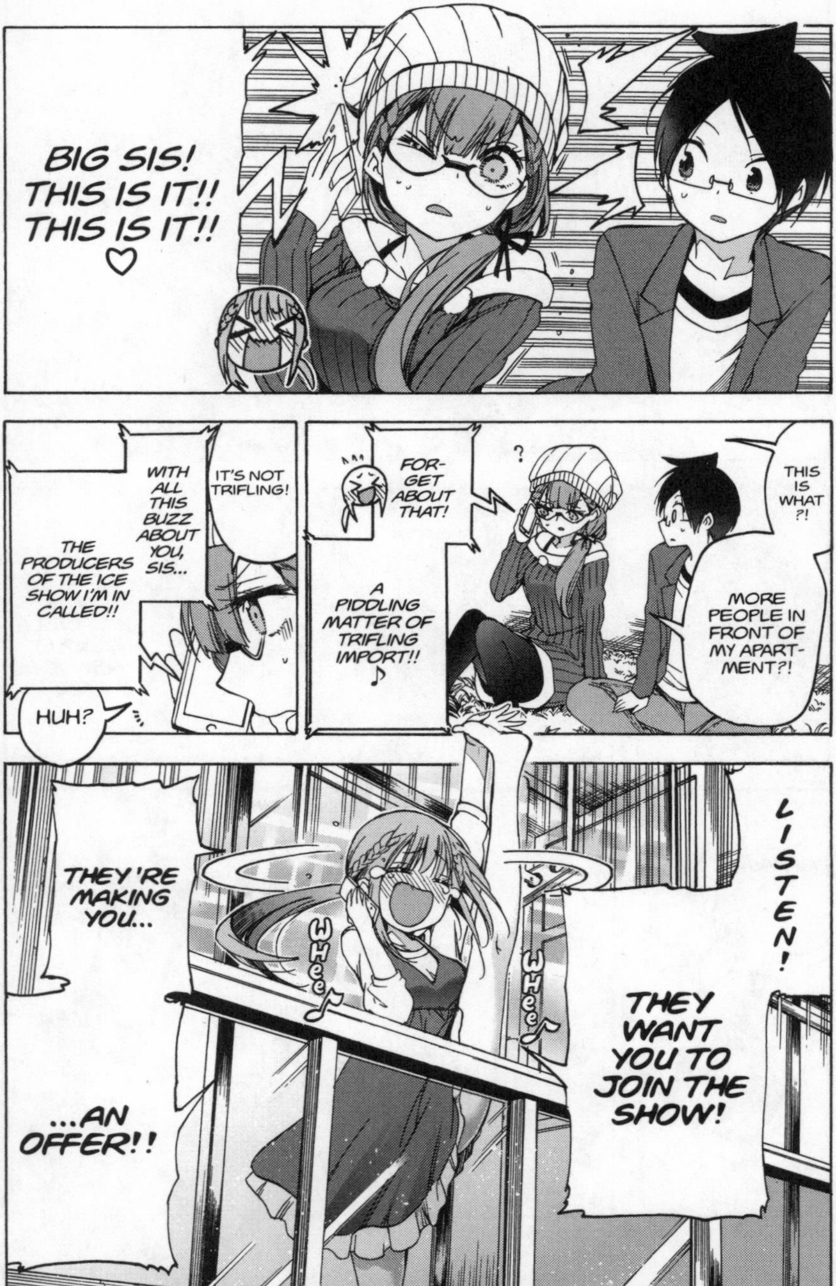
BIG SIS! THIS IS IT!! THIS IS IT!! ♡
THIS IS WHAT?!
MORE PEOPLE IN FRONT OF MY APART-MENT?!
FOR-GET ABOUT THAT!
A PIDDLING MATTER OF TRIFLING IMPORT!! ♪
IT'S NOT TRIFLING!
WITH ALL THIS BUZZ ABOUT YOU, SIS...
THE PRODUCERS OF THE ICE SHOW I'M IN CALLED!!
HUH?
LISTEN!
THEY WANT YOU TO JOIN THE SHOW!
WHEE♪
WHEE♪
THEY'RE MAKING YOU...
...AN OFFER!!

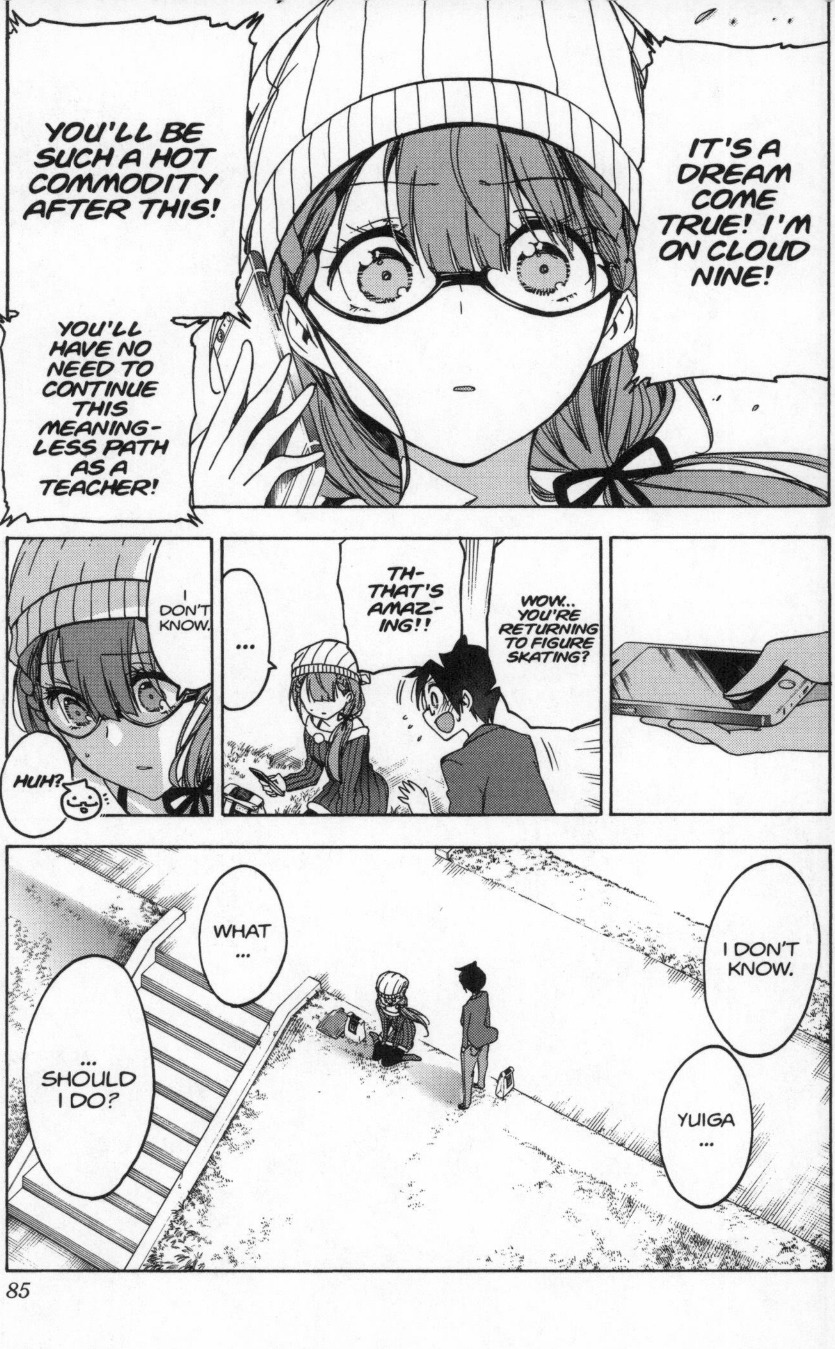
IT'S A DREAM COME TRUE! I'M ON CLOUD NINE!
YOU'LL BE SUCH A HOT COMMODITY AFTER THIS!
YOU'LL HAVE NO NEED TO CONTINUE THIS MEANING-LESS PATH AS A TEACHER!
WOW... YOU'RE RETURNING TO FIGURE SKATING?
TH-THAT'S AMAZ-ING!!
...
I DON'T KNOW.
HUH?
I DON'T KNOW.
YUIGA...
WHAT...
...SHOULD I DO?

Now that I think about it, I don't know how long it's been...

...since I bought clothes that weren't tracksuits.

That long?

Question 101: The Ice Flower Dances with [X] at Twilight, Part 2

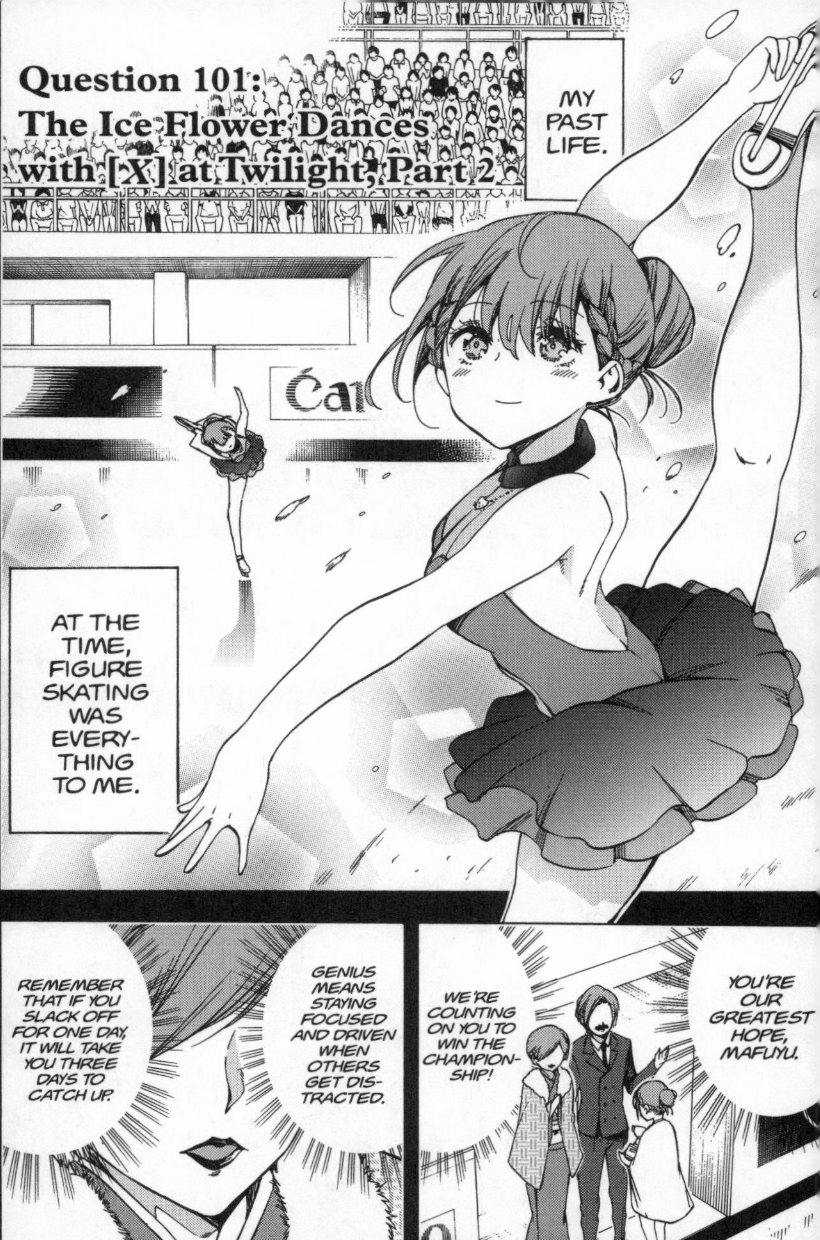
MY PAST LIFE.
AT THE TIME, FIGURE SKATING WAS EVERY-THING TO ME.
YOU'RE OUR GREATEST HOPE, MAFUYU.
WE'RE COUNTING ON YOU TO WIN THE CHAMPION-SHIP!
GENIUS MEANS STAYING FOCUSED AND DRIVEN WHEN OTHERS GET DIS-TRACTED.
REMEMBER THAT IF YOU SLACK OFF FOR ONE DAY, IT WILL TAKE YOU THREE DAYS TO CATCH UP.

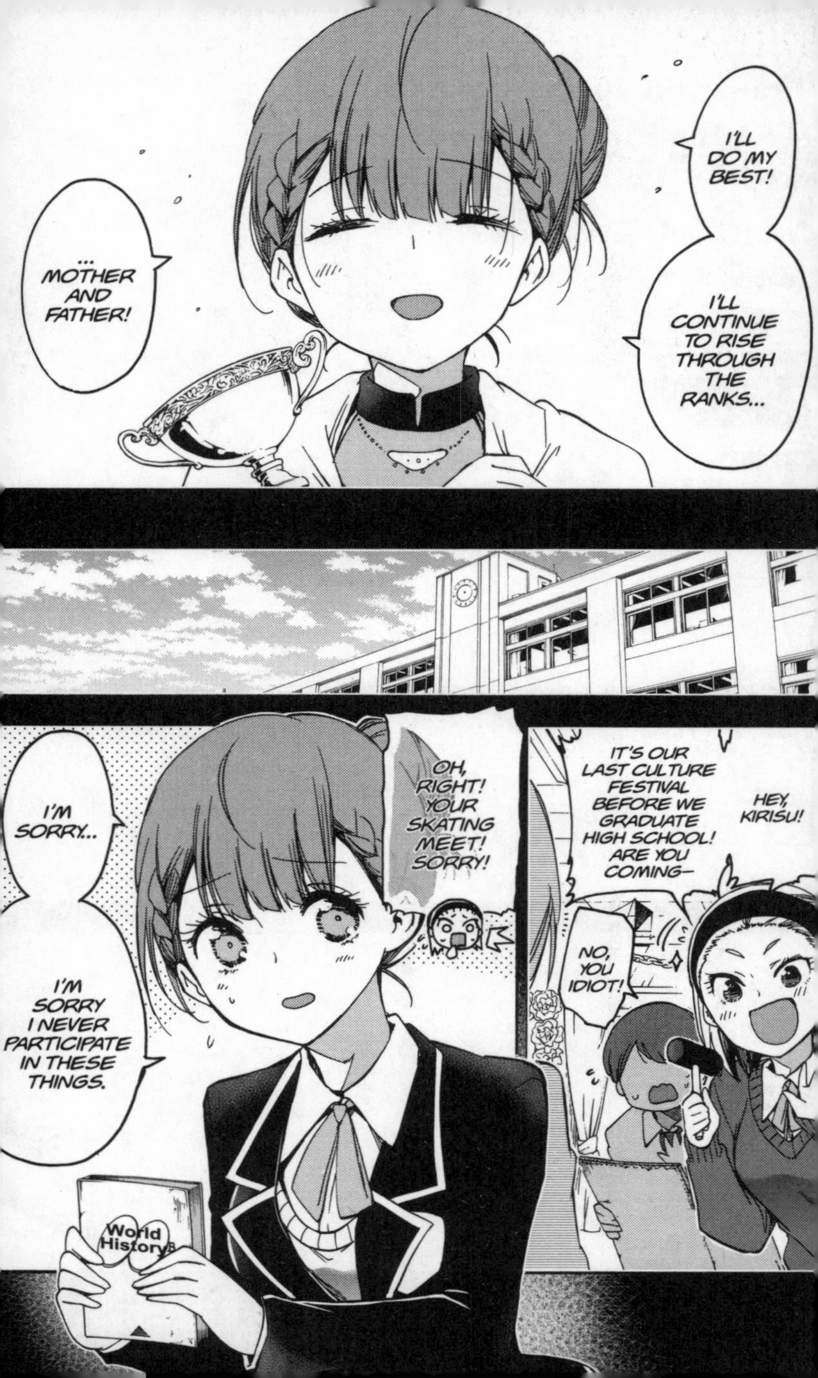
I'LL DO MY BEST!
I'LL CONTINUE TO RISE THROUGH THE RANKS...
... MOTHER AND FATHER!
HEY, KIRISU!
IT'S OUR LAST CULTURE FESTIVAL BEFORE WE GRADUATE HIGH SCHOOL! ARE YOU COMING—
NO, YOU IDIOT!
OH, RIGHT! YOUR SKATING MEET! SORRY!
I'M SORRY...
I'M SORRY I NEVER PARTICIPATE IN THESE THINGS.
World History B

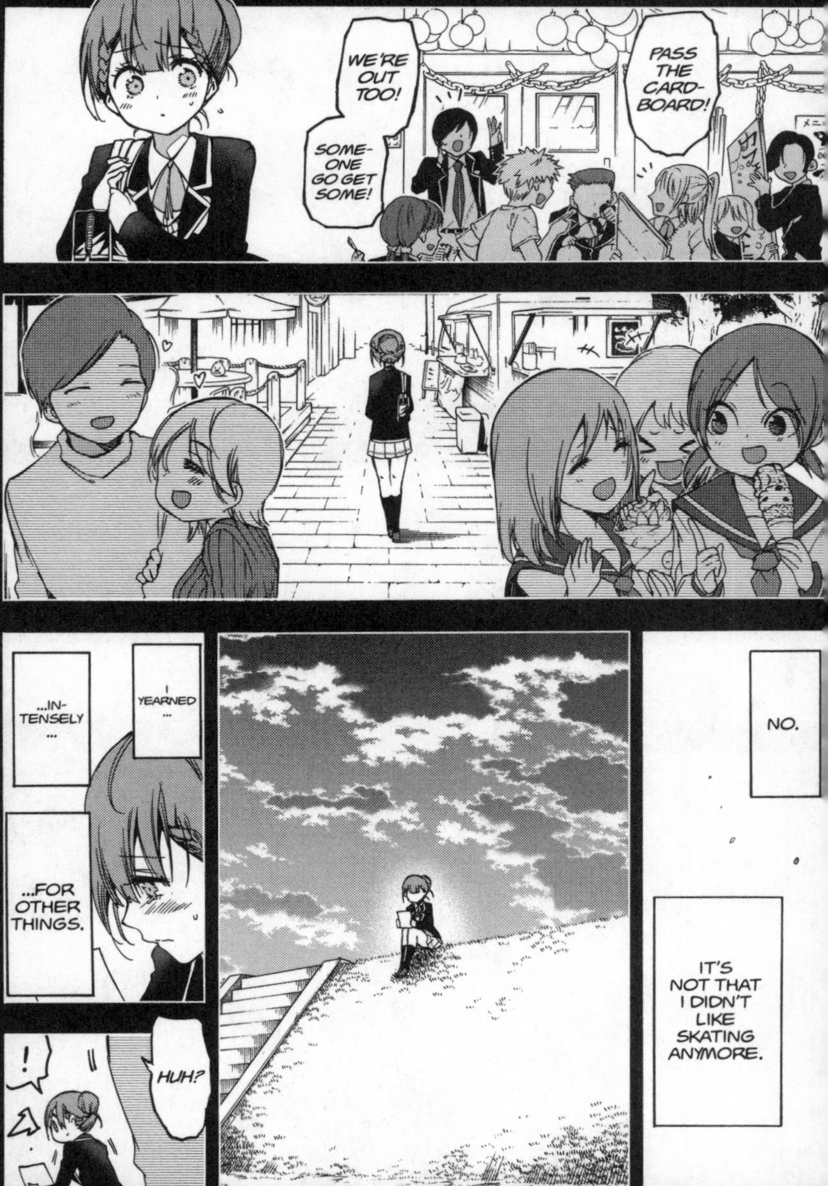
PASS THE CARD-BOARD!
WE'RE OUT TOO!
SOME-ONE GO GET SOME!
NO.
IT'S NOT THAT I DIDN'T LIKE SKATING ANYMORE.
I YEARNED...
...IN-TENSELY...
...FOR OTHER THINGS.
HUH?
!

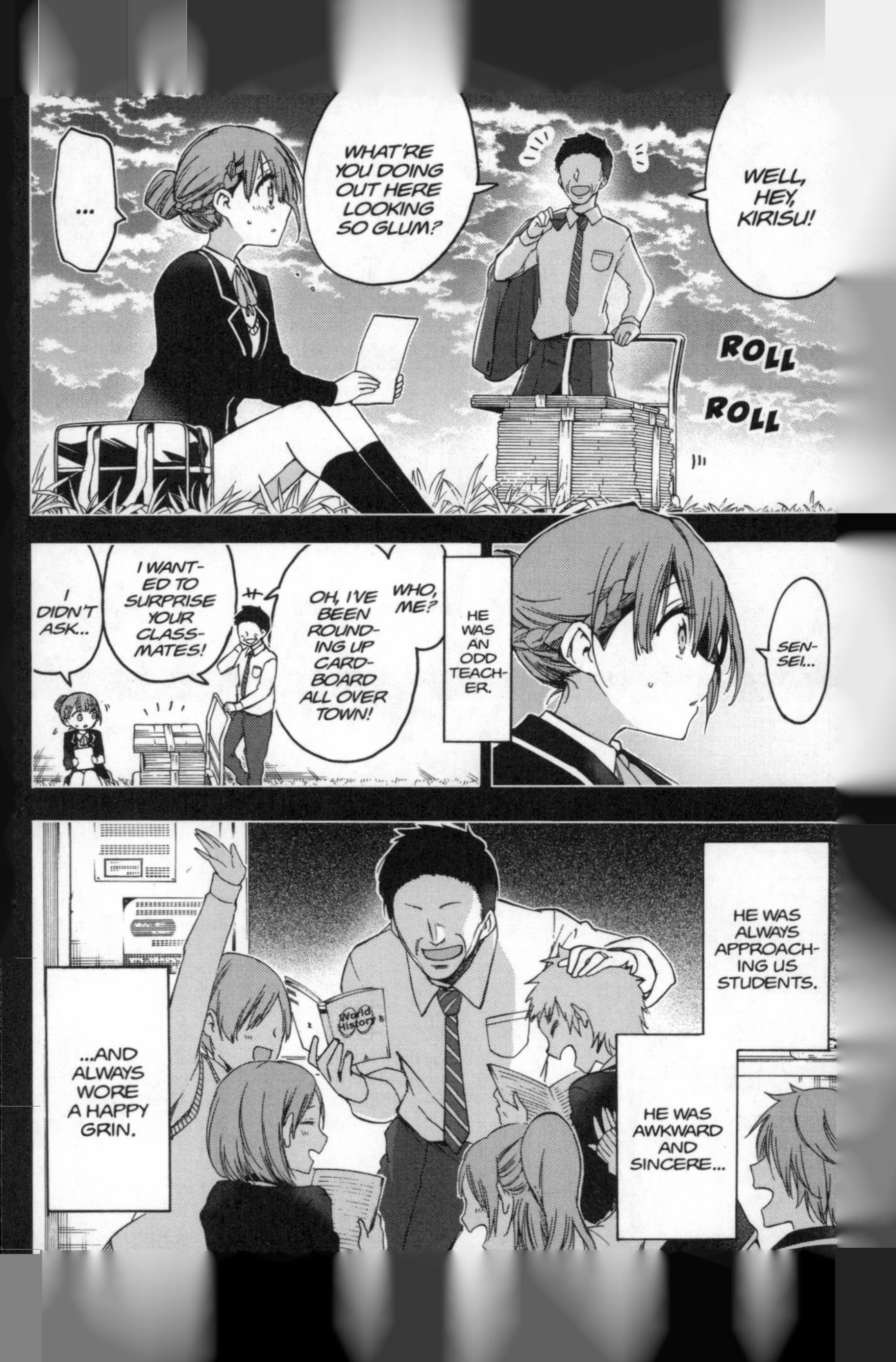
WELL, HEY, KIRISU!
ROLL
ROLL
WHAT'RE YOU DOING OUT HERE LOOKING SO GLUM?
...
SENSEI...
HE WAS AN ODD TEACHER.
WHO, ME?
OH, I'VE BEEN ROUNDING UP CARDBOARD ALL OVER TOWN!
I WANTED TO SURPRISE YOUR CLASSMATES!
I DIDN'T ASK...
HE WAS ALWAYS APPROACHING US STUDENTS.
HE WAS AWKWARD AND SINCERE...
World History B
...AND ALWAYS WORE A HAPPY GRIN.

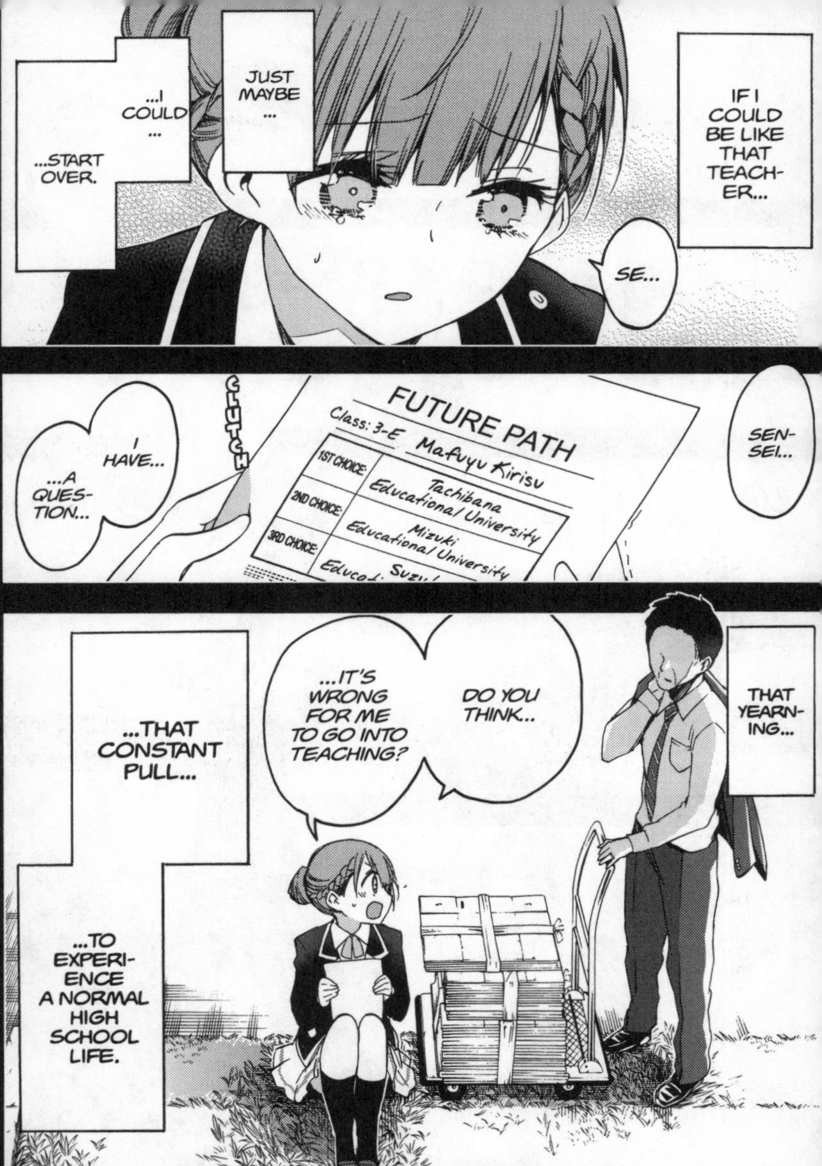
IF I COULD BE LIKE THAT TEACHER...
SE...
JUST MAYBE ...
...I COULD ...
...START OVER.
SEN-SEI...
FUTURE PATH
Class: 3-E Mafuyu Kirisu
1ST CHOICE: Tachibana Educational/University
2ND CHOICE: Mizuki Educational/University
3RD CHOICE:
CLUTCH
I HAVE...
...A QUESTION...
THAT YEARNING...
DO YOU THINK...
...IT'S WRONG FOR ME TO GO INTO TEACHING?
...THAT CONSTANT PULL...
...TO EXPERIENCE A NORMAL HIGH SCHOOL LIFE.

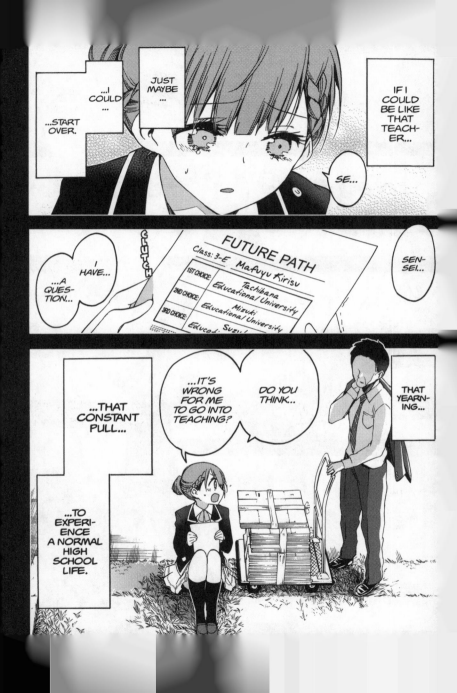

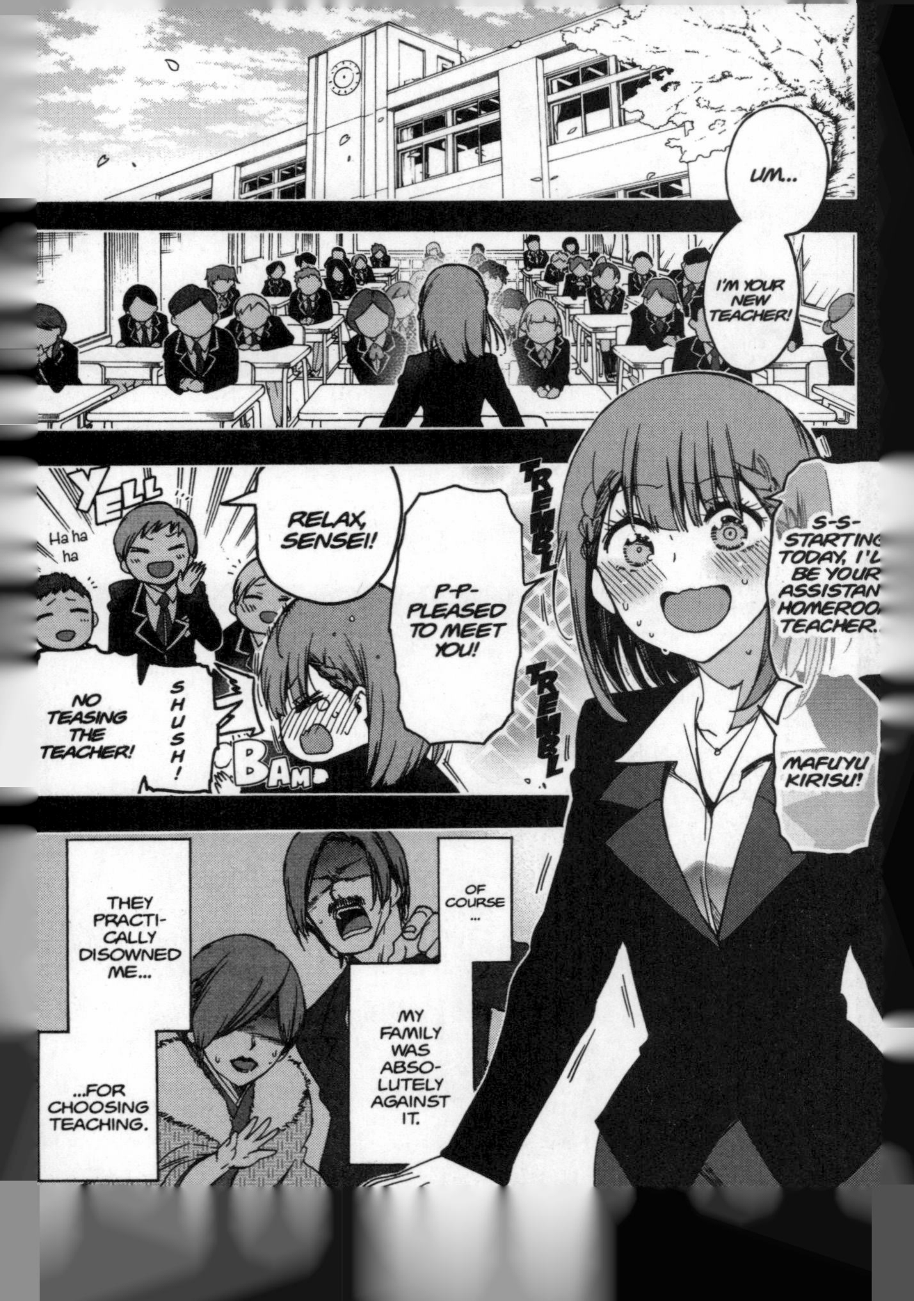
UM...
I'M YOUR NEW TEACHER!
S-S-STARTING TODAY, I'L BE YOUR ASSISTAN HOMEROO TEACHER...
MAFUYU KIRISU!
TREMBL
TREMBL
P-P-PLEASED TO MEET YOU!
RELAX, SENSEI!
YELL
Ha ha ha
SHUSH!
BAM
NO TEASING THE TEACHER!
OF COURSE...
MY FAMILY WAS ABSO-LUTELY AGAINST IT.
THEY PRACTI-CALLY DISOWNED ME...
...FOR CHOOSING TEACHING.

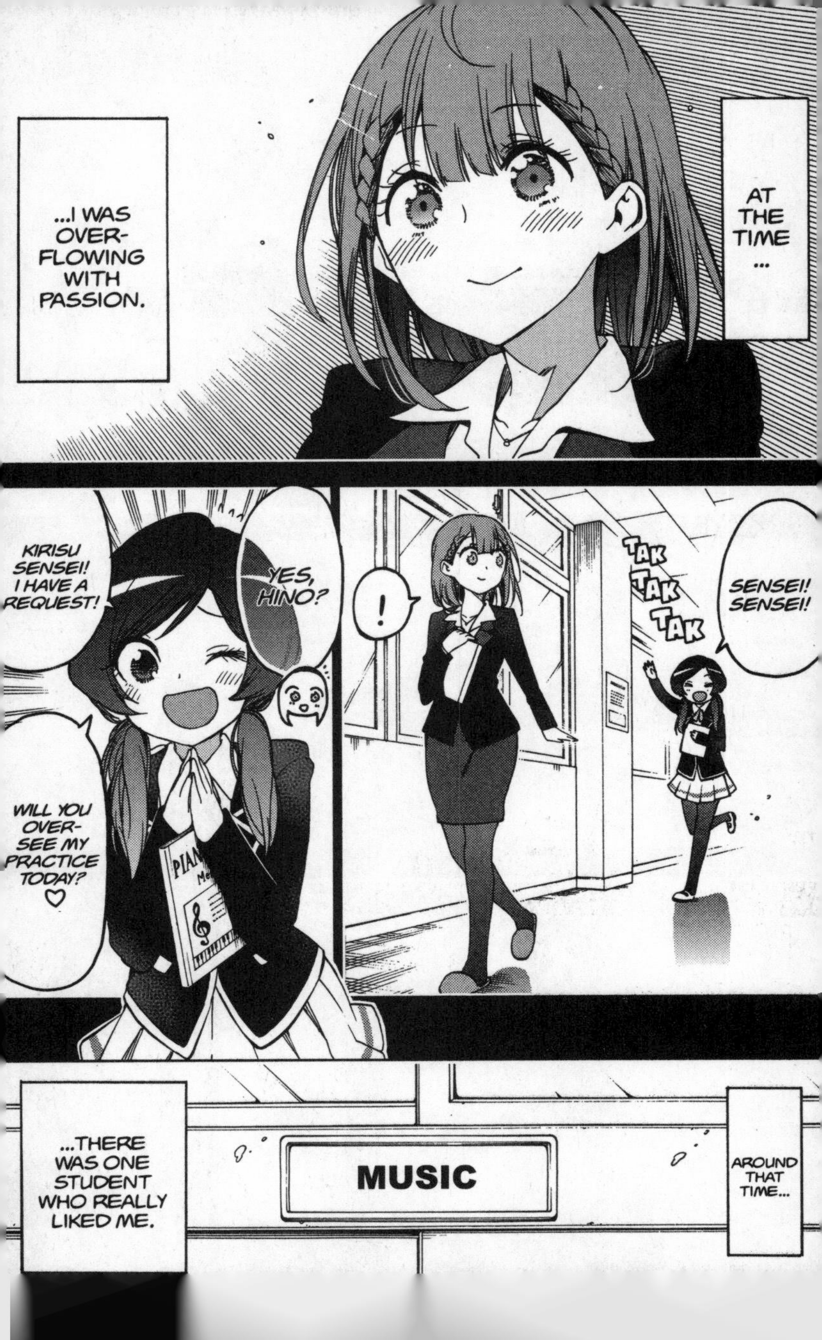
AT THE TIME...
...I WAS OVER-FLOWING WITH PASSION.
SENSEI! SENSEI!
TAK TAK TAK
!
YES, HINO?
KIRISU SENSEI! I HAVE A REQUEST!
WILL YOU OVER-SEE MY PRACTICE TODAY? ♡
AROUND THAT TIME...
MUSIC
...THERE WAS ONE STUDENT WHO REALLY LIKED ME.

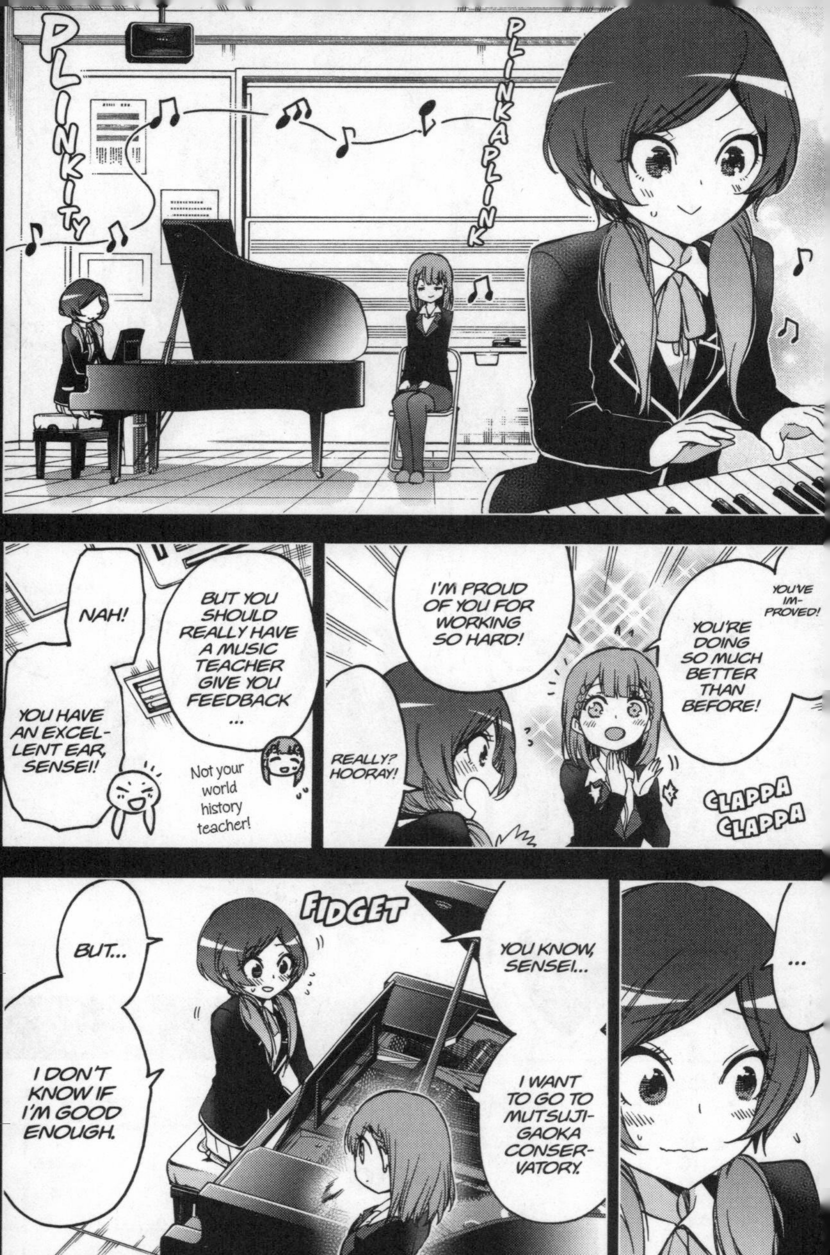
PLINKAPLINK
PLINKITY
YOU'VE IM-PROVED!
YOU'RE DOING SO MUCH BETTER THAN BEFORE!
I'M PROUD OF YOU FOR WORKING SO HARD!
CLAPPA CLAPPA
REALLY? HOORAY!
BUT YOU SHOULD REALLY HAVE A MUSIC TEACHER GIVE YOU FEEDBACK ...
NAH!
YOU HAVE AN EXCEL-LENT EAR, SENSEI!
Not your world history teacher!
...
YOU KNOW, SENSEI...
I WANT TO GO TO MUTSUJI-GAOKA CONSER-VATORY.
FIDGET
BUT...
I DON'T KNOW IF I'M GOOD ENOUGH.

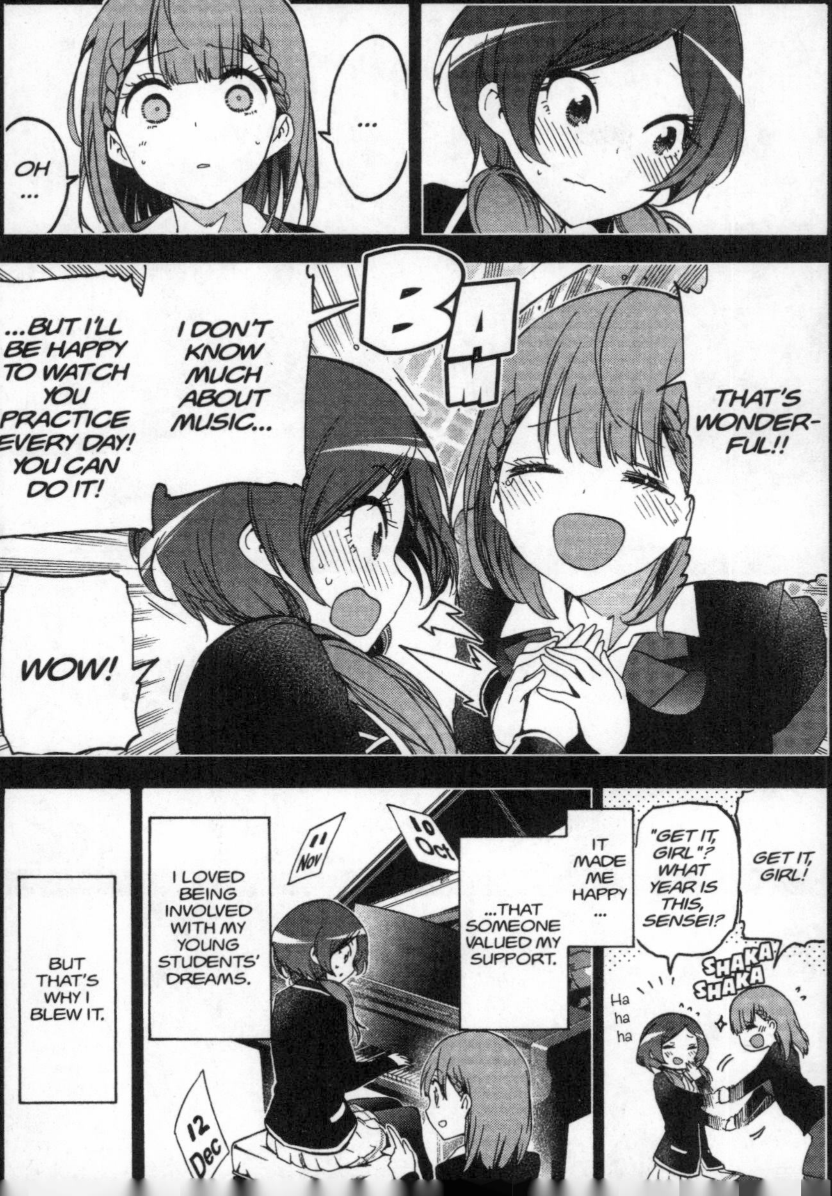
...
OH ...
THAT'S WONDERFUL!!
BAM
I DON'T KNOW MUCH ABOUT MUSIC...
...BUT I'LL BE HAPPY TO WATCH YOU PRACTICE EVERY DAY! YOU CAN DO IT!
WOW!
GET IT, GIRL!
"GET IT, GIRL"? WHAT YEAR IS THIS, SENSEI?
SHAKA SHAKA
Ha ha ha
IT MADE ME HAPPY ...
...THAT SOMEONE VALUED MY SUPPORT.
10 Oct
11 Nov
I LOVED BEING INVOLVED WITH MY YOUNG STUDENTS' DREAMS.
12 Dec
BUT THAT'S WHY I BLEW IT.

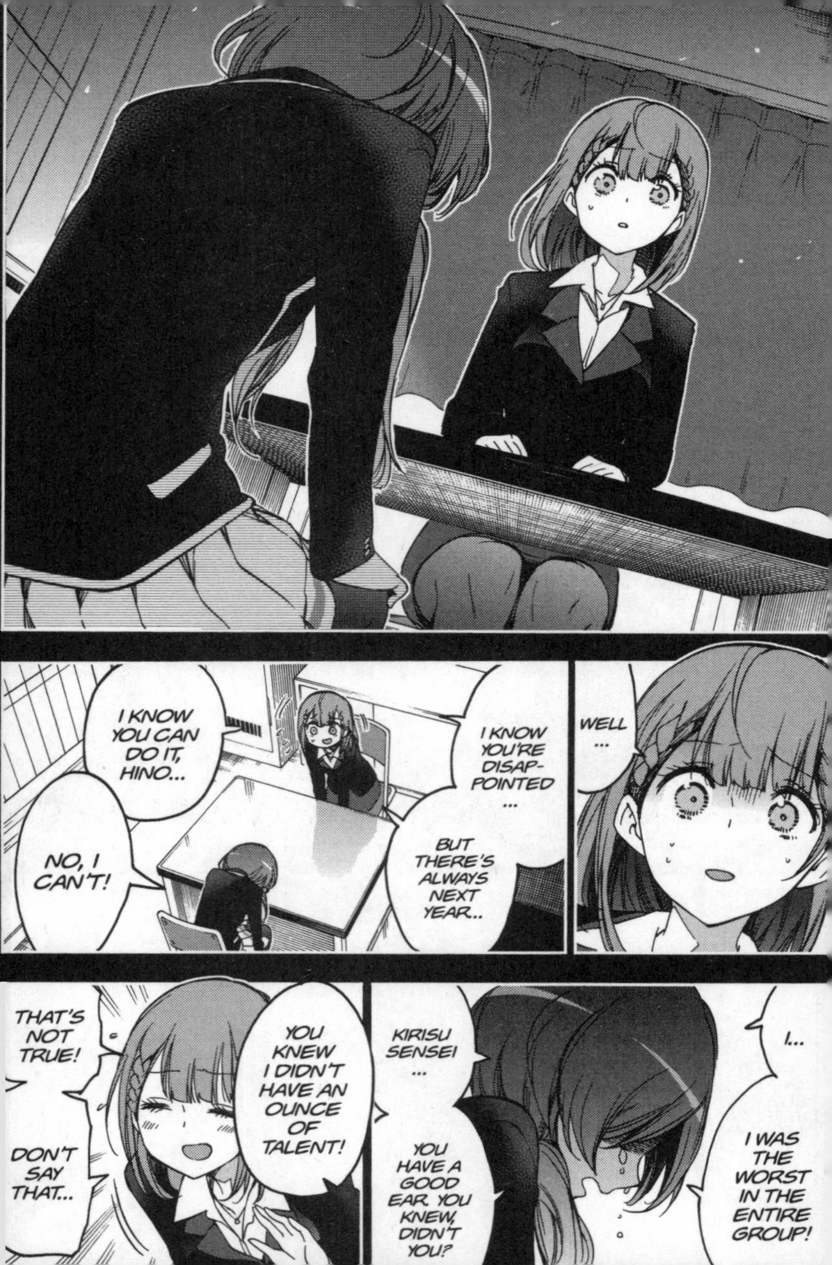
WELL ...
I KNOW YOU'RE DISAPPOINTED ...
BUT THERE'S ALWAYS NEXT YEAR...
I KNOW YOU CAN DO IT, HINO...
NO, I CAN'T!
I...
I WAS THE WORST IN THE ENTIRE GROUP!
KIRISU SENSEI ...
YOU HAVE A GOOD EAR. YOU KNEW, DIDN'T YOU?
YOU KNEW I DIDN'T HAVE AN OUNCE OF TALENT!
THAT'S NOT TRUE!
DON'T SAY THAT...

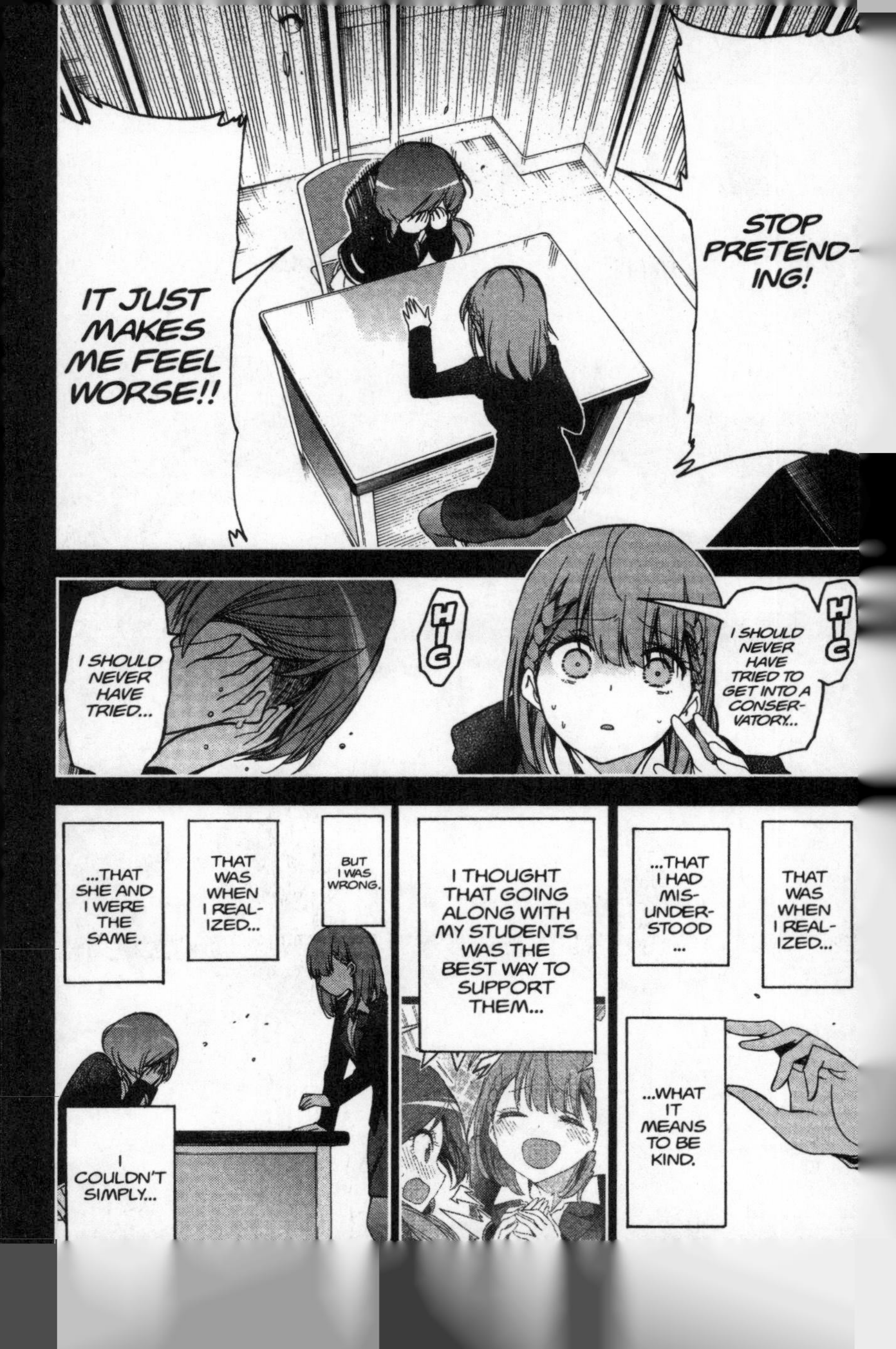
STOP PRETEND-ING!
IT JUST MAKES ME FEEL WORSE!!
HIC
I SHOULD NEVER HAVE TRIED TO GET INTO A CONSER-VATORY...
HIC
I SHOULD NEVER HAVE TRIED...
THAT WAS WHEN I REAL-IZED...
...THAT I HAD MIS-UNDER-STOOD ...
...WHAT IT MEANS TO BE KIND.
I THOUGHT THAT GOING ALONG WITH MY STUDENTS WAS THE BEST WAY TO SUPPORT THEM...
BUT I WAS WRONG.
THAT WAS WHEN I REAL-IZED...
...THAT SHE AND I WERE THE SAME.
I COULDN'T SIMPLY...

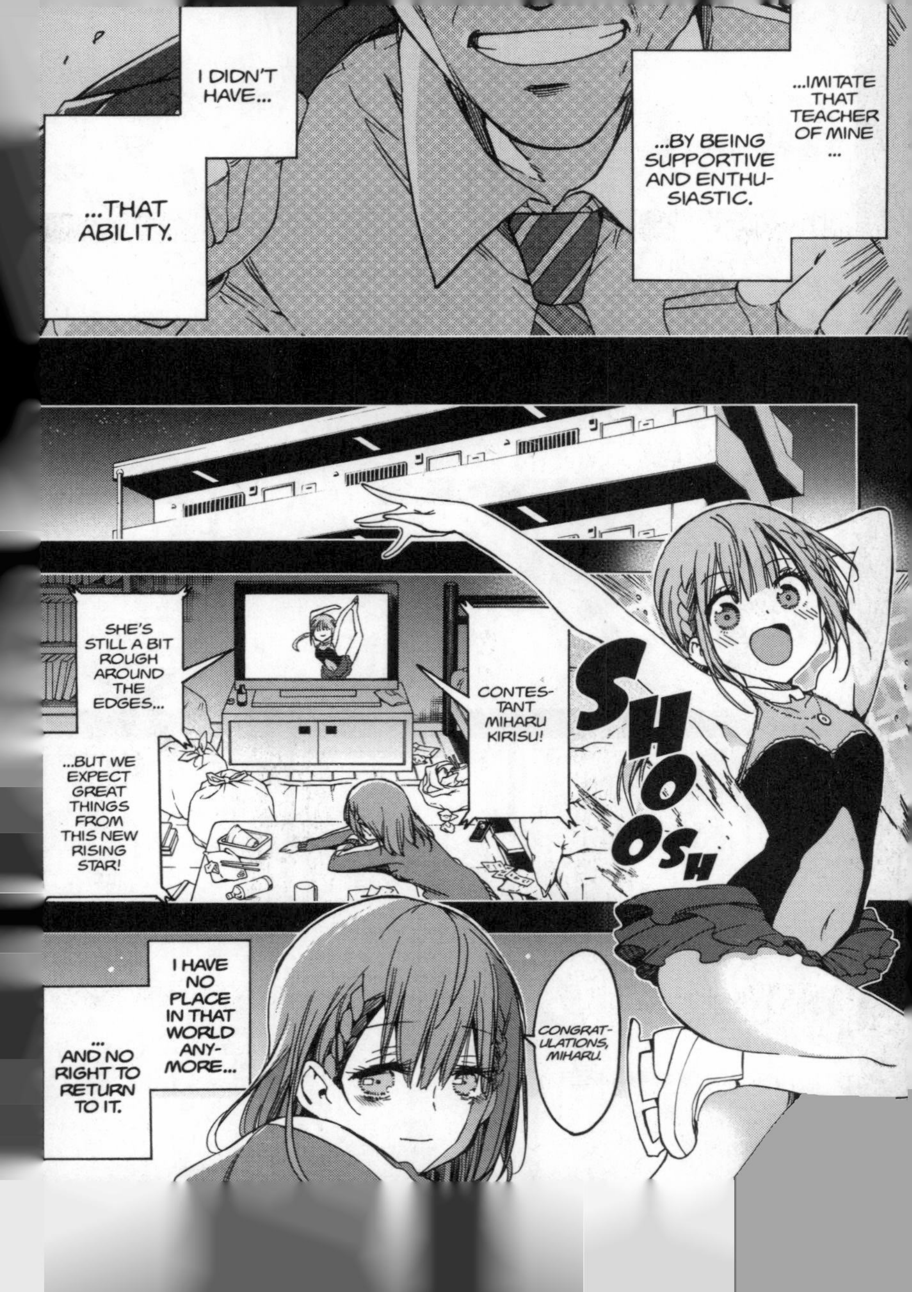
...IMITATE THAT TEACHER OF MINE ...
...BY BEING SUPPORTIVE AND ENTHUSIASTIC.
I DIDN'T HAVE...
...THAT ABILITY.
SHOOOSH
CONTESTANT MIHARU KIRISU!
SHE'S STILL A BIT ROUGH AROUND THE EDGES...
...BUT WE EXPECT GREAT THINGS FROM THIS NEW RISING STAR!
CONGRATULATIONS, MIHARU.
I HAVE NO PLACE IN THAT WORLD ANYMORE...
...AND NO RIGHT TO RETURN TO IT.

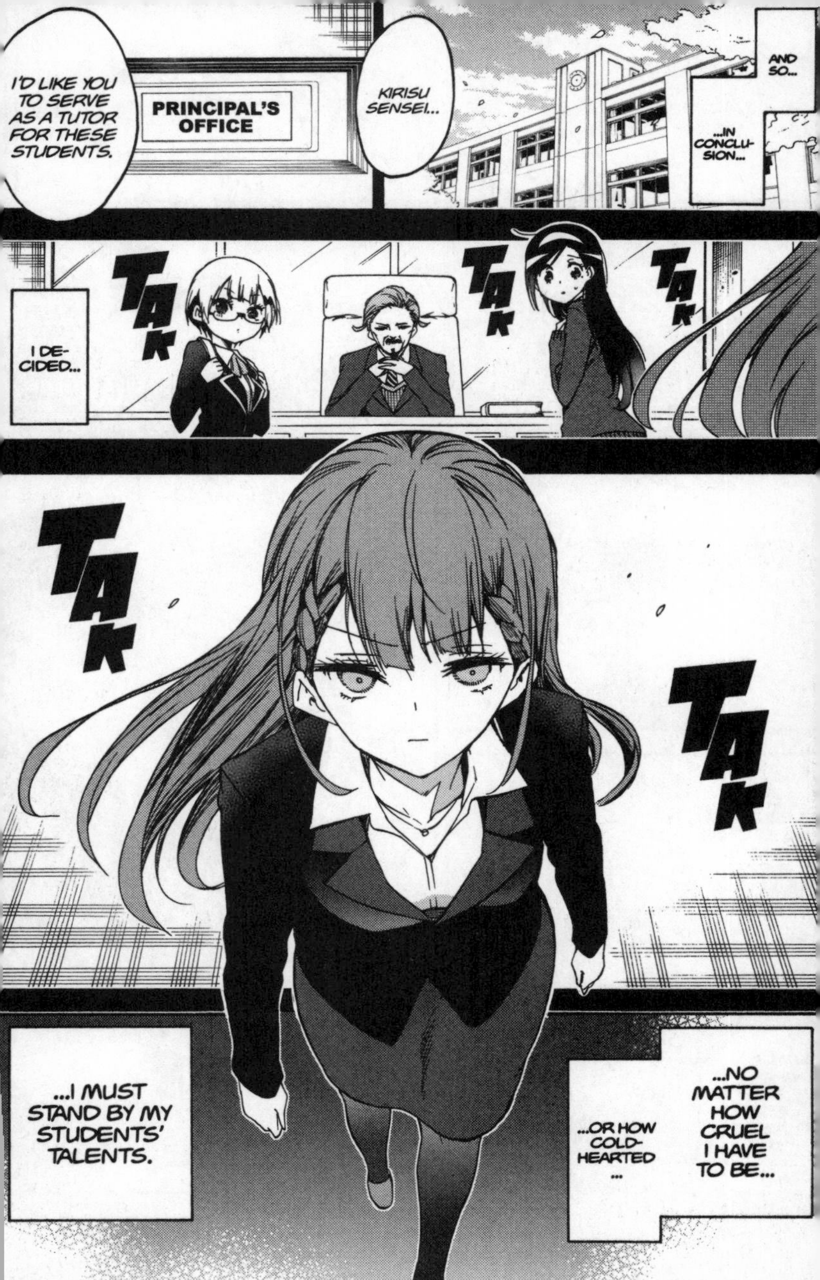
AND SO...
...IN CONCLUSION...
KIRISU SENSEI...
PRINCIPAL'S OFFICE
I'D LIKE YOU TO SERVE AS A TUTOR FOR THESE STUDENTS.
TAK
TAK
TAK
I DECIDED...
TAK
TAK
...NO MATTER HOW CRUEL I HAVE TO BE...
...OR HOW COLD-HEARTED...
...I MUST STAND BY MY STUDENTS' TALENTS.

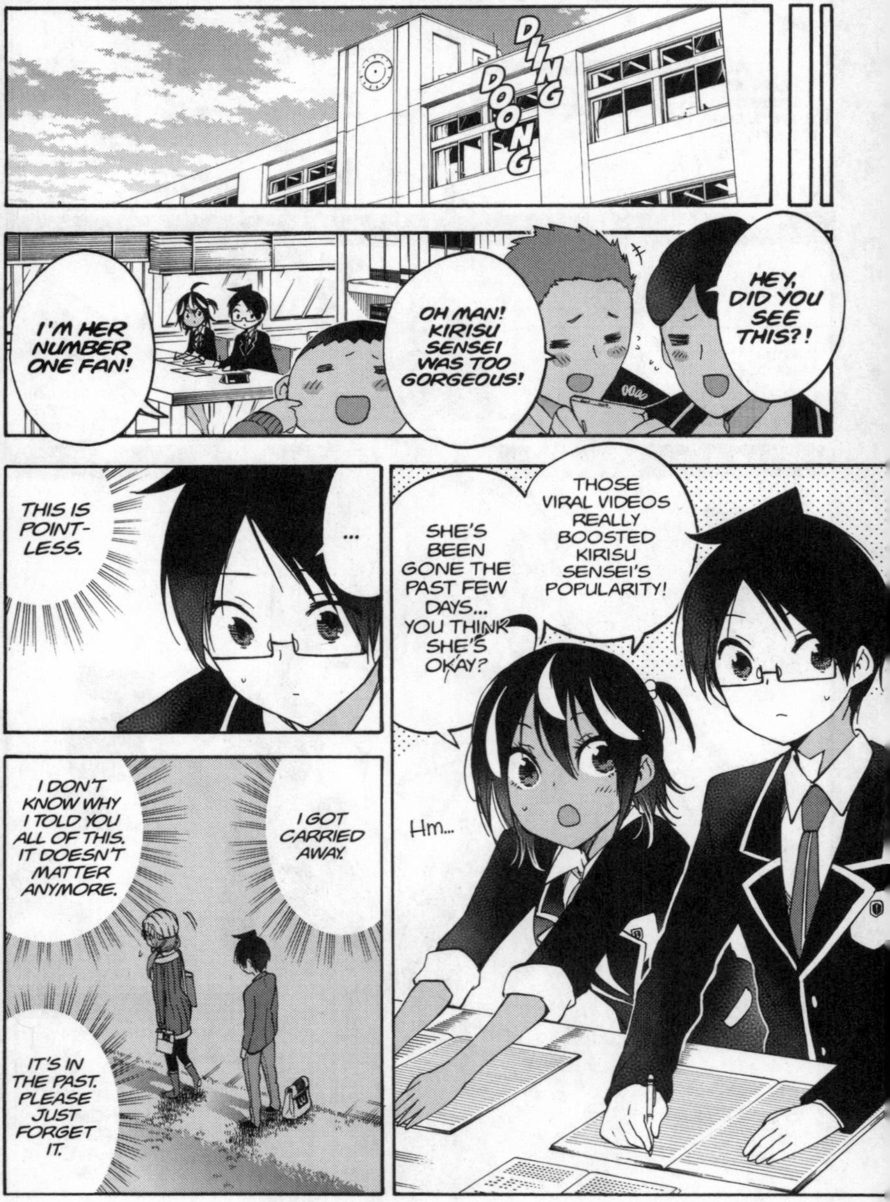
DING DOONG
HEY, DID YOU SEE THIS?!
OH MAN! KIRISU SENSEI WAS TOO GORGEOUS!
I'M HER NUMBER ONE FAN!
THOSE VIRAL VIDEOS REALLY BOOSTED KIRISU SENSEI'S POPULARITY!
SHE'S BEEN GONE THE PAST FEW DAYS... YOU THINK SHE'S OKAY?
Hm...
...
THIS IS POINT-LESS.
I GOT CARRIED AWAY.
I DON'T KNOW WHY I TOLD YOU ALL OF THIS. IT DOESN'T MATTER ANYMORE.
IT'S IN THE PAST. PLEASE JUST FORGET IT.

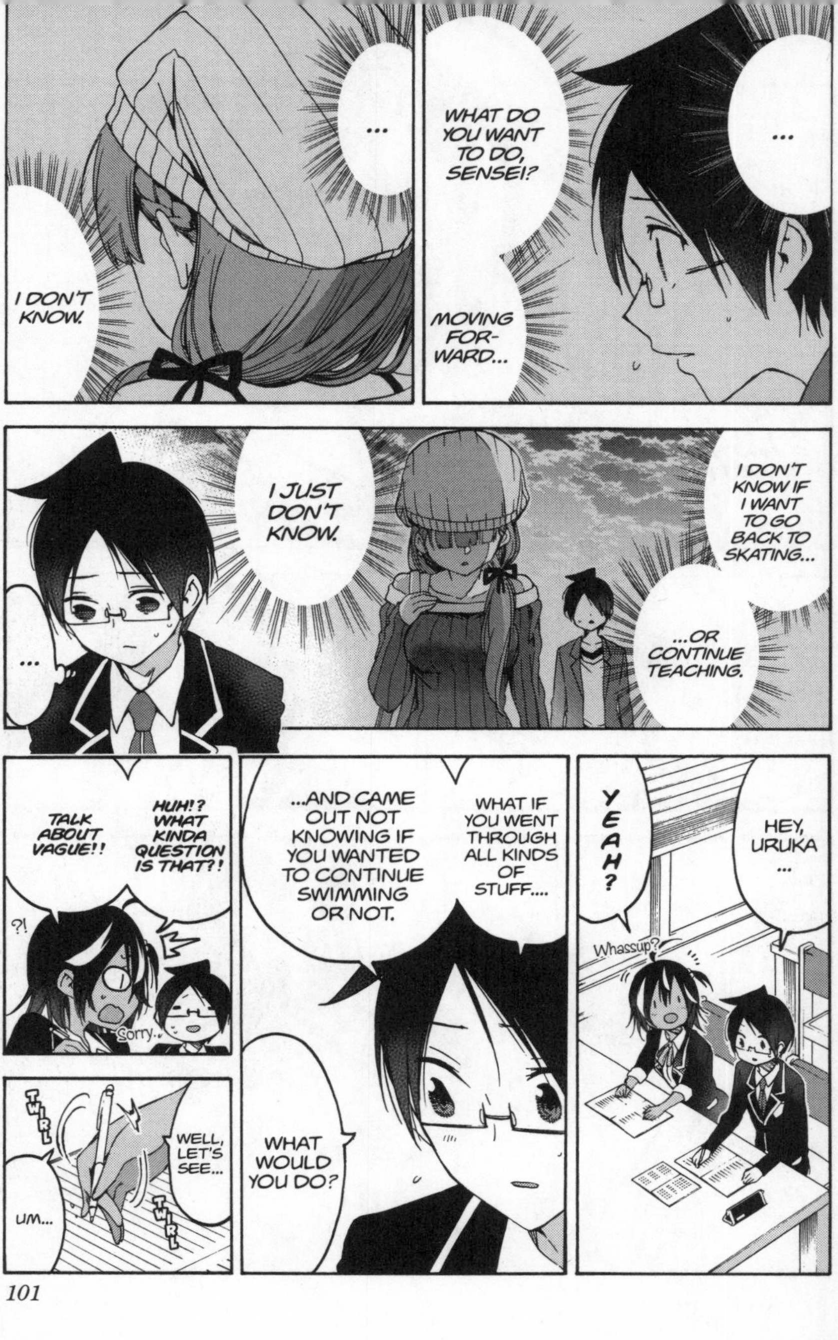
...
WHAT DO YOU WANT TO DO, SENSEI?
MOVING FOR-WARD...
...
I DON'T KNOW.
I DON'T KNOW IF I WANT TO GO BACK TO SKATING...
...OR CONTINUE TEACHING.
I JUST DON'T KNOW.
...
HEY, URUKA...
YEAH?
Whassup?
WHAT IF YOU WENT THROUGH ALL KINDS OF STUFF....
...AND CAME OUT NOT KNOWING IF YOU WANTED TO CONTINUE SWIMMING OR NOT.
WHAT WOULD YOU DO?
HUH!? WHAT KINDA QUESTION IS THAT?!
TALK ABOUT VAGUE!!
?!
Sorry.
WELL, LET'S SEE...
TWIRL
TWIRL
UM...

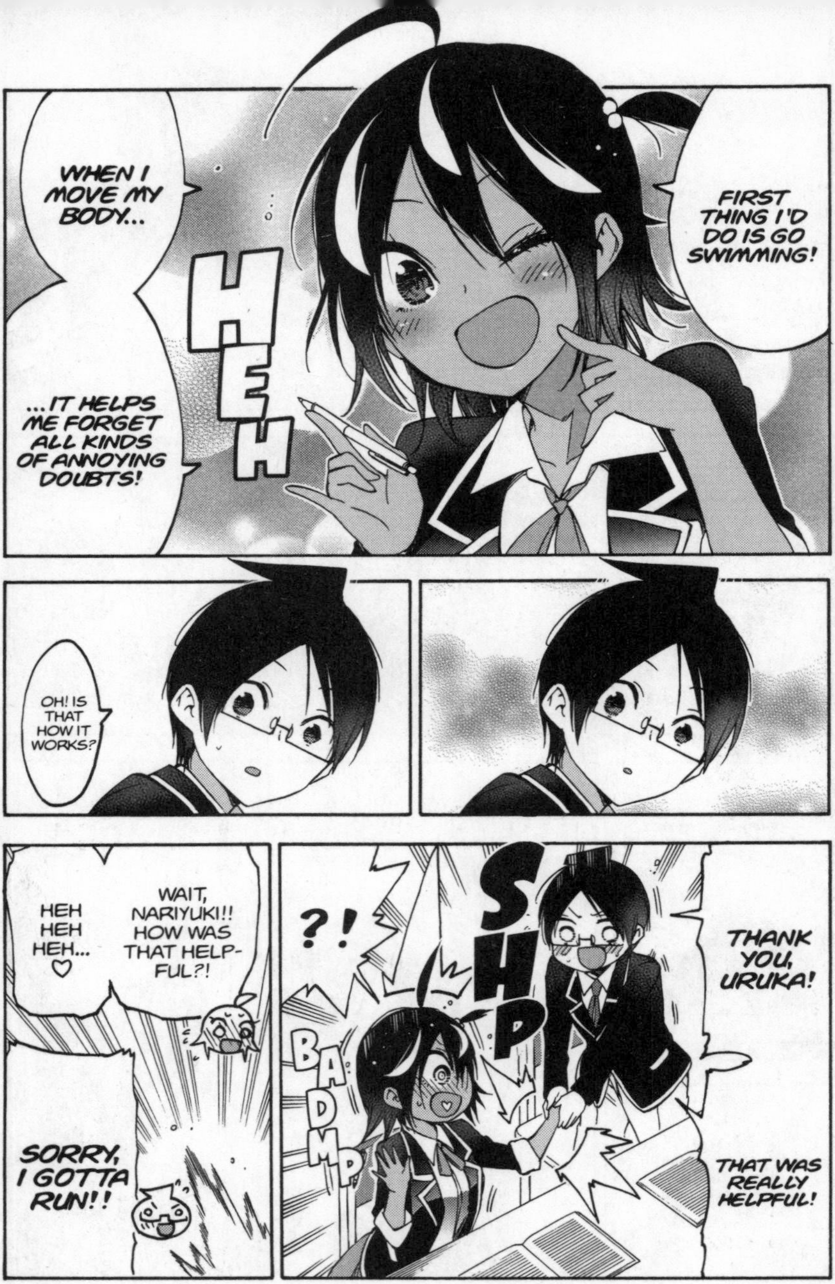
FIRST THING I'D DO IS GO SWIMMING!
HEH
WHEN I MOVE MY BODY...
...IT HELPS ME FORGET ALL KINDS OF ANNOYING DOUBTS!
OH! IS THAT HOW IT WORKS?
SHP
THANK YOU, URUKA!
?!
BADMP
THAT WAS REALLY HELPFUL!
WAIT, NARIYUKI!! HOW WAS THAT HELP-FUL?!
HEH HEH HEH... ♡
SORRY, I GOTTA RUN!!

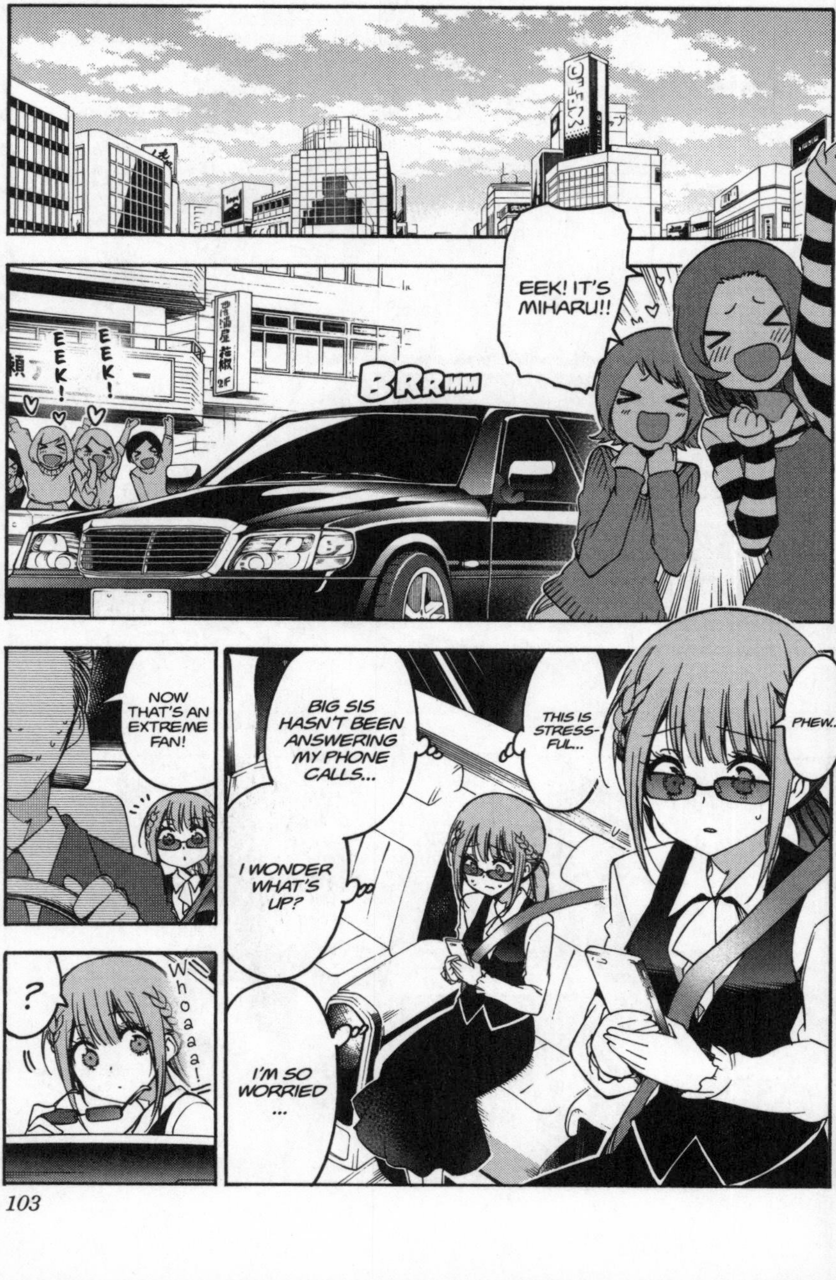
EEK! IT'S MIHARU!!
BRRMM
EEK!
EEK!
PHEW...
THIS IS STRESSFUL...
BIG SIS HASN'T BEEN ANSWERING MY PHONE CALLS...
I WONDER WHAT'S UP?
I'M SO WORRIED...
NOW THAT'S AN EXTREME FAN!
?
Whoaaa!

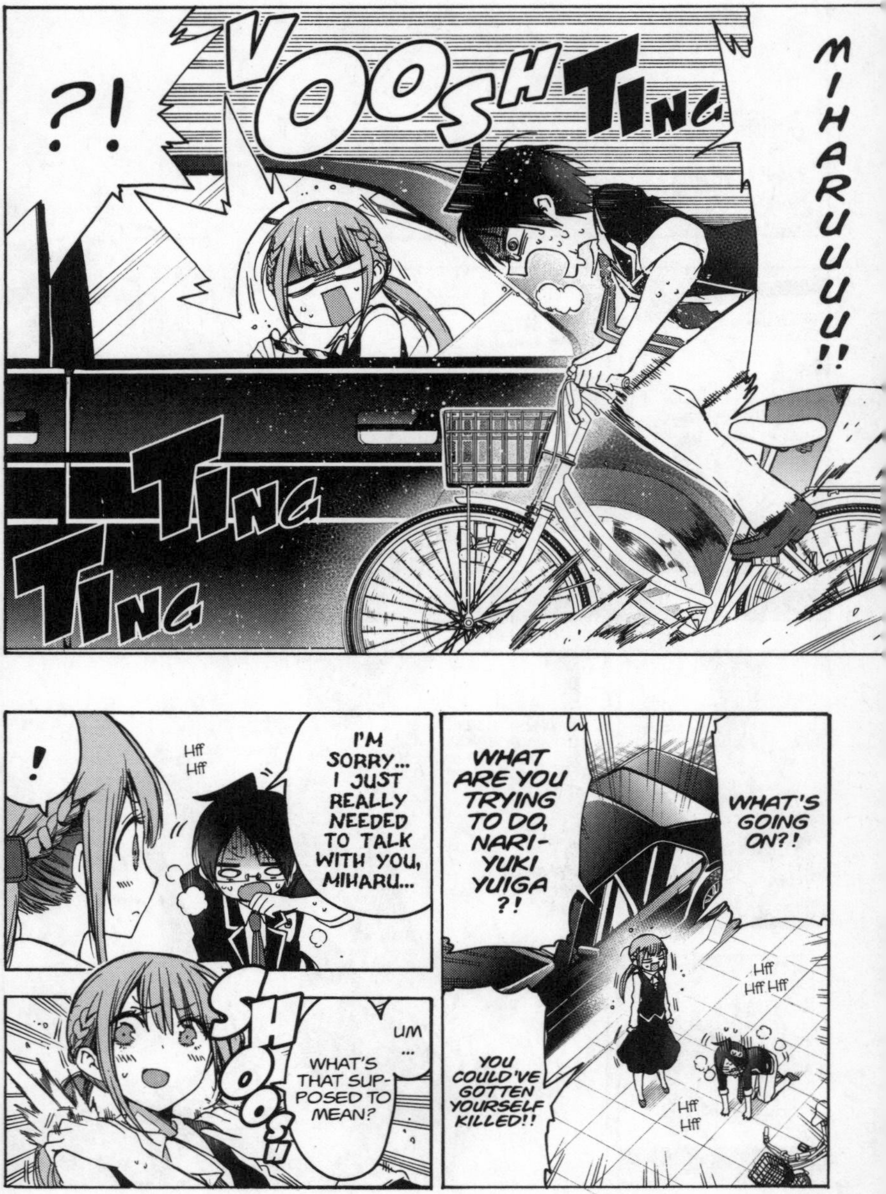
MIHARUUUUU!!
VOOSHTING
?!
TING TING
WHAT'S GOING ON?!
WHAT ARE YOU TRYING TO DO, NARI-YUKI YUIGA ?!
Hff Hff Hff
YOU COULD'VE GOTTEN YOURSELF KILLED!!
Hff Hff
I'M SORRY... I JUST REALLY NEEDED TO TALK WITH YOU, MIHARU...
Hff Hff
!
UM ...
WHAT'S THAT SUP-POSED TO MEAN?
SHOOOSH

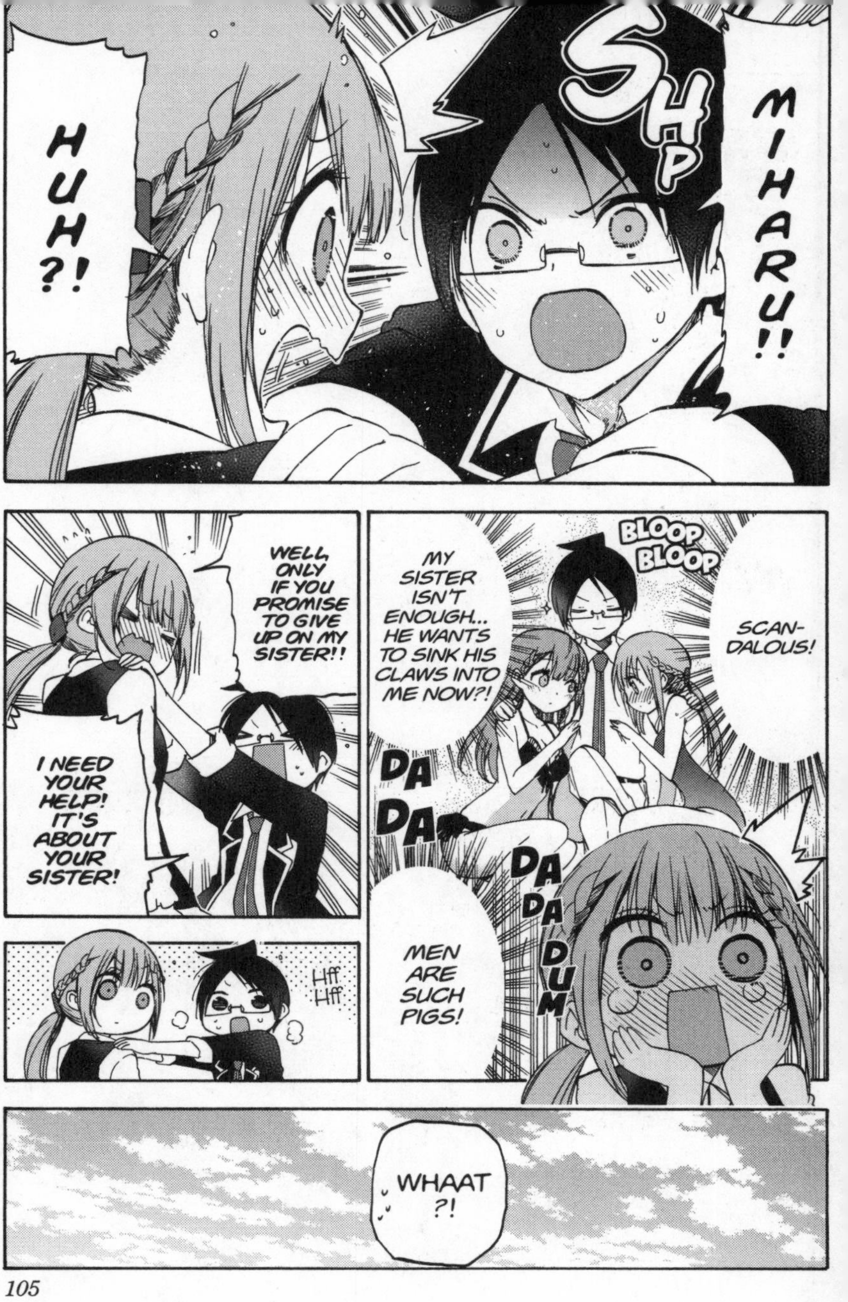
SHP
MIHARU!!
HUH?!
BLOOP BLOOP
SCAN-DALOUS!
MY SISTER ISN'T ENOUGH... HE WANTS TO SINK HIS CLAWS INTO ME NOW?!
DA DA
DA DA DA DUM
MEN ARE SUCH PIGS!
WELL, ONLY IF YOU PROMISE TO GIVE UP ON MY SISTER!!
I NEED YOUR HELP! IT'S ABOUT YOUR SISTER!
Hff Hff
WHAAT?!

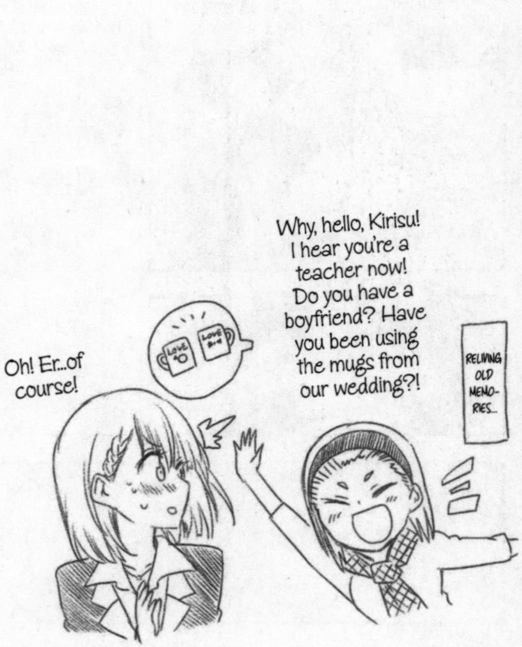
RELIVING OLD MEMO-RIES...
Why, hello, Kirisu! I hear you're a teacher now! Do you have a boyfriend? Have you been using the mugs from our wedding?!
Oh! Er...of course!

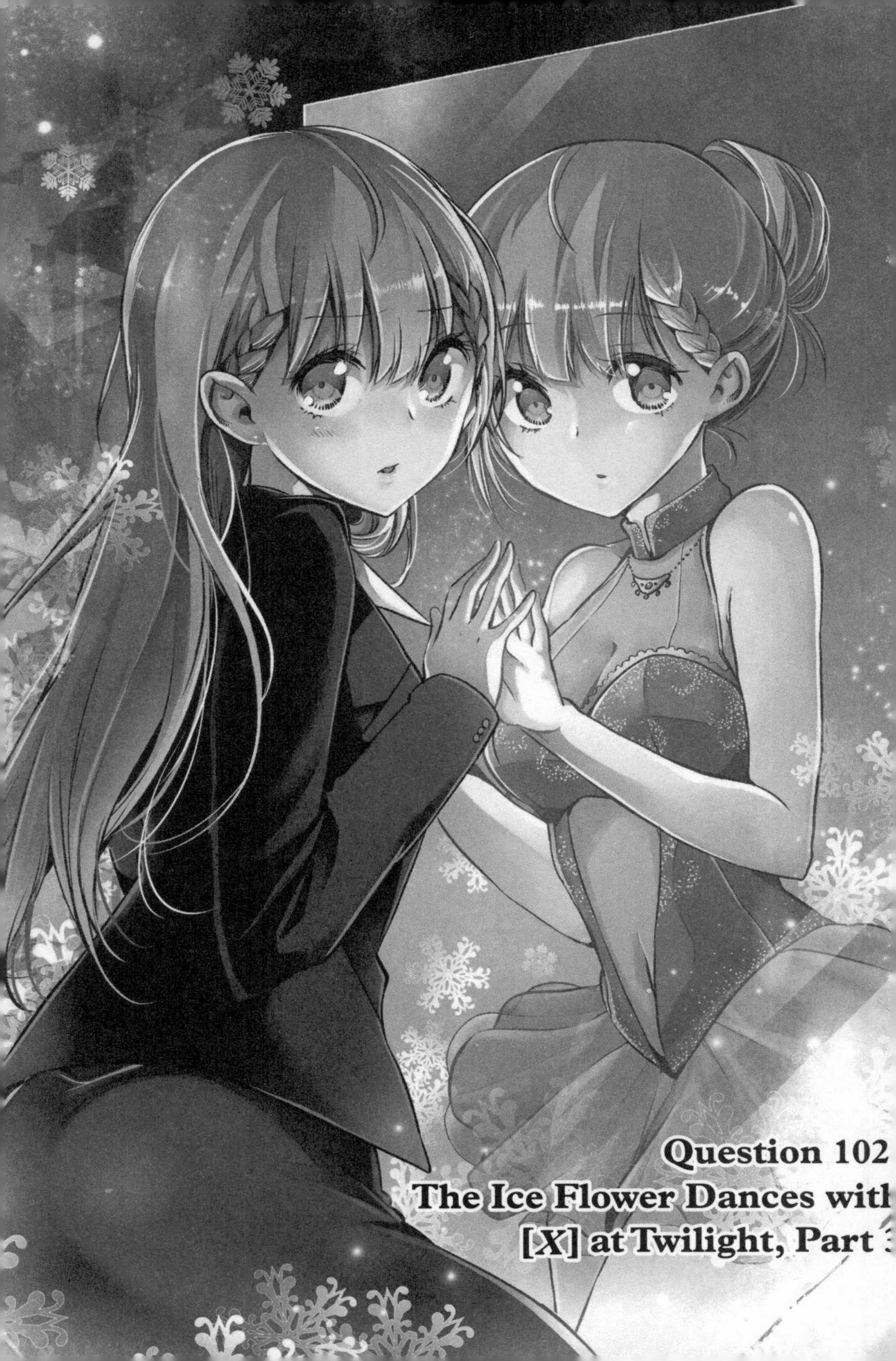
Question 102
The Ice Flower Dances with
[X] at Twilight, Part 3

[x] We + Never ÷ × Learn

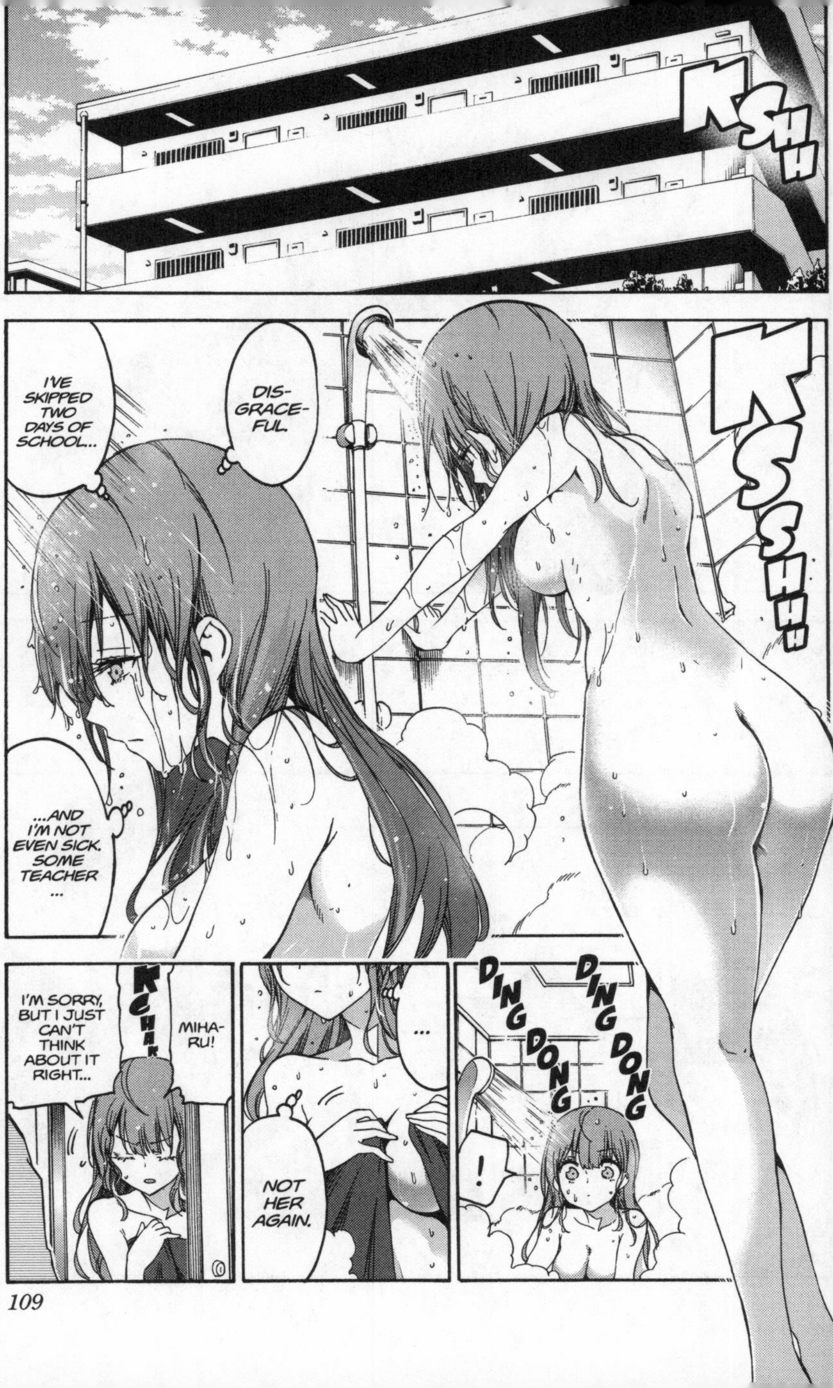
KSHH
KSSSHHH
DIS-GRACE-FUL.
I'VE SKIPPED TWO DAYS OF SCHOOL...
...AND I'M NOT EVEN SICK. SOME TEACHER ...
DING DONG
DING DONG
!
...
NOT HER AGAIN.
KCHA
MIHA-RU!
I'M SORRY, BUT I JUST CAN'T THINK ABOUT IT RIGHT...

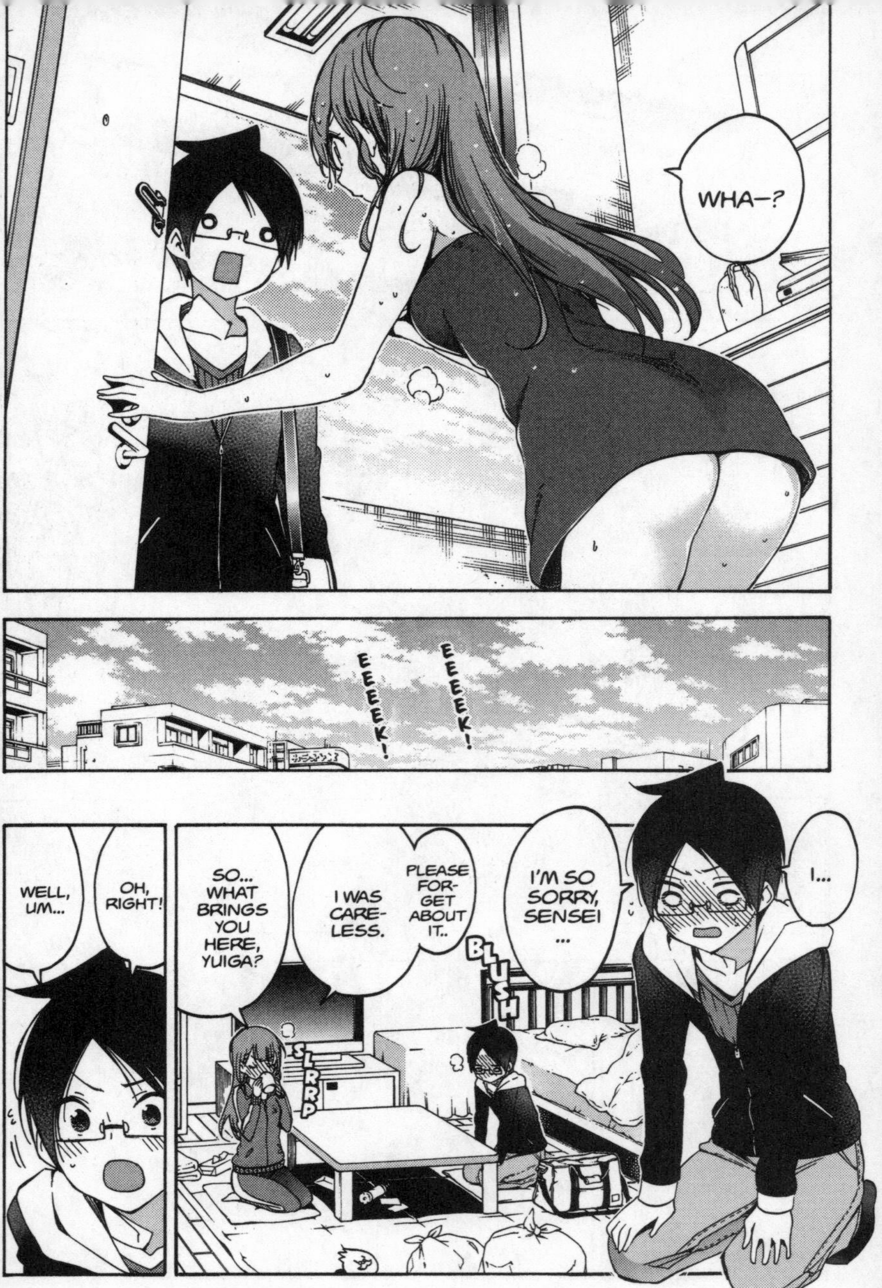
WHA–?
EEEEK!
EEEEK!
I...
I'M SO SORRY, SENSEI ...
BLUSH
PLEASE FOR-GET ABOUT IT..
I WAS CARE-LESS.
SO... WHAT BRINGS YOU HERE, YUIGA?
SLRRP
OH, RIGHT!
WELL, UM...

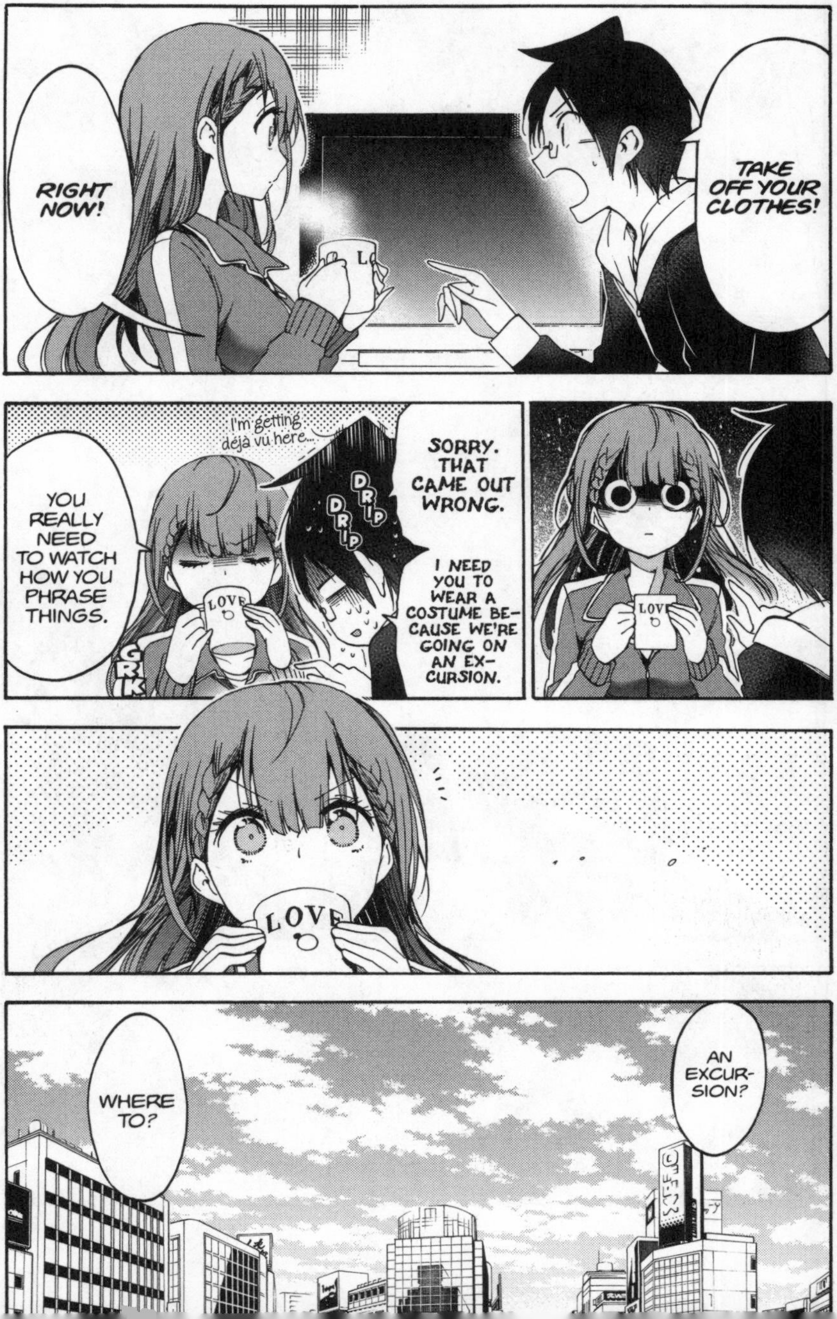
TAKE OFF YOUR CLOTHES!
RIGHT NOW!
SORRY. THAT CAME OUT WRONG.
I NEED YOU TO WEAR A COSTUME BE- CAUSE WE'RE GOING ON AN EX- CURSION.
I'm getting déjà vu here...
DRIP
DRIP
YOU REALLY NEED TO WATCH HOW YOU PHRASE THINGS.
GRK
LOVE
LOVE
LOVE
AN EXCUR- SION?
WHERE TO?

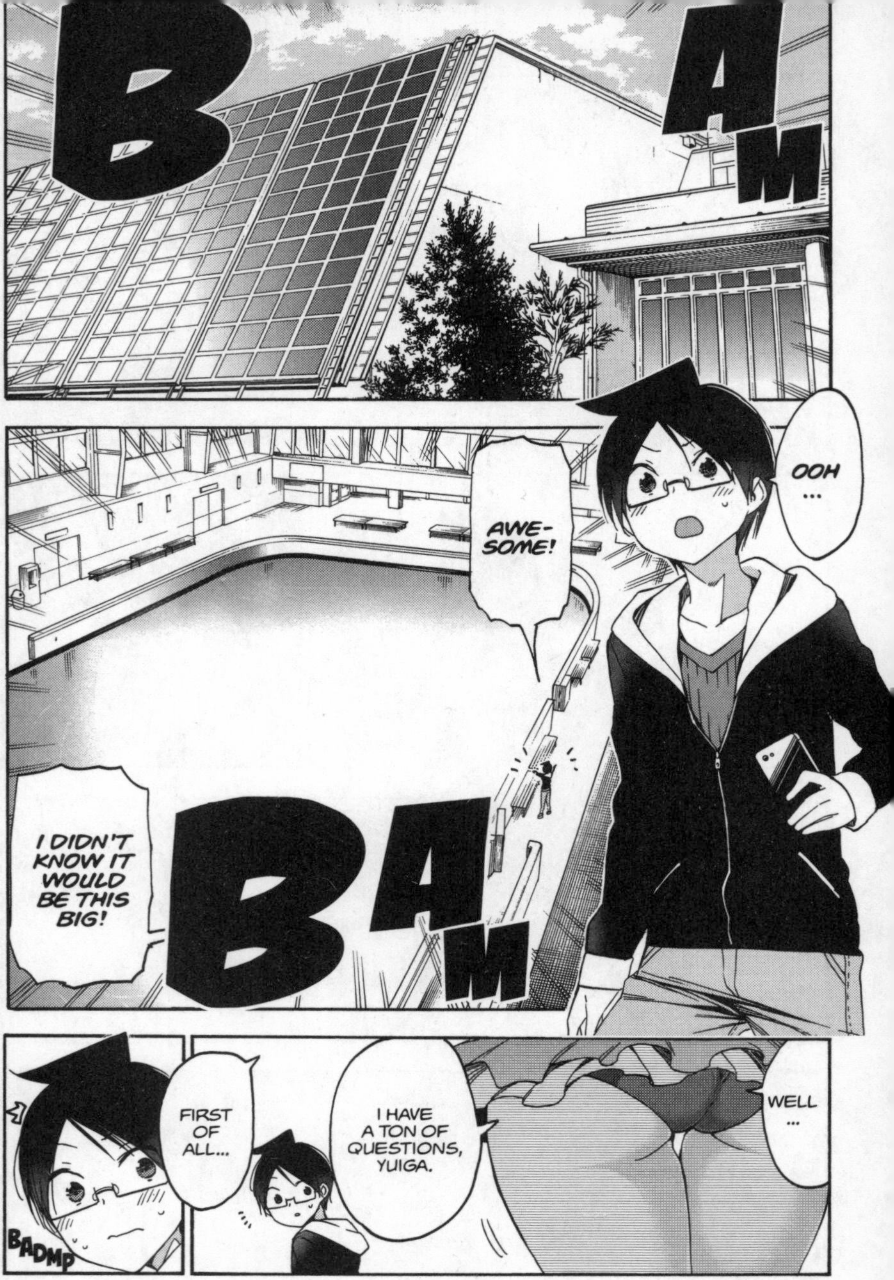
BAM
OOH ...
AWESOME!
I DIDN'T KNOW IT WOULD BE THIS BIG!
BAM
WELL ...
I HAVE A TON OF QUESTIONS, YUIGA.
FIRST OF ALL...
BADMP

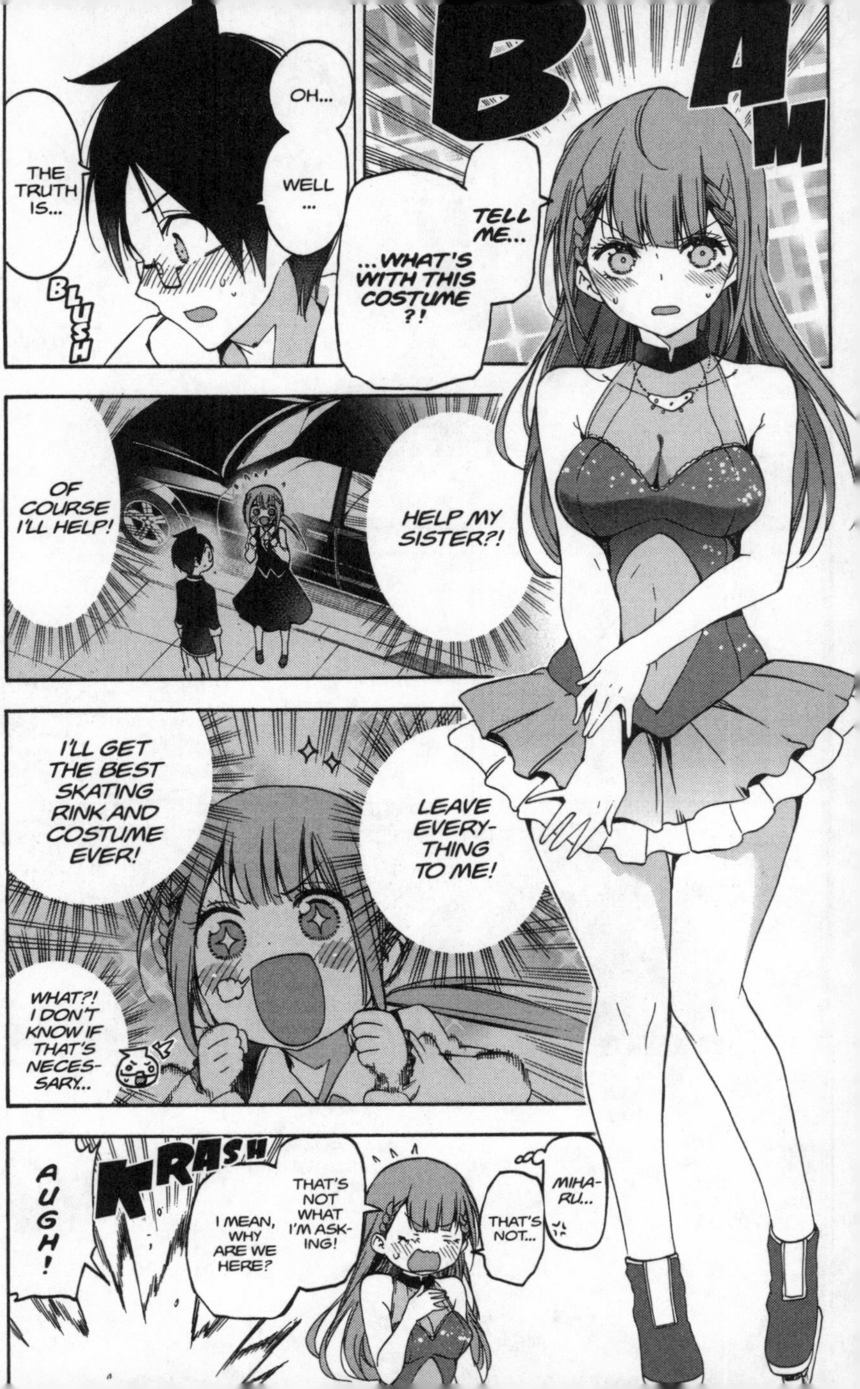
BAM
TELL ME...
...WHAT'S WITH THIS COSTUME?!
OH... WELL...
THE TRUTH IS...
BLUSH
HELP MY SISTER?!
OF COURSE I'LL HELP!
LEAVE EVERYTHING TO ME!
I'LL GET THE BEST SKATING RINK AND COSTUME EVER!
WHAT?! I DON'T KNOW IF THAT'S NECESSARY...
MIHARU...
THAT'S NOT...
THAT'S NOT WHAT I'M ASKING!
I MEAN, WHY ARE WE HERE?
KRASH
AUGH!

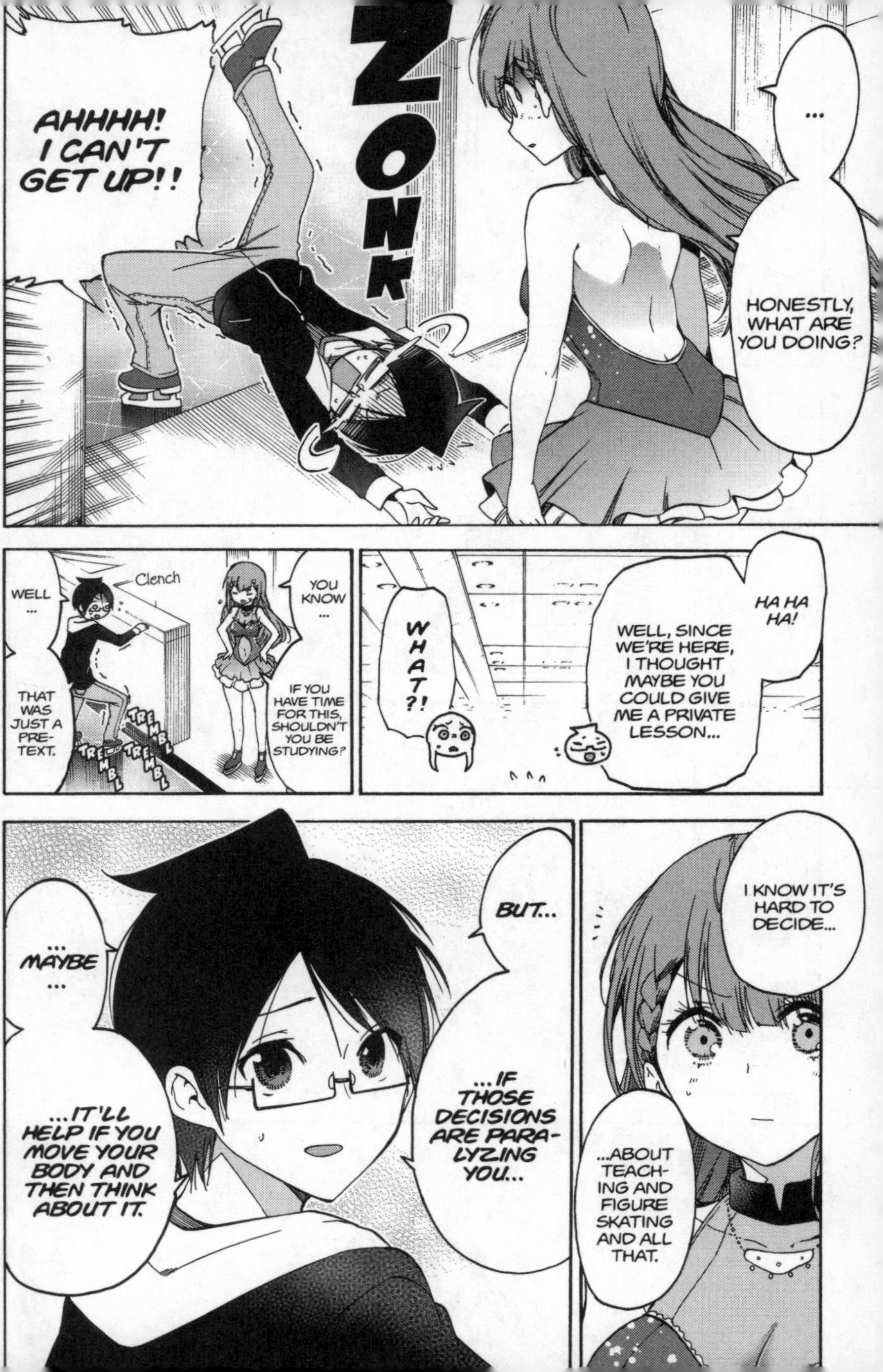
...
HONESTLY, WHAT ARE YOU DOING?
ZONK
AHHHH! I CAN'T GET UP!!
HA HA HA!
WELL, SINCE WE'RE HERE, I THOUGHT MAYBE YOU COULD GIVE ME A PRIVATE LESSON...
WHAT?!
YOU KNOW ...
IF YOU HAVE TIME FOR THIS, SHOULDN'T YOU BE STUDYING?
Clench
WELL ...
THAT WAS JUST A PRE-TEXT.
TREMBL
TREMBL
TREMBL
I KNOW IT'S HARD TO DECIDE...
...ABOUT TEACHING AND FIGURE SKATING AND ALL THAT.
BUT...
...IF THOSE DECISIONS ARE PARA-LYZING YOU...
... MAYBE ...
...IT'LL HELP IF YOU MOVE YOUR BODY AND THEN THINK ABOUT IT.

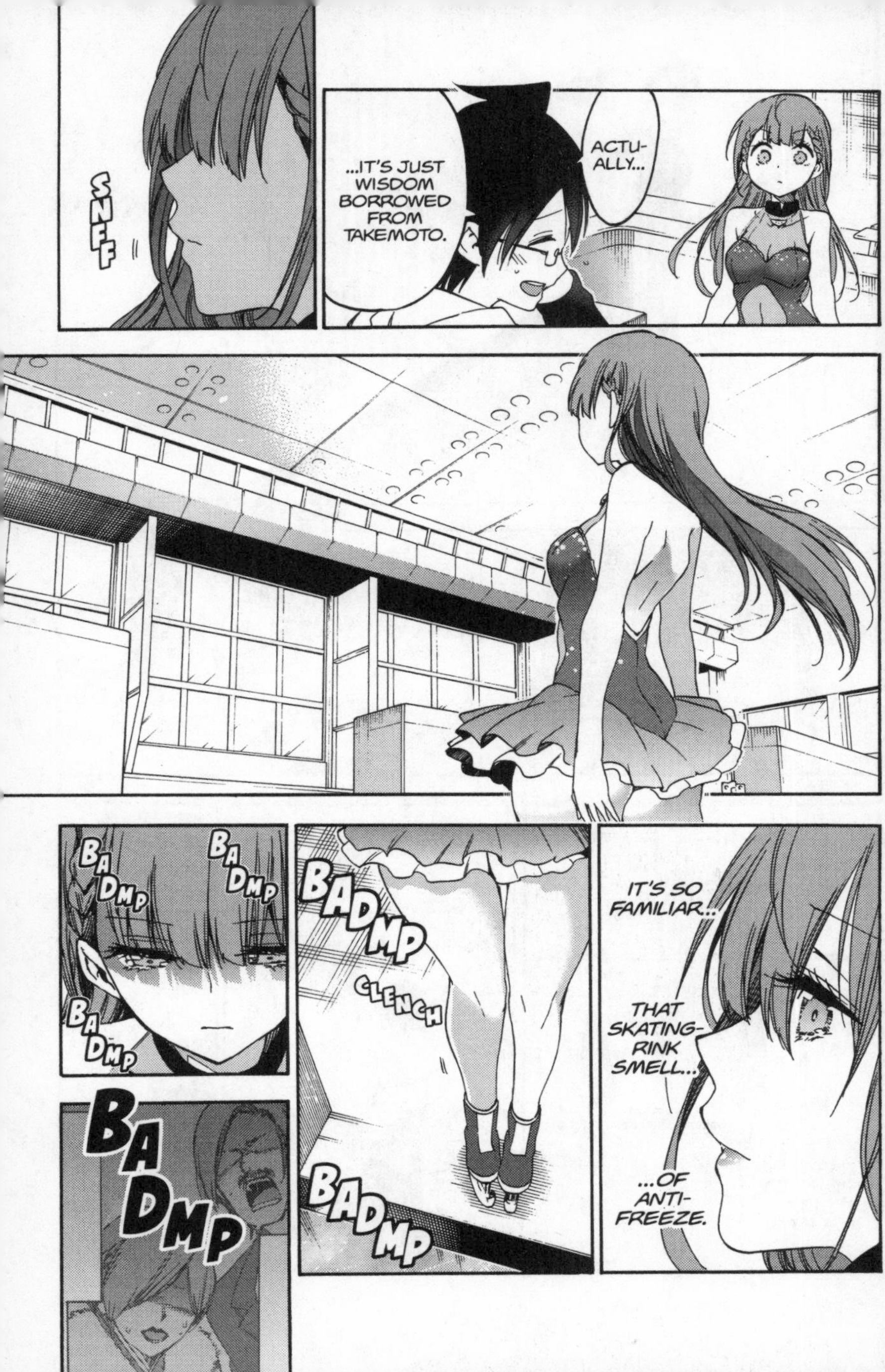
ACTU-
ALLY...
...IT'S JUST WISDOM BORROWED FROM TAKEMOTO.
SNFF
IT'S SO FAMILIAR...
THAT SKATING-RINK SMELL...
...OF ANTI-FREEZE.
BADMP
CLENCH
BADMP
BADMP
BADMP
BADMP
BADMP

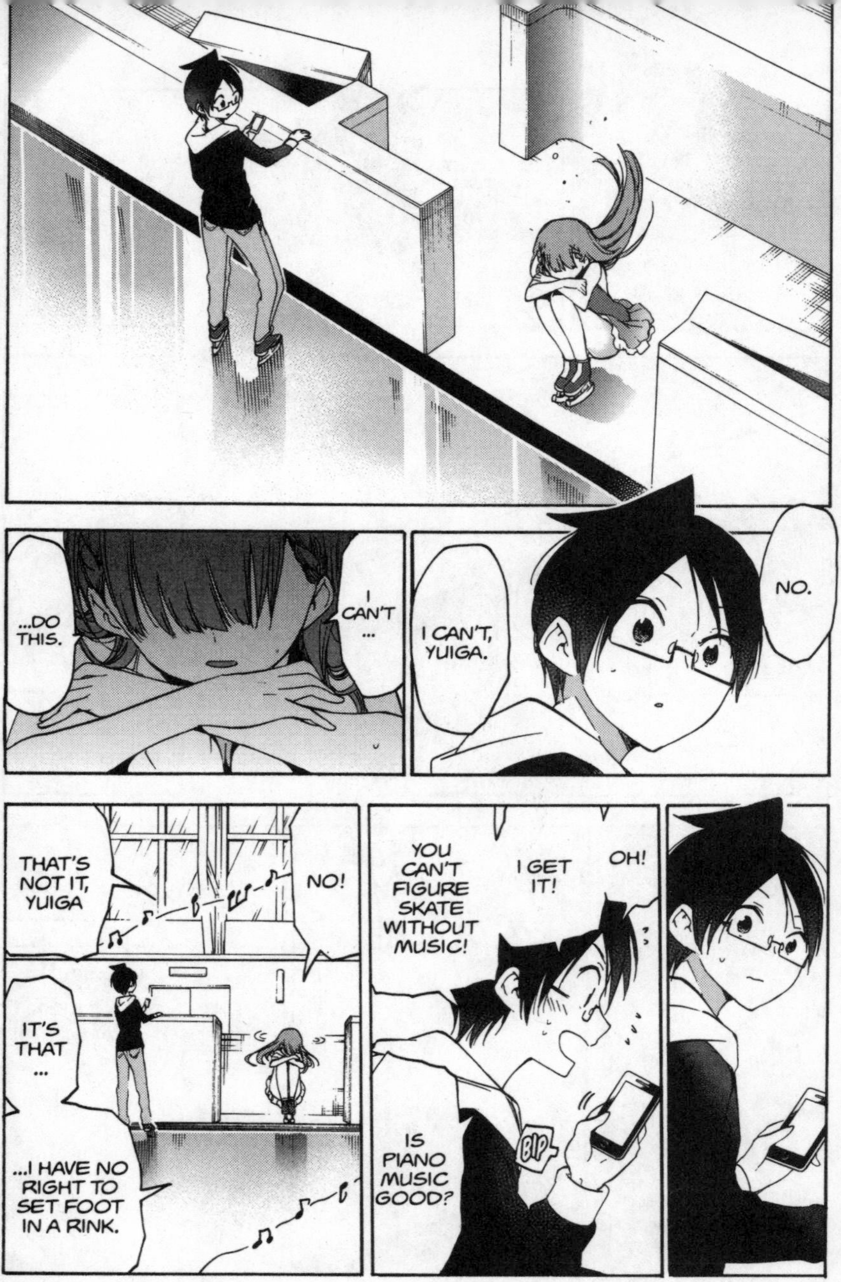
NO.
I CAN'T, YUIGA.
I CAN'T ...
...DO THIS.
OH!
I GET IT!
YOU CAN'T FIGURE SKATE WITHOUT MUSIC!
BIP
IS PIANO MUSIC GOOD?
NO!
THAT'S NOT IT, YUIGA
IT'S THAT ...
...I HAVE NO RIGHT TO SET FOOT IN A RINK.

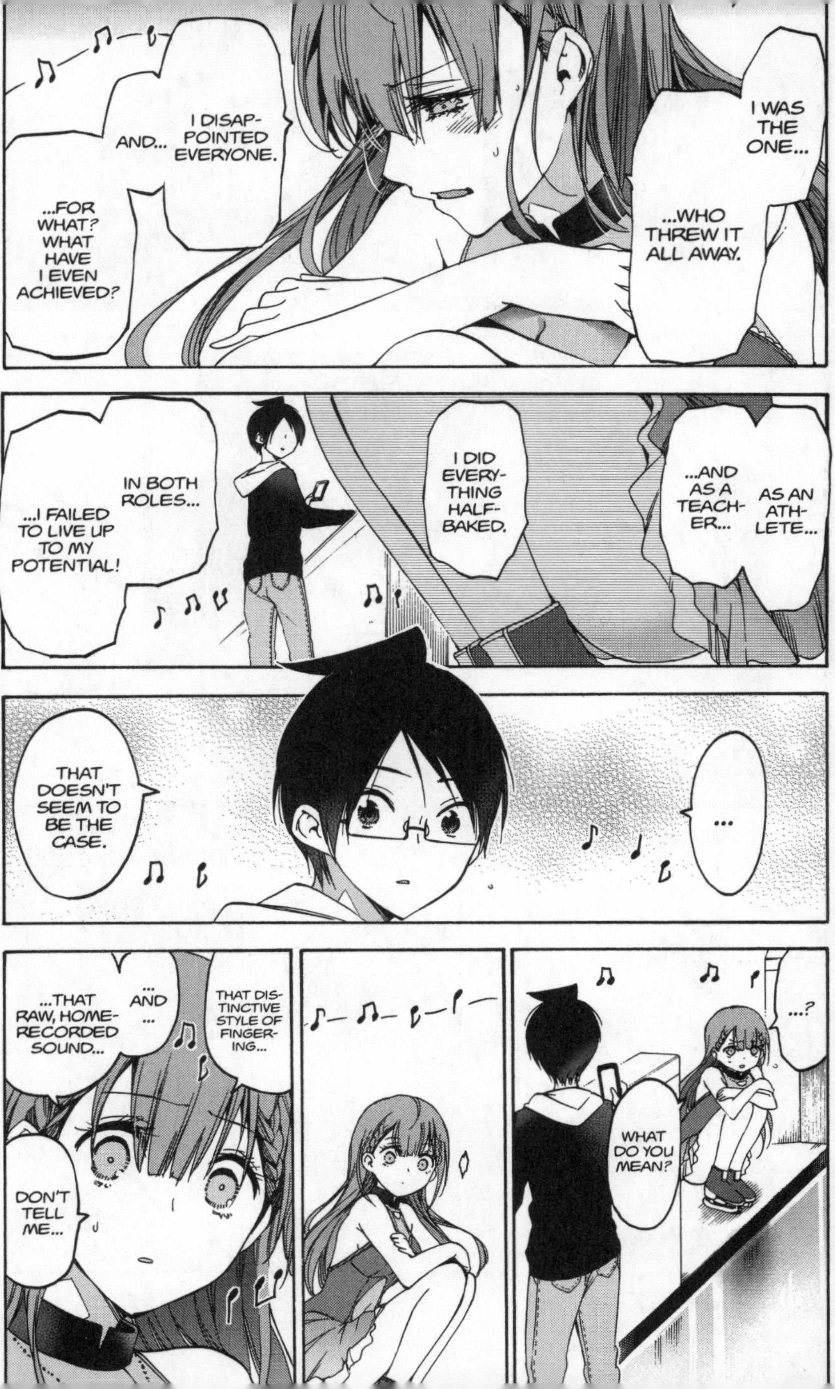
I WAS THE ONE...
...WHO THREW IT ALL AWAY.
I DISAPPOINTED EVERYONE.
AND...
...FOR WHAT? WHAT HAVE I EVEN ACHIEVED?
AS AN ATHLETE...
...AND AS A TEACHER...
I DID EVERYTHING HALF-BAKED.
IN BOTH ROLES...
...I FAILED TO LIVE UP TO MY POTENTIAL!
...
THAT DOESN'T SEEM TO BE THE CASE.
...?
WHAT DO YOU MEAN?
THAT DISTINCTIVE STYLE OF FINGERING...
...AND...
...THAT RAW, HOME-RECORDED SOUND...
DON'T TELL ME...

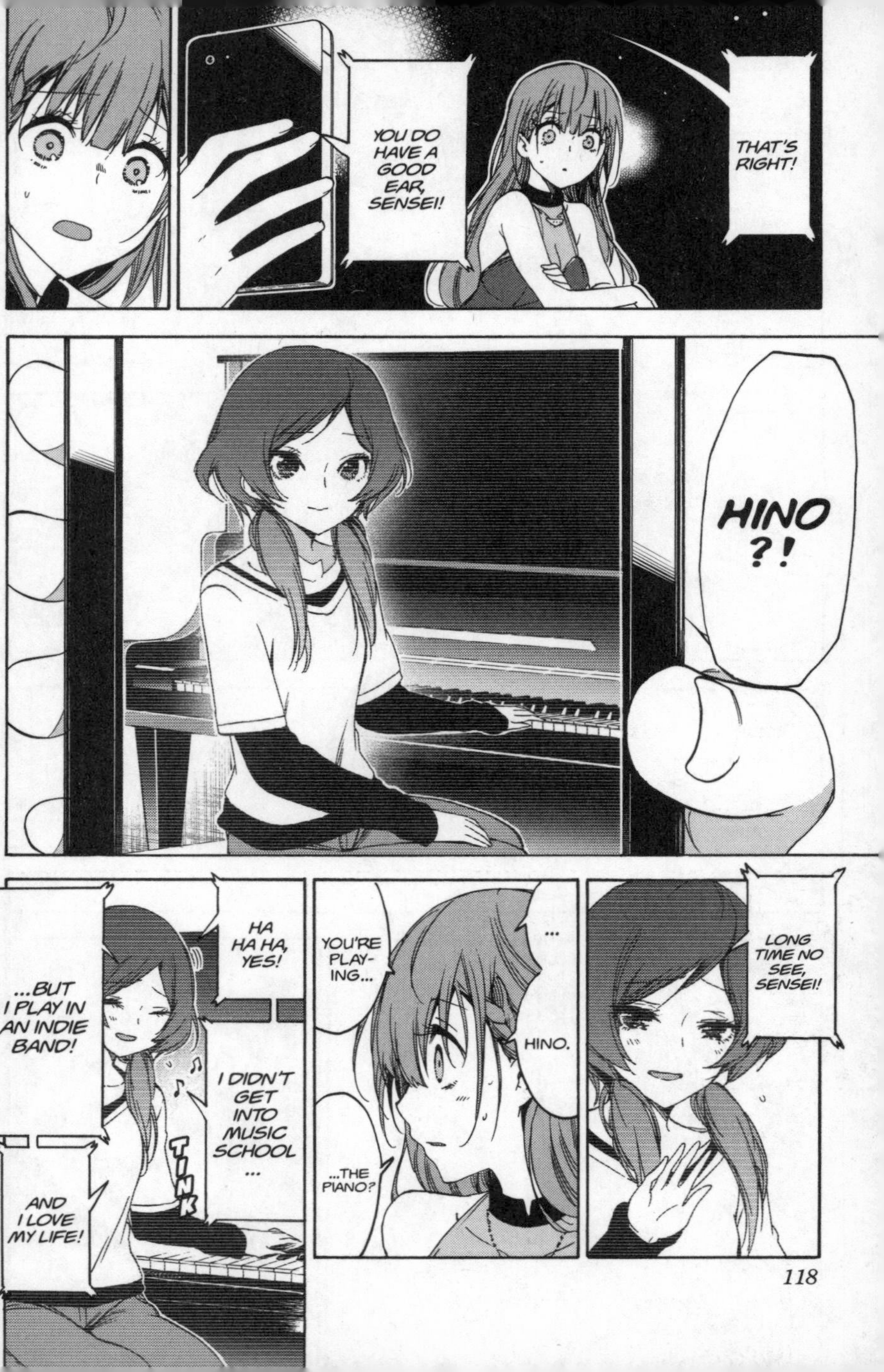
THAT'S RIGHT!
YOU DO HAVE A GOOD EAR, SENSEI!
HINO ?!
LONG TIME NO SEE, SENSEI!
...
HINO.
YOU'RE PLAY-ING...
...THE PIANO?
HA HA HA, YES!
I DIDN'T GET INTO MUSIC SCHOOL ...
TINK
...BUT I PLAY IN AN INDIE BAND!
AND I LOVE MY LIFE!

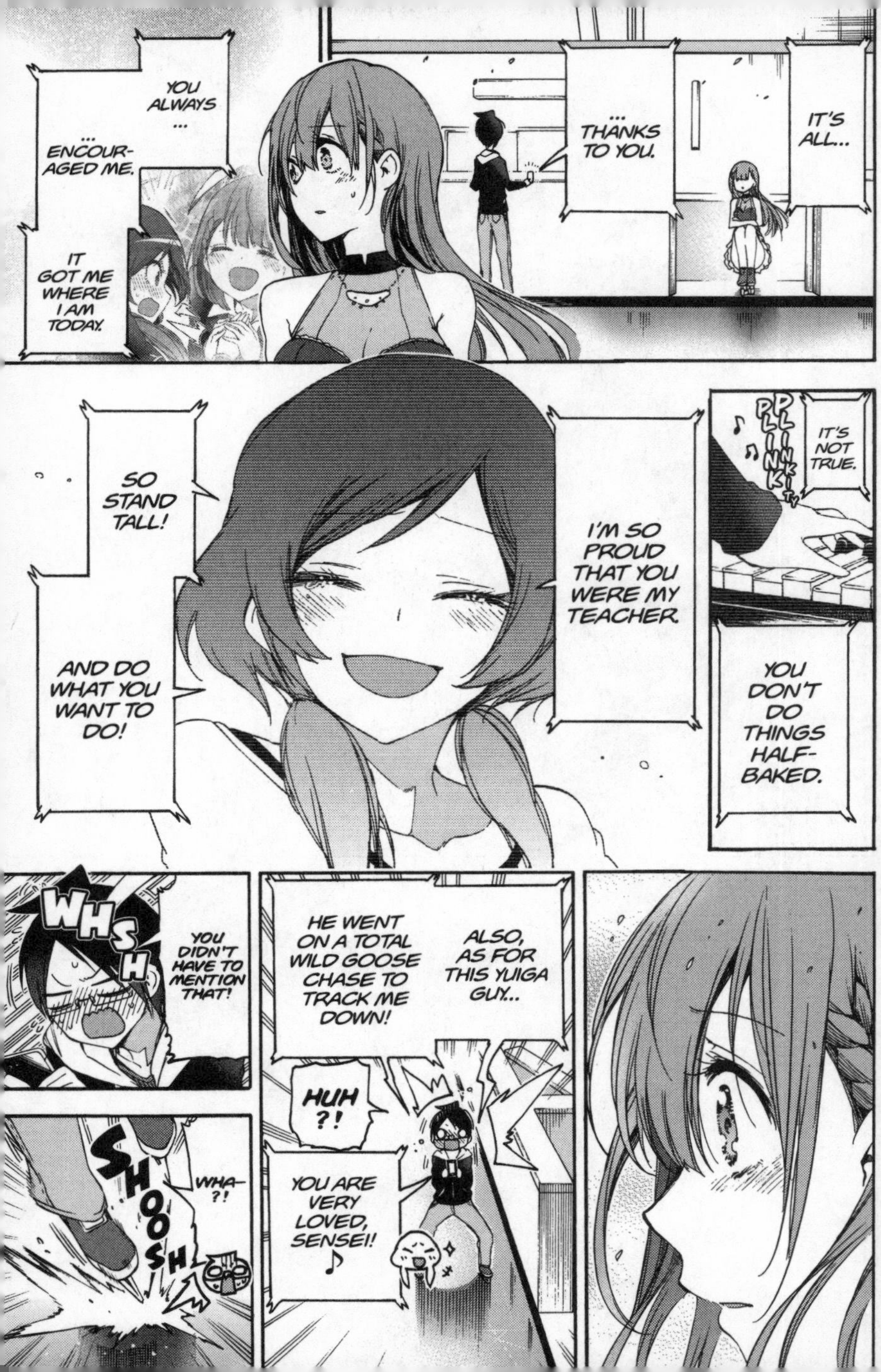
IT'S ALL...
...THANKS TO YOU.
YOU ALWAYS ...
...ENCOURAGED ME.
IT GOT ME WHERE I AM TODAY.
PLINK PLINKITY
IT'S NOT TRUE.
YOU DON'T DO THINGS HALF-BAKED.
I'M SO PROUD THAT YOU WERE MY TEACHER.
SO STAND TALL!
AND DO WHAT YOU WANT TO DO!
ALSO, AS FOR THIS YUIGA GUY...
HE WENT ON A TOTAL WILD GOOSE CHASE TO TRACK ME DOWN!
HUH?!
YOU ARE VERY LOVED, SENSEI! ♪
WHSH
YOU DIDN'T HAVE TO MENTION THAT!
SHOOSH
WHA-?!

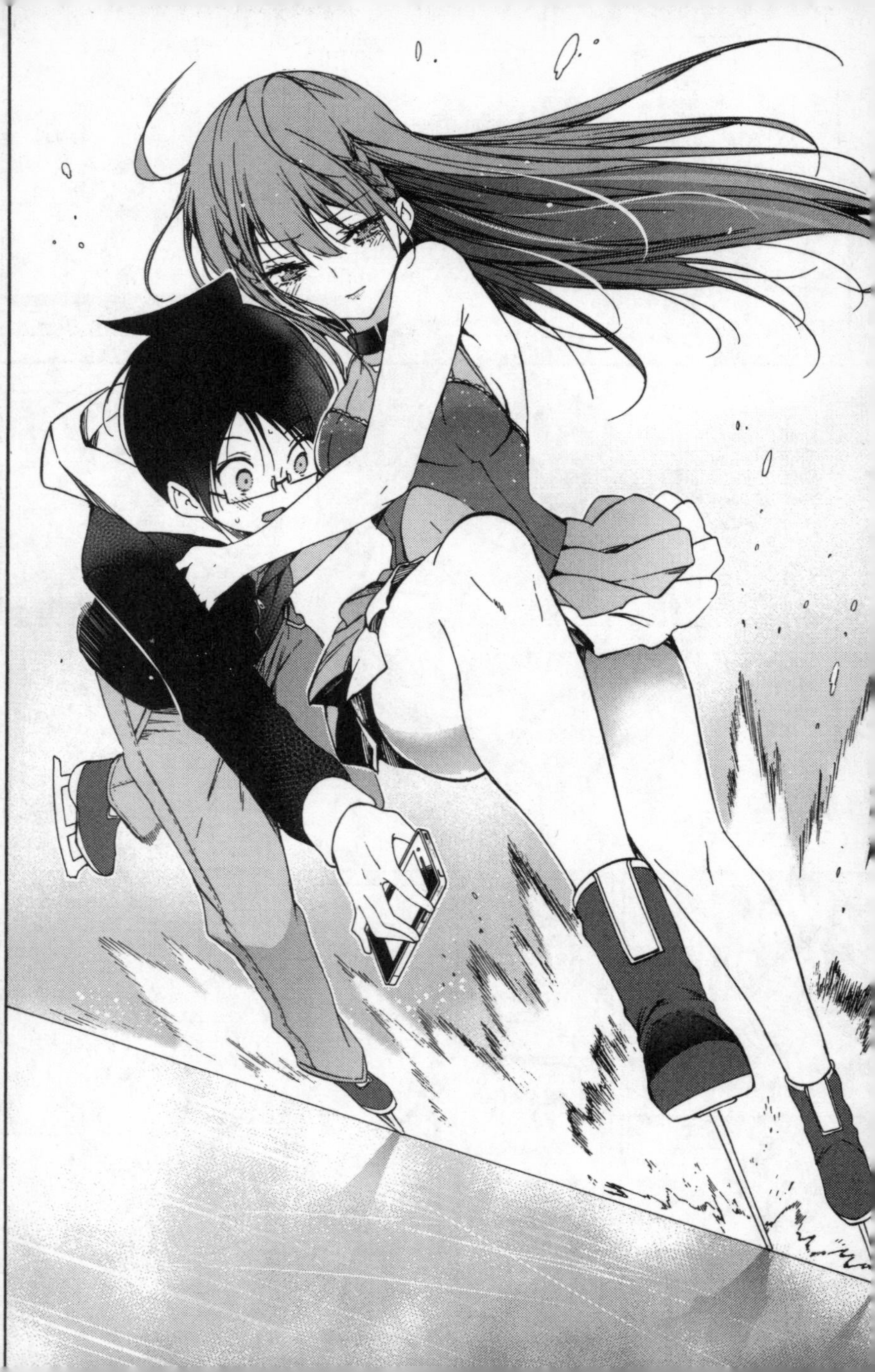

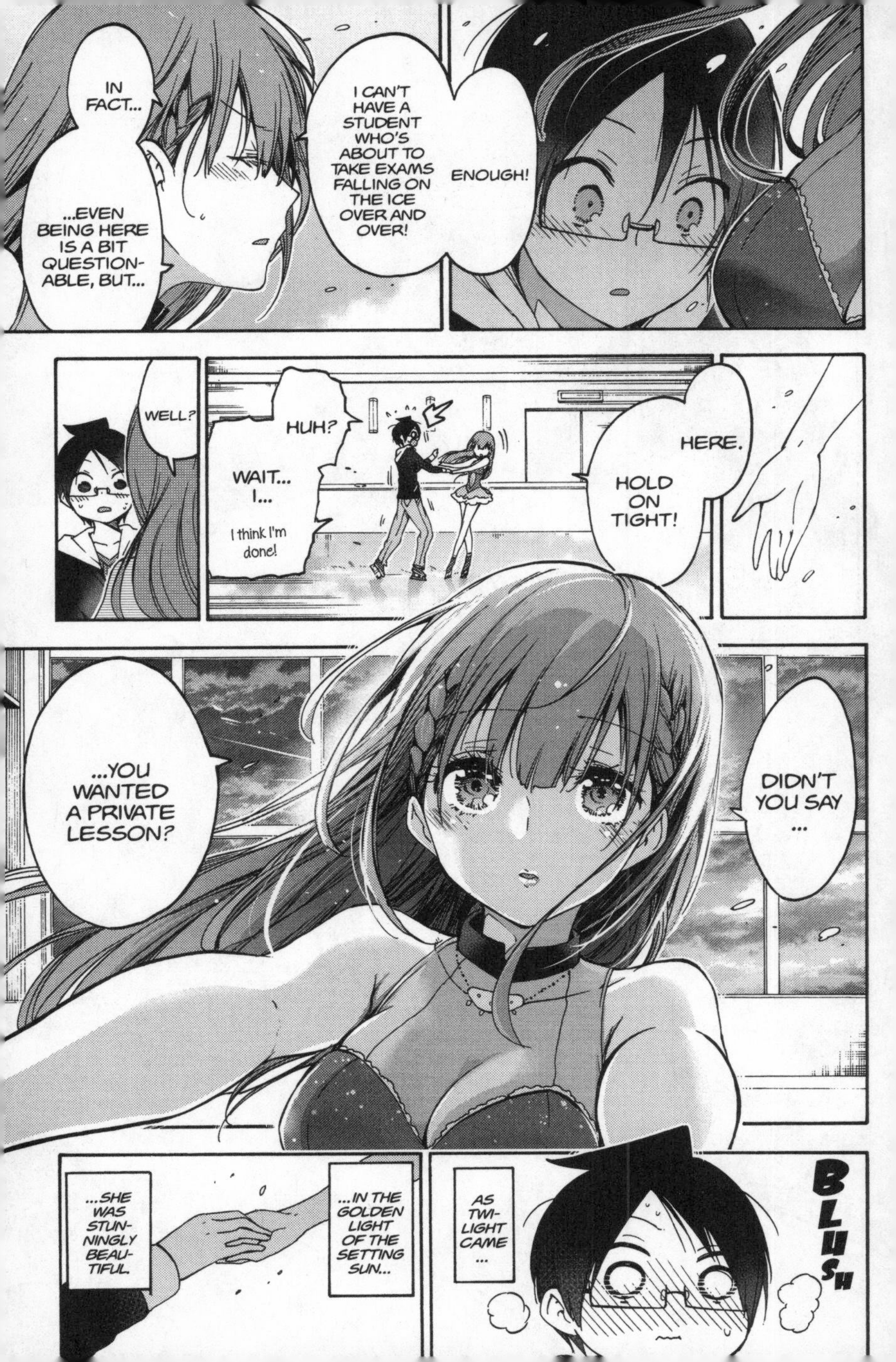
ENOUGH!
I CAN'T HAVE A STUDENT WHO'S ABOUT TO TAKE EXAMS FALLING ON THE ICE OVER AND OVER!
IN FACT...
...EVEN BEING HERE IS A BIT QUESTION-ABLE, BUT...
HERE.
HOLD ON TIGHT!
HUH?
WAIT... I...
I think I'm done!
WELL?
DIDN'T YOU SAY ...
...YOU WANTED A PRIVATE LESSON?
BLUSH
AS TWI-LIGHT CAME ...
...IN THE GOLDEN LIGHT OF THE SETTING SUN...
...SHE WAS STUN-NINGLY BEAU-TIFUL.

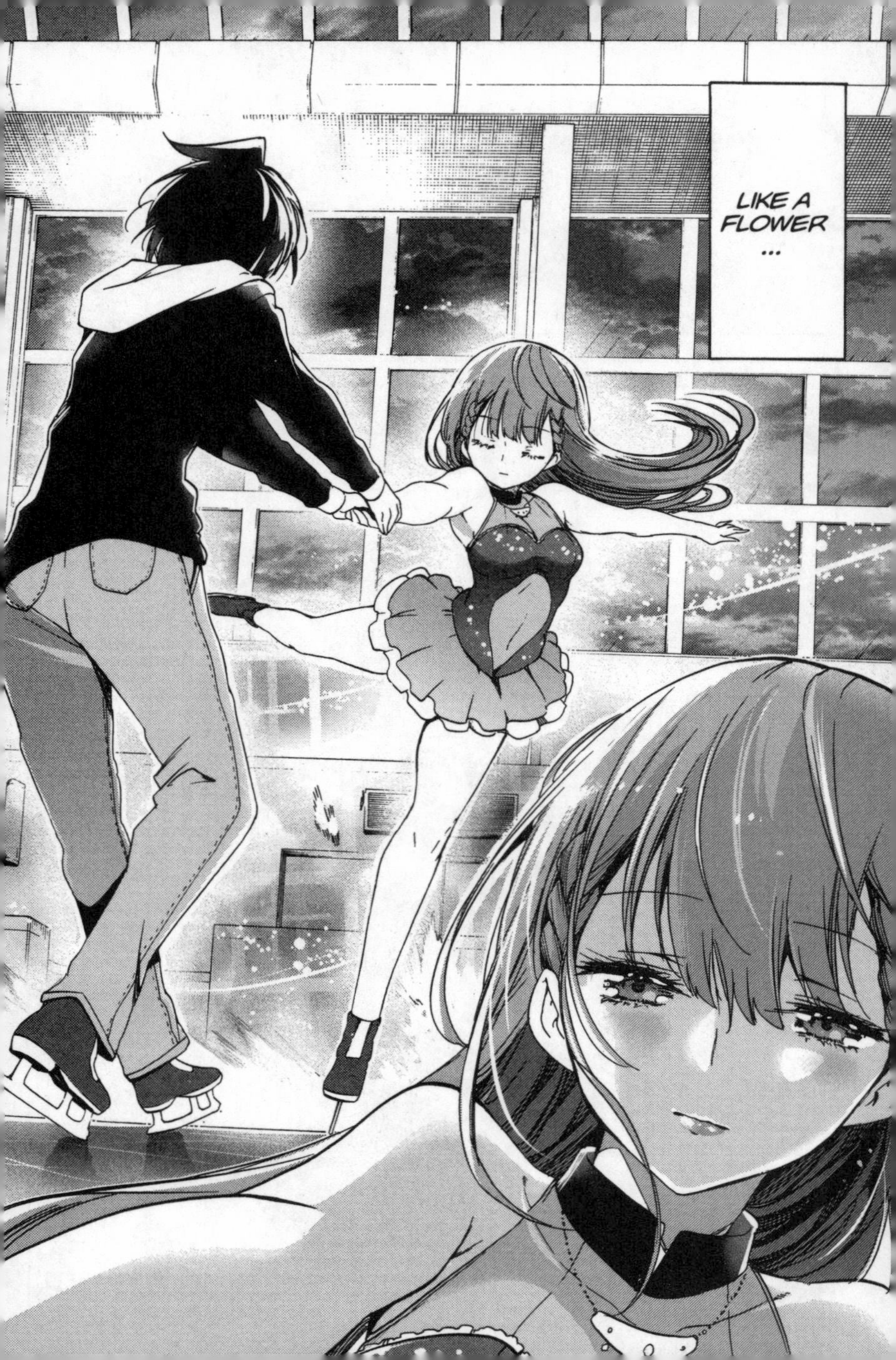
LIKE A FLOWER ...

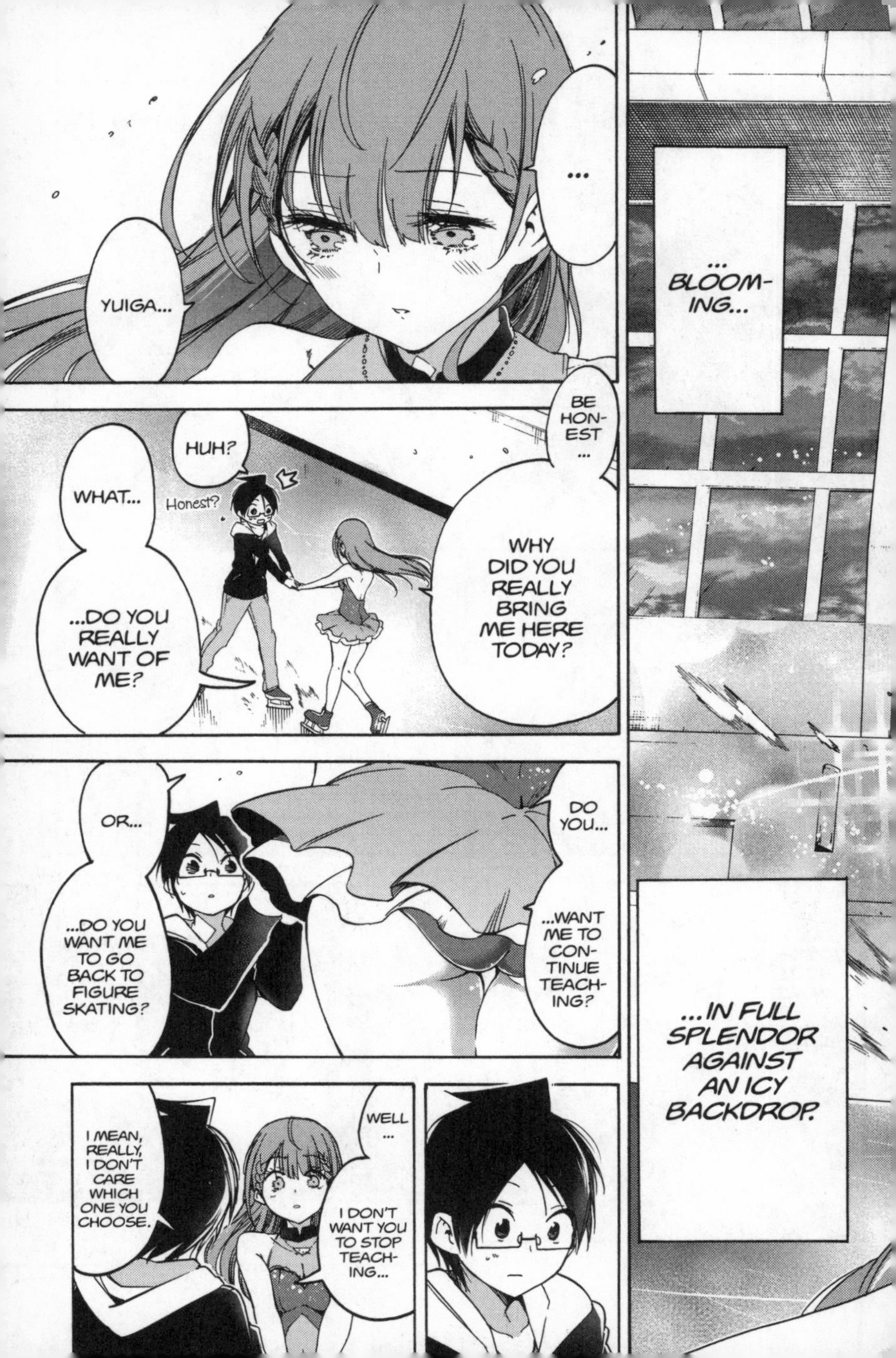
...BLOOMING...
...IN FULL SPLENDOR AGAINST AN ICY BACKDROP.
...
YUIGA...
BE HONEST...
WHY DID YOU REALLY BRING ME HERE TODAY?
HUH?
Honest?
WHAT... ...DO YOU REALLY WANT OF ME?
DO YOU... ...WANT ME TO CONTINUE TEACHING?
OR... ...DO YOU WANT ME TO GO BACK TO FIGURE SKATING?
WELL ...
I DON'T WANT YOU TO STOP TEACHING...
I MEAN, REALLY, I DON'T CARE WHICH ONE YOU CHOOSE.

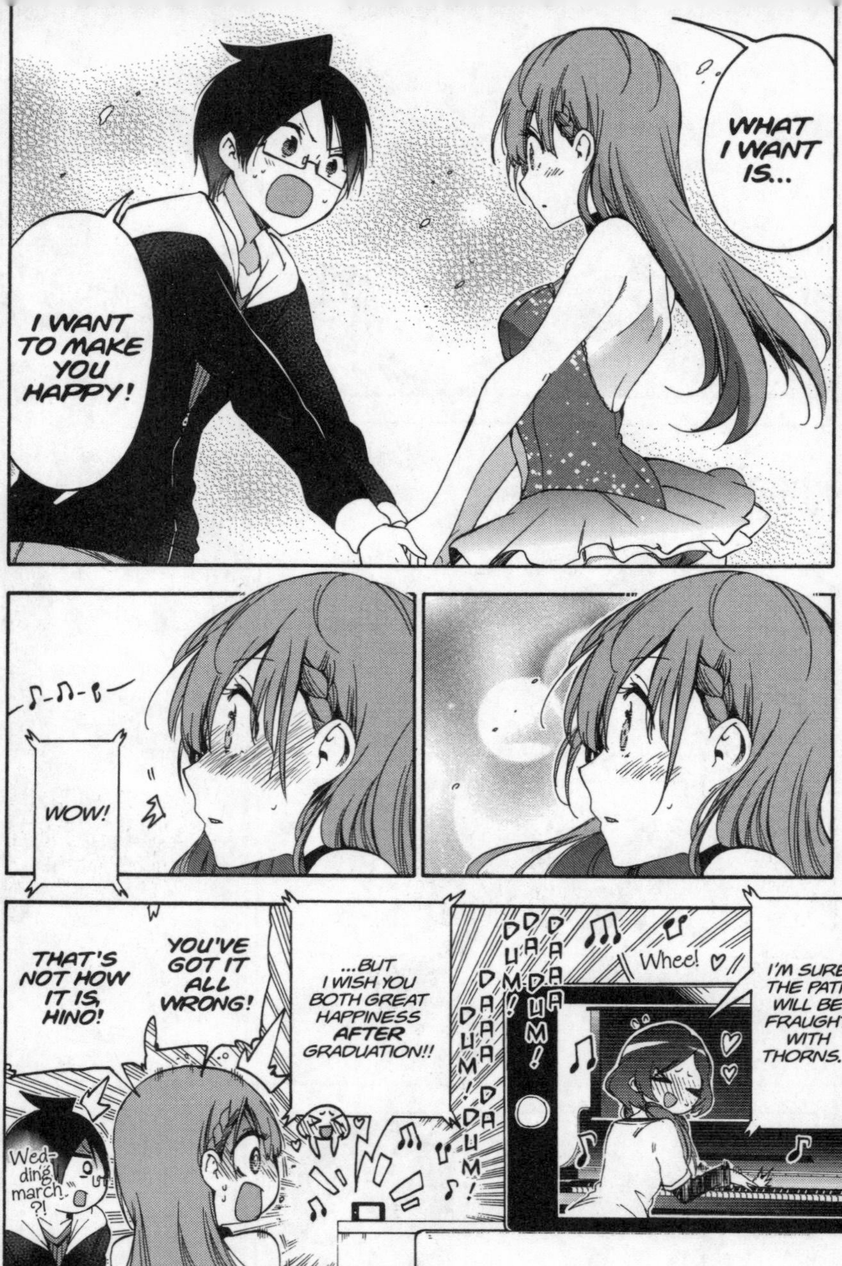
WHAT I WANT IS...
I WANT TO MAKE YOU HAPPY!
WOW!
I'M SURE THE PATH WILL BE FRAUGHT WITH THORNS...
Whee! ♡
DA DUM! DAA DUM! DAAA
DAAA DUM! DA DUM!
...BUT I WISH YOU BOTH GREAT HAPPINESS AFTER GRADUATION!!
YOU'VE GOT IT ALL WRONG!
THAT'S NOT HOW IT IS, HINO!
Wedding march?!

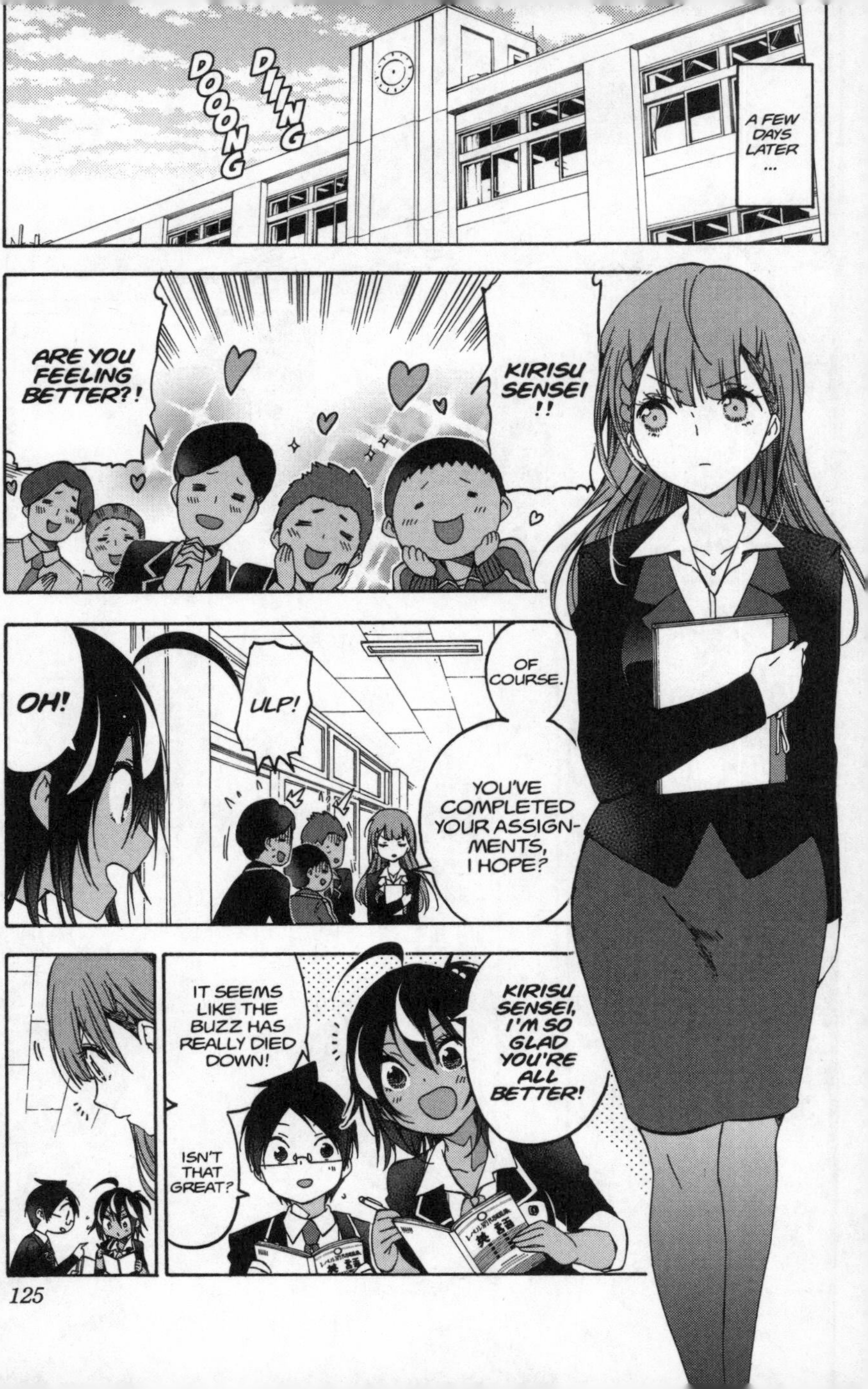
A FEW DAYS LATER ...
DIIING
DOOONG
KIRISU SENSEI !!
ARE YOU FEELING BETTER?!
OF COURSE.
YOU'VE COMPLETED YOUR ASSIGN-MENTS, I HOPE?
ULP!
OH!
KIRISU SENSEI, I'M SO GLAD YOU'RE ALL BETTER!
IT SEEMS LIKE THE BUZZ HAS REALLY DIED DOWN!
ISN'T THAT GREAT?

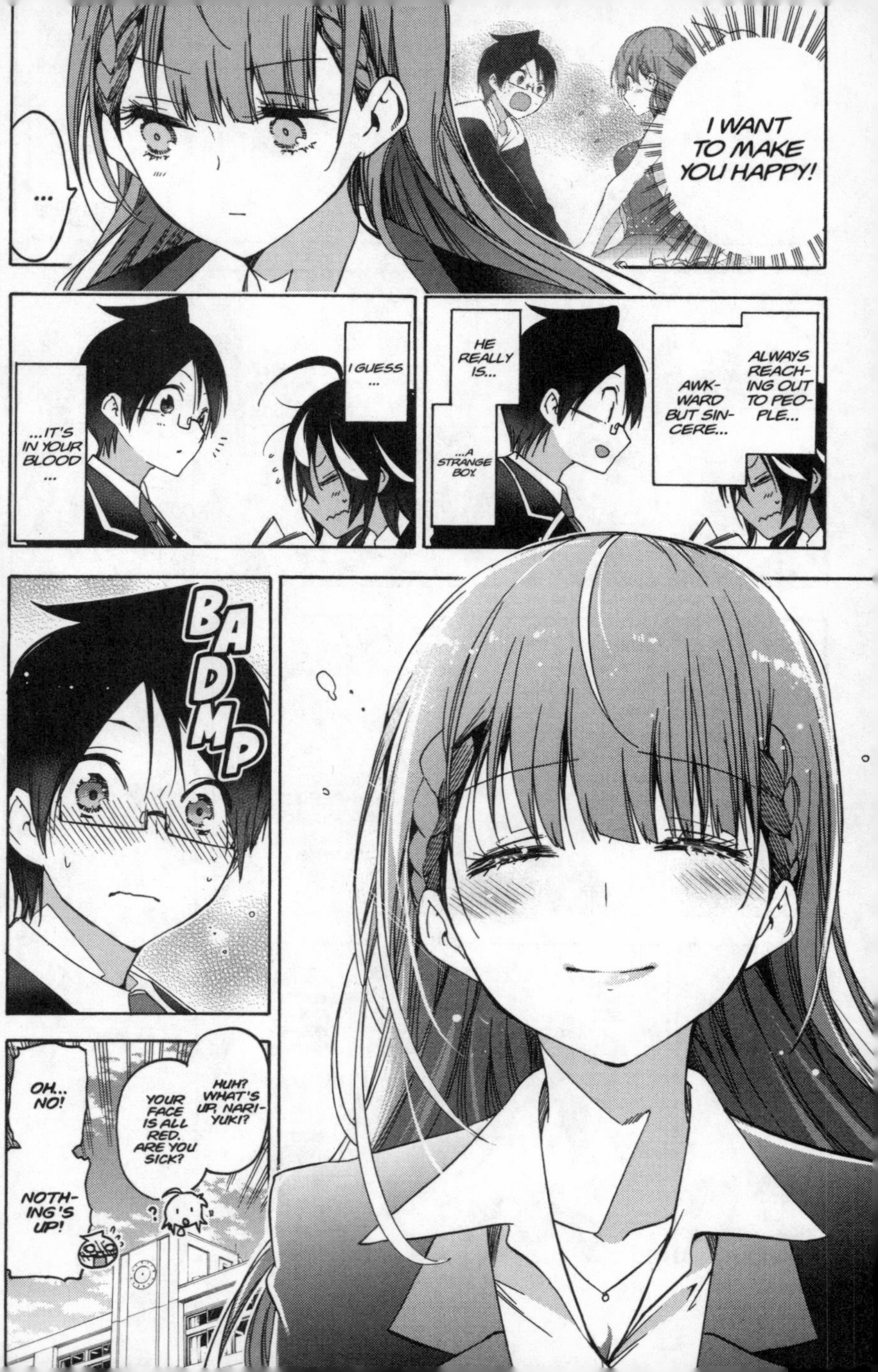
I WANT TO MAKE YOU HAPPY!
...
ALWAYS REACHING OUT TO PEOPLE...
AWKWARD BUT SINCERE...
HE REALLY IS...
...A STRANGE BOY.
I GUESS...
...IT'S IN YOUR BLOOD...
BADMP
HUH? WHAT'S UP, NARIYUKI?
YOUR FACE IS ALL RED. ARE YOU SICK?
OH... NO!
NOTHING'S UP!

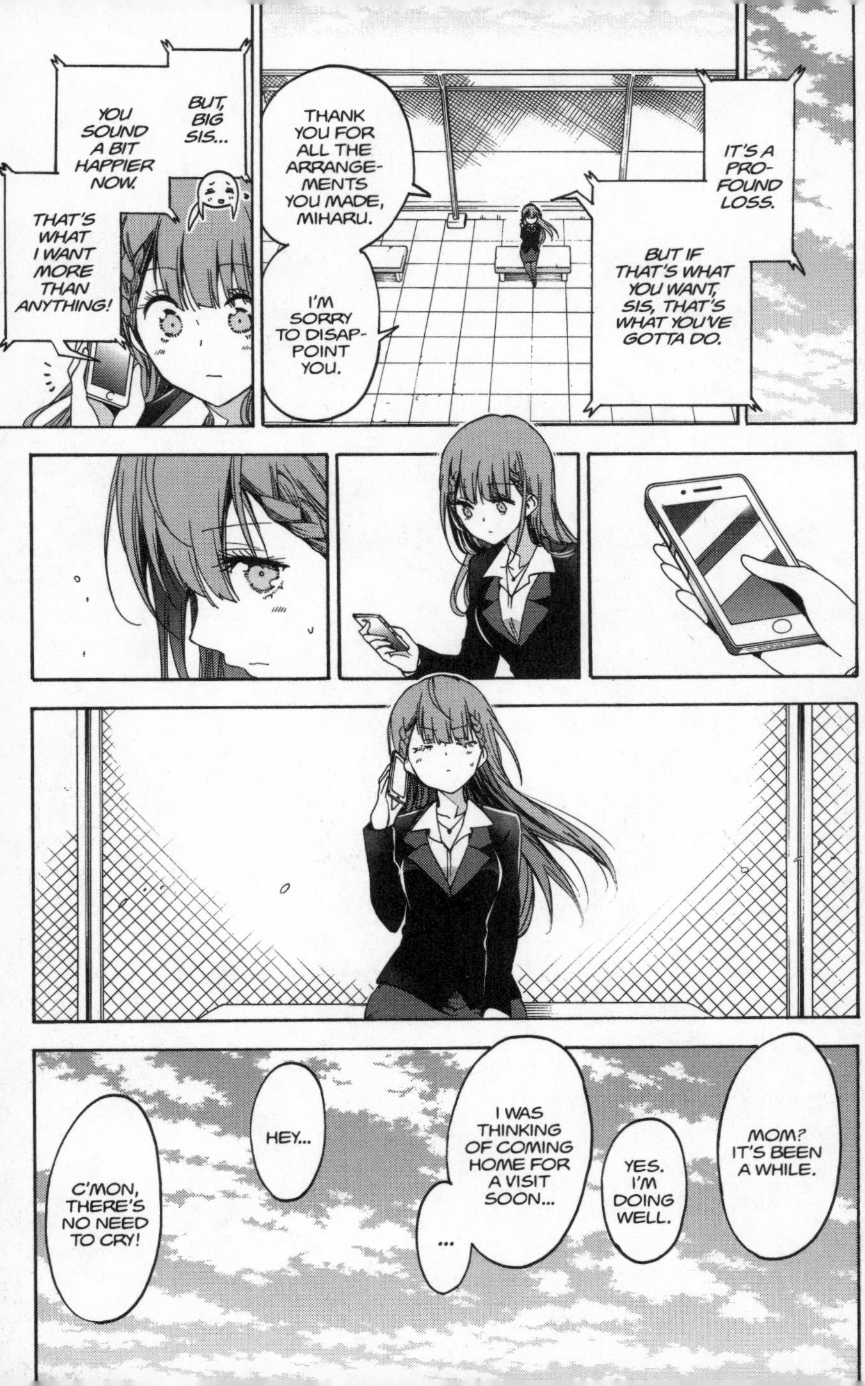

IT'S A PRO-FOUND LOSS.
BUT IF THAT'S WHAT YOU WANT, SIS, THAT'S WHAT YOU'VE GOTTA DO.
THANK YOU FOR ALL THE ARRANGE-MENTS YOU MADE, MIHARU.
I'M SORRY TO DISAP-POINT YOU.
BUT, BIG SIS...
YOU SOUND A BIT HAPPIER NOW.
THAT'S WHAT I WANT MORE THAN ANYTHING!
MOM? IT'S BEEN A WHILE.
YES. I'M DOING WELL.
I WAS THINKING OF COMING HOME FOR A VISIT SOON...
...
HEY...
C'MON, THERE'S NO NEED TO CRY!

What an odd question. But I do have a guy who comes and cleans my place...

Boyfriend?!   Huh?

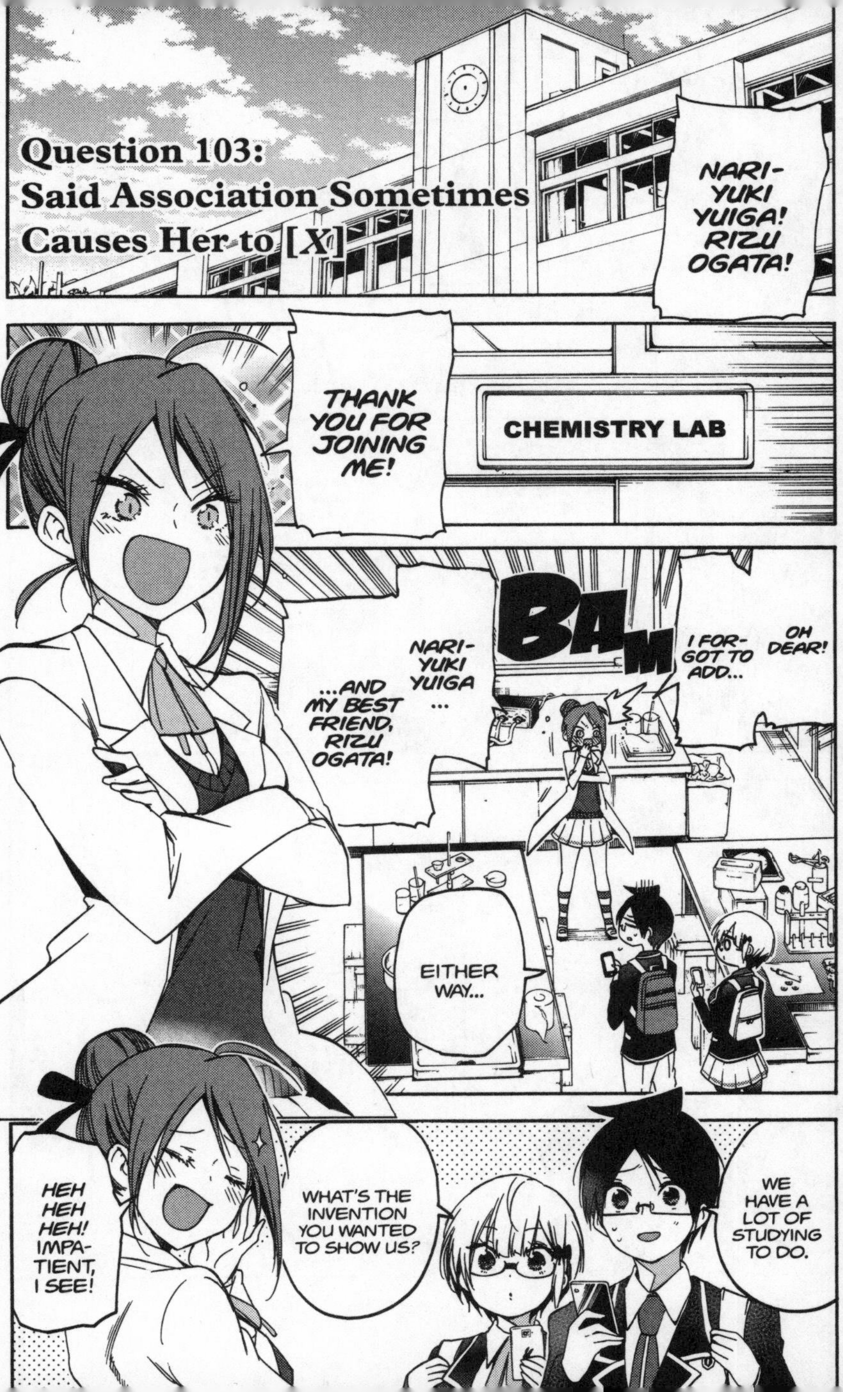
Question 103: Said Association Sometimes Causes Her to [X]
NARI-YUKI YUIGA! RIZU OGATA!
CHEMISTRY LAB
THANK YOU FOR JOINING ME!
OH DEAR!
I FOR-GOT TO ADD...
BAM
NARI-YUKI YUIGA ...
...AND MY BEST FRIEND, RIZU OGATA!
EITHER WAY...
WE HAVE A LOT OF STUDYING TO DO.
WHAT'S THE INVENTION YOU WANTED TO SHOW US?
HEH HEH HEH! IMPA-TIENT, I SEE!

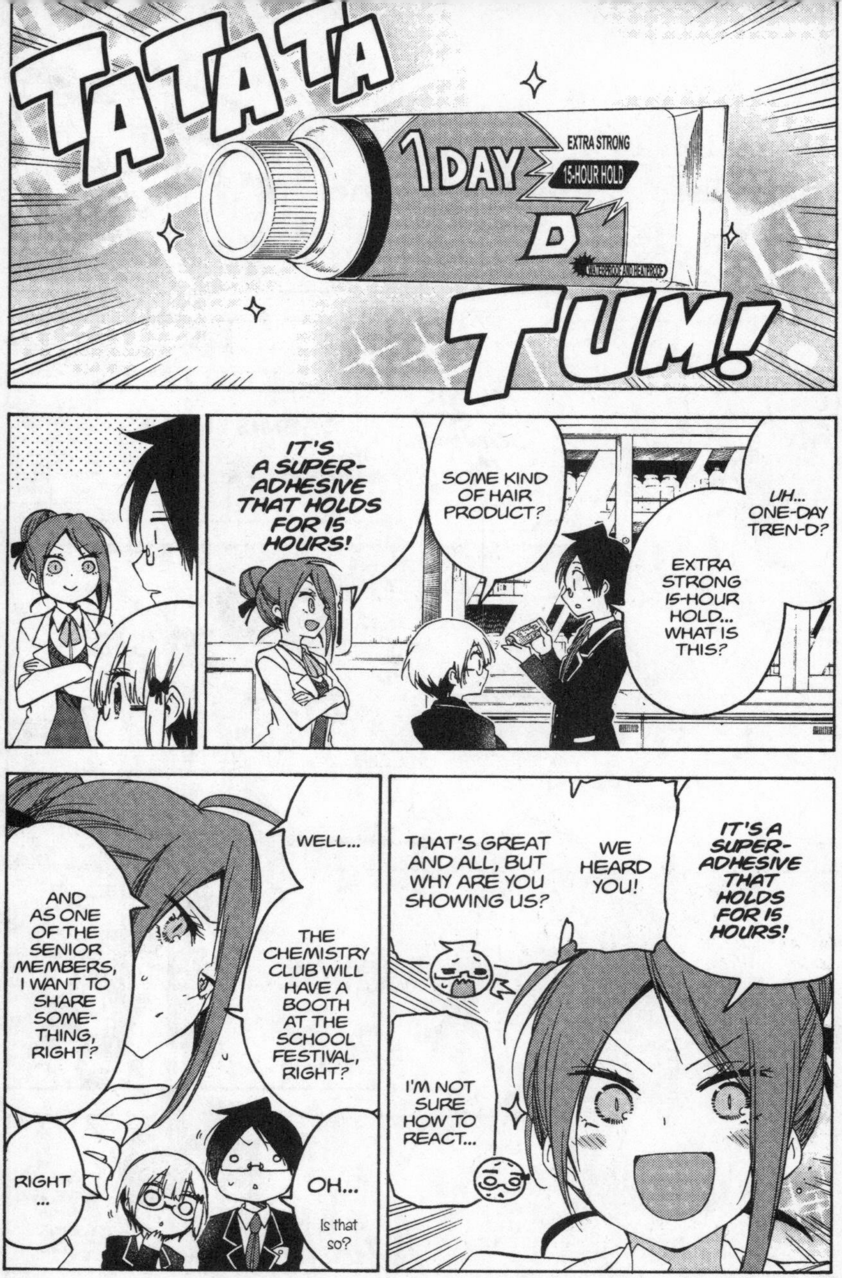
TATATA
1DAY
EXTRA STRONG
15-HOUR HOLD
D
WATERPROOF AND HEATPROOF
TUM!
UH... ONE-DAY TREN-D?
EXTRA STRONG 15-HOUR HOLD... WHAT IS THIS?
SOME KIND OF HAIR PRODUCT?
IT'S A SUPER-ADHESIVE THAT HOLDS FOR 15 HOURS!
IT'S A SUPER-ADHESIVE THAT HOLDS FOR 15 HOURS!
WE HEARD YOU!
THAT'S GREAT AND ALL, BUT WHY ARE YOU SHOWING US?
I'M NOT SURE HOW TO REACT...
WELL...
THE CHEMISTRY CLUB WILL HAVE A BOOTH AT THE SCHOOL FESTIVAL, RIGHT?
OH...
Is that so?
AND AS ONE OF THE SENIOR MEMBERS, I WANT TO SHARE SOMETHING, RIGHT?
RIGHT...

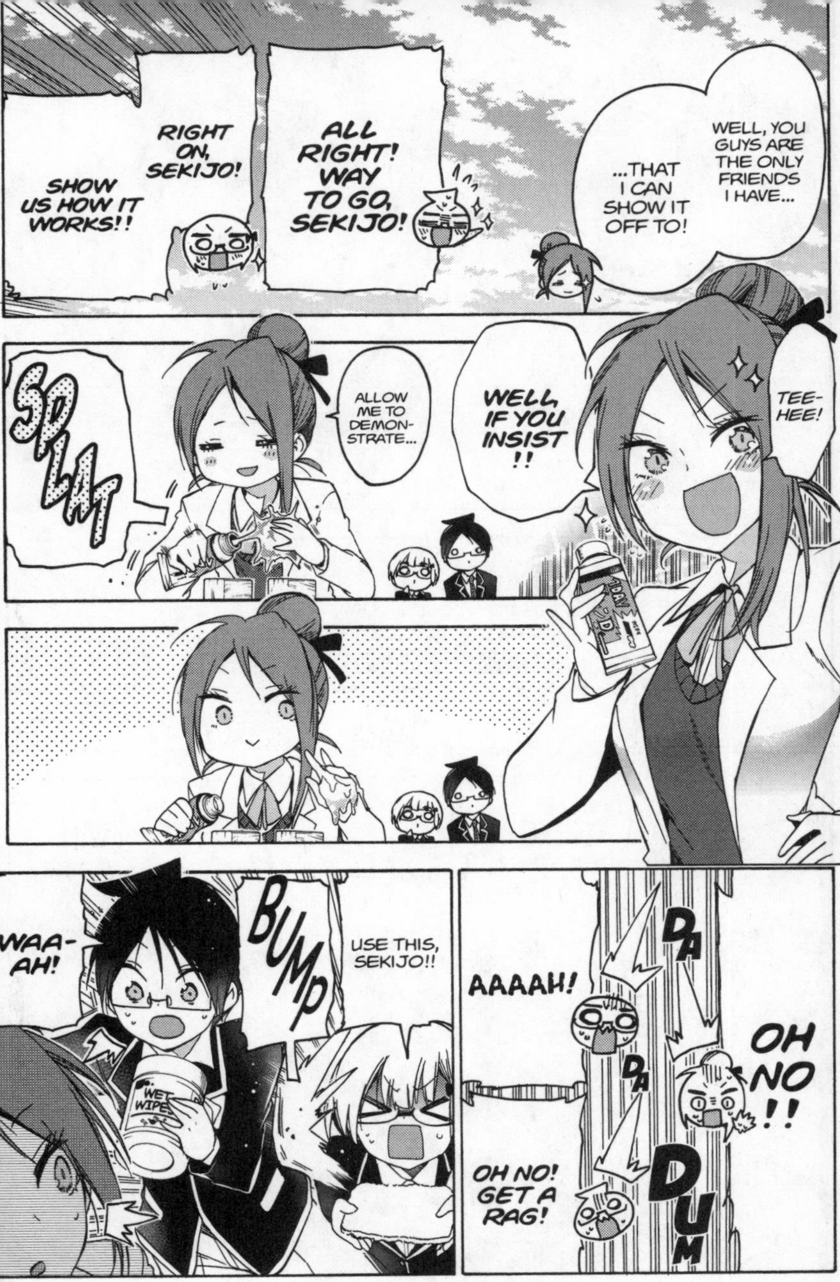
WELL, YOU GUYS ARE THE ONLY FRIENDS I HAVE...
...THAT I CAN SHOW IT OFF TO!
ALL RIGHT! WAY TO GO, SEKIJO!
RIGHT ON, SEKIJO!
SHOW US HOW IT WORKS!!
TEE-HEE!
WELL, IF YOU INSIST!!
ALLOW ME TO DEMONSTRATE...
SPLAT
OH NO!!
DA
AAAAH!
DA
DUM
OH NO! GET A RAG!
USE THIS, SEKIJO!!
BUMP
WAA-AH!
WET WIPES

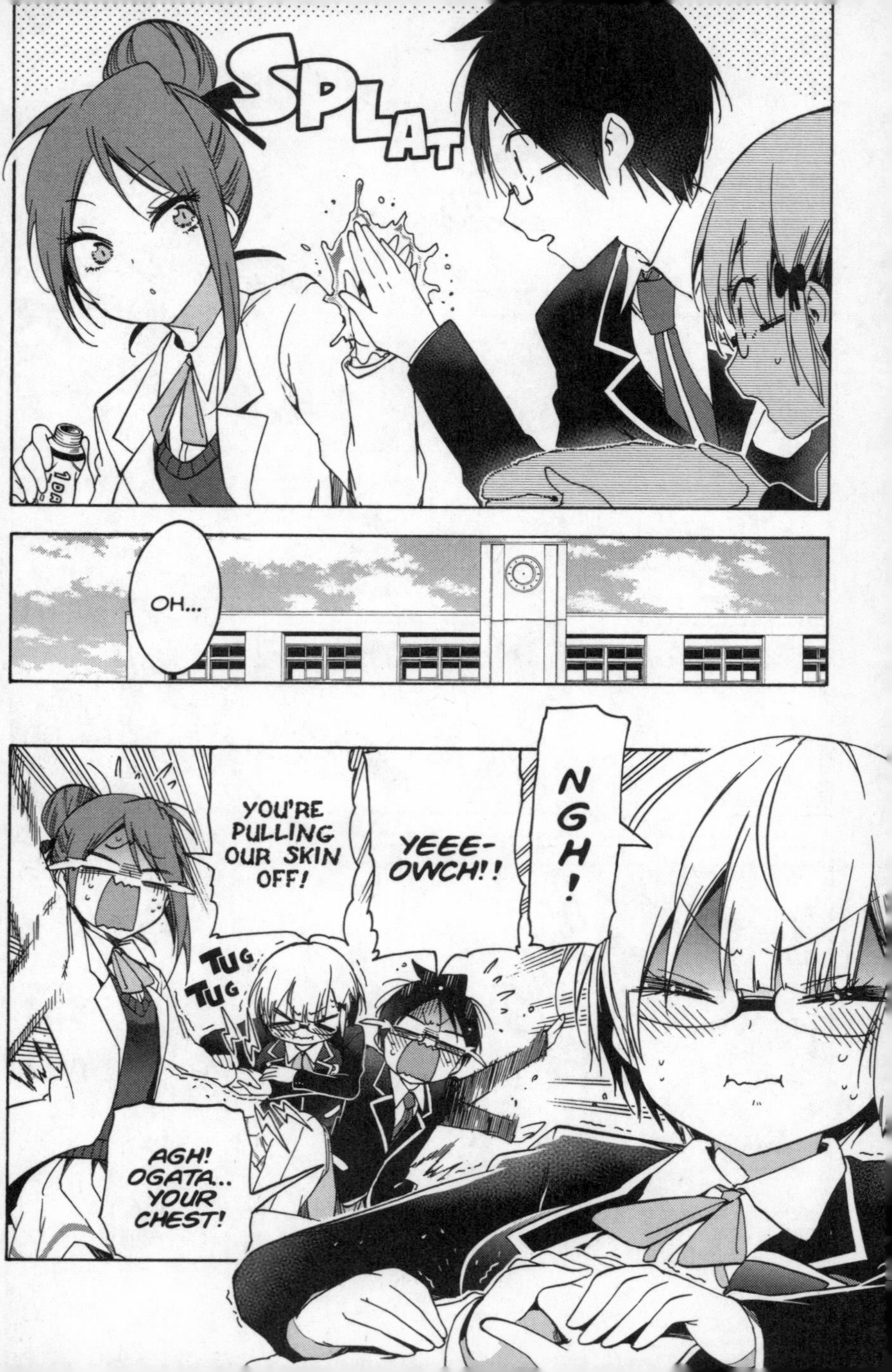
SPLAT
OH...
NGH!
YEEE-OWCH!!
YOU'RE PULLING OUR SKIN OFF!
TUG TUG
AGH! OGATA... YOUR CHEST!

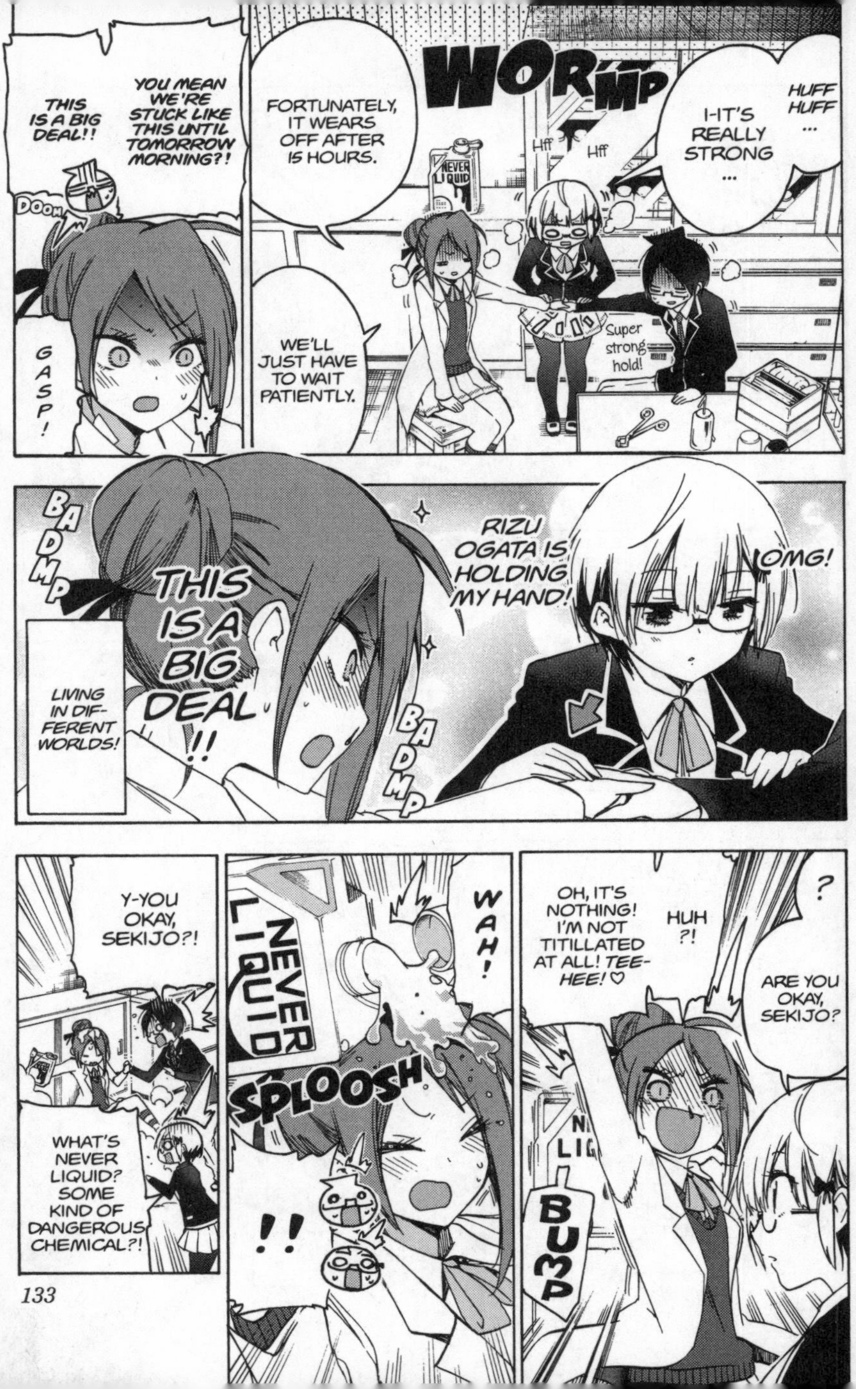

WORMP
I-IT'S REALLY STRONG ...
HUFF HUFF ...
Hff Hff
NEVER LIQUID
FORTUNATELY, IT WEARS OFF AFTER 15 HOURS.
WE'LL JUST HAVE TO WAIT PATIENTLY.
Super strong hold!
YOU MEAN WE'RE STUCK LIKE THIS UNTIL TOMORROW MORNING?!
THIS IS A BIG DEAL!!
DOOM
GASP!
RIZU OGATA IS HOLDING MY HAND!
OMG!
THIS IS A BIG DEAL!!
BADMP
LIVING IN DIFFERENT WORLDS!
BADMP
?
ARE YOU OKAY, SEKIJO?
HUH?!
OH, IT'S NOTHING! I'M NOT TITILLATED AT ALL! TEE-HEE! ♡
NE LIQ
BUMP
WAH!
NEVER LIQUID
SPLOOSH
!!
Y-YOU OKAY, SEKIJO?!
WHAT'S NEVER LIQUID? SOME KIND OF DANGEROUS CHEMICAL?!

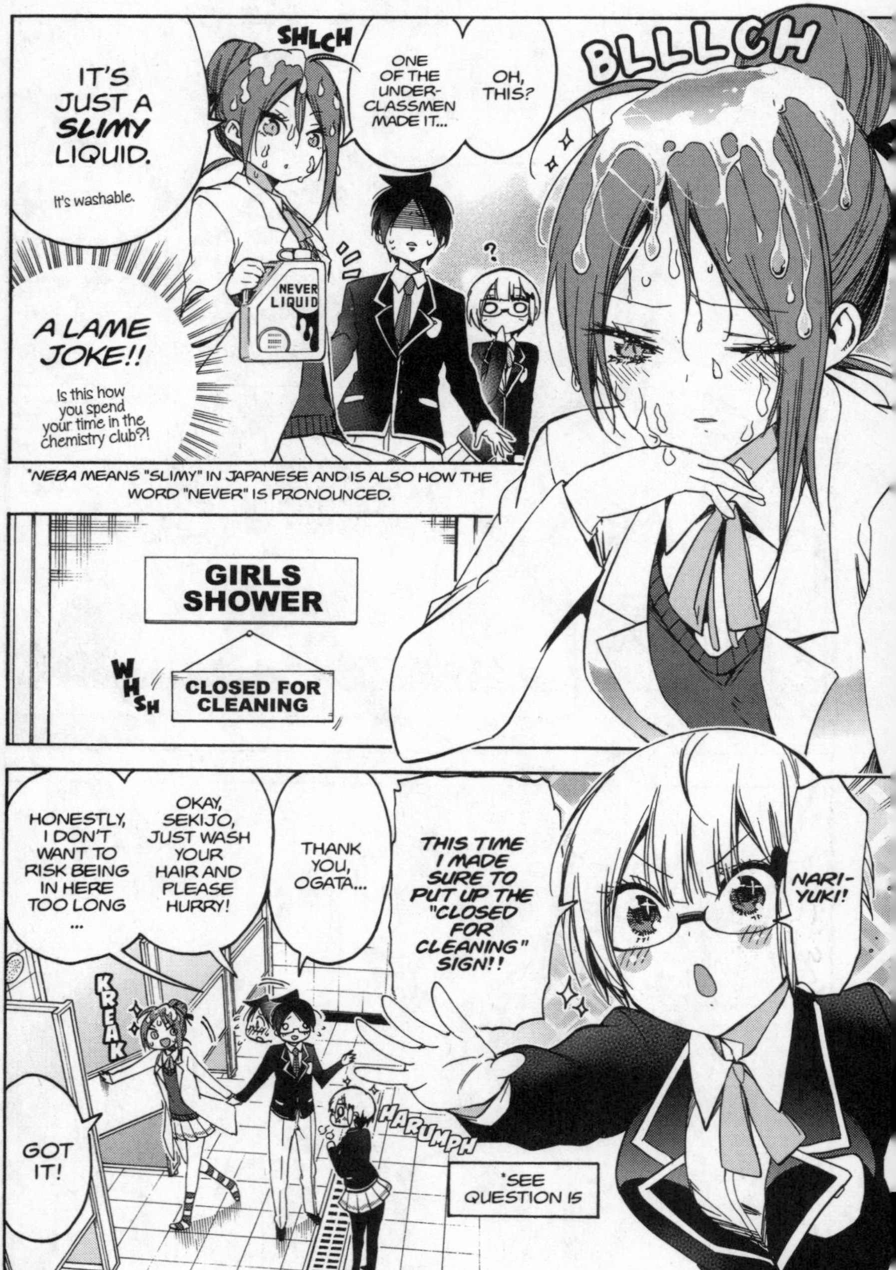
BLLLCH
OH, THIS?
ONE OF THE UNDER-CLASSMEN MADE IT...
SHLCH
IT'S JUST A SLIMY LIQUID.
It's washable.
A LAME JOKE!!
Is this how you spend your time in the chemistry club?!
NEVER LIQUID
*NEBA MEANS "SLIMY" IN JAPANESE AND IS ALSO HOW THE WORD "NEVER" IS PRONOUNCED.
GIRLS SHOWER
CLOSED FOR CLEANING
WHSH
NARI-YUKI!
THIS TIME I MADE SURE TO PUT UP THE "CLOSED FOR CLEANING" SIGN!!
*SEE QUESTION 15
THANK YOU, OGATA...
OKAY, SEKIJO, JUST WASH YOUR HAIR AND PLEASE HURRY!
HONESTLY, I DON'T WANT TO RISK BEING IN HERE TOO LONG ...
KREAK
HARUMPH
GOT IT!

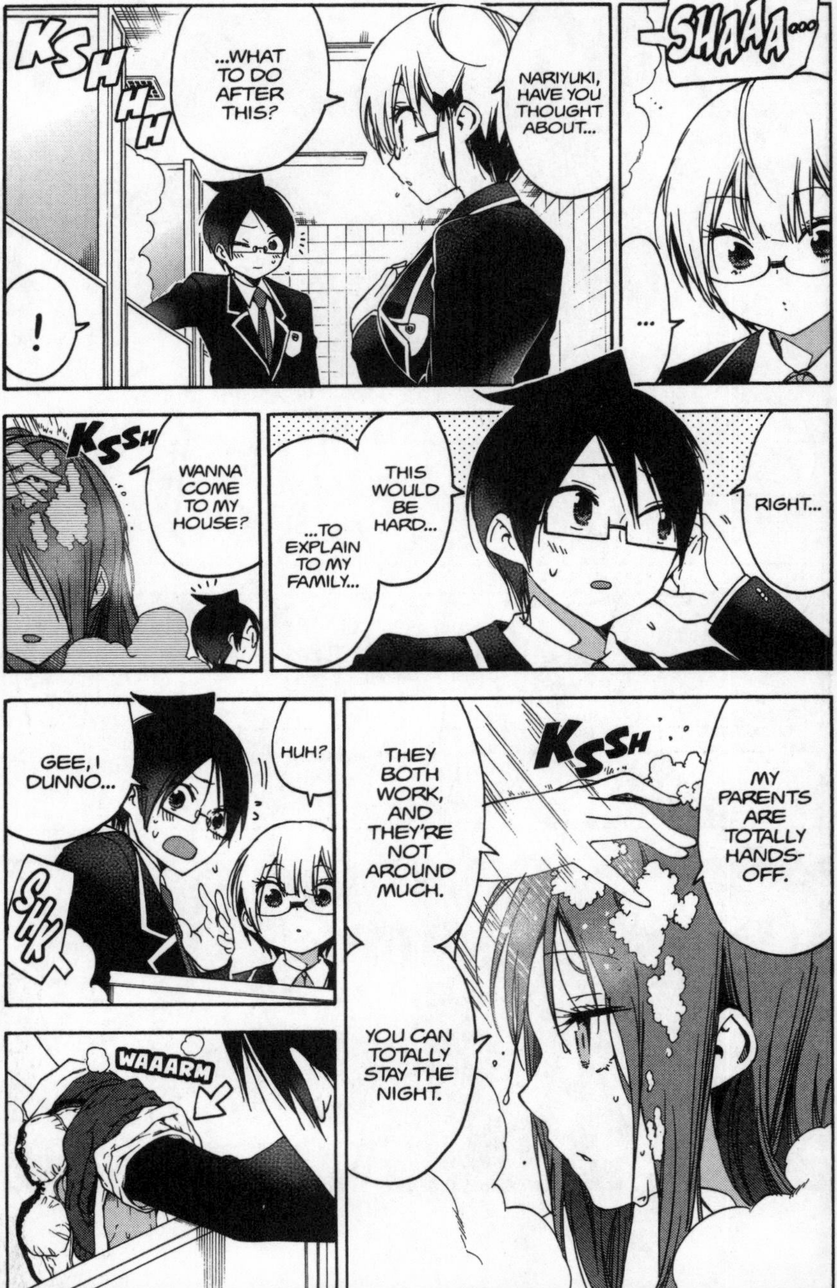
SHAAA...
...
NARIYUKI, HAVE YOU THOUGHT ABOUT...
...WHAT TO DO AFTER THIS?
KSHHHH
!
RIGHT...
THIS WOULD BE HARD...
...TO EXPLAIN TO MY FAMILY...
KSSH
WANNA COME TO MY HOUSE?
MY PARENTS ARE TOTALLY HANDS-OFF.
KSSH
THEY BOTH WORK, AND THEY'RE NOT AROUND MUCH.
YOU CAN TOTALLY STAY THE NIGHT.
HUH?
GEE, I DUNNO...
SHK
WAAARM

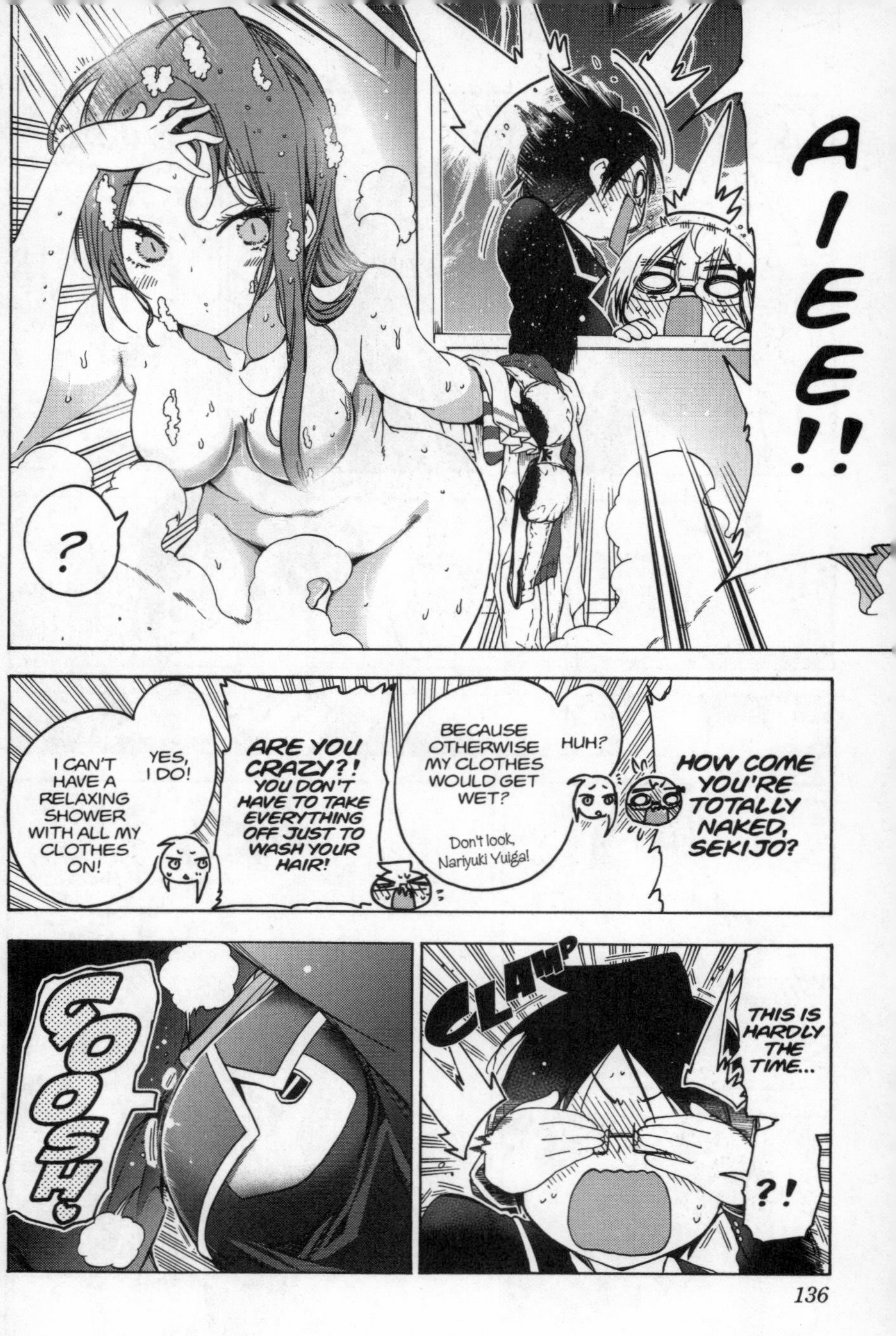
AIEEE!!
?
HOW COME YOU'RE TOTALLY NAKED, SEKIJO?
HUH?
BECAUSE OTHERWISE MY CLOTHES WOULD GET WET?
Don't look, Nariyuki Yuiga!
ARE YOU CRAZY?! YOU DON'T HAVE TO TAKE EVERYTHING OFF JUST TO WASH YOUR HAIR!
YES, I DO!
I CAN'T HAVE A RELAXING SHOWER WITH ALL MY CLOTHES ON!
CLAMP
THIS IS HARDLY THE TIME...
?!
GOOSH!

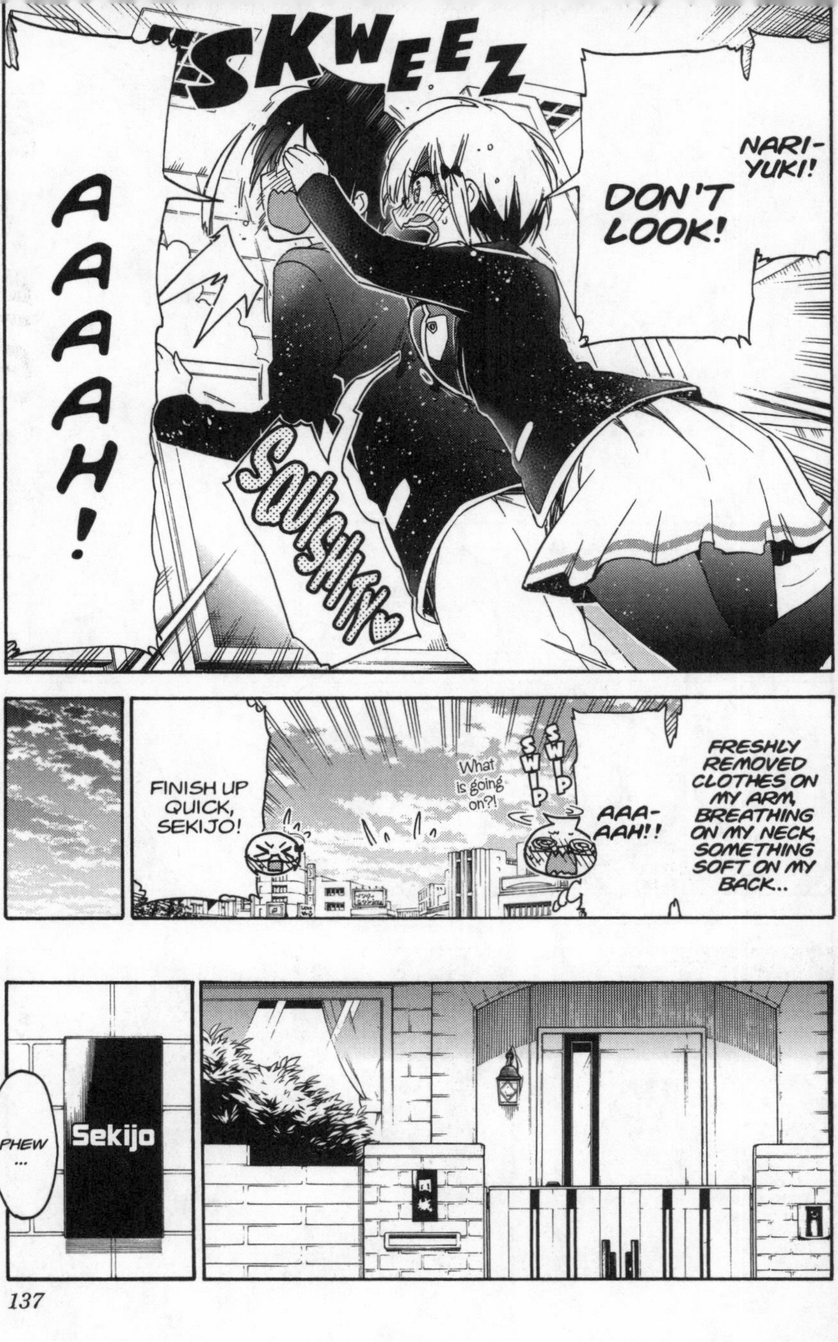
SKWEEZ
NARI-YUKI!
DON'T LOOK!
AAAAAH!
SQUISHY♥
FRESHLY REMOVED CLOTHES ON MY ARM, BREATHING ON MY NECK, SOMETHING SOFT ON MY BACK...
SWIP SWIP
AAA-AAH!!
What is going on?!
FINISH UP QUICK, SEKIJO!
Sekijo
PHEW...

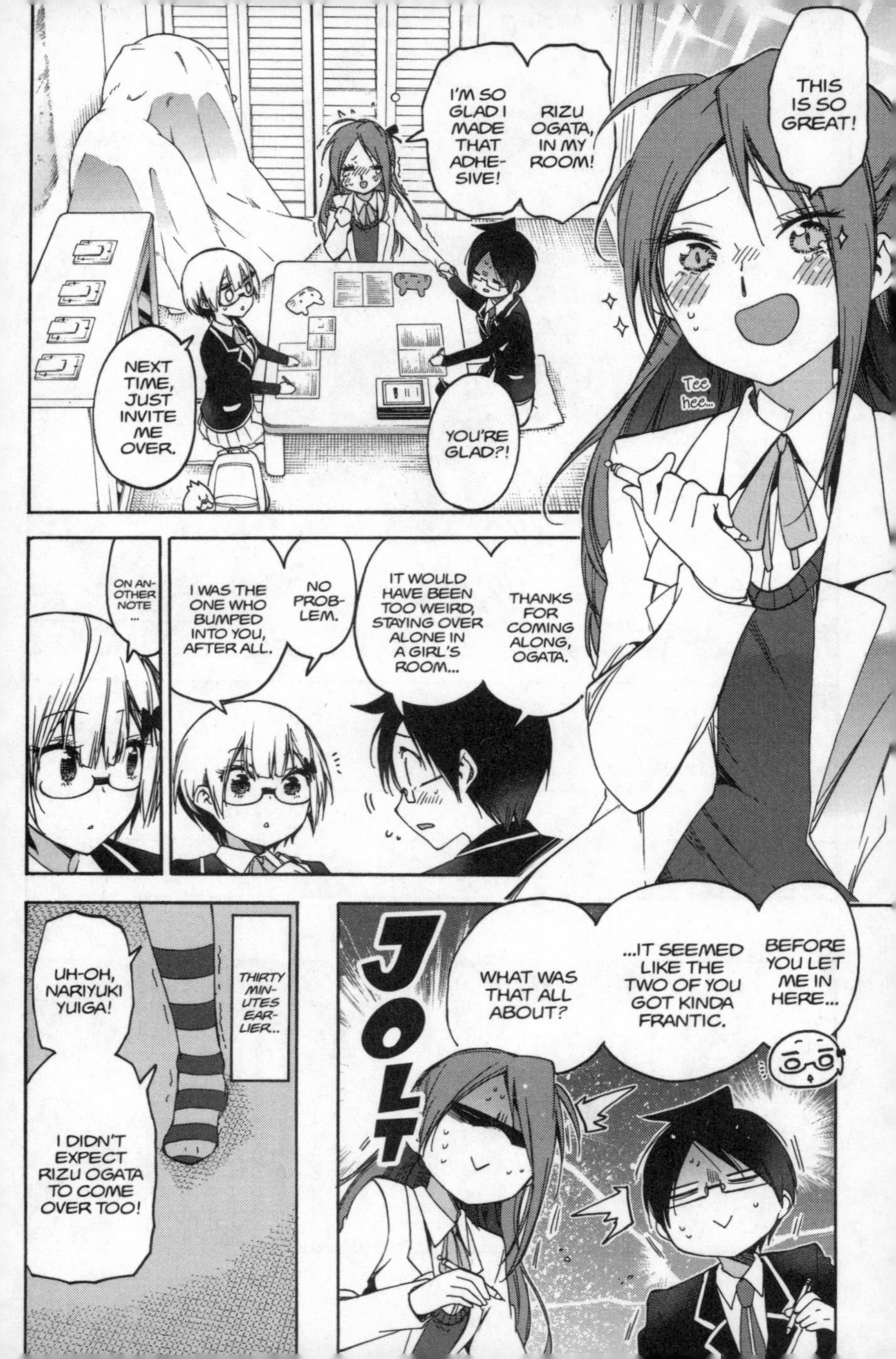
THIS IS SO GREAT!
Tee hee...
RIZU OGATA, IN MY ROOM!
I'M SO GLAD I MADE THAT ADHESIVE!
YOU'RE GLAD?!
NEXT TIME, JUST INVITE ME OVER.
THANKS FOR COMING ALONG, OGATA.
IT WOULD HAVE BEEN TOO WEIRD, STAYING OVER ALONE IN A GIRL'S ROOM...
NO PROBLEM.
I WAS THE ONE WHO BUMPED INTO YOU, AFTER ALL.
ON ANOTHER NOTE...
BEFORE YOU LET ME IN HERE...
...IT SEEMED LIKE THE TWO OF YOU GOT KINDA FRANTIC.
WHAT WAS THAT ALL ABOUT?
JOLT
THIRTY MINUTES EARLIER...
UH-OH, NARIYUKI YUIGA!
I DIDN'T EXPECT RIZU OGATA TO COME OVER TOO!

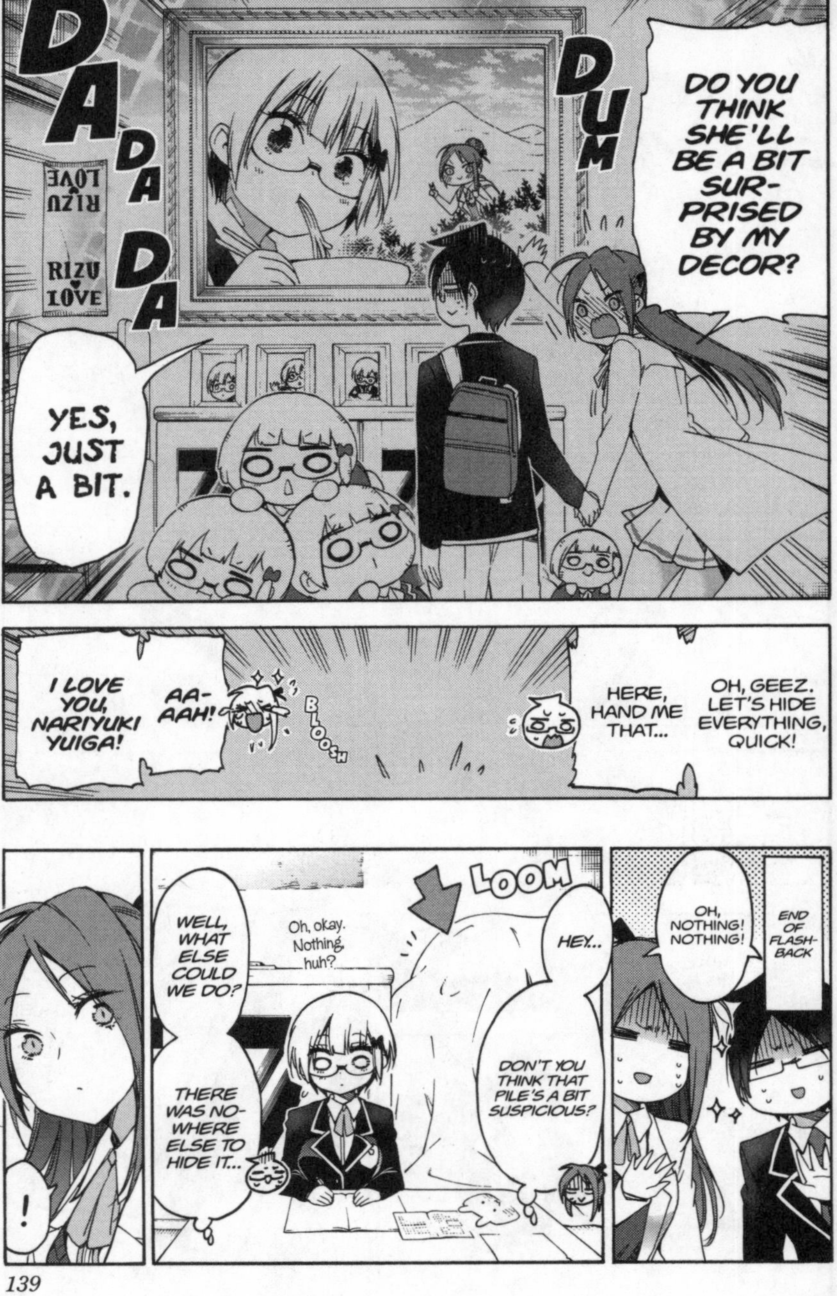
DO YOU THINK SHE'LL BE A BIT SUR-PRISED BY MY DECOR?
DA DA DA DA DUM
RIZU LOVE
RIZU LOVE
YES, JUST A BIT.
OH, GEEZ. LET'S HIDE EVERYTHING, QUICK!
HERE, HAND ME THAT...
BLOOSH
AA-AAH!
I LOVE YOU, NARIYUKI YUIGA!
END OF FLASH-BACK
OH, NOTHING! NOTHING!
LOOM
HEY...
DON'T YOU THINK THAT PILE'S A BIT SUSPICIOUS?
Oh, okay. Nothing, huh?
WELL, WHAT ELSE COULD WE DO?
THERE WAS NO-WHERE ELSE TO HIDE IT...
!

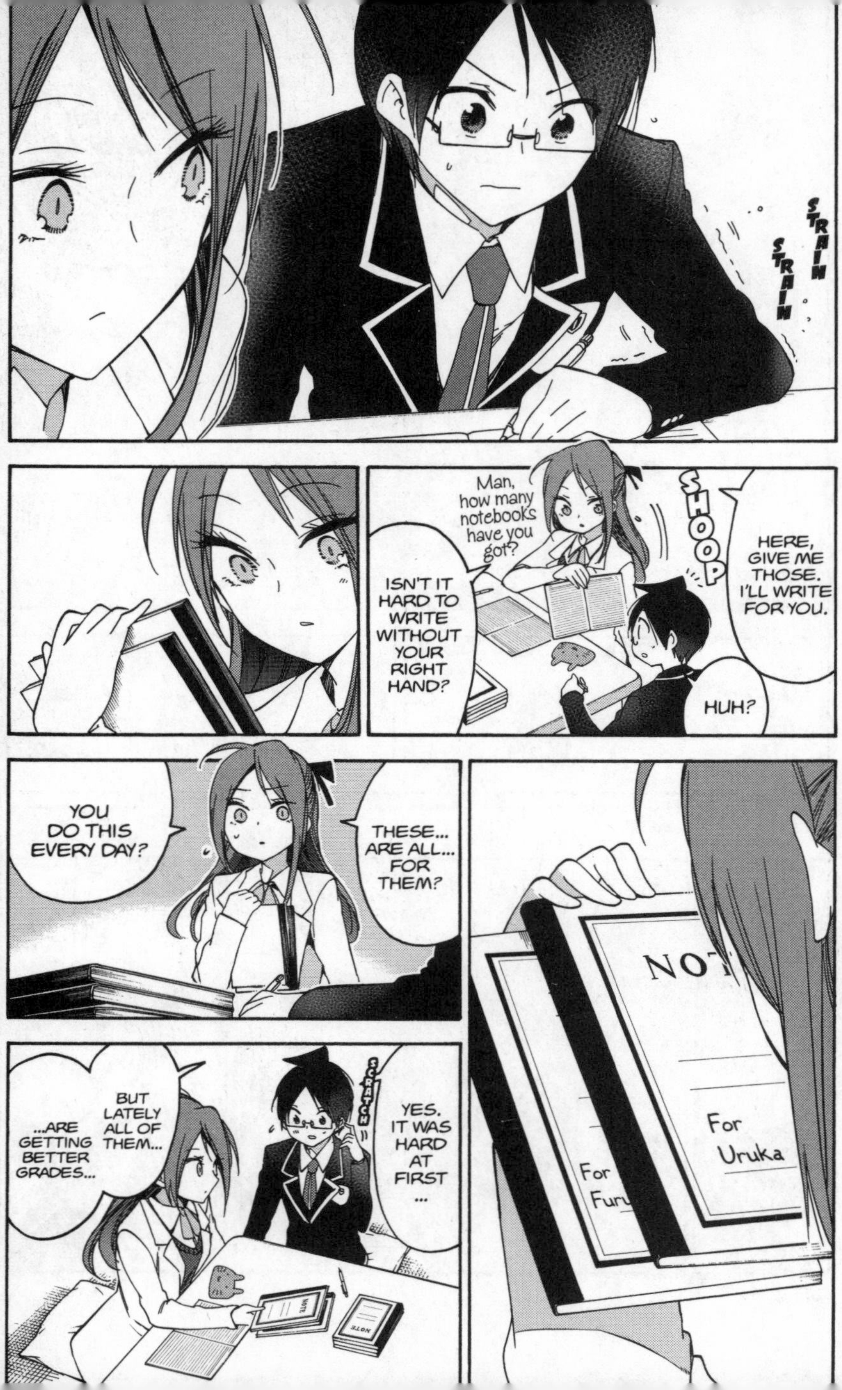
STRAIN
STRAIN
HERE, GIVE ME THOSE. I'LL WRITE FOR YOU.
SHOOP
Man, how many notebooks have you got?
HUH?
ISN'T IT HARD TO WRITE WITHOUT YOUR RIGHT HAND?
NOT
For Uruka
For Furu
THESE... ARE ALL... FOR THEM?
YOU DO THIS EVERY DAY?
YES. IT WAS HARD AT FIRST ...
SCRATCH
BUT LATELY ALL OF THEM...
...ARE GETTING BETTER GRADES...

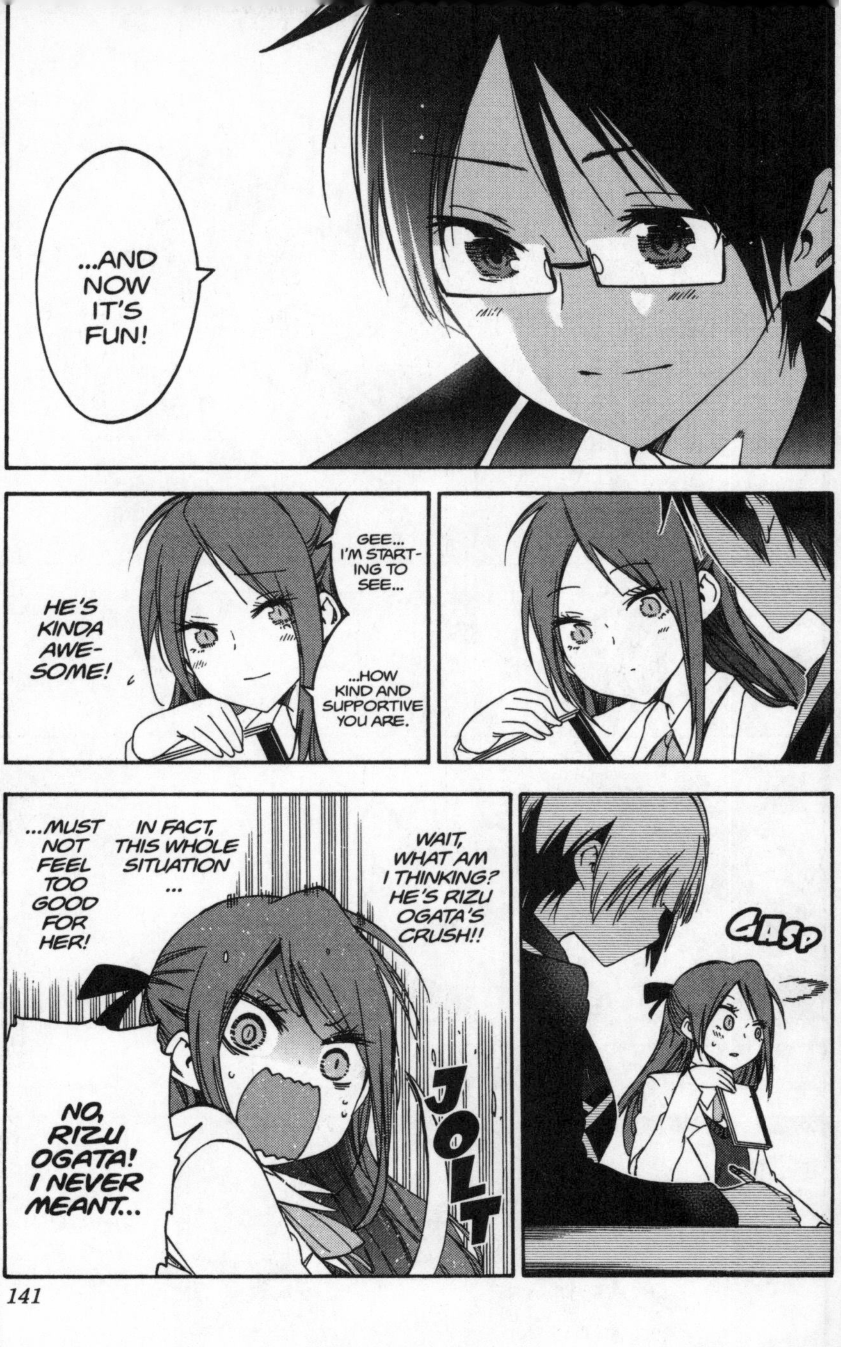
...AND NOW IT'S FUN!
GEE... I'M STARTING TO SEE...
...HOW KIND AND SUPPORTIVE YOU ARE.
HE'S KINDA AWESOME!
GASP
WAIT, WHAT AM I THINKING? HE'S RIZU OGATA'S CRUSH!!
IN FACT, THIS WHOLE SITUATION ...
...MUST NOT FEEL TOO GOOD FOR HER!
JOLT
NO, RIZU OGATA! I NEVER MEANT...

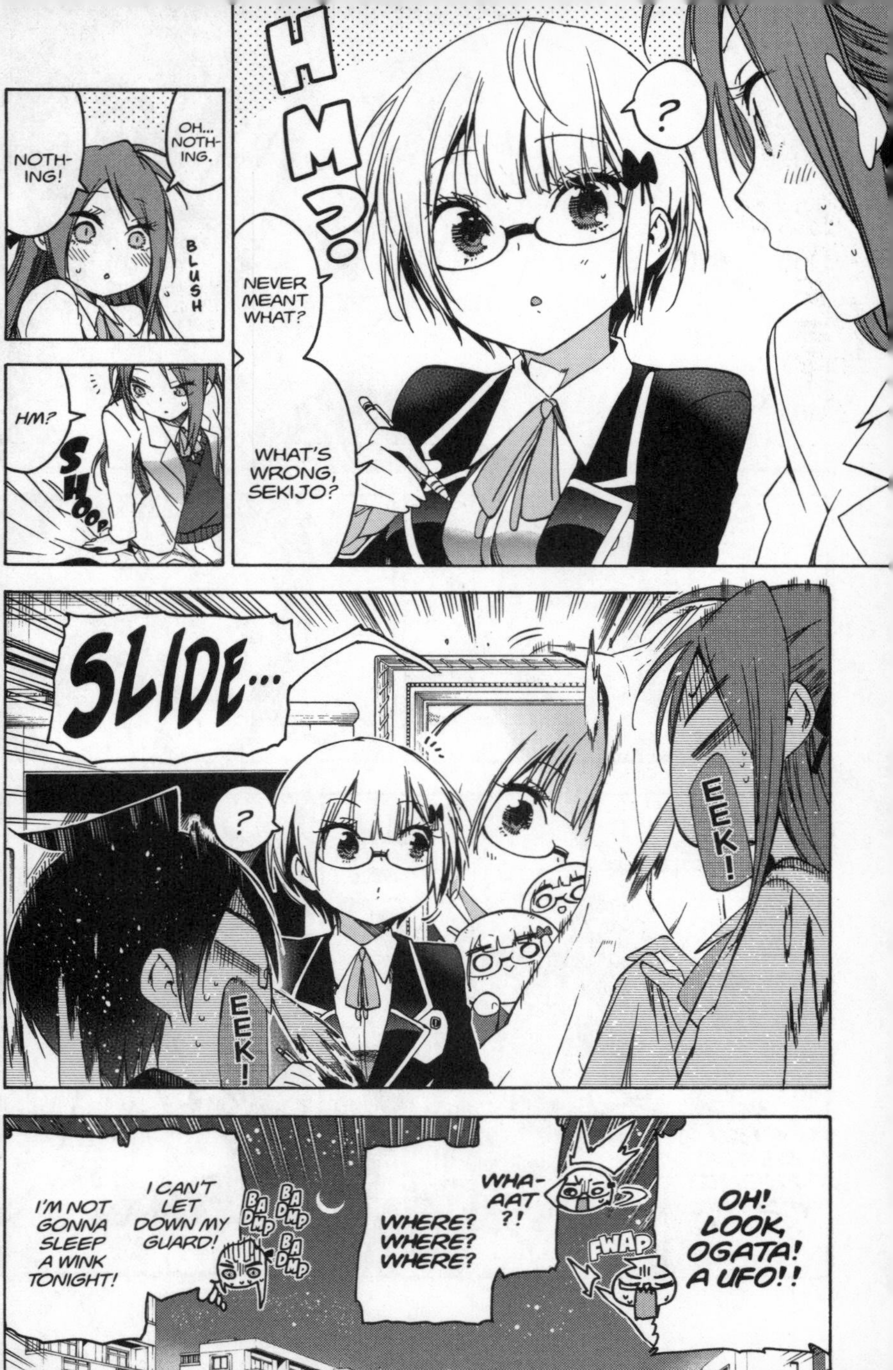
HM?
?
NEVER MEANT WHAT?
WHAT'S WRONG, SEKIJO?
OH... NOTHING.
NOTHING!
BLUSH
HM?
SHOOOP
SLIDE...
EEK!
?
EEK!
OH! LOOK, OGATA! A UFO!!
FWAP
WHA-AAT?!
WHERE? WHERE? WHERE?
BADMP BADMP
BADMP BADMP
I CAN'T LET DOWN MY GUARD!
I'M NOT GONNA SLEEP A WINK TONIGHT!

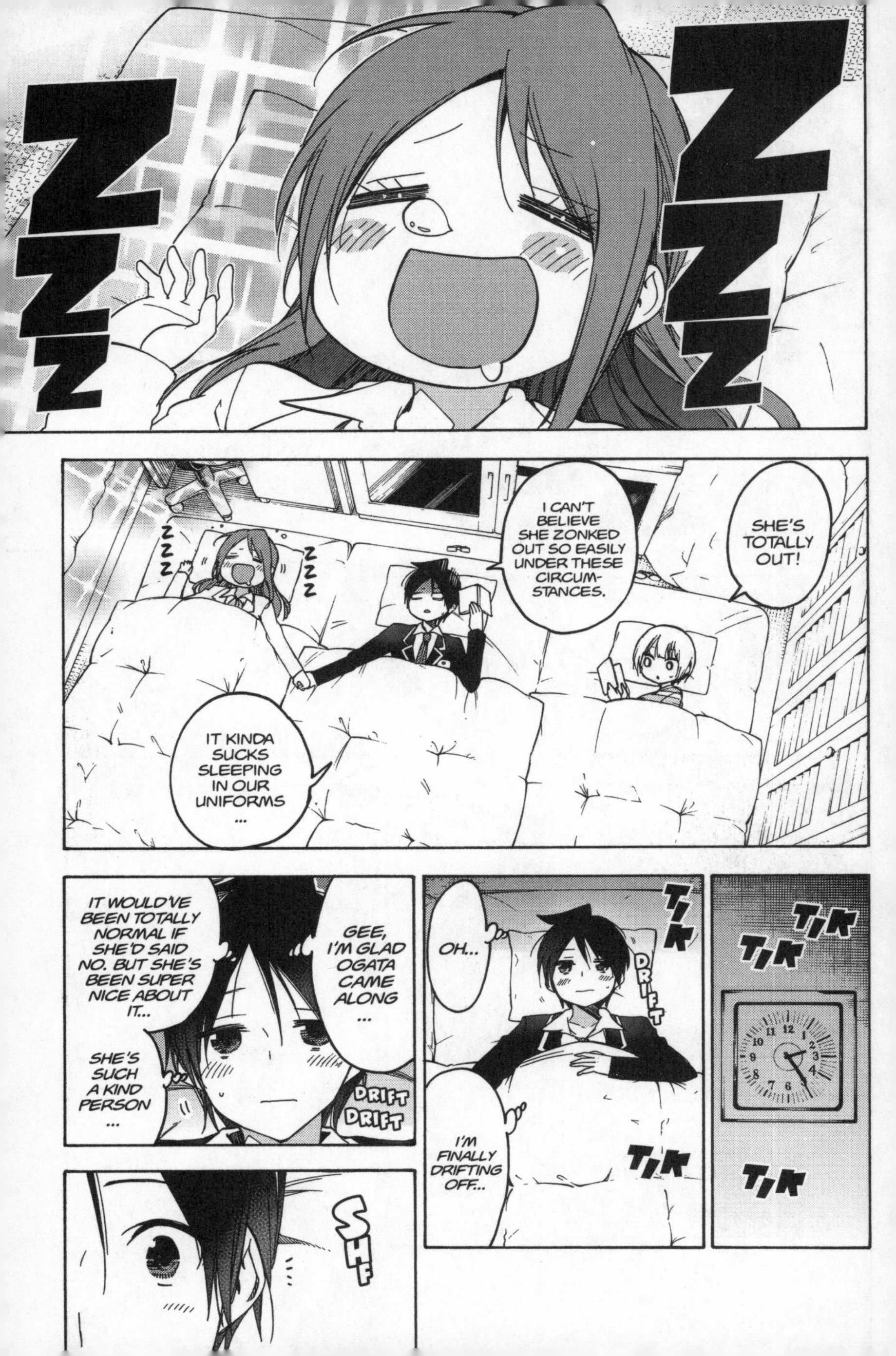
ZZZ
ZZZ
SHE'S TOTALLY OUT!
I CAN'T BELIEVE SHE ZONKED OUT SO EASILY UNDER THESE CIRCUM-STANCES.
ZZZ
ZZZ
IT KINDA SUCKS SLEEPING IN OUR UNIFORMS ...
TIK TIK
TIK
TIK
DRIFT
OH...
I'M FINALLY DRIFTING OFF...
TIK
GEE, I'M GLAD OGATA CAME ALONG ...
IT WOULD'VE BEEN TOTALLY NORMAL IF SHE'D SAID NO. BUT SHE'S BEEN SUPER NICE ABOUT IT...
SHE'S SUCH A KIND PERSON ...
DRIFT DRIFT
SHF

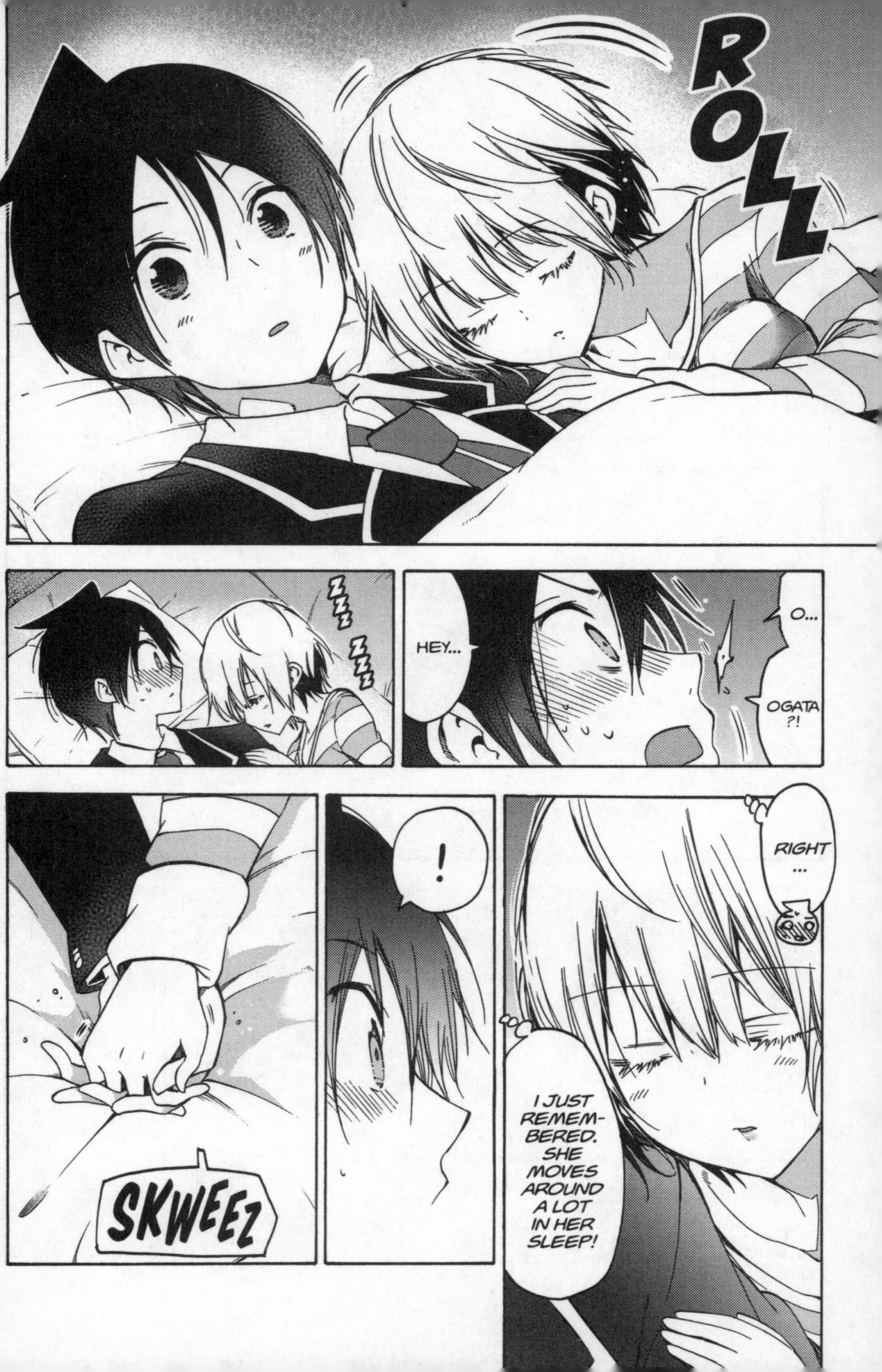
ROLL
O...
HEY...
OGATA ?!
ZZZ
ZZZ
RIGHT ...
I JUST REMEMBERED. SHE MOVES AROUND A LOT IN HER SLEEP!
!
SKWEEZ

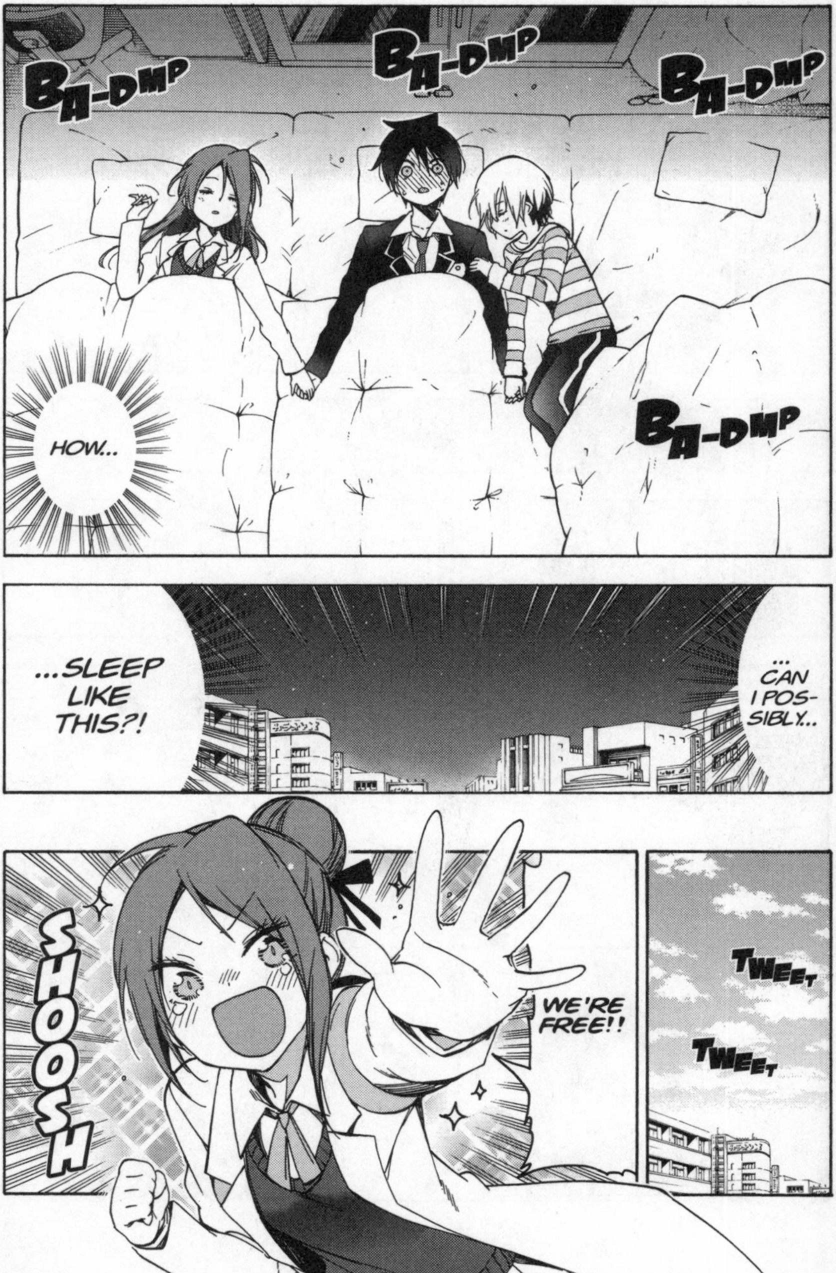
BA-DMP
BA-DMP
BA-DMP
BA-DMP
HOW...
... CAN I POS-SIBLY...
...SLEEP LIKE THIS?!
TWEET
TWEET
WE'RE FREE!!
SHOOSH

ARE YOU OKAY, NARIYUKI?

THANK GOODNESS IT'S THE WEEKEND...

I'M THE ONE WHO COULDN'T SLEEP!

Not a wink!

WAVE WAVE

I BARELY SLEPT A WINK ALL NIGHT!

GEE, THAT WAS ROUGH!

ABOUT LAST NIGHT...

UM, OGATA?

...

SEE YA LATER!

OKAY, BYE!

FLAIL FLAIL

UM... JUST... THANKS FOR EVERY-THING!

HM?

WHAT ABOUT IT?

SHE WAS ASLEEP, THAT'S ALL!!

SLAP SLAP

GAH! WHAT AM I DOING?!

I'M SORRY. THAT WAS...

Question 104: A Little Pale Pink Evokes Memories of [X]

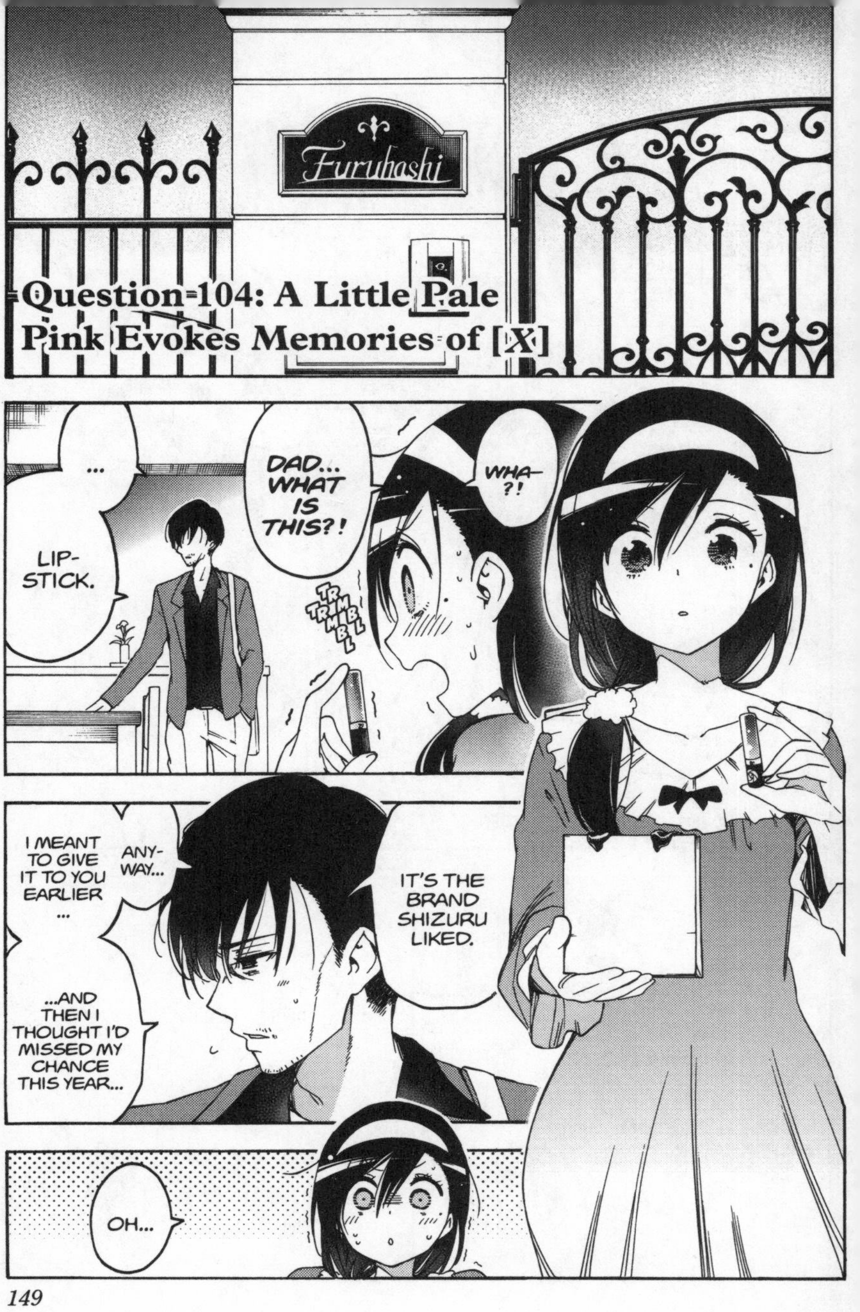
Furuhashi
WHA-?!
DAD... WHAT IS THIS?!
TRMBL TRMBL
...
LIP-STICK.
IT'S THE BRAND SHIZURU LIKED.
ANY-WAY...
I MEANT TO GIVE IT TO YOU EARLIER...
...AND THEN I THOUGHT I'D MISSED MY CHANCE THIS YEAR...
OH...

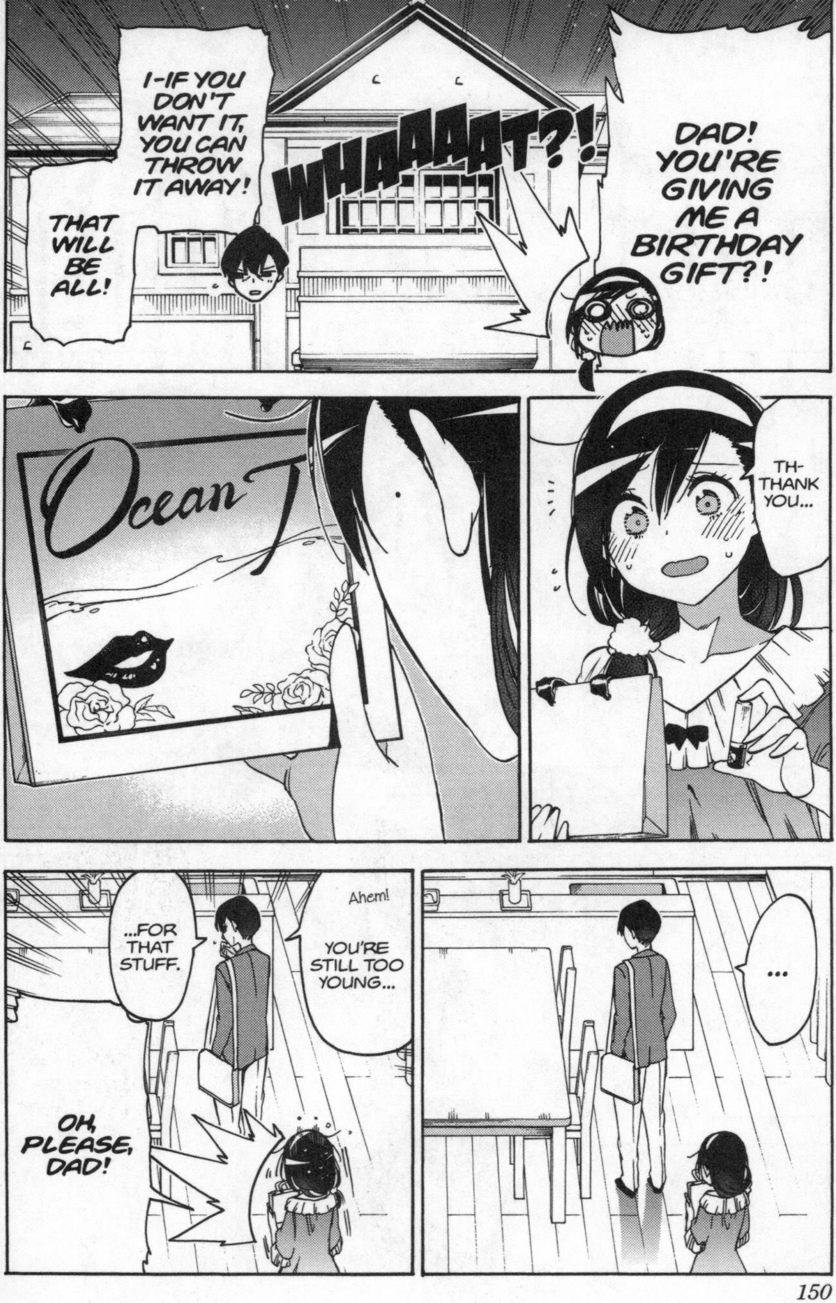
DAD! YOU'RE GIVING ME A BIRTHDAY GIFT?!
WHAAAAT?!
I-IF YOU DON'T WANT IT, YOU CAN THROW IT AWAY!
THAT WILL BE ALL!
TH- THANK YOU...
Ocean
...
Ahem!
YOU'RE STILL TOO YOUNG...
...FOR THAT STUFF.
OH, PLEASE, DAD!

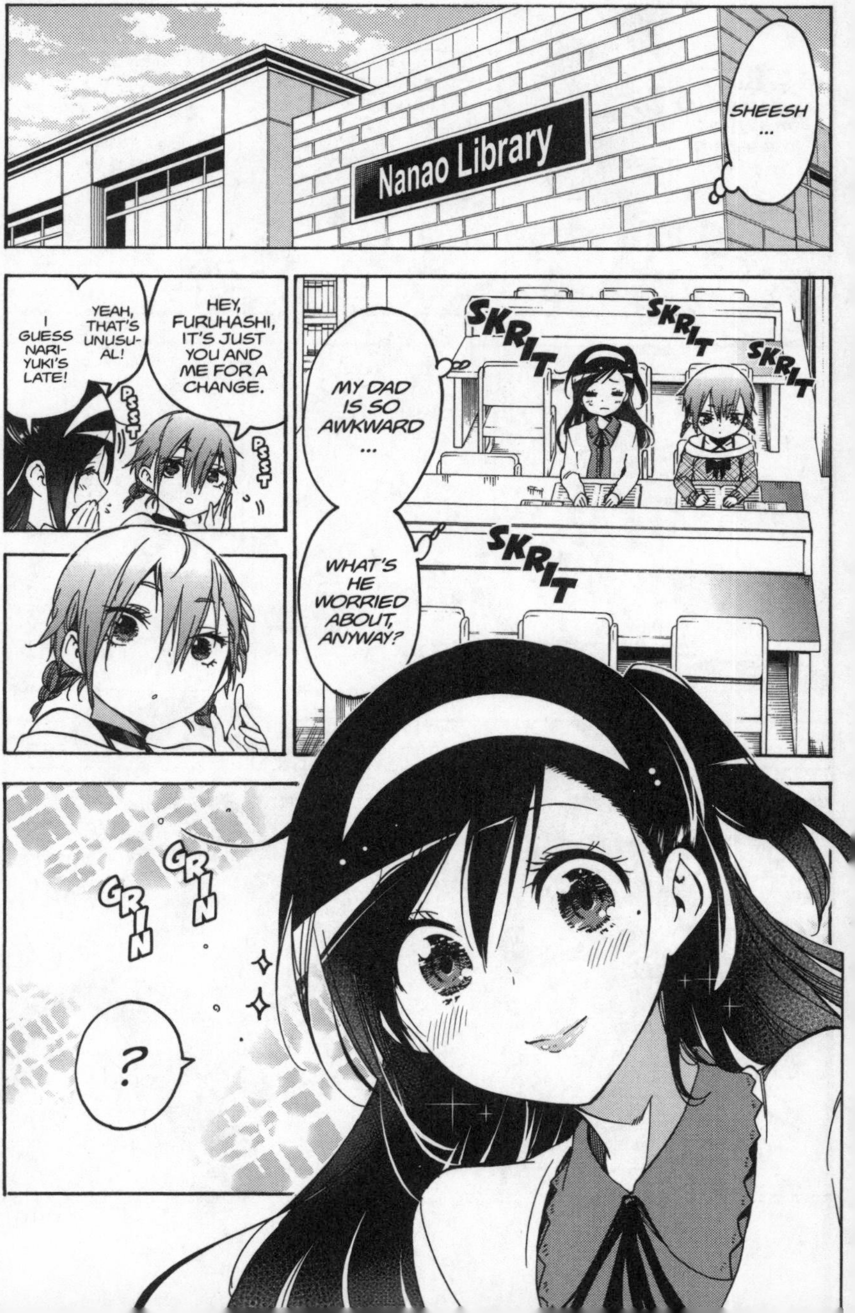
Nanao Library
SHEESH ...
SKRIT
SKRIT
SKRIT
SKRIT
MY DAD IS SO AWKWARD ...
WHAT'S HE WORRIED ABOUT, ANYWAY?
HEY, FURUHASHI, IT'S JUST YOU AND ME FOR A CHANGE.
PSST
YEAH, THAT'S UNUSU-AL!
I GUESS NARI-YUKI'S LATE!
PSST
GRIN
GRIN
?

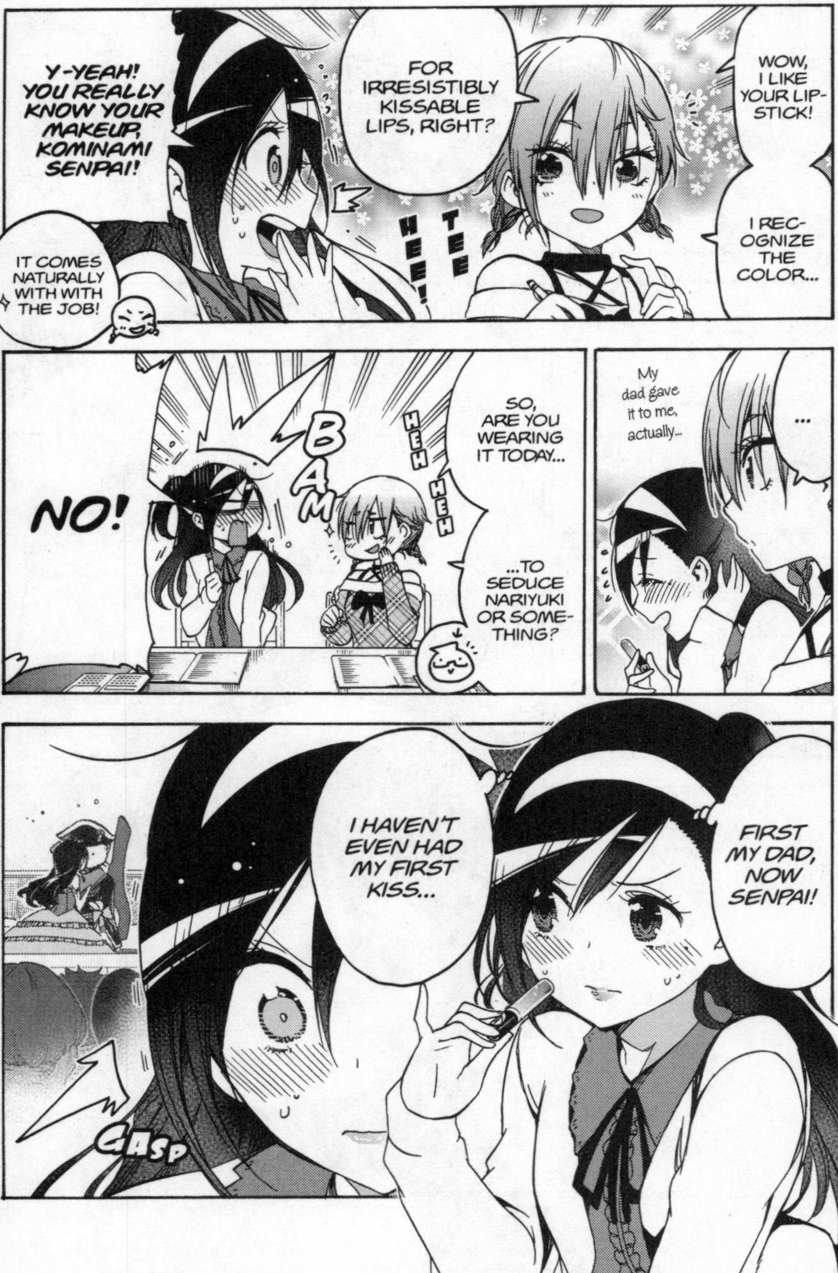
WOW, I LIKE YOUR LIP-STICK!
I REC-OGNIZE THE COLOR...
FOR IRRESISTIBLY KISSABLE LIPS, RIGHT?
TEE HEE!
Y-YEAH! YOU REALLY KNOW YOUR MAKEUP, KOMINAMI SENPAI!
IT COMES NATURALLY WITH WITH THE JOB!
My dad gave it to me, actually...
...
SO, ARE YOU WEARING IT TODAY...
...TO SEDUCE NARIYUKI OR SOME-THING?
HEH HEH
BAM
NO!
FIRST MY DAD, NOW SENPAI!
I HAVEN'T EVEN HAD MY FIRST KISS...
GASP

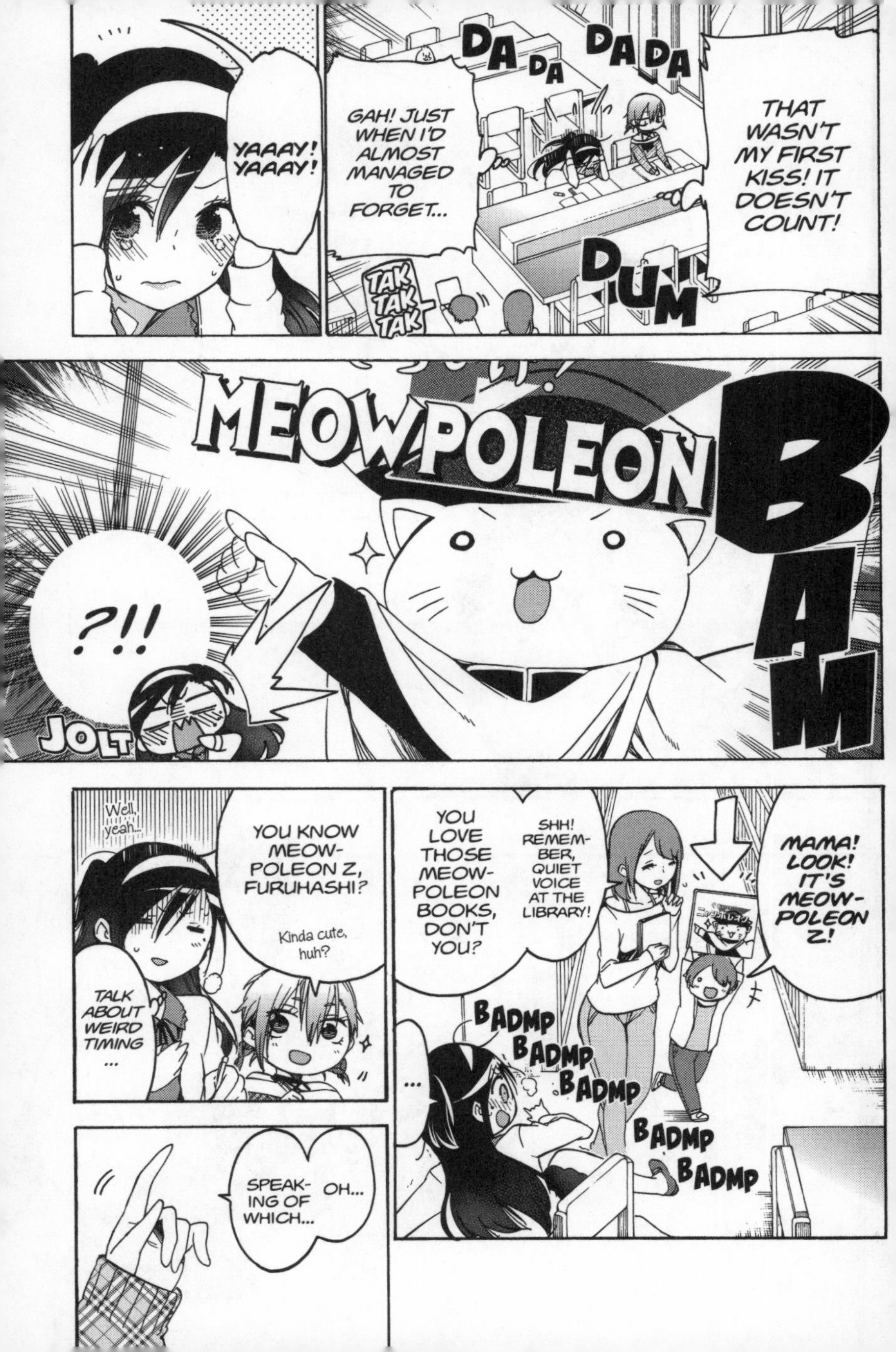
THAT WASN'T MY FIRST KISS! IT DOESN'T COUNT!
DA DA DA DA
GAH! JUST WHEN I'D ALMOST MANAGED TO FORGET...
DUM
TAK TAK TAK
YAAAY! YAAAY!
MEOWPOLEON
BAM
?!!
JOLT
MAMA! LOOK! IT'S MEOW-POLEON Z!
SHH! REMEM-BER, QUIET VOICE AT THE LIBRARY!
YOU LOVE THOSE MEOW-POLEON BOOKS, DON'T YOU?
BADMP BADMP BADMP
BADMP BADMP
...
YOU KNOW MEOW-POLEON Z, FURUHASHI?
Well, yeah...
Kinda cute, huh?
TALK ABOUT WEIRD TIMING...
OH...
SPEAK-ING OF WHICH...

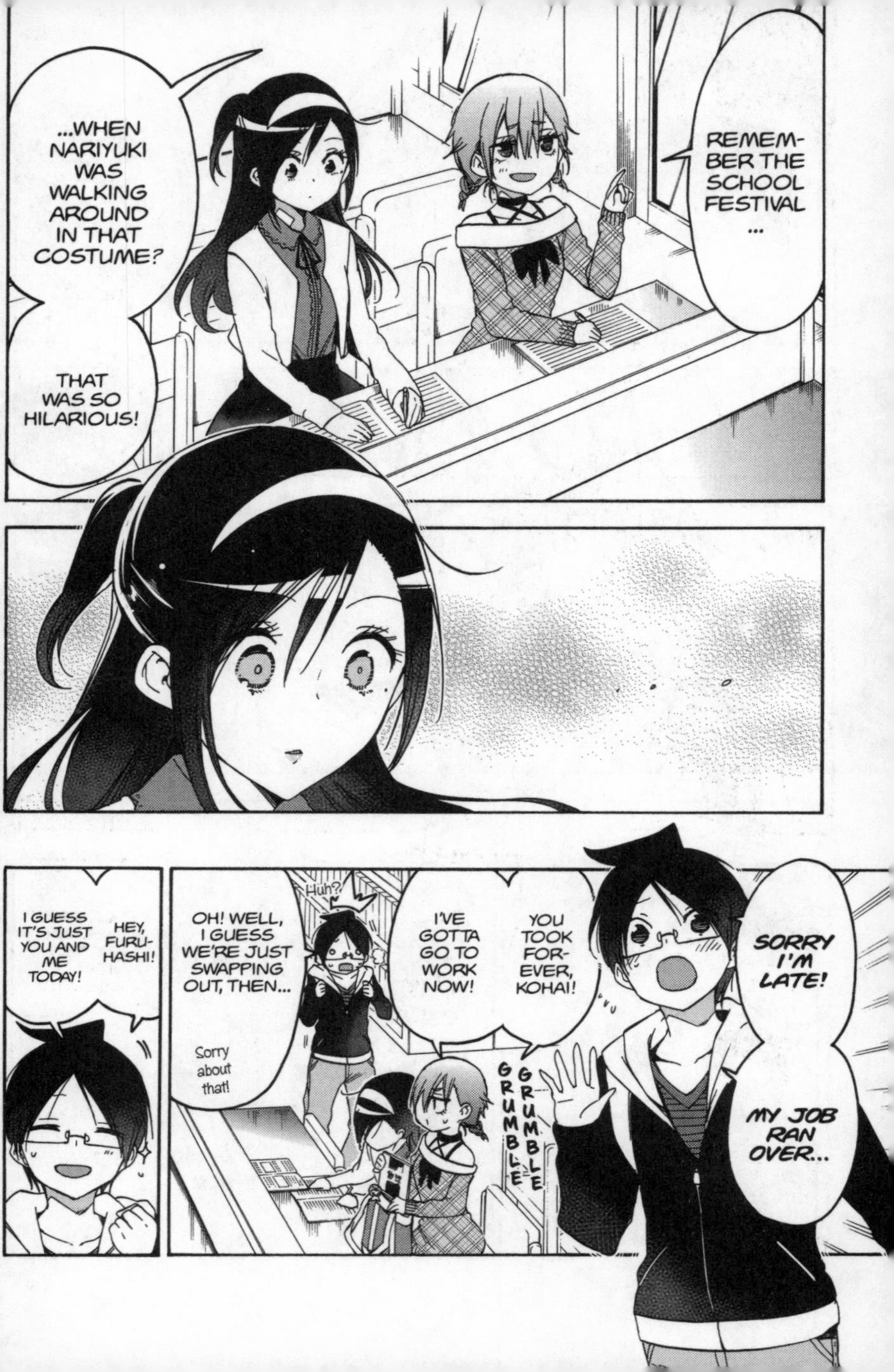
REMEM-
BER THE
SCHOOL
FESTIVAL
...
...WHEN
NARIYUKI
WAS
WALKING
AROUND
IN THAT
COSTUME?
THAT
WAS SO
HILARIOUS!
SORRY
I'M
LATE!
MY JOB
RAN
OVER...
YOU
TOOK
FOR-
EVER,
KOHAI!
I'VE
GOTTA
GO TO
WORK
NOW!
GRUMBLE
GRUMBLE
Huh?
OH! WELL,
I GUESS
WE'RE JUST
SWAPPING
OUT, THEN...
Sorry
about
that!
HEY,
FURU-
HASHI!
I GUESS
IT'S JUST
YOU AND
ME
TODAY!

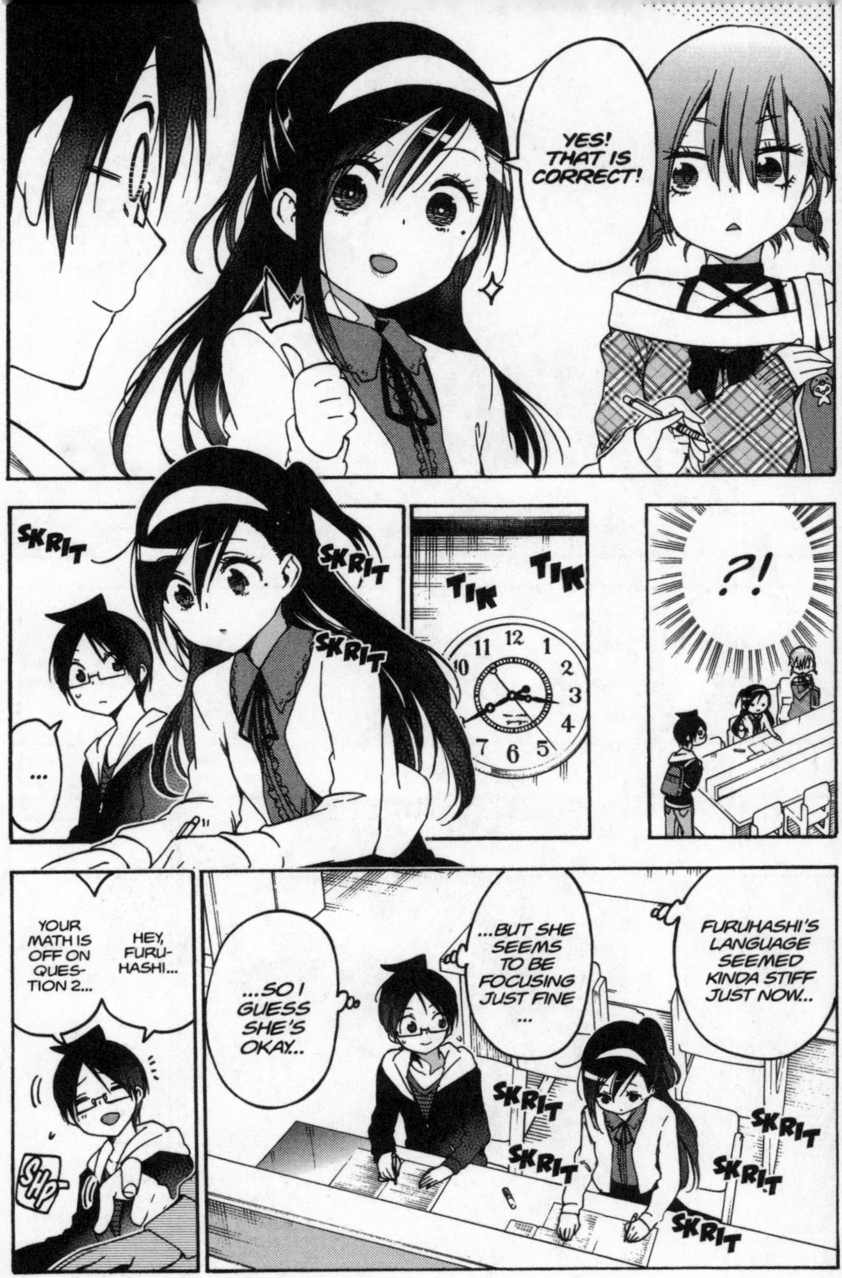
YES! THAT IS CORRECT!
?!
TIK
TIK
SKRIT
SKRIT
SKRIT
...
FURUHASHI'S LANGUAGE SEEMED KINDA STIFF JUST NOW...
...BUT SHE SEEMS TO BE FOCUSING JUST FINE ...
...SO I GUESS SHE'S OKAY...
SKRIT
SKRIT
SKRIT
SKRIT
SKRIT
HEY, FURU-HASHI...
YOUR MATH IS OFF ON QUES-TION 2...
SHP

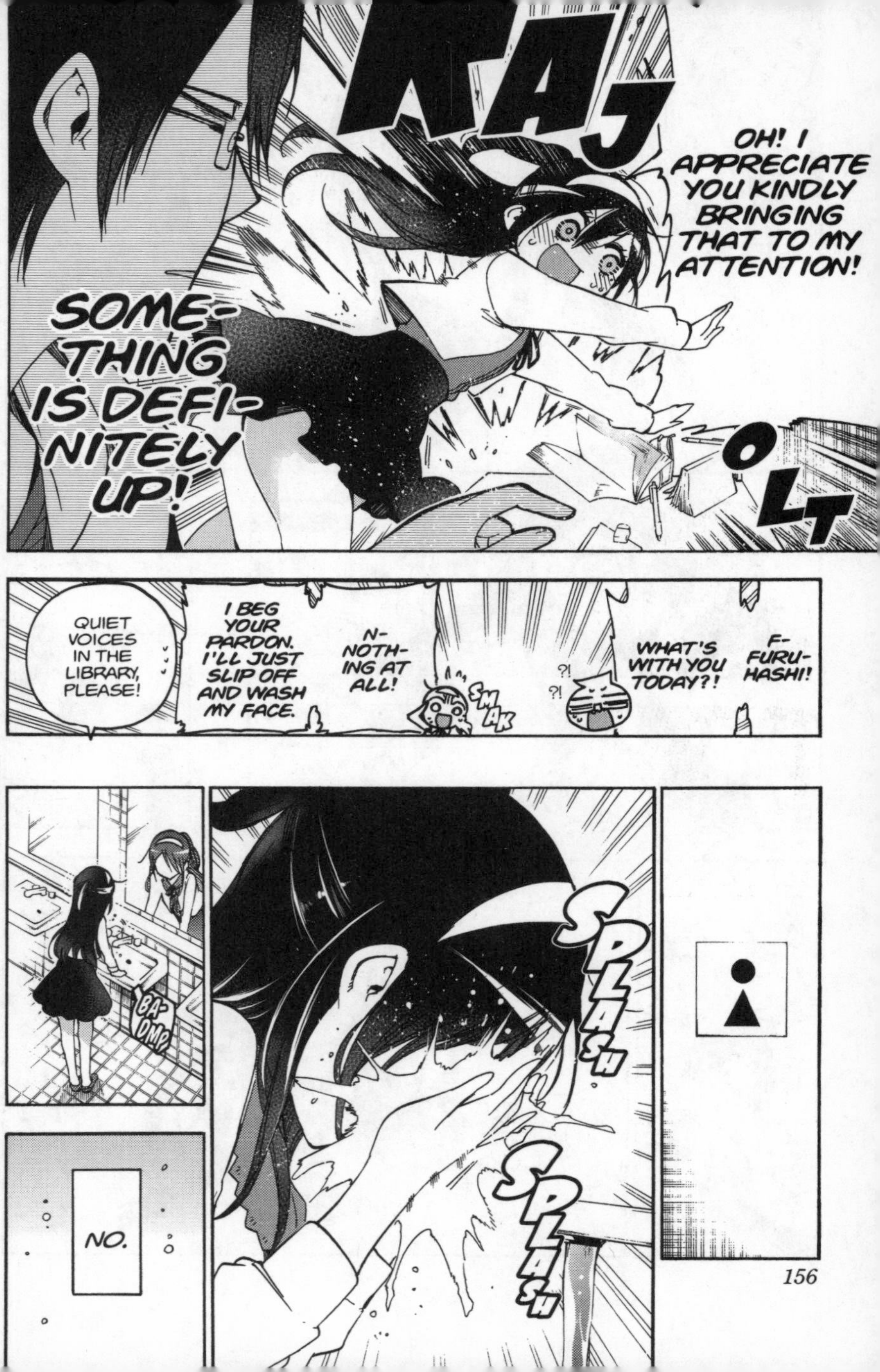
KAJ
OH! I APPRECIATE YOU KINDLY BRINGING THAT TO MY ATTENTION!
SOME-THING IS DEFI-NITELY UP!
OLT
F-FURU-HASHI!
WHAT'S WITH YOU TODAY?!
?! ?!
N-NOTHING AT ALL!
SMAK
I BEG YOUR PARDON. I'LL JUST SLIP OFF AND WASH MY FACE.
QUIET VOICES IN THE LIBRARY, PLEASE!
SPLASH
SPLASH
BA-DMP
NO.

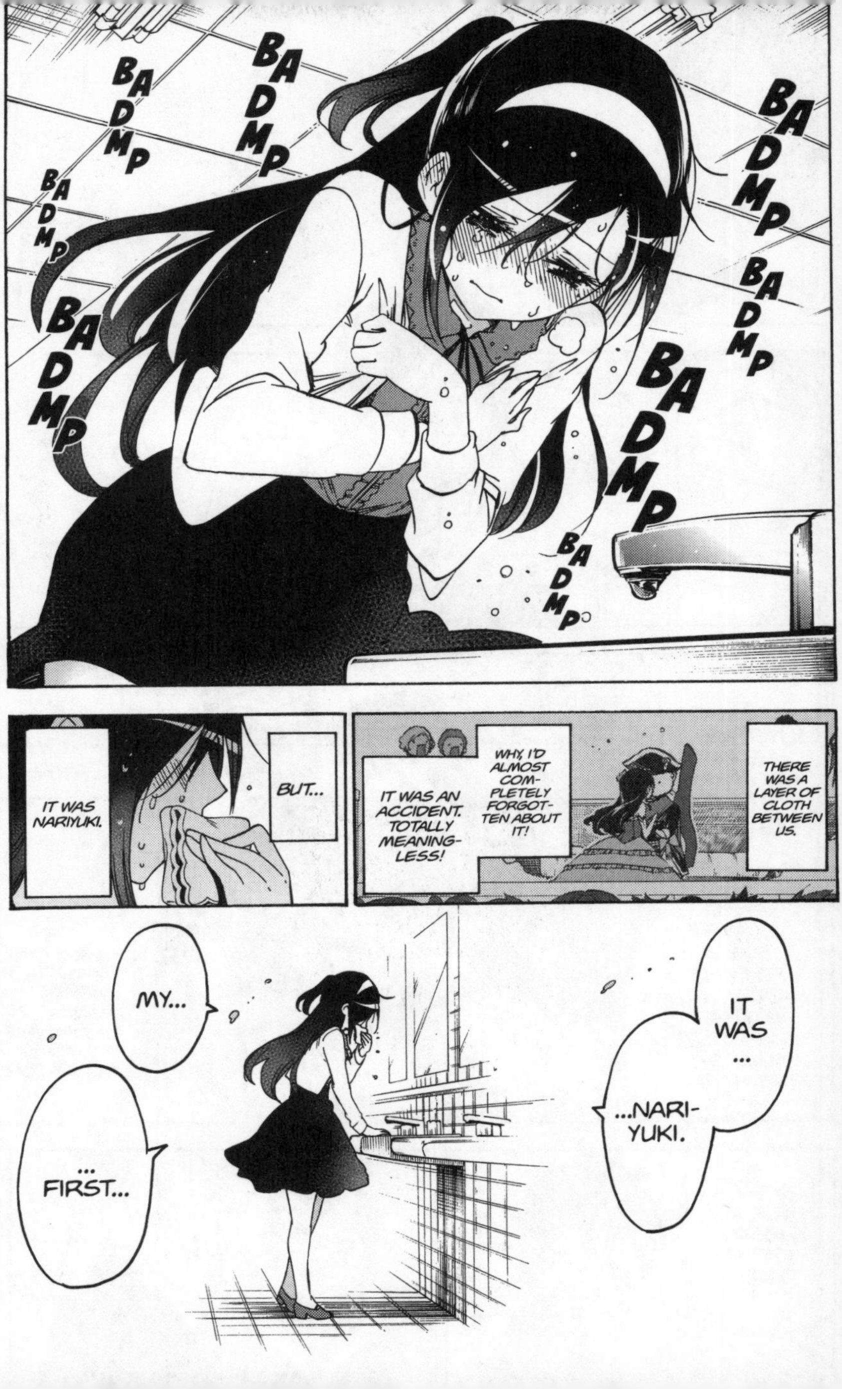
BADMP
BADMP
BADMP
BADMP
BADMP
BADMP
BADMP
BADMP
THERE WAS A LAYER OF CLOTH BETWEEN US.
WHY, I'D ALMOST COMPLETELY FORGOTTEN ABOUT IT!
IT WAS AN ACCIDENT. TOTALLY MEANINGLESS!
BUT...
IT WAS NARIYUKI.
IT WAS ...
...NARI-YUKI.
MY...
... FIRST...

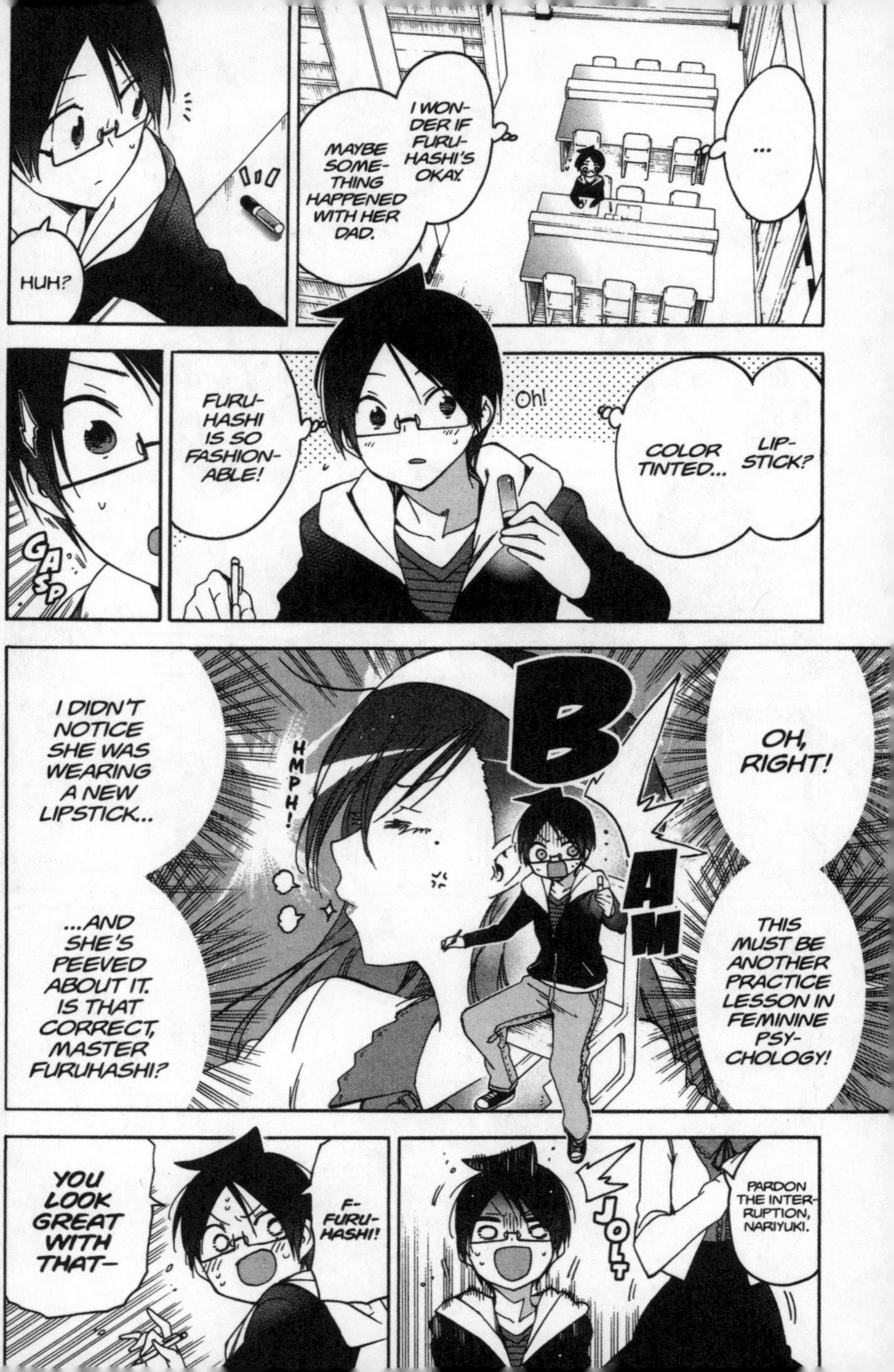
...
I WONDER IF FURUHASHI'S OKAY.
MAYBE SOMETHING HAPPENED WITH HER DAD.
HUH?
COLOR TINTED... LIPSTICK?
Oh!
FURUHASHI IS SO FASHIONABLE!
GASP
OH, RIGHT!
THIS MUST BE ANOTHER PRACTICE LESSON IN FEMININE PSYCHOLOGY!
BAM
HMPH!
I DIDN'T NOTICE SHE WAS WEARING A NEW LIPSTICK...
...AND SHE'S PEEVED ABOUT IT. IS THAT CORRECT, MASTER FURUHASHI?
PARDON THE INTERRUPTION, NARIYUKI.
JOLT
F-FURUHASHI!
YOU LOOK GREAT WITH THAT–

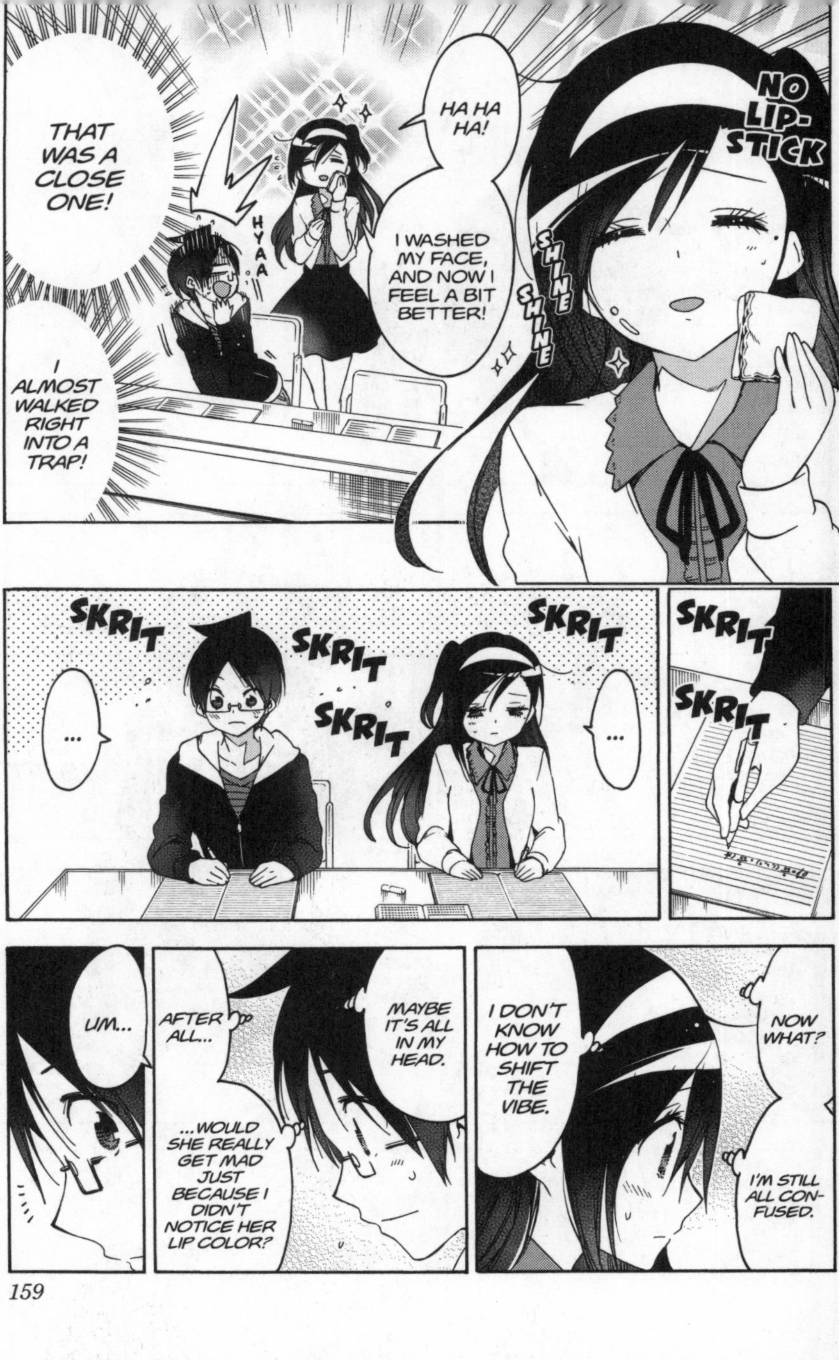
NO LIP-STICK
SHINE SHINE
HA HA HA!
I WASHED MY FACE, AND NOW I FEEL A BIT BETTER!
HYAA
THAT WAS A CLOSE ONE!
I ALMOST WALKED RIGHT INTO A TRAP!
SKRIT
SKRIT
...
SKRIT
SKRIT
SKRIT
SKRIT
...
NOW WHAT?
I'M STILL ALL CON-FUSED.
I DON'T KNOW HOW TO SHIFT THE VIBE.
MAYBE IT'S ALL IN MY HEAD.
AFTER ALL...
...WOULD SHE REALLY GET MAD JUST BECAUSE I DIDN'T NOTICE HER LIP COLOR?
UM...

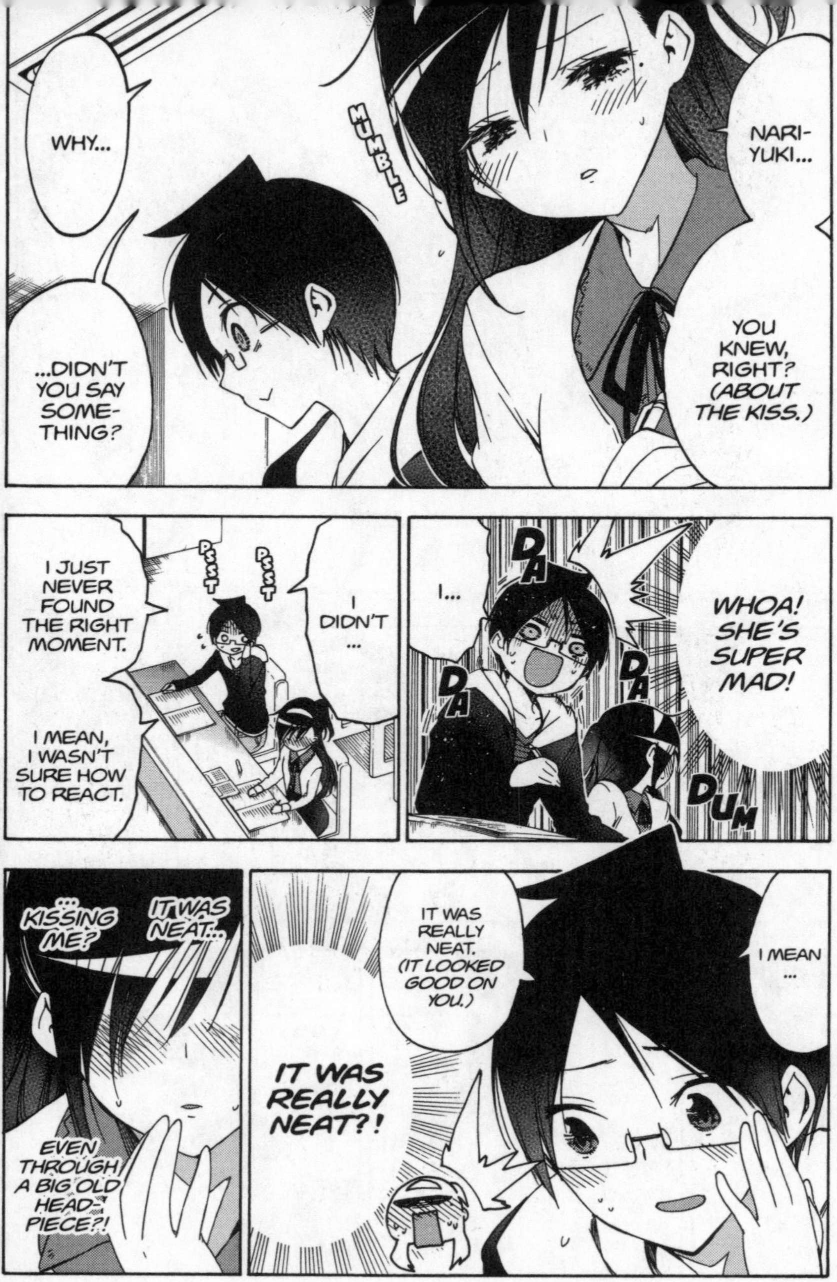
NARI-YUKI...
YOU KNEW, RIGHT? (ABOUT THE KISS.)
MUMBLE
WHY...
...DIDN'T YOU SAY SOME-THING?
WHOA! SHE'S SUPER MAD!
DA
DA
DA
DUM
I...
I DIDN'T ...
PSST
PSST
I JUST NEVER FOUND THE RIGHT MOMENT.
I MEAN, I WASN'T SURE HOW TO REACT.
I MEAN ...
IT WAS REALLY NEAT. (IT LOOKED GOOD ON YOU.)
IT WAS REALLY NEAT?!
IT WAS NEAT...
...KISSING ME?
EVEN THROUGH A BIG OLD HEAD-PIECE?!

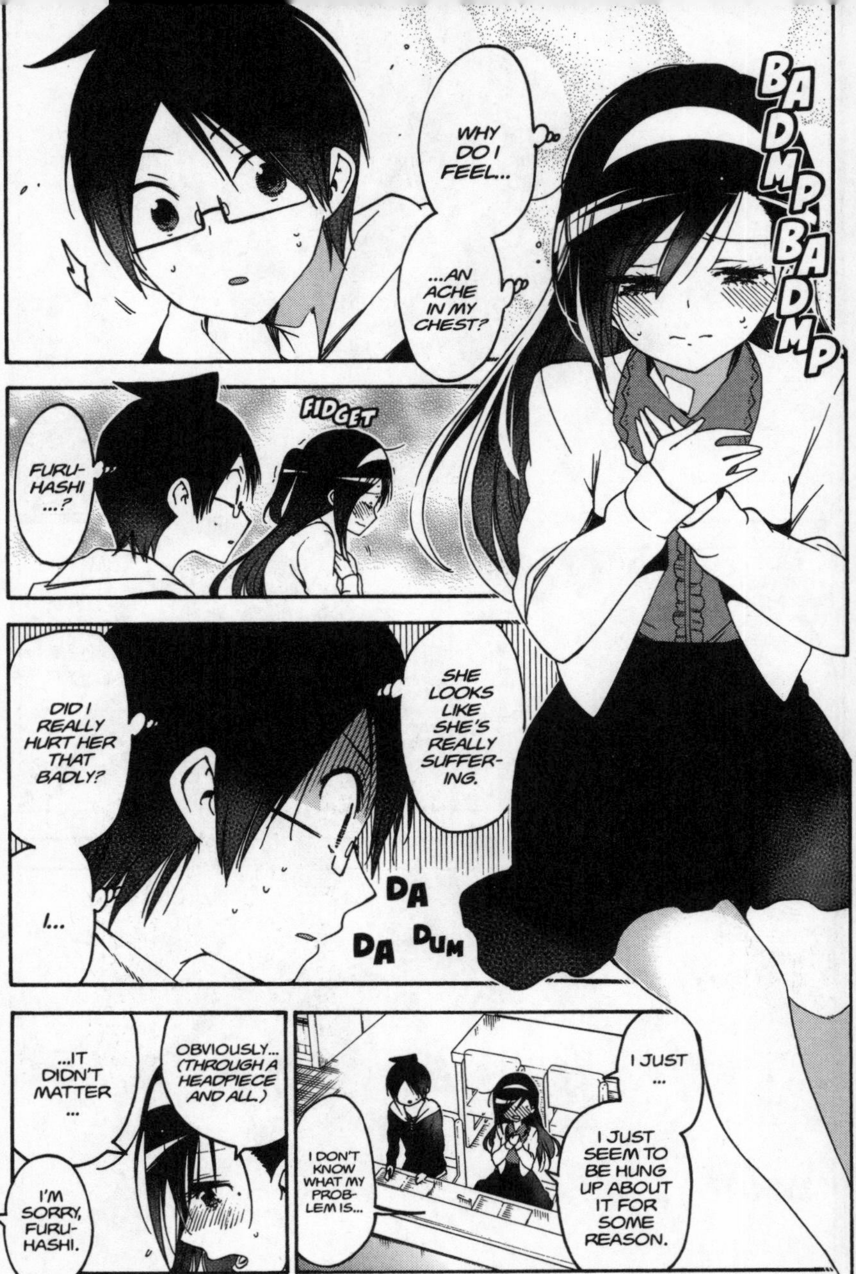
BADMP BADMP
WHY DO I FEEL...
...AN ACHE IN MY CHEST?
FIDGET
FURU-HASHI ...?
SHE LOOKS LIKE SHE'S REALLY SUFFER-ING.
DID I REALLY HURT HER THAT BADLY?
I...
DA DA DUM
I JUST ...
I JUST SEEM TO BE HUNG UP ABOUT IT FOR SOME REASON.
I DON'T KNOW WHAT MY PROB-LEM IS...
OBVIOUSLY... (THROUGH A HEADPIECE AND ALL.)
...IT DIDN'T MATTER ...
I'M SORRY, FURU-HASHI.

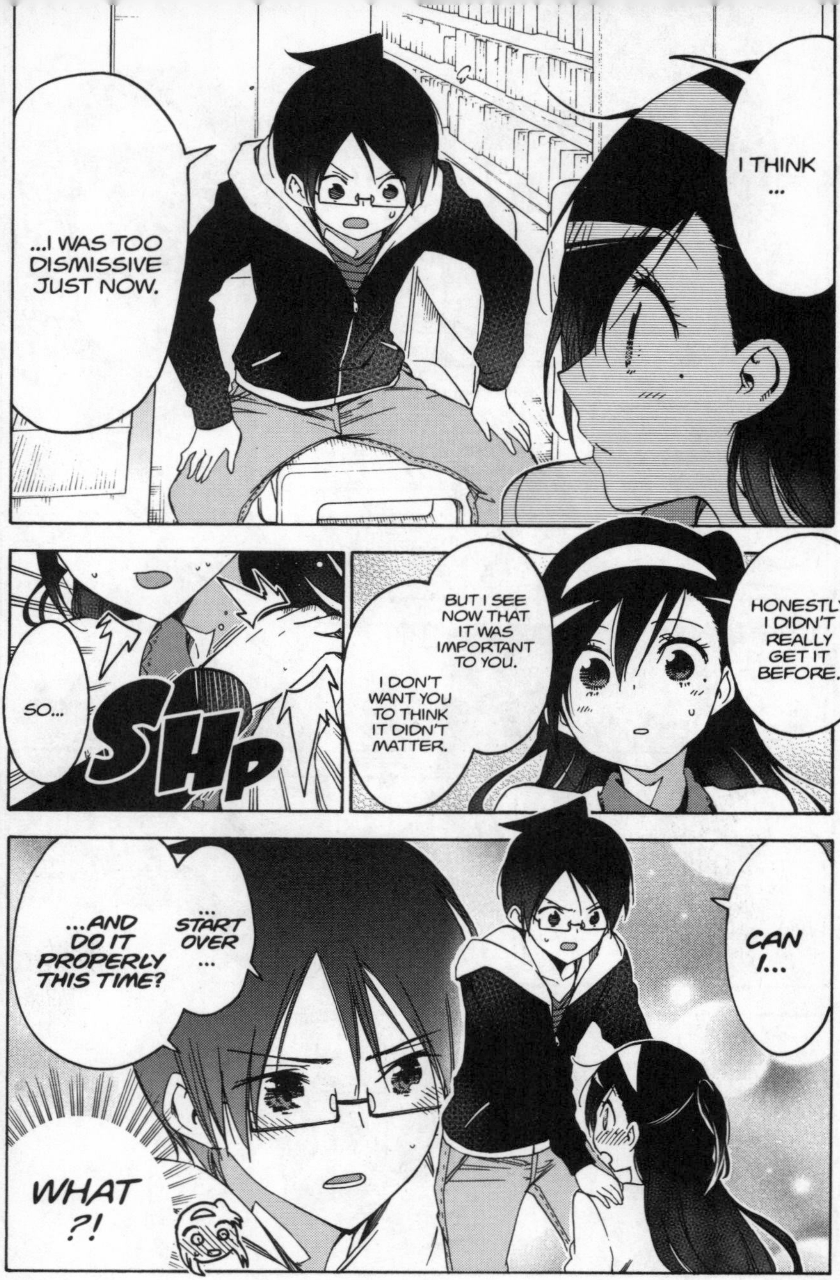
I THINK ...
...I WAS TOO DISMISSIVE JUST NOW.
HONESTLY, I DIDN'T REALLY GET IT BEFORE.
BUT I SEE NOW THAT IT WAS IMPORTANT TO YOU.
I DON'T WANT YOU TO THINK IT DIDN'T MATTER.
SO...
SHP
CAN I...
... START OVER ...
...AND DO IT PROPERLY THIS TIME?
WHAT ?!

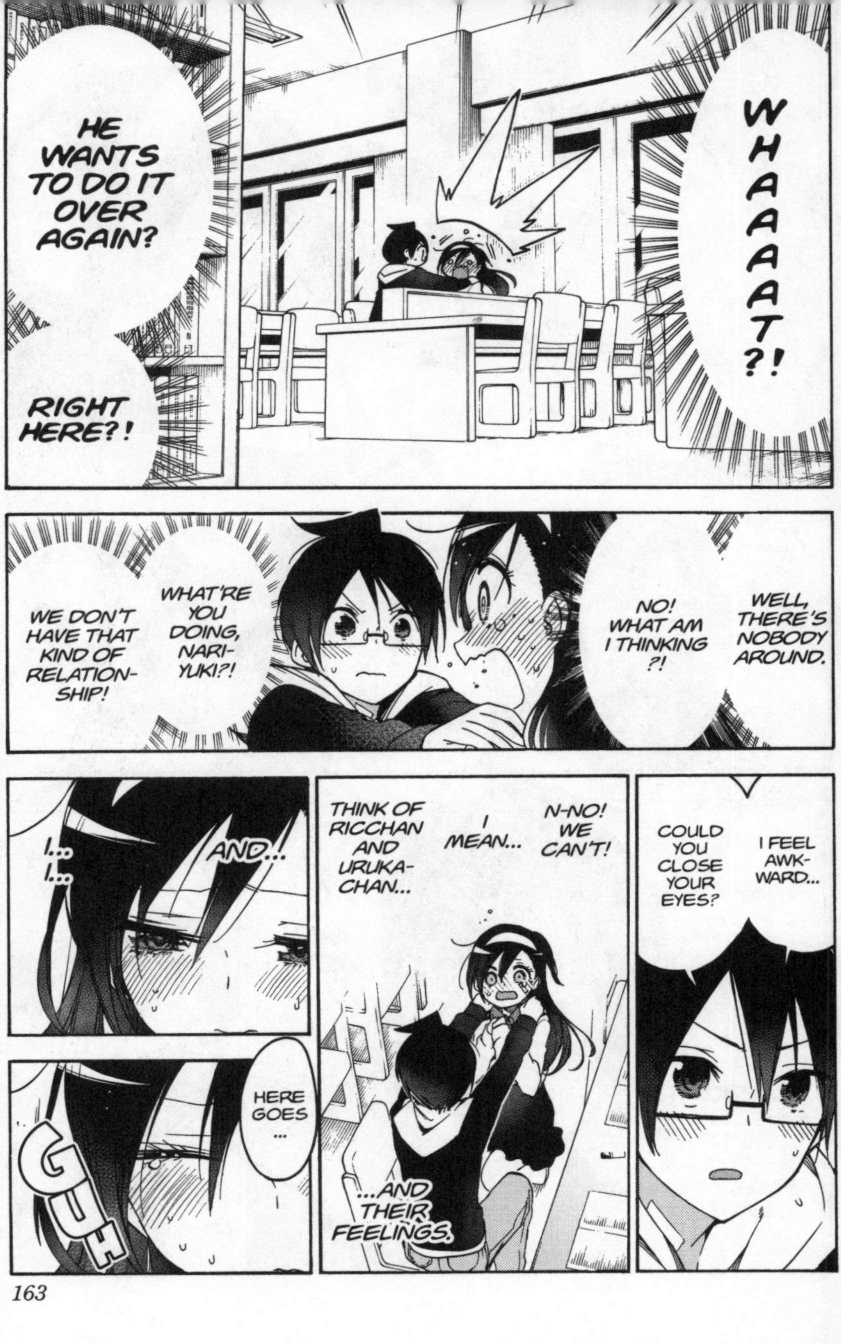
WHAAAAAT?!
HE WANTS TO DO IT OVER AGAIN?
RIGHT HERE?!
WELL, THERE'S NOBODY AROUND.
NO! WHAT AM I THINKING?!
WHAT'RE YOU DOING, NARI-YUKI?!
WE DON'T HAVE THAT KIND OF RELATION-SHIP!
I FEEL AWK-WARD...
COULD YOU CLOSE YOUR EYES?
N-NO! WE CAN'T!
I MEAN...
THINK OF RICCHAN AND URUKA-CHAN...
...AND THEIR FEELINGS.
AND...
I... I...
HERE GOES...
GUH

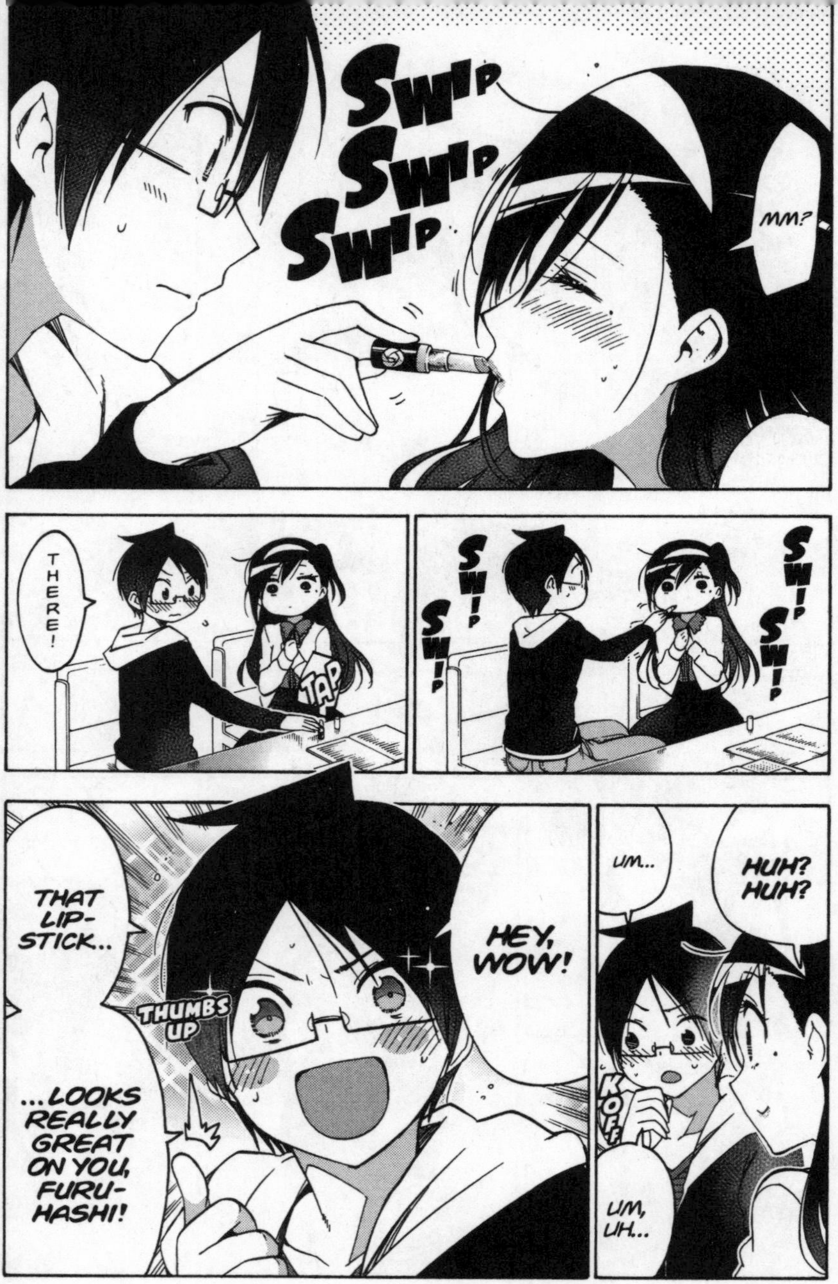
MM?
SWIP
SWIP
SWIP
SWIP
SWIP
SWIP
SWIP
THERE!
TAP
HUH? HUH?
UM...
KOFF
UM, UH...
HEY, WOW!
THAT LIP-STICK...
THUMBS UP
...LOOKS REALLY GREAT ON YOU, FURU-HASHI!

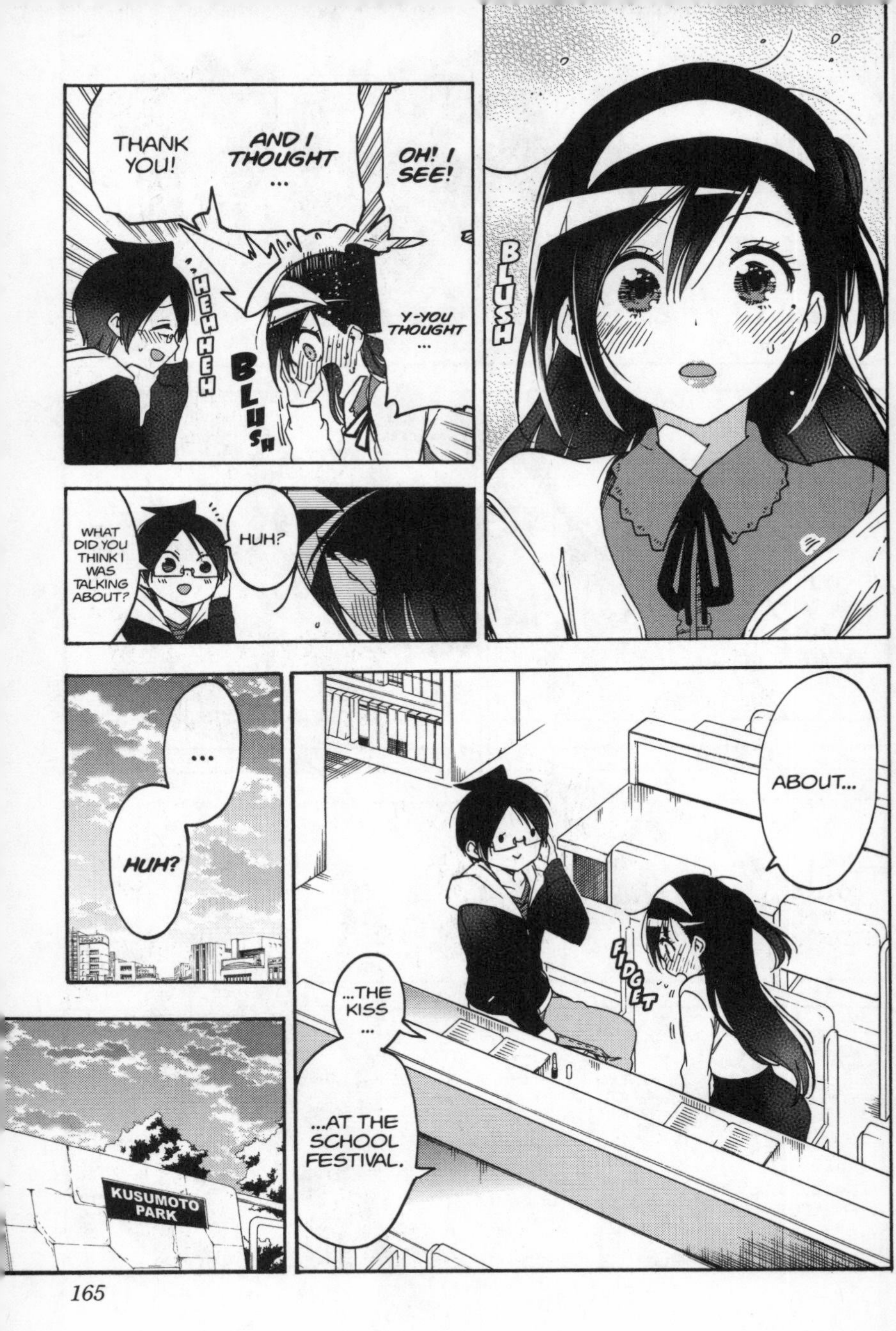
BLUSH
OH! I SEE!
AND I THOUGHT ...
THANK YOU!
Y-YOU THOUGHT ...
BLUSH
HEH HEH HEH
HUH?
WHAT DID YOU THINK I WAS TALKING ABOUT?
ABOUT...
FIDGET
...THE KISS ...
...AT THE SCHOOL FESTIVAL.
... HUH?
KUSUMOTO PARK

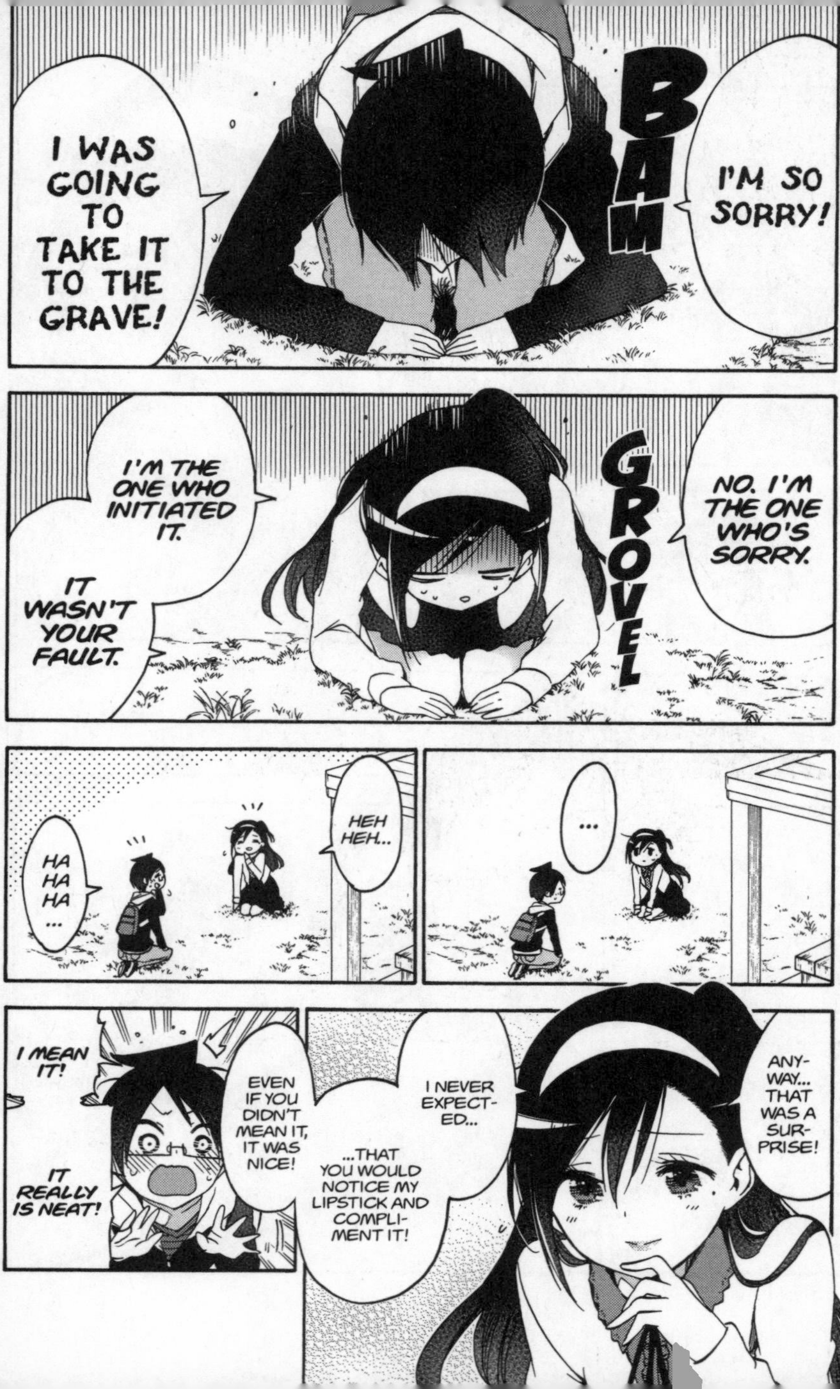
I'M SO SORRY!
BAM
I WAS GOING TO TAKE IT TO THE GRAVE!
NO. I'M THE ONE WHO'S SORRY.
GROVEL
I'M THE ONE WHO INITIATED IT.
IT WASN'T YOUR FAULT.
...
HEH HEH...
HA HA HA ...
ANY-WAY... THAT WAS A SUR-PRISE!
I NEVER EXPECT-ED...
...THAT YOU WOULD NOTICE MY LIPSTICK AND COMPLI-MENT IT!
EVEN IF YOU DIDN'T MEAN IT, IT WAS NICE!
I MEAN IT!
IT REALLY IS NEAT!

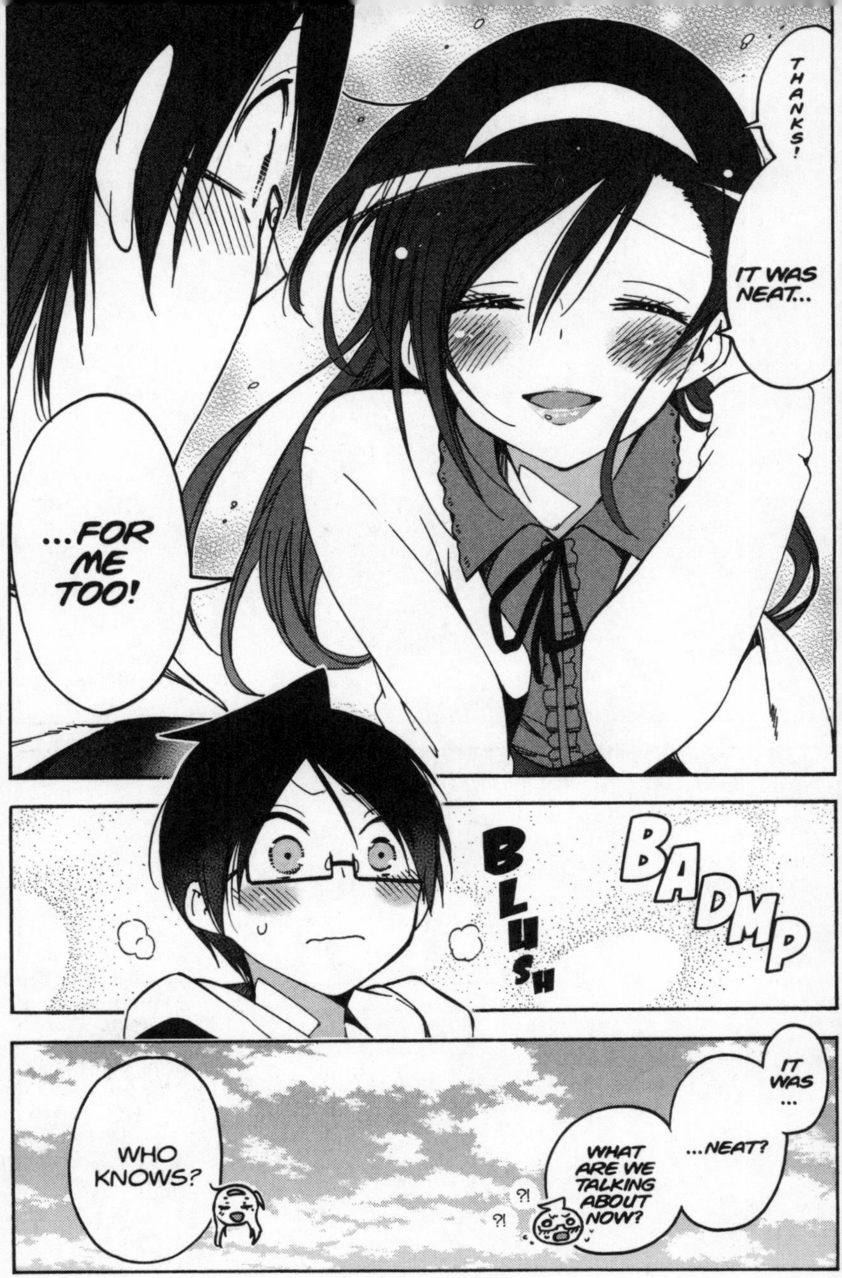
THANKS!
IT WAS NEAT...
...FOR ME TOO!
BADMP
BLUSH
IT WAS ...
...NEAT?
WHAT ARE WE TALKING ABOUT NOW?
?!
?!
WHO KNOWS?

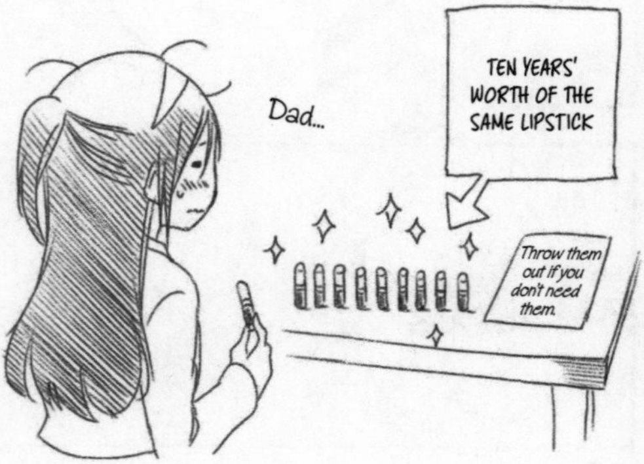
TEN YEARS' WORTH OF THE SAME LIPSTICK
Dad...
Throw them out if you don't need them.

Question 105. A Maiden's Invitation Inadvertently Reflects [*X*]

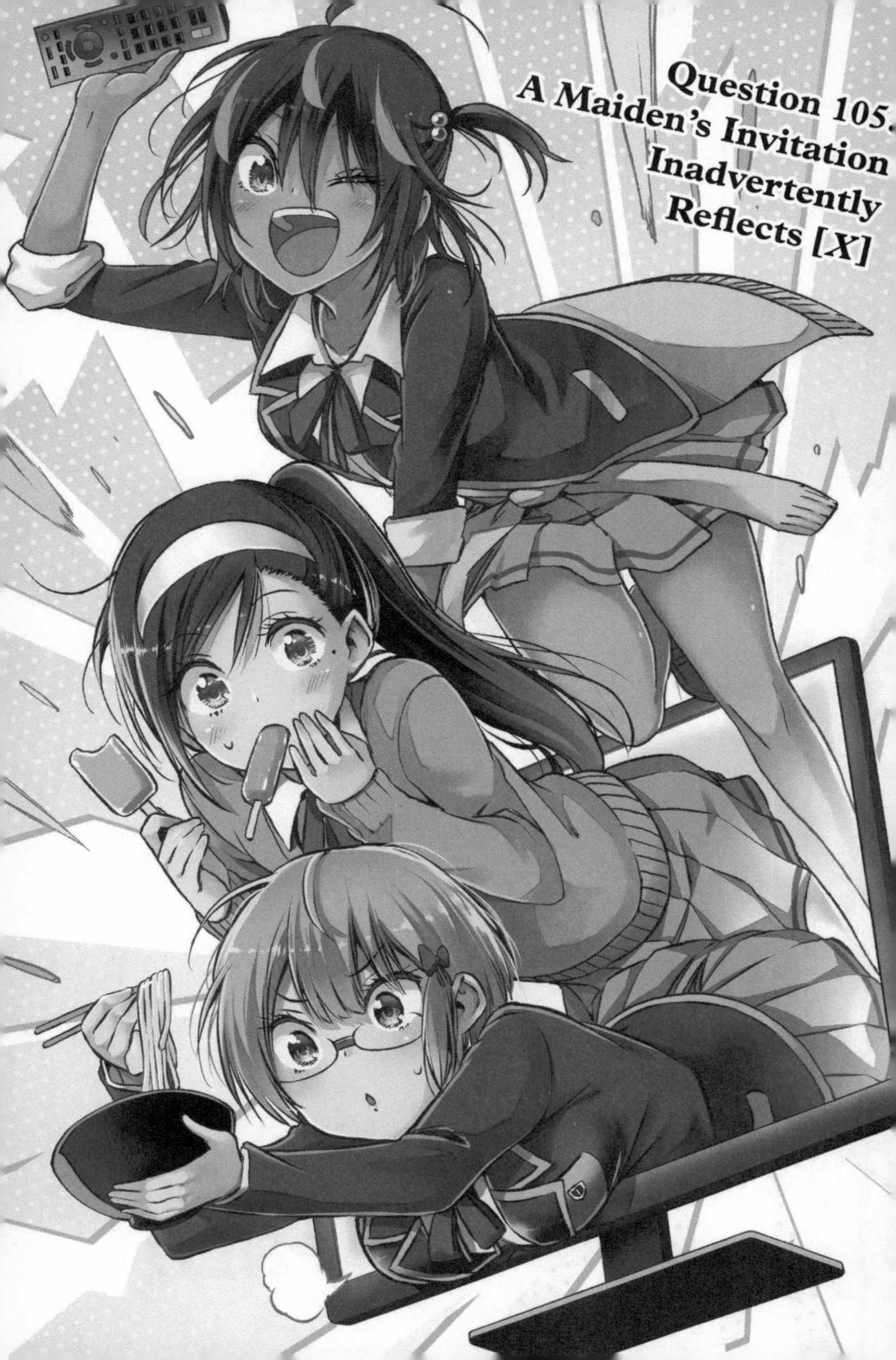

We Never Learn

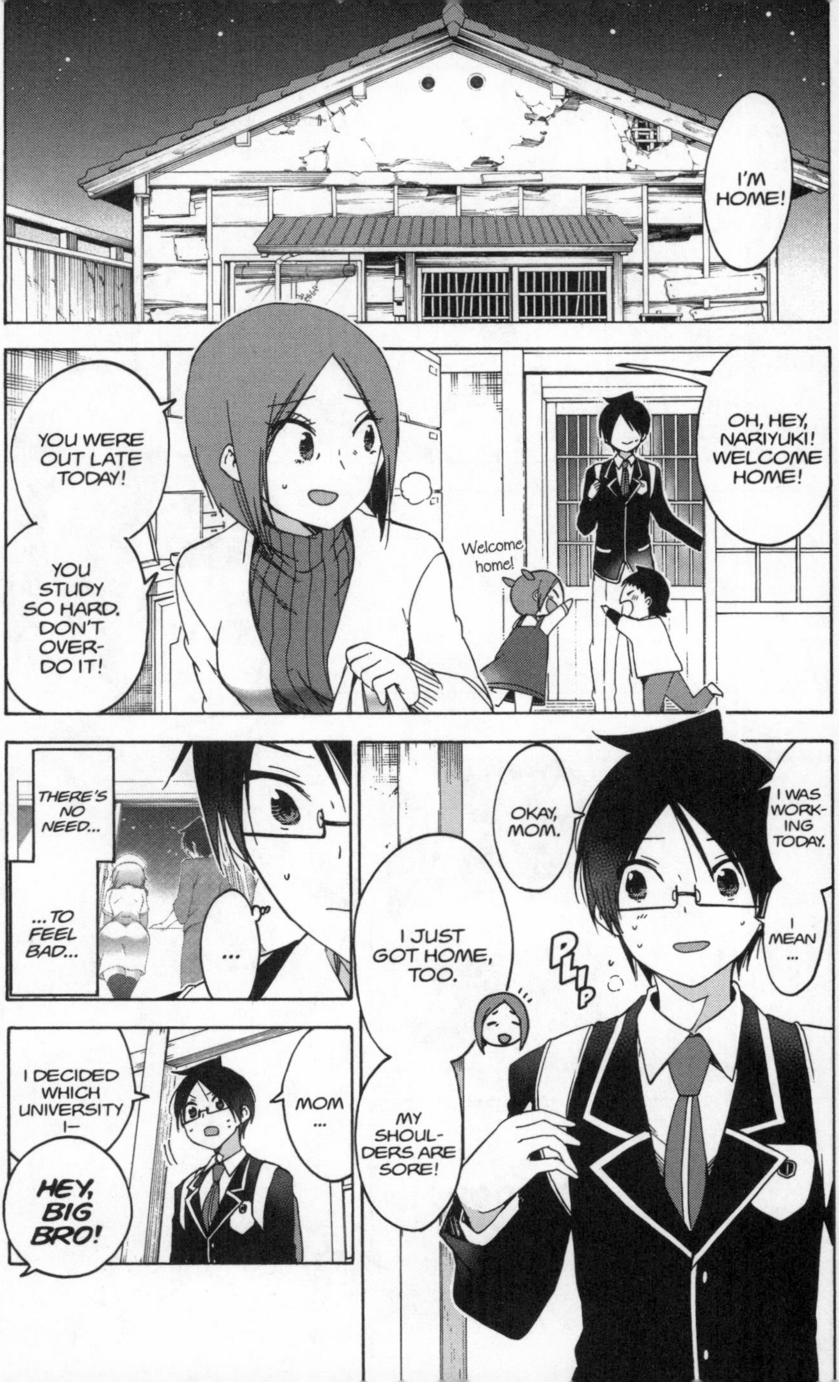
I'M HOME!
OH, HEY, NARIYUKI! WELCOME HOME!
Welcome home!
YOU WERE OUT LATE TODAY!
YOU STUDY SO HARD. DON'T OVER-DO IT!
I WAS WORKING TODAY.
OKAY, MOM.
I MEAN ...
PLIP
I JUST GOT HOME, TOO.
MY SHOUL-DERS ARE SORE!
THERE'S NO NEED...
...
...TO FEEL BAD...
MOM ...
I DECIDED WHICH UNIVERSITY I—
HEY, BIG BRO!

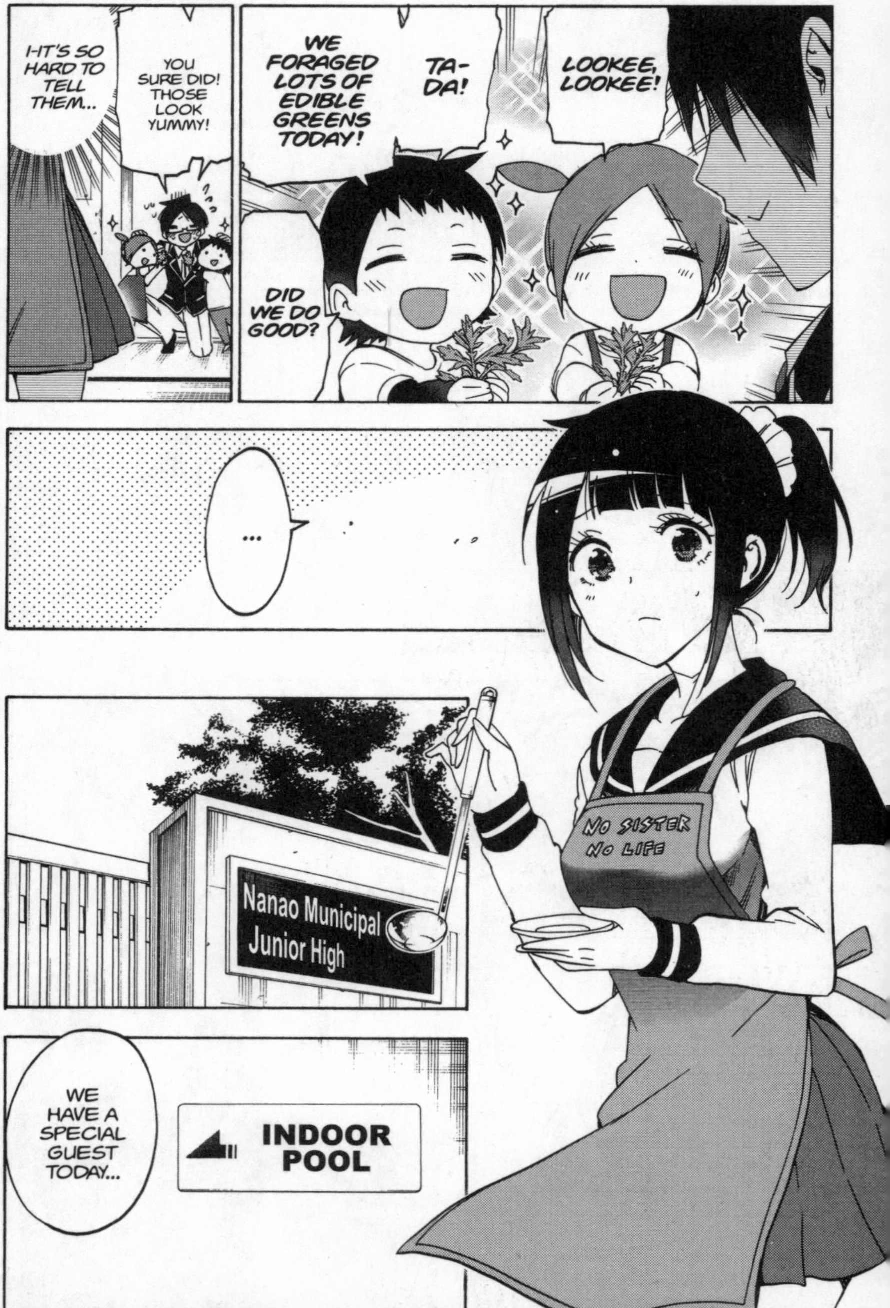
LOOKEE, LOOKEE!
TA-DA!
WE FORAGED LOTS OF EDIBLE GREENS TODAY!
DID WE DO GOOD?
YOU SURE DID! THOSE LOOK YUMMY!
I-IT'S SO HARD TO TELL THEM...
...
NO SISTER NO LIFE
Nanao Municipal Junior High
INDOOR POOL
WE HAVE A SPECIAL GUEST TODAY...

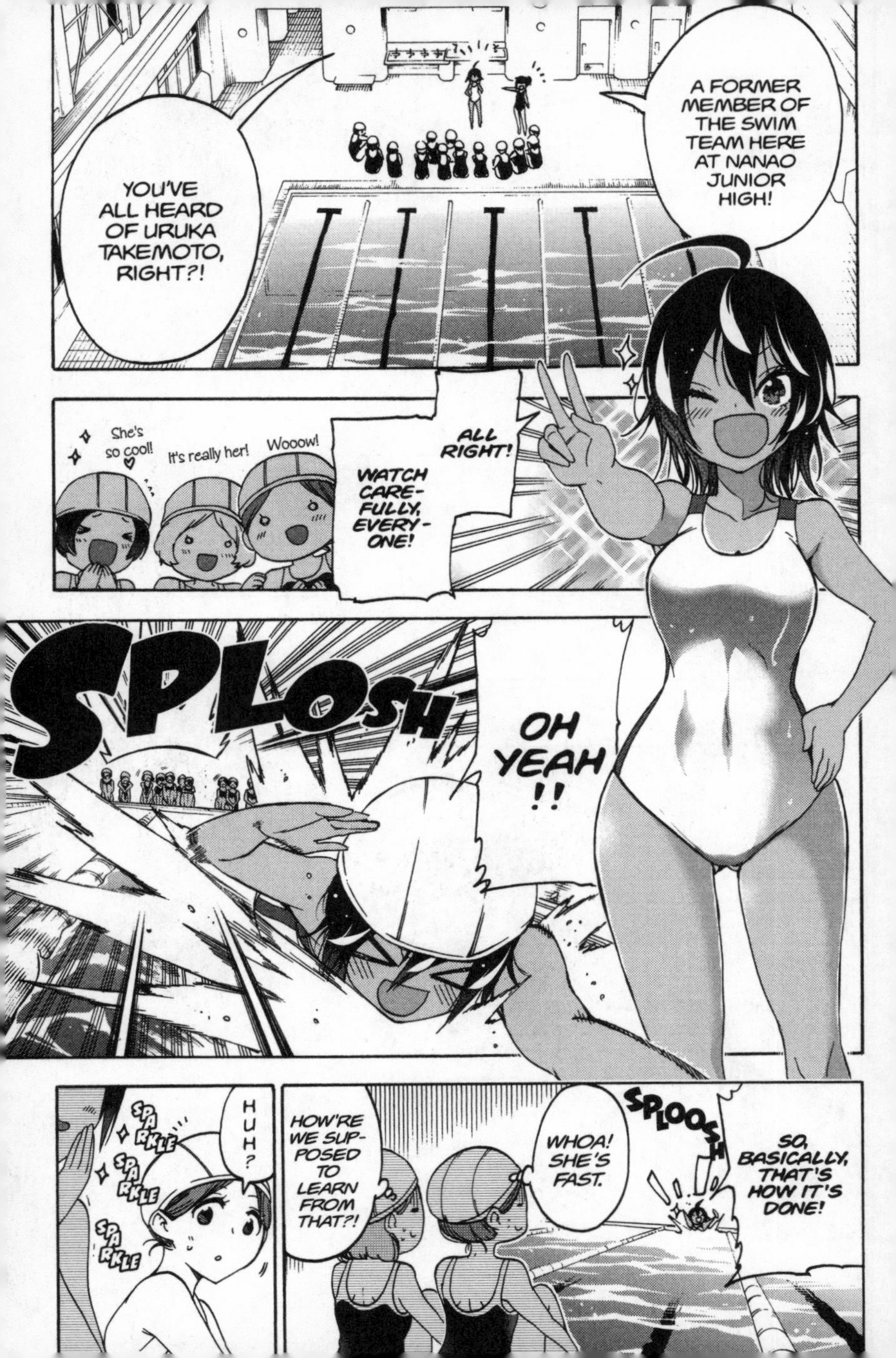
A FORMER MEMBER OF THE SWIM TEAM HERE AT NANAO JUNIOR HIGH!
YOU'VE ALL HEARD OF URUKA TAKEMOTO, RIGHT?!
ALL RIGHT!
WATCH CAREFULLY, EVERYONE!
Wooow!
It's really her!
She's so cool!
OH YEAH!!
SPLOSH
SO, BASICALLY, THAT'S HOW IT'S DONE!
SPLOOSH
WHOA! SHE'S FAST.
HOW'RE WE SUPPOSED TO LEARN FROM THAT?!
HUH?
SPARKLE
SPARKLE
SPARKLE

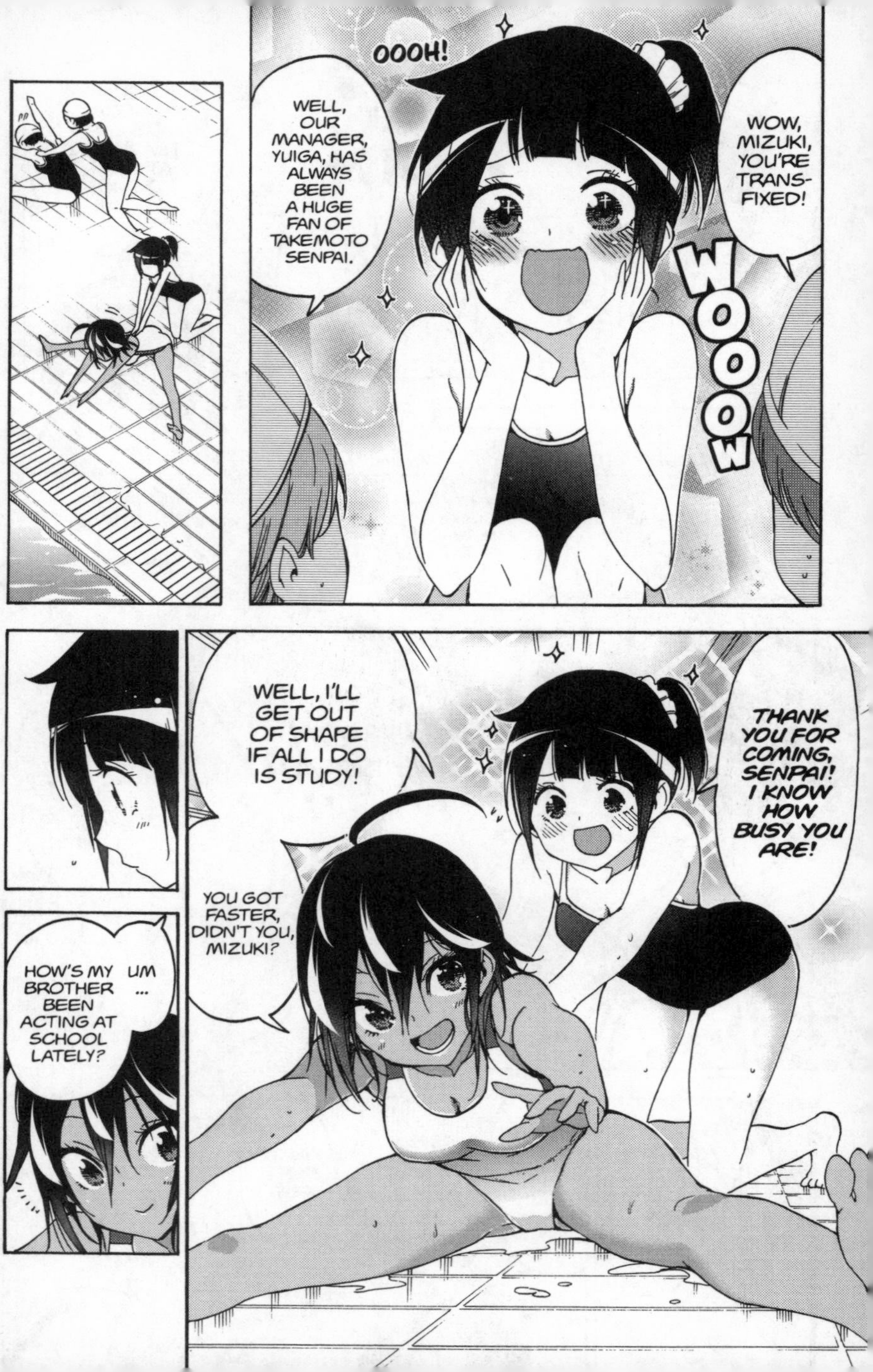
WOW, MIZUKI, YOU'RE TRANS-FIXED!
WOOOOW
OOOH!
WELL, OUR MANAGER, YUIGA, HAS ALWAYS BEEN A HUGE FAN OF TAKEMOTO SENPAI.
THANK YOU FOR COMING, SENPAI! I KNOW HOW BUSY YOU ARE!
WELL, I'LL GET OUT OF SHAPE IF ALL I DO IS STUDY!
YOU GOT FASTER, DIDN'T YOU, MIZUKI?
UM ...
HOW'S MY BROTHER BEEN ACTING AT SCHOOL LATELY?

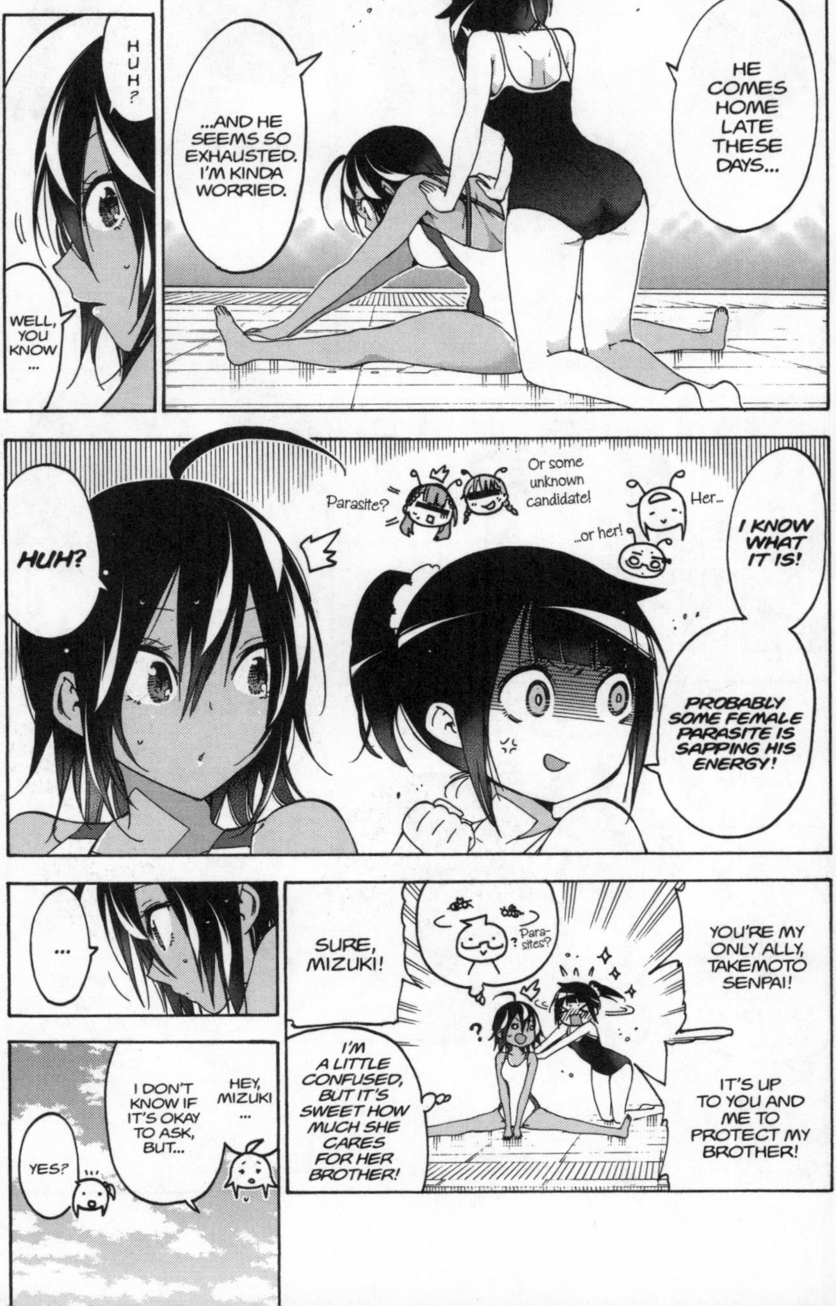
HE COMES HOME LATE THESE DAYS...
...AND HE SEEMS SO EXHAUSTED. I'M KINDA WORRIED.
HUH?
WELL, YOU KNOW ...
I KNOW WHAT IT IS!
Her...
...or her!
Or some unknown candidate!
Parasite?
PROBABLY SOME FEMALE PARASITE IS SAPPING HIS ENERGY!
HUH?
YOU'RE MY ONLY ALLY, TAKEMOTO SENPAI!
IT'S UP TO YOU AND ME TO PROTECT MY BROTHER!
SURE, MIZUKI!
Para-sites?
I'M A LITTLE CONFUSED, BUT IT'S SWEET HOW MUCH SHE CARES FOR HER BROTHER!
...
HEY, MIZUKI ...
I DON'T KNOW IF IT'S OKAY TO ASK, BUT...
YES?

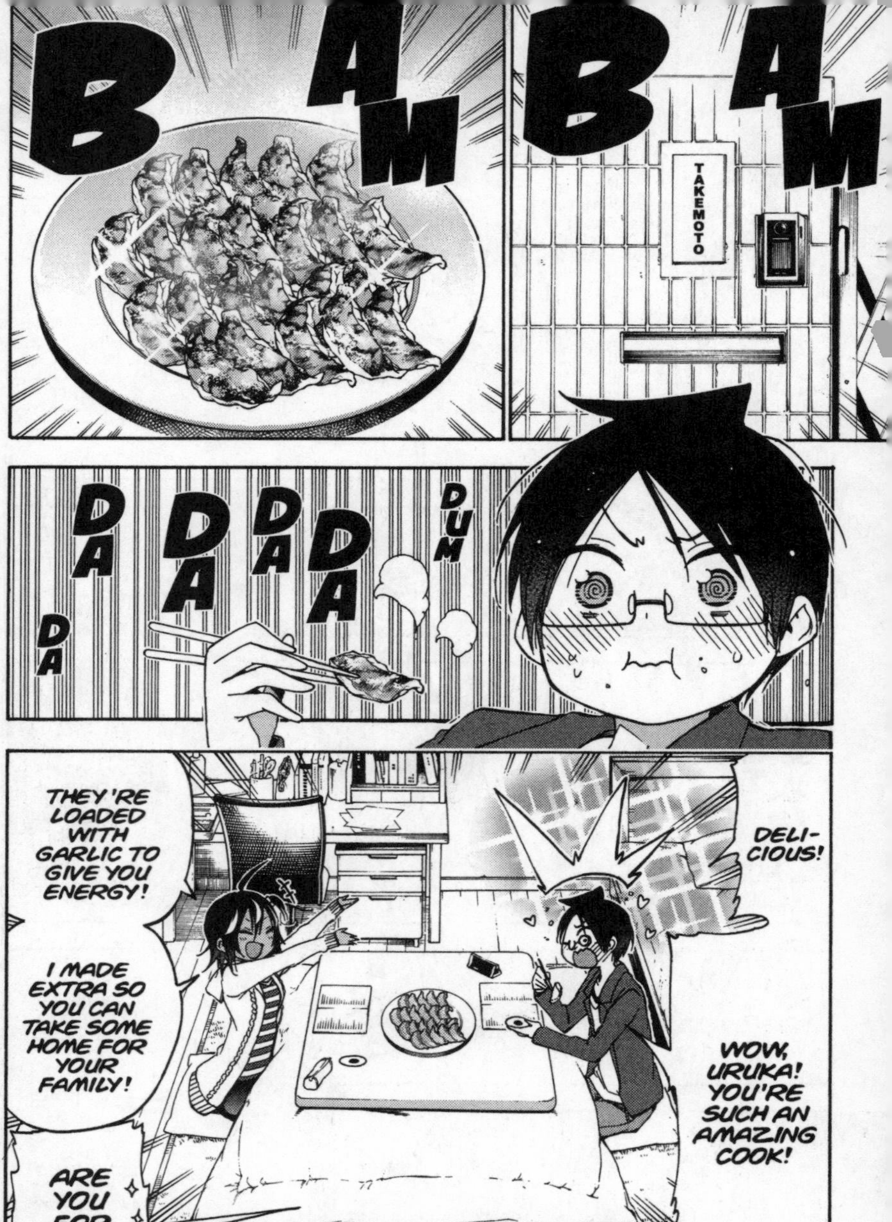
BAM
TAKEMOTO
BAM
DUM
DA DA DA DA DA
DELI-CIOUS!
WOW, URUKA! YOU'RE SUCH AN AMAZING COOK!
THEY'RE LOADED WITH GARLIC TO GIVE YOU ENERGY!
I MADE EXTRA SO YOU CAN TAKE SOME HOME FOR YOUR FAMILY!
ARE YOU FOR REAL?!

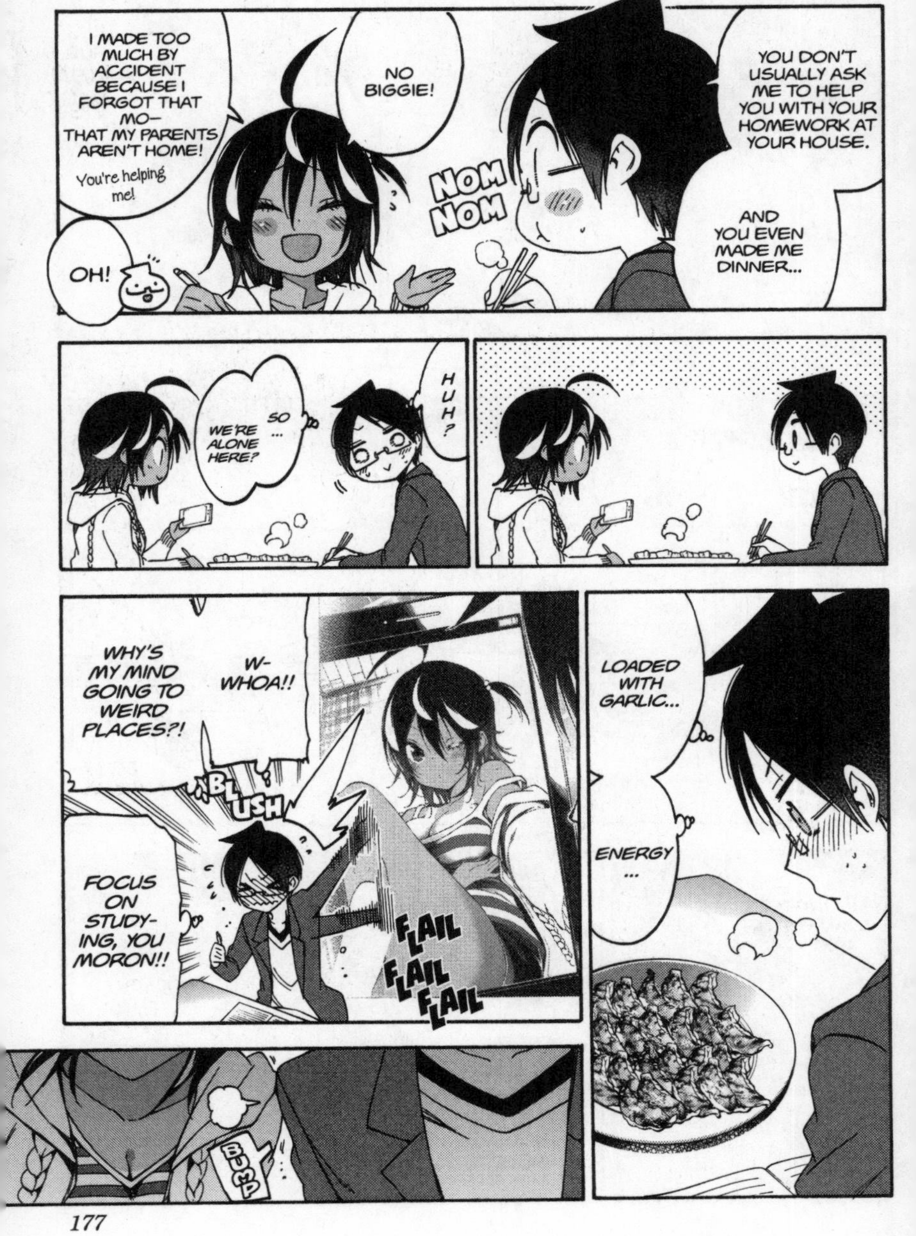
YOU DON'T USUALLY ASK ME TO HELP YOU WITH YOUR HOMEWORK AT YOUR HOUSE.
AND YOU EVEN MADE ME DINNER...
NOM NOM
NO BIGGIE!
I MADE TOO MUCH BY ACCIDENT BECAUSE I FORGOT THAT MO— THAT MY PARENTS AREN'T HOME!
You're helping me!
OH!
HUH?
SO ... WE'RE ALONE HERE?
LOADED WITH GARLIC...
ENERGY ...
W- WHOA!!
WHY'S MY MIND GOING TO WEIRD PLACES?!
BLUSH
FOCUS ON STUDY- ING, YOU MORON!!
FLAIL FLAIL FLAIL
BUMP

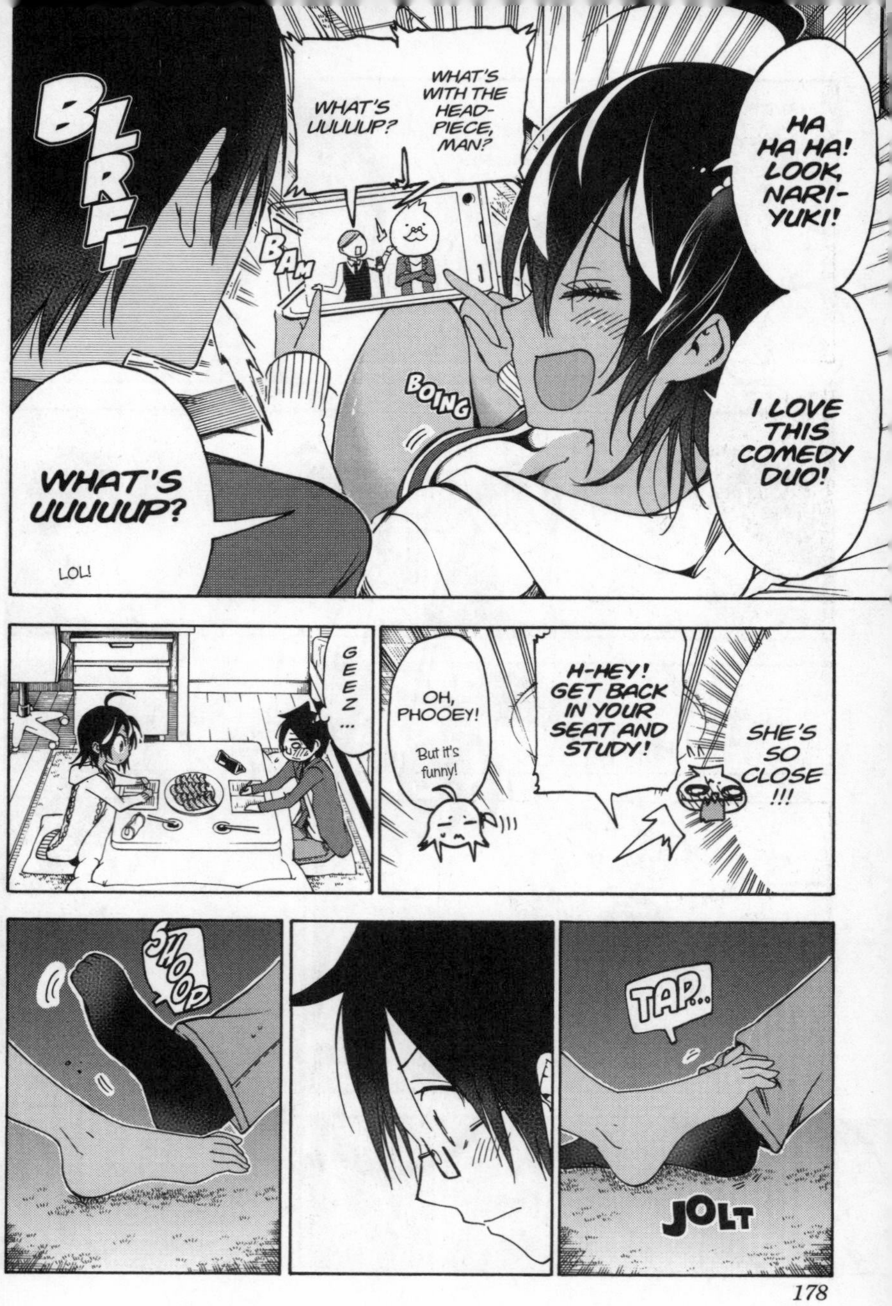
HA HA HA! LOOK, NARI-YUKI!
I LOVE THIS COMEDY DUO!
WHAT'S WITH THE HEAD-PIECE, MAN?
WHAT'S UUUUUP?
BAM
BOING
BLRFF
WHAT'S UUUUUP?
LOL!
SHE'S SO CLOSE !!!
H-HEY! GET BACK IN YOUR SEAT AND STUDY!
OH, PHOOEY!
But it's funny!
GEEZ ...
TAP...
JOLT
SHOOP

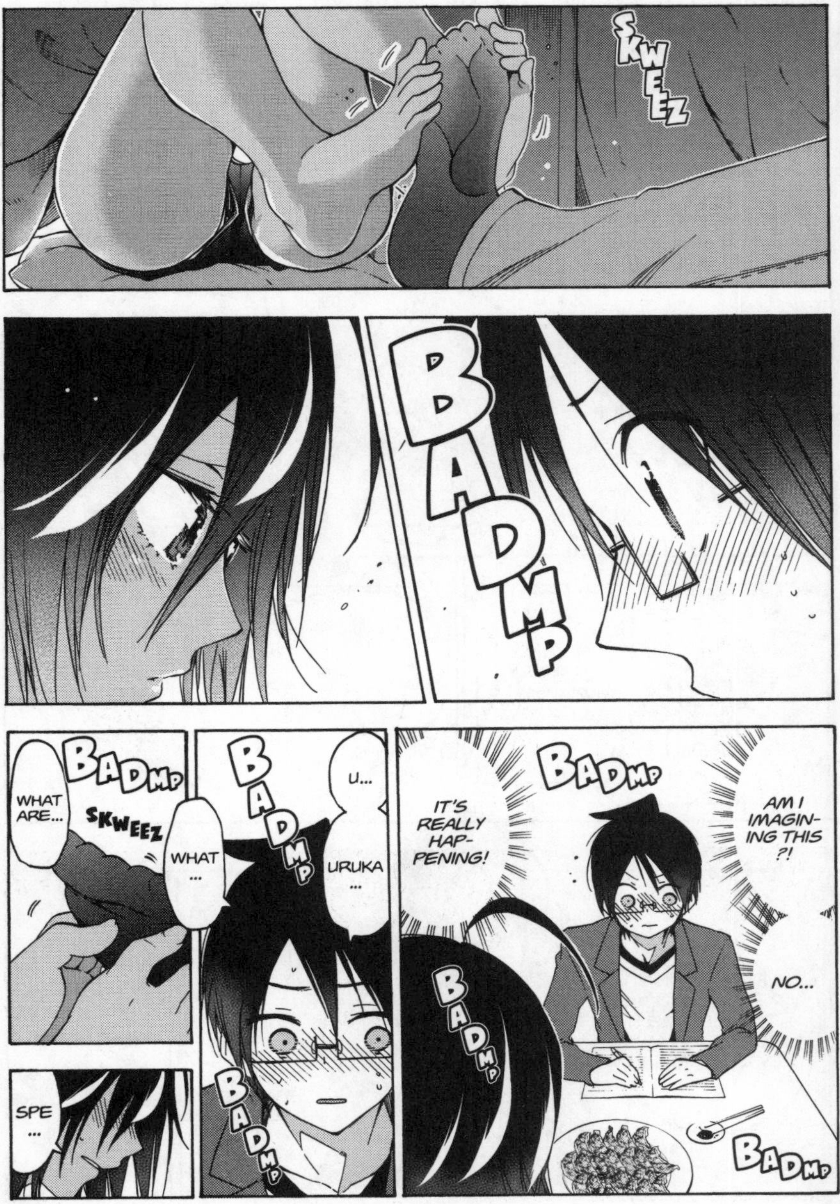
SKWEEZ
BADMP
AM I IMAGINING THIS ?!
BADMP
IT'S REALLY HAP-PENING!
NO...
BADMP
BADMP
U...
URUKA ...
BADMP
WHAT ...
BADMP
BADMP
WHAT ARE...
SKWEEZ
SPE ...

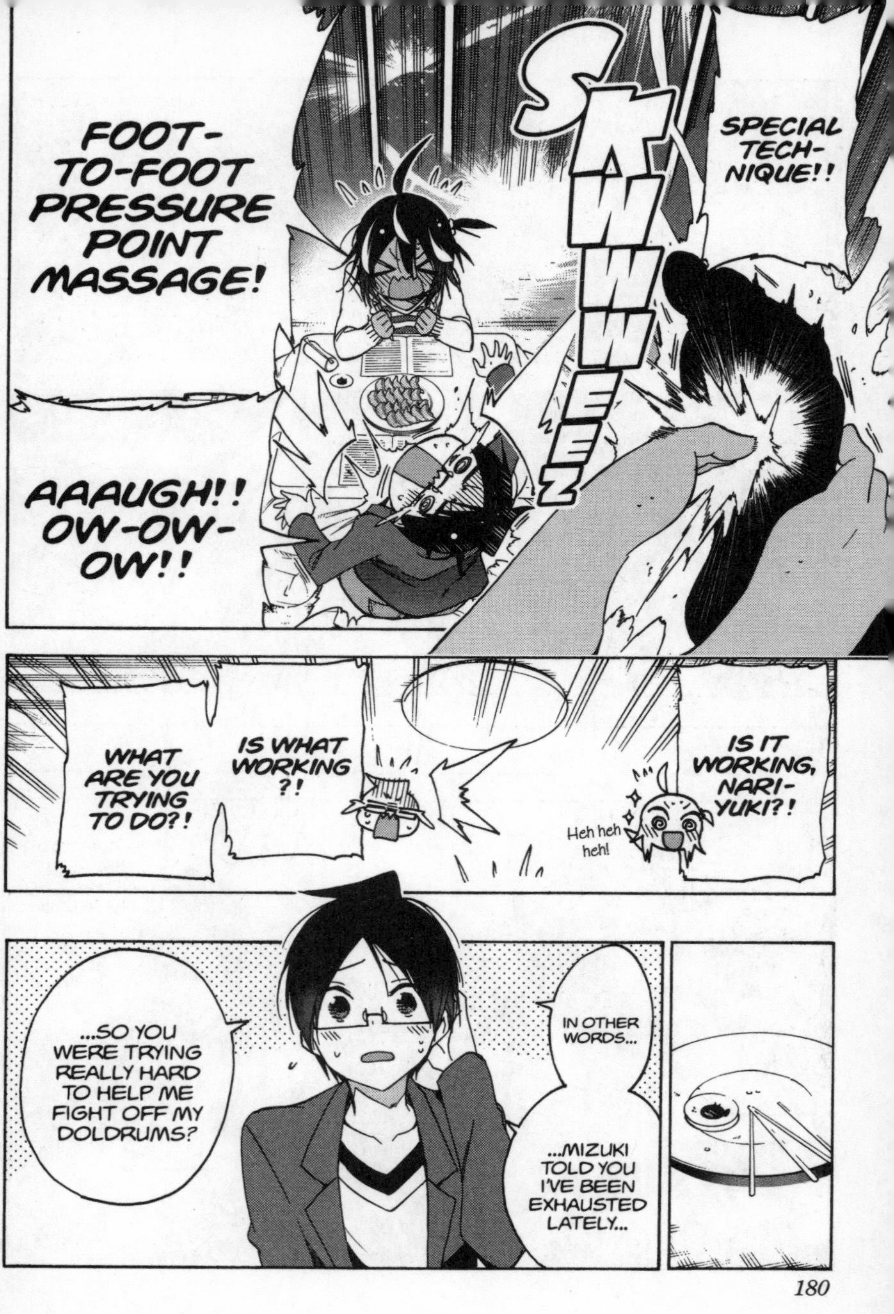
SPECIAL TECHNIQUE!!
SKWWWEEZ
FOOT-TO-FOOT PRESSURE POINT MASSAGE!
AAAUGH!! OW-OW-OW!!
IS IT WORKING, NARIYUKI?!
Heh heh heh!
IS WHAT WORKING?!
WHAT ARE YOU TRYING TO DO?!
IN OTHER WORDS...
...MIZUKI TOLD YOU I'VE BEEN EXHAUSTED LATELY...
...SO YOU WERE TRYING REALLY HARD TO HELP ME FIGHT OFF MY DOLDRUMS?

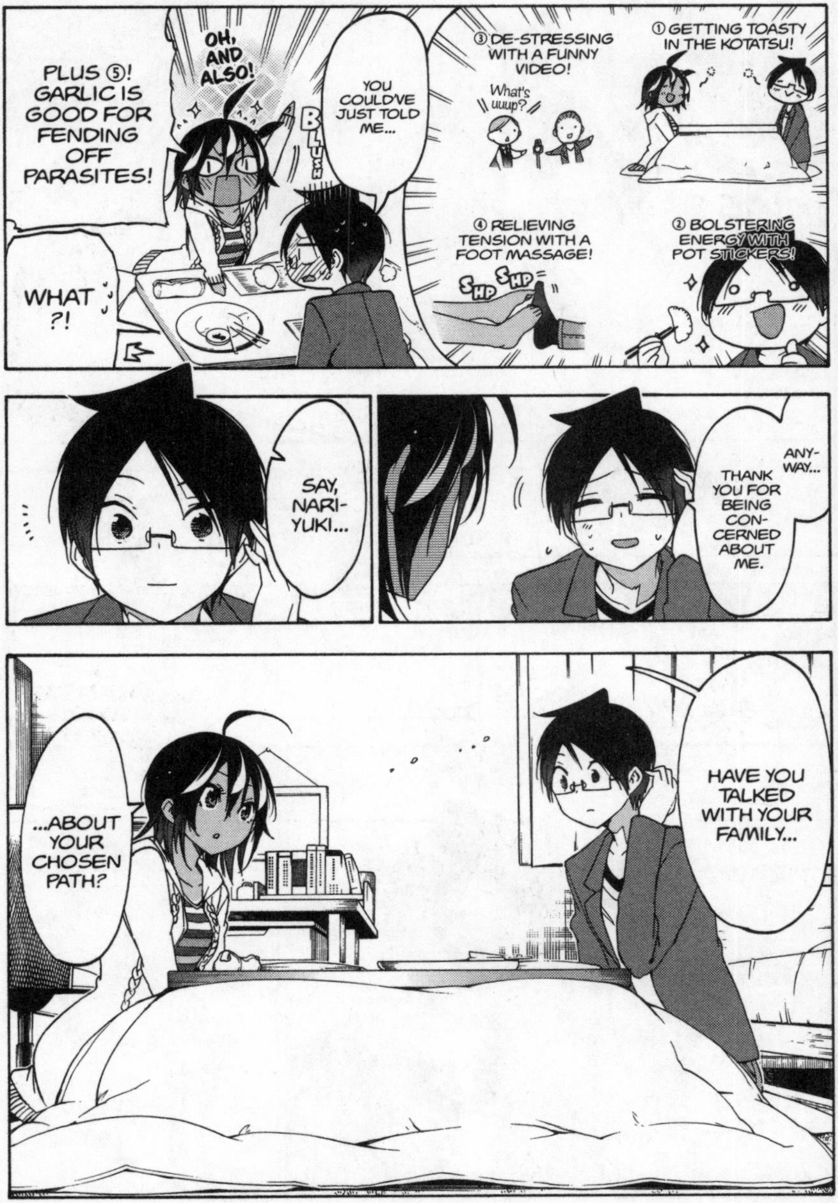
① GETTING TOASTY IN THE KOTATSU!
② BOLSTERING ENERGY WITH POT STICKERS!
③ DE-STRESSING WITH A FUNNY VIDEO!
What's uuup?
④ RELIEVING TENSION WITH A FOOT MASSAGE!
SHP SHP
YOU COULD'VE JUST TOLD ME...
BLUSH
OH, AND ALSO!
PLUS ⑤! GARLIC IS GOOD FOR FENDING OFF PARASITES!
WHAT?!
ANY-WAY...
THANK YOU FOR BEING CON-CERNED ABOUT ME.
SAY, NARI-YUKI...
HAVE YOU TALKED WITH YOUR FAMILY...
...ABOUT YOUR CHOSEN PATH?

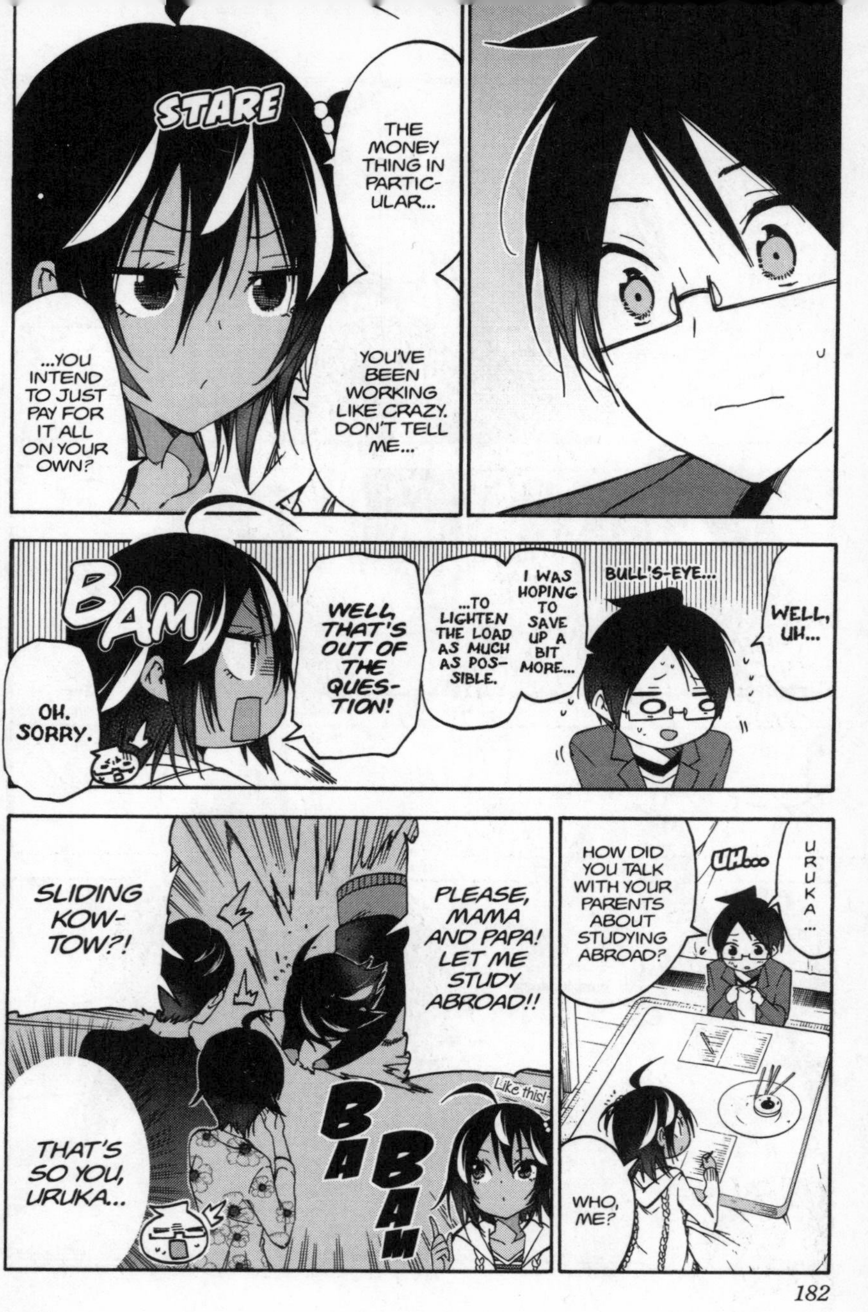
THE MONEY THING IN PARTICULAR...
STARE
YOU'VE BEEN WORKING LIKE CRAZY. DON'T TELL ME...
...YOU INTEND TO JUST PAY FOR IT ALL ON YOUR OWN?
WELL, UH...
BULL'S-EYE...
I WAS HOPING TO SAVE UP A BIT MORE...
...TO LIGHTEN THE LOAD AS MUCH AS POSSIBLE.
WELL, THAT'S OUT OF THE QUESTION!
BAM
OH. SORRY.
URUKA...
UH...
HOW DID YOU TALK WITH YOUR PARENTS ABOUT STUDYING ABROAD?
WHO, ME?
PLEASE, MAMA AND PAPA! LET ME STUDY ABROAD!!
SLIDING KOWTOW?!
Like this!
BABAM
THAT'S SO YOU, URUKA...

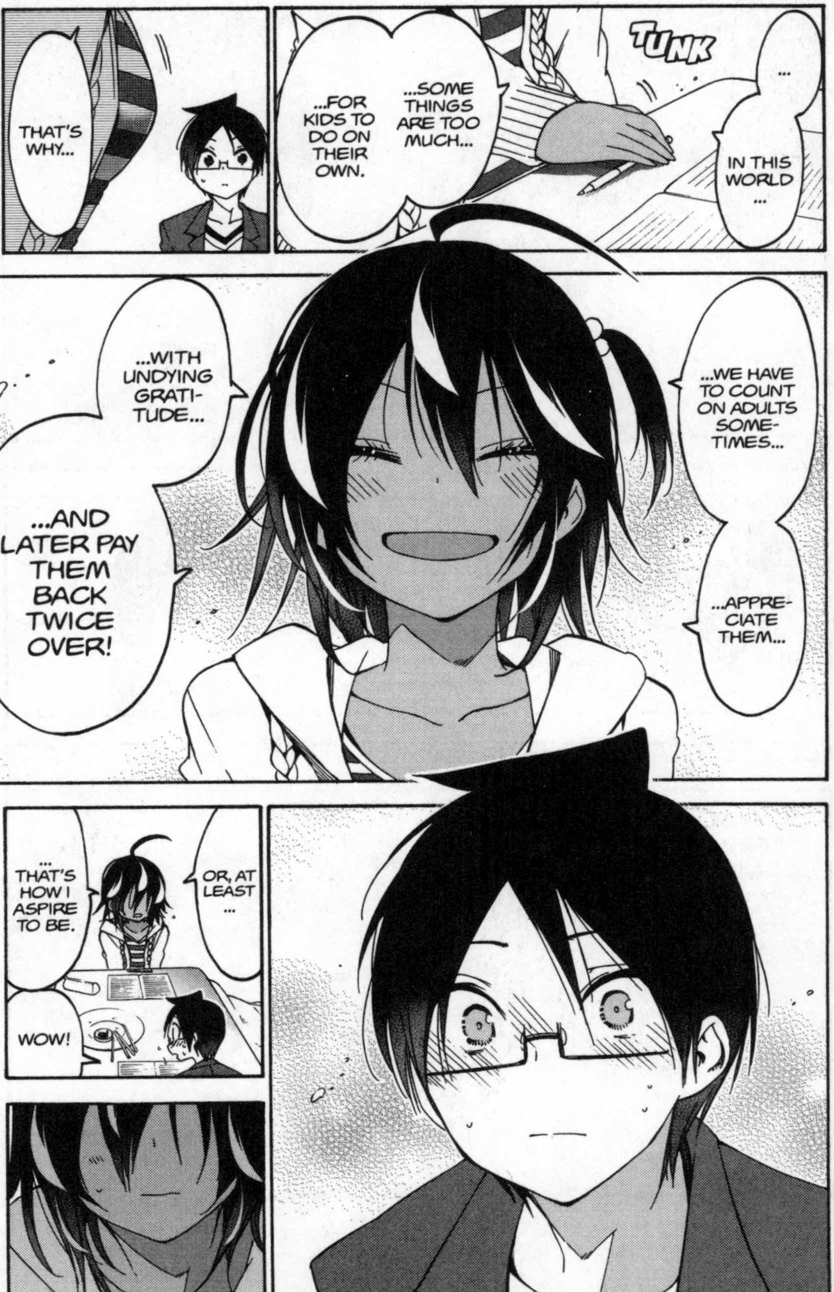
TUNK
... IN THIS WORLD ...
...SOME THINGS ARE TOO MUCH...
...FOR KIDS TO DO ON THEIR OWN.
THAT'S WHY...
...WE HAVE TO COUNT ON ADULTS SOMETIMES...
...APPRECIATE THEM...
...WITH UNDYING GRATITUDE...
...AND LATER PAY THEM BACK TWICE OVER!
OR, AT LEAST ...
... THAT'S HOW I ASPIRE TO BE.
WOW!

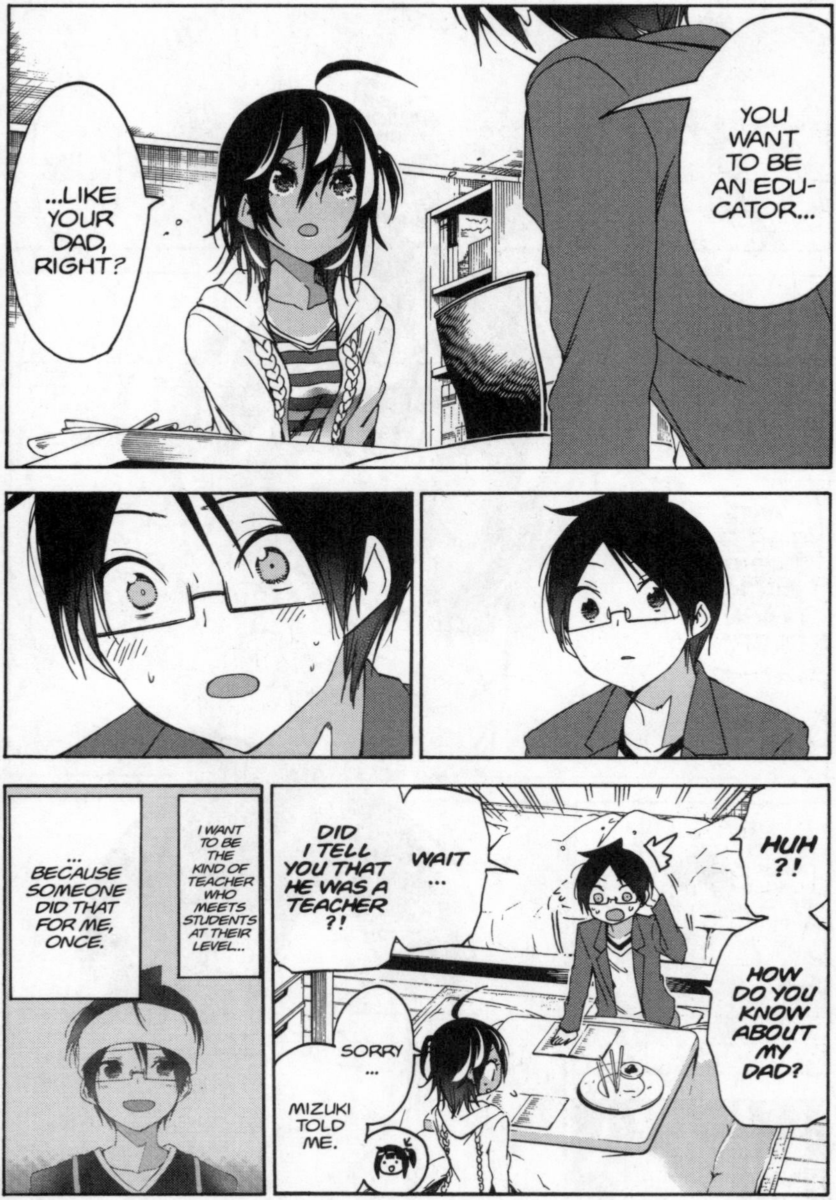
YOU WANT TO BE AN EDU-CATOR...
...LIKE YOUR DAD, RIGHT?
HUH ?!
HOW DO YOU KNOW ABOUT MY DAD?
WAIT ...
DID I TELL YOU THAT HE WAS A TEACHER ?!
SORRY ...
MIZUKI TOLD ME.
I WANT TO BE THE KIND OF TEACHER WHO MEETS STUDENTS AT THEIR LEVEL...
... BECAUSE SOMEONE DID THAT FOR ME, ONCE.

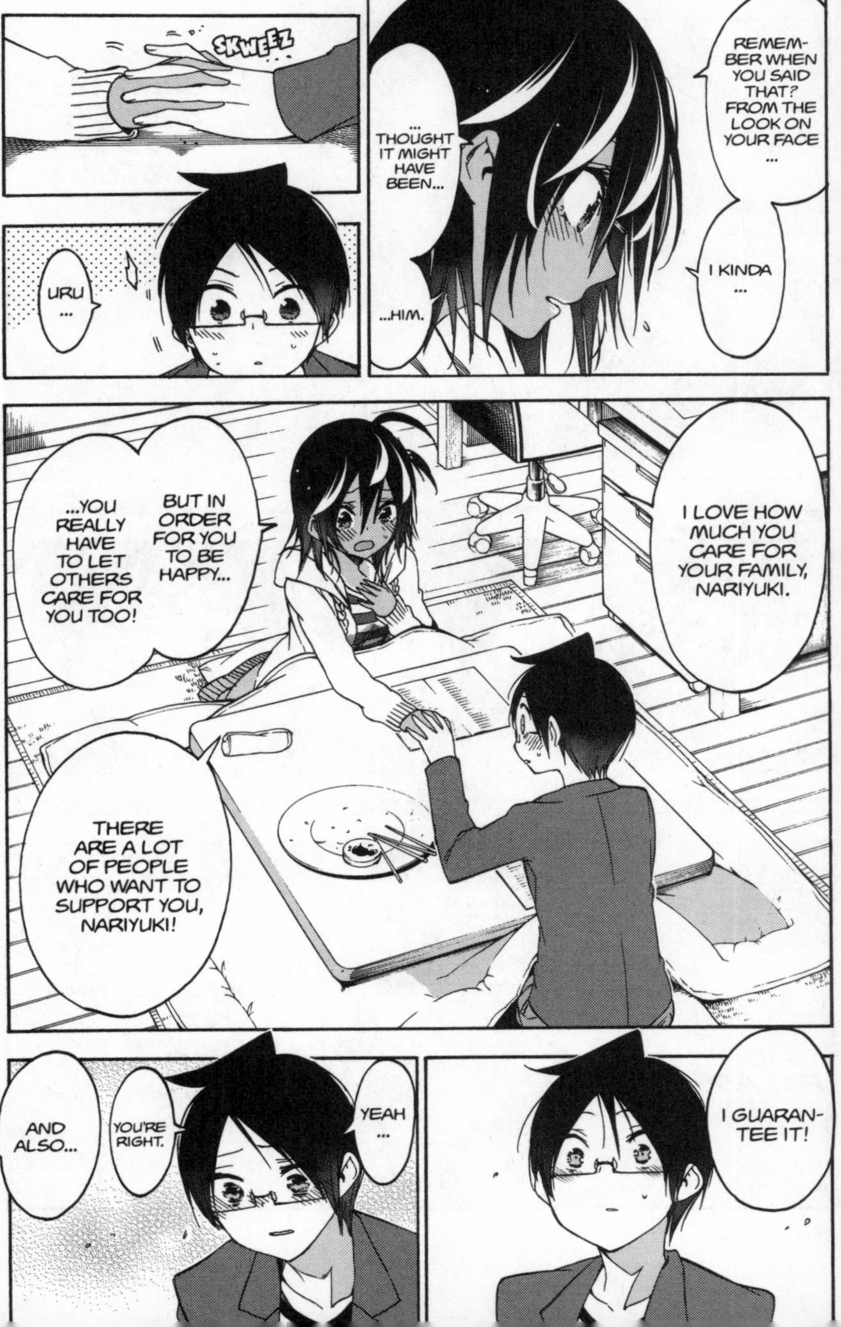
REMEMBER WHEN YOU SAID THAT? FROM THE LOOK ON YOUR FACE ...
I KINDA ...
... THOUGHT IT MIGHT HAVE BEEN...
...HIM.
SKWEEZ
URU ...
I LOVE HOW MUCH YOU CARE FOR YOUR FAMILY, NARIYUKI.
BUT IN ORDER FOR YOU TO BE HAPPY...
...YOU REALLY HAVE TO LET OTHERS CARE FOR YOU TOO!
THERE ARE A LOT OF PEOPLE WHO WANT TO SUPPORT YOU, NARIYUKI!
I GUARANTEE IT!
YEAH ...
YOU'RE RIGHT.
AND ALSO...

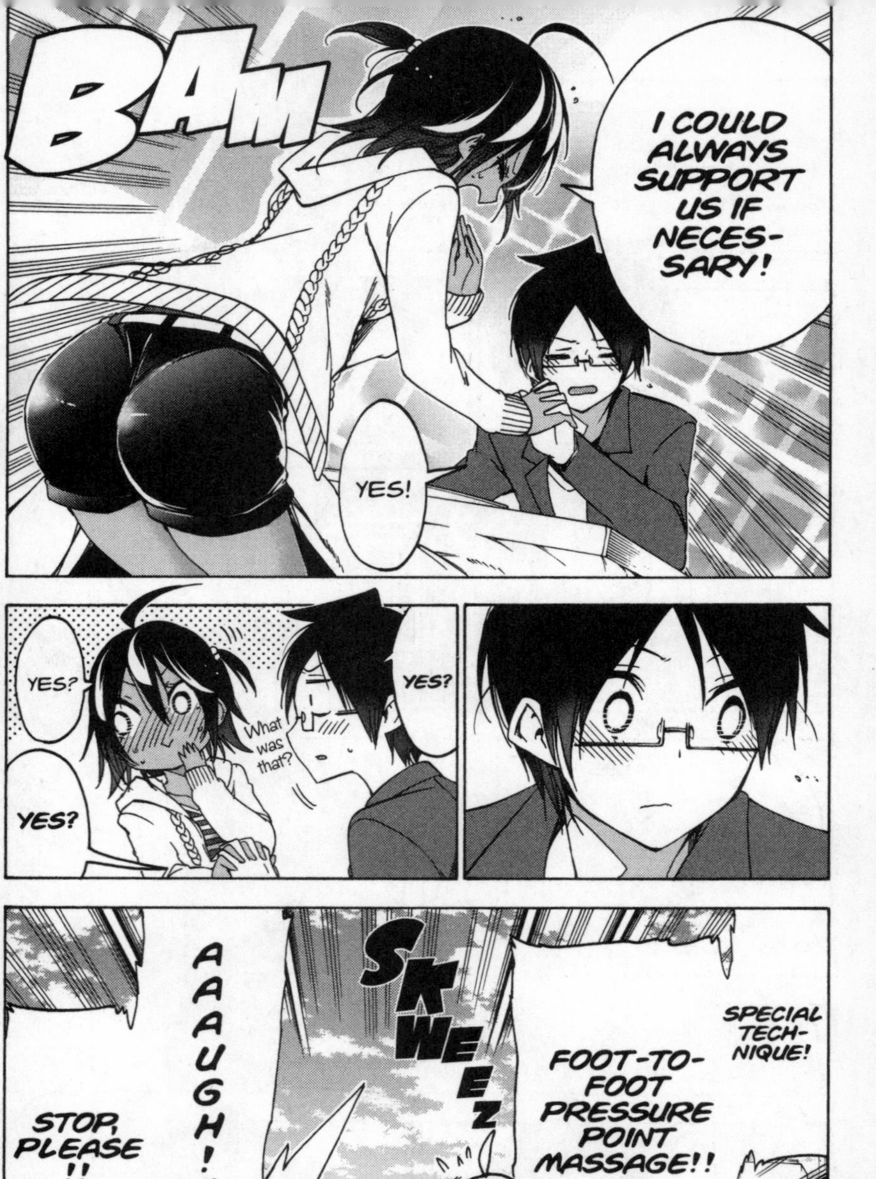
I COULD ALWAYS SUPPORT US IF NECES-SARY!
BAM
YES!
...
YES?
What was that?
YES?
YES?
SPECIAL TECH-NIQUE!
FOOT-TO-FOOT PRESSURE POINT MASSAGE!!
SKWEEZ
AAAAUGH!
STOP, PLEASE!!

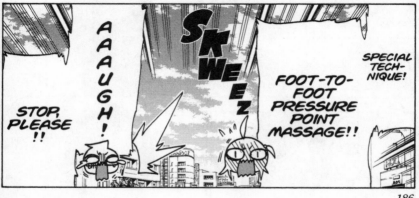

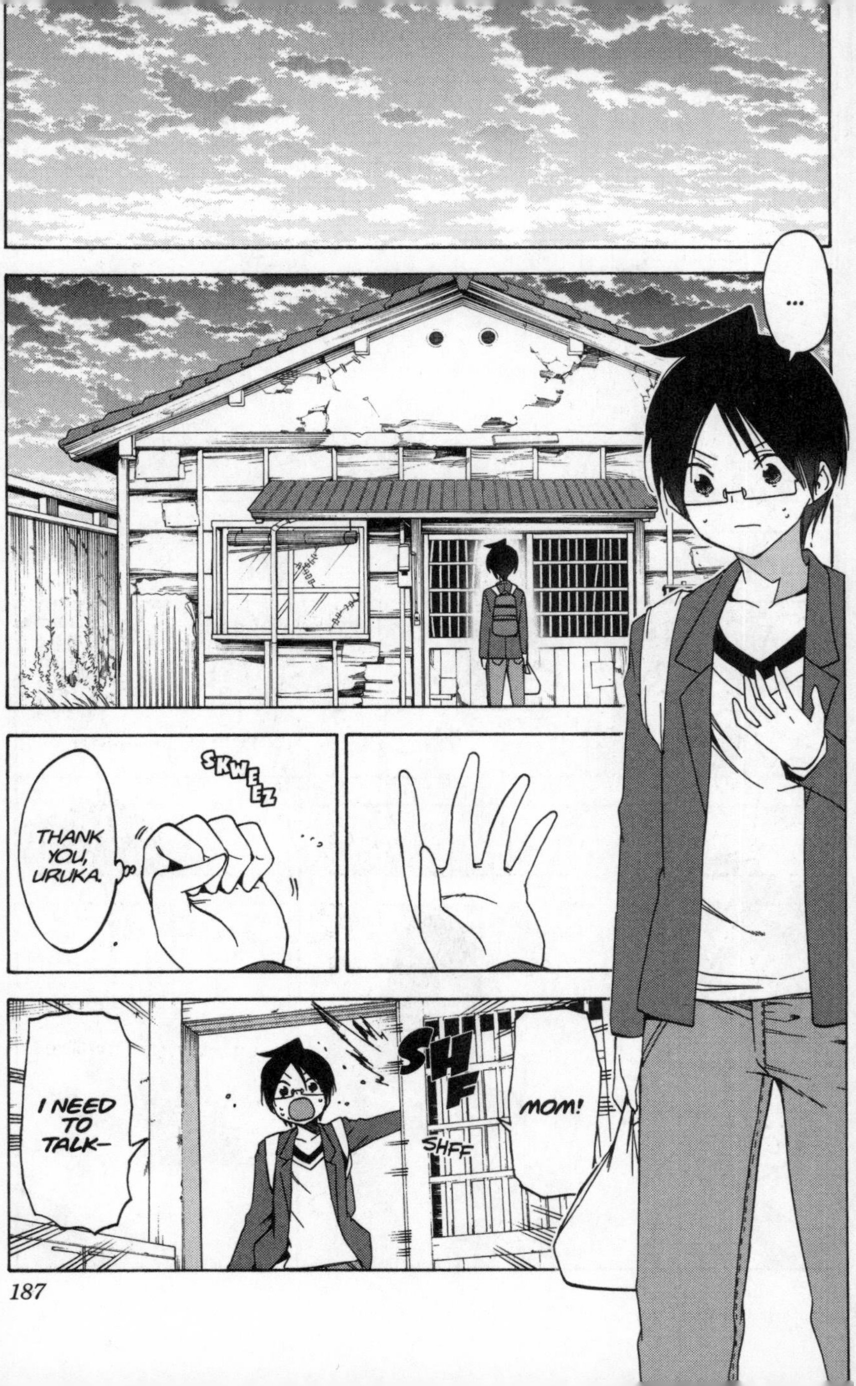
...
SKWEEZ
THANK YOU, URUKA.
MOM!
SHF
SHFF
I NEED TO TALK—

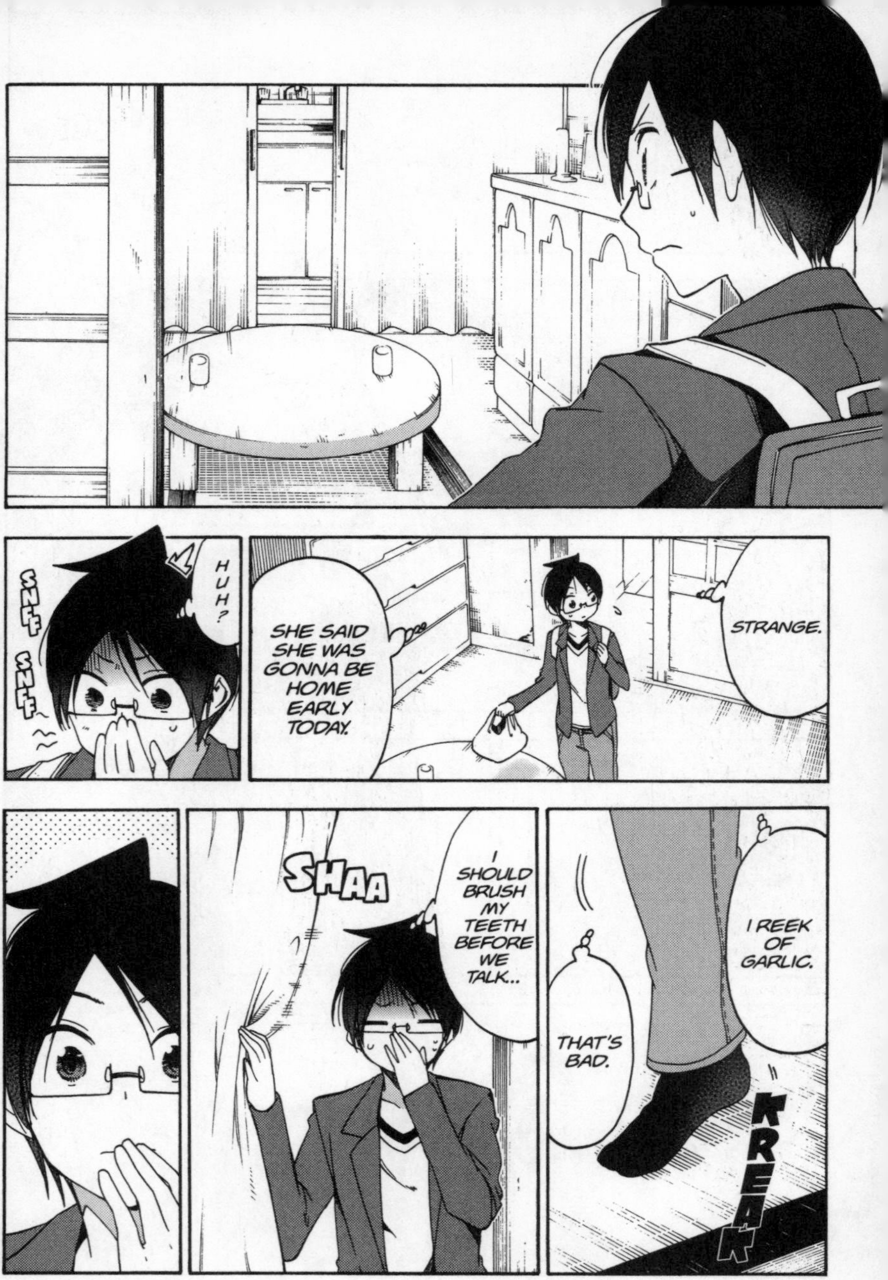
STRANGE.
SHE SAID SHE WAS GONNA BE HOME EARLY TODAY.
HUH?
SNFF SNFF
I REEK OF GARLIC.
THAT'S BAD.
KREAK
I SHOULD BRUSH MY TEETH BEFORE WE TALK...
SHAA

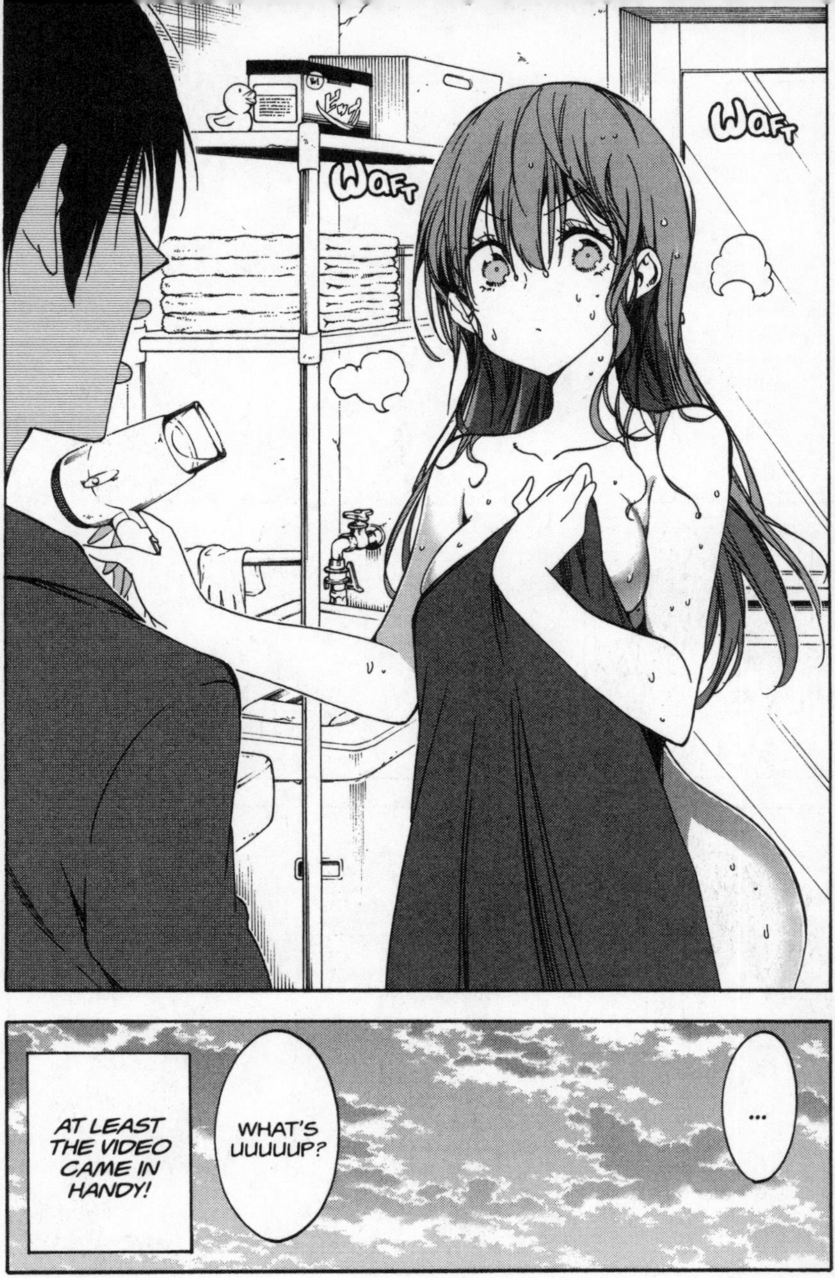
WAFT
WAFT
...
WHAT'S UUUUUP?
AT LEAST THE VIDEO CAME IN HANDY!

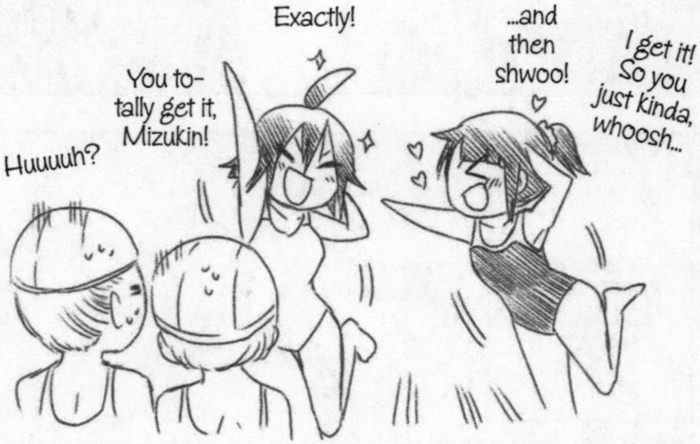
I get it! So you just kinda, whoosh...
...and then shwoo!
Exactly!
You to-tally get it, Mizukin!
Huuuuh?

[x] We
+
Never
×
×Learn×

To celebrate the two-year anniversary of *We Never Learn* and the three-year anniversary of *Yuuna and the Haunted Hot Springs,* we created a collaborative illustration. Thank you, Miura Sensei! It was so much fun to collaborate! Let's do it again for sure!

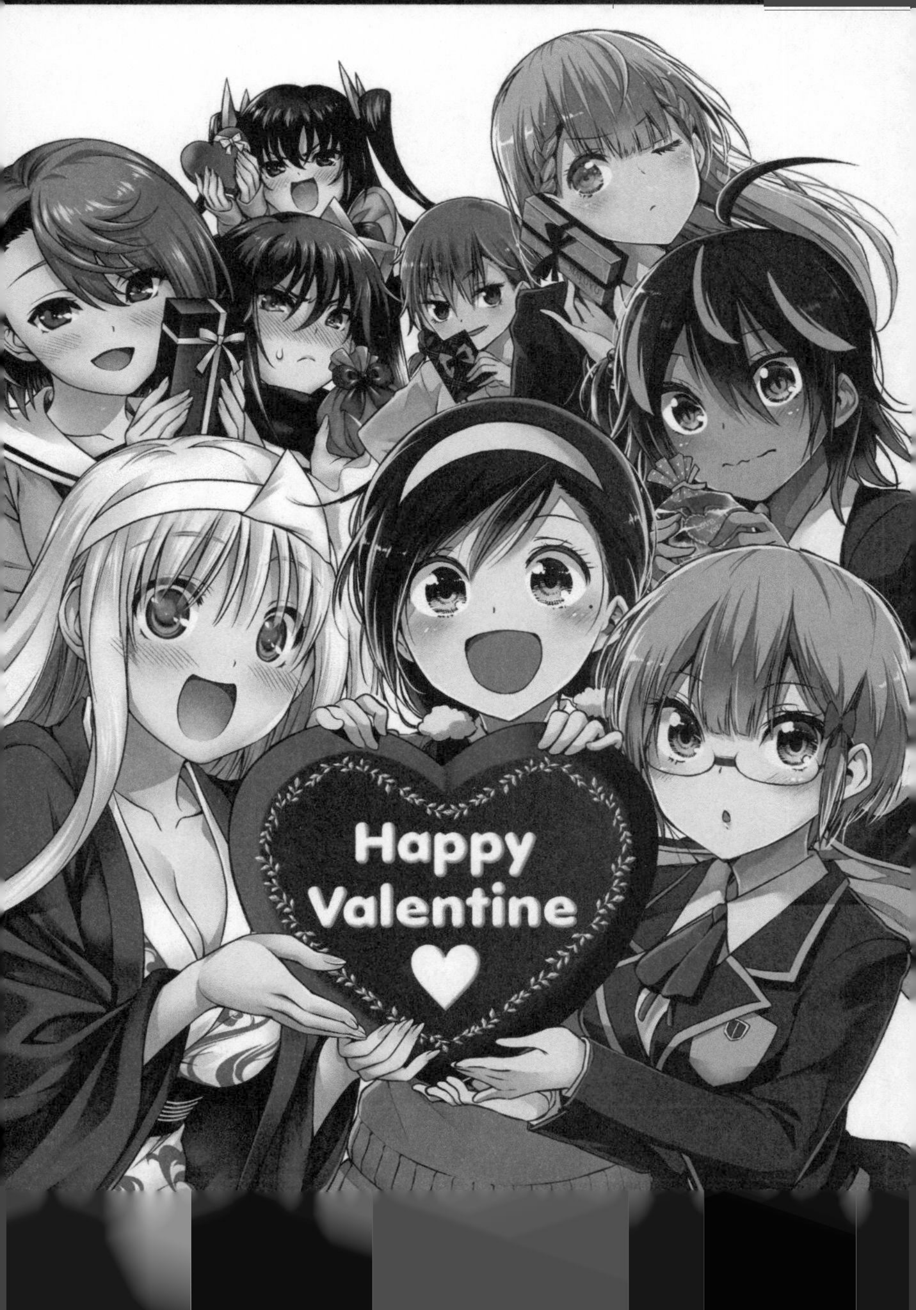
Happy
Valentine

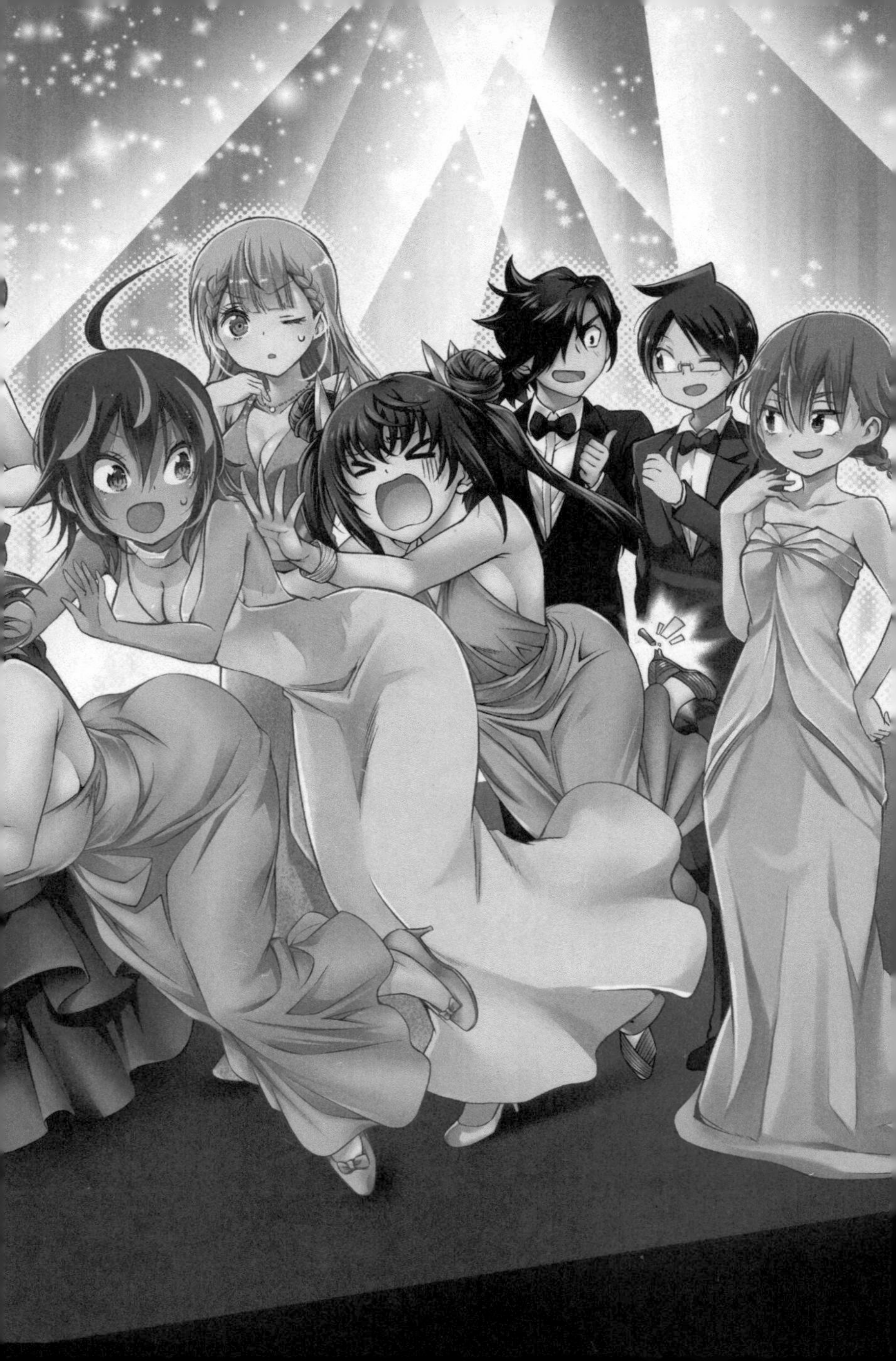

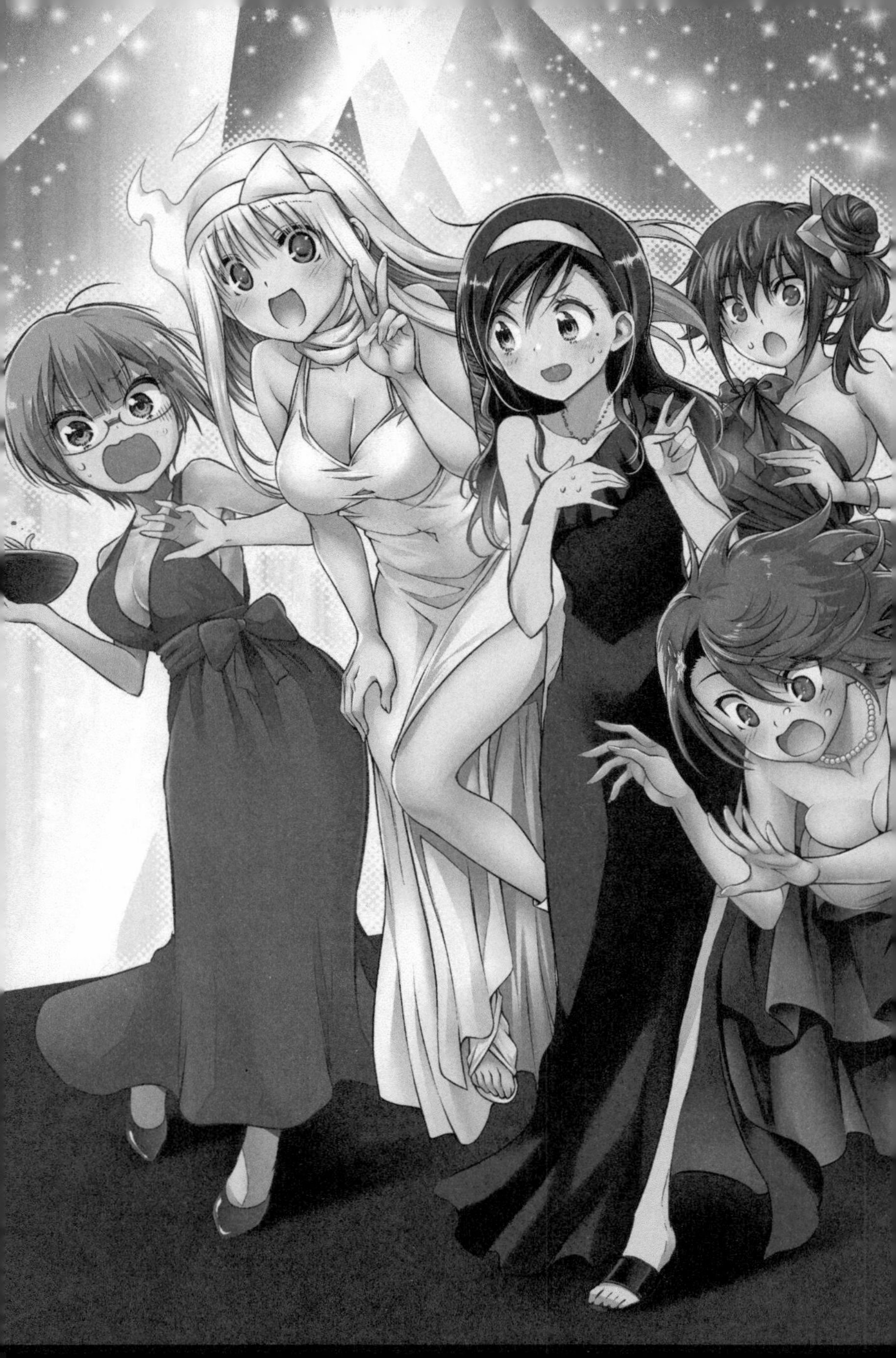

We
Never
Learn

We Never Learn

12

STAFF

Taishi Tsutsui

Yu Kato

Naoki Ochiai

Sachiko

Yukki

Satoshi Okazaki

HELP

Paripoi

Shinobu Irooki

Chikomichi

STAFF LIST

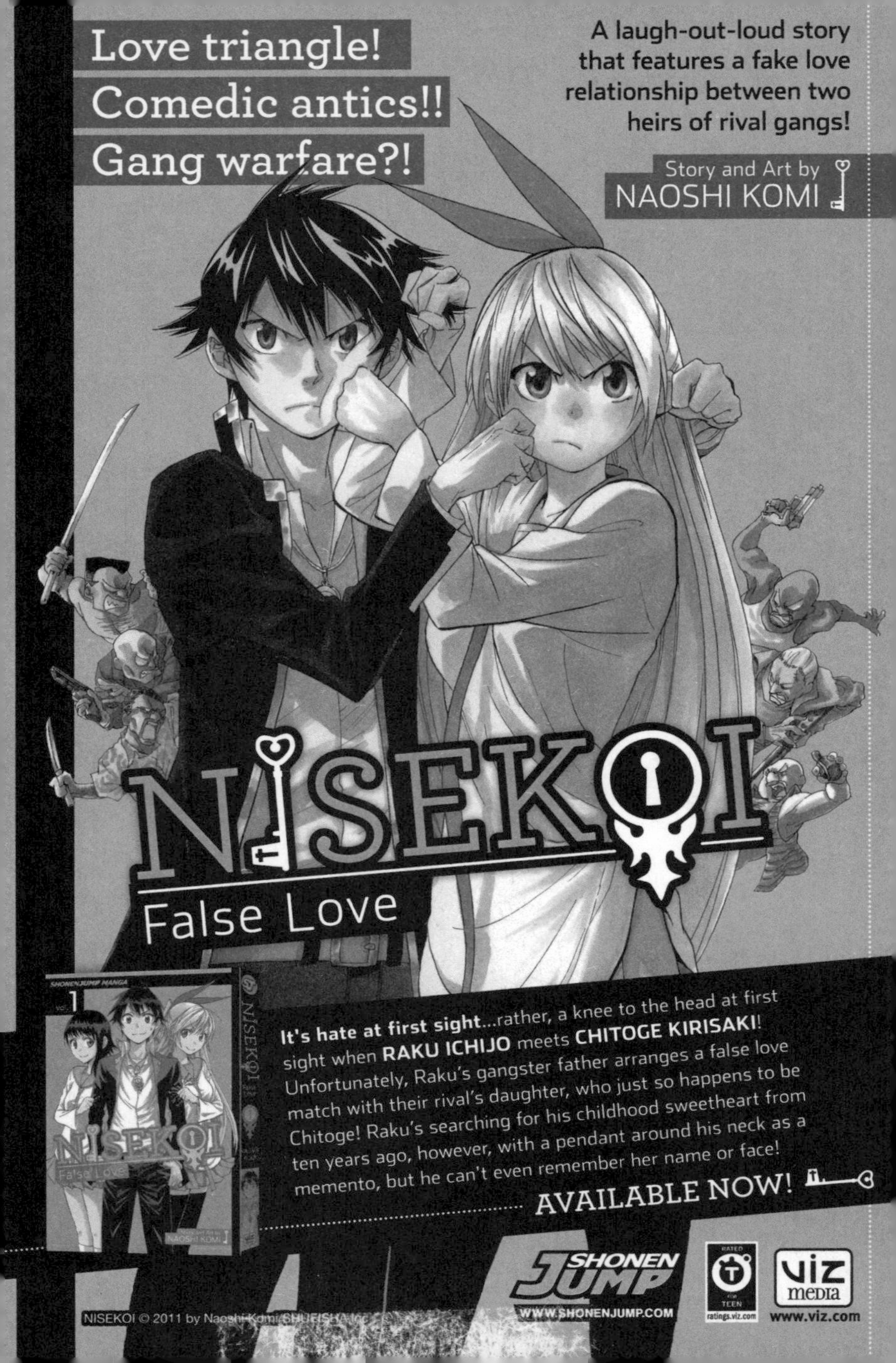
Love triangle!
Comedic antics!!
Gang warfare?!
A laugh-out-loud story that features a fake love relationship between two heirs of rival gangs!
Story and Art by
NAOSHI KOMI
NISEKOI
False Love
SHONENJUMP MANGA
vol. 1
NISEKOI
False Love
NAOSHI KOMI
It's hate at first sight...rather, a knee to the head at first sight when RAKU ICHIJO meets CHITOGE KIRISAKI! Unfortunately, Raku's gangster father arranges a false love match with their rival's daughter, who just so happens to be Chitoge! Raku's searching for his childhood sweetheart from ten years ago, however, with a pendant around his neck as a memento, but he can't even remember her name or face!
AVAILABLE NOW!
SHONEN JUMP
WWW.SHONENJUMP.COM
RATED T FOR TEEN
ratings.viz.com
viz media
www.viz.com
NISEKOI © 2011 by Naoshi Komi/SHUEISHA Inc.

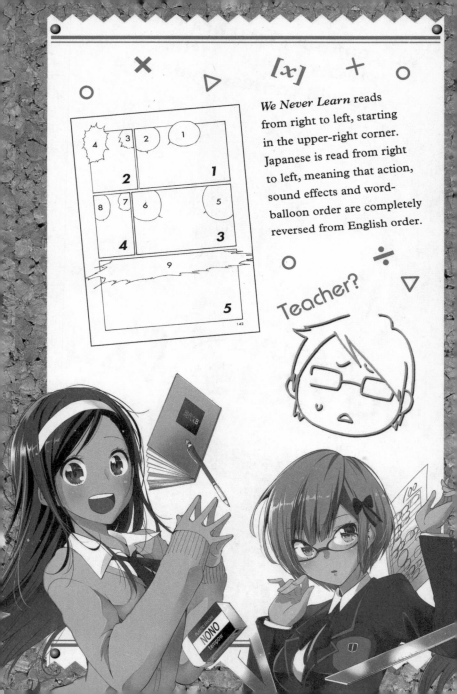

We Never Learn **reads from right to left, starting in the upper-right corner. Japanese is read from right to left, meaning that action, word-sound effects and word-balloon order are completely reversed from English order.**

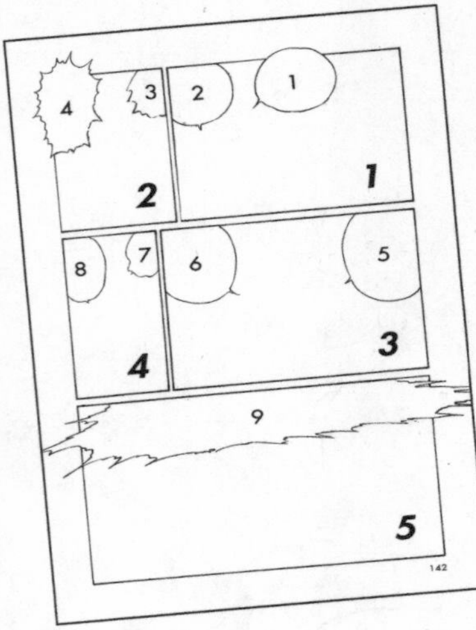
1
2
3
4
1
2
5
6
7
8
3
4
9
5
142

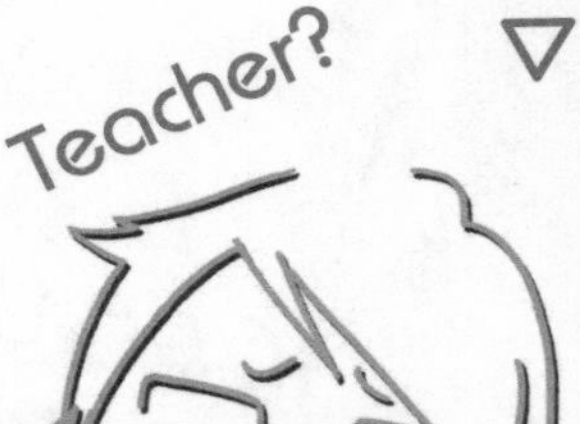
Teacher?

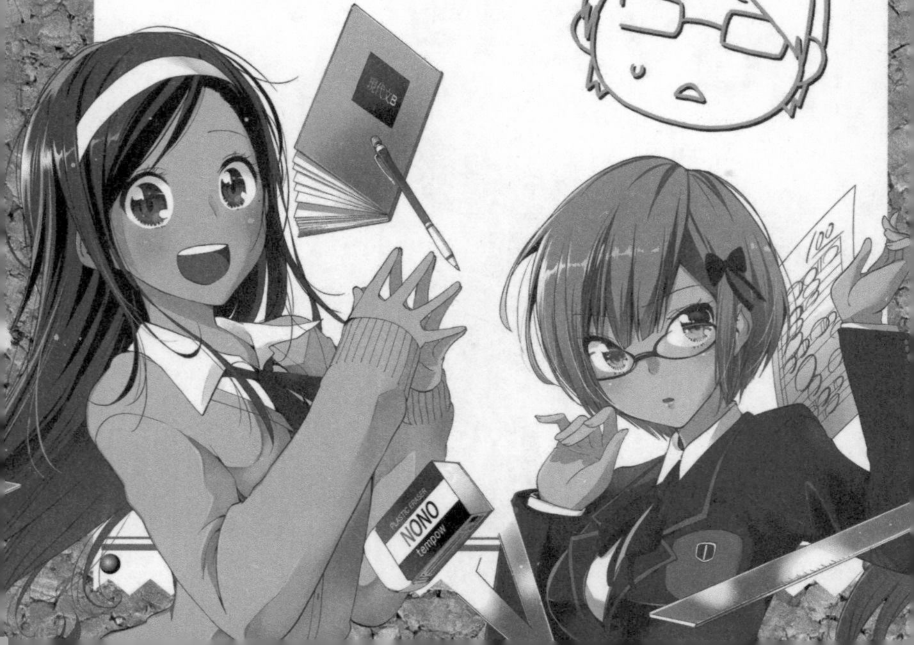
現代文B
NONO
tempow